D1383841

LEADERSHIP
AND POWER
IN THE
BOS-WASH
MEGALOPOLIS

THE WILEY SERIES IN URBAN RESEARCH

TERRY N. CLARK, Editor

LEADERSHIP AND POWER IN THE BOS-WASH MEGALOPOLIS

Environment, Ecology, and Urban Organization

DELBERT C. MILLER

A WILEY-INTERSCIENCE PUBLICATION

JOHN WILEY & SONS, New York • London • Sydney • Toronto

Library of Congress Cataloging in Publication Data:

Miller, Delbert Charles, 1913-
    Leadership and power in the Bos-Wash megalopolis.

    (The Wiley series in urban research)
    "A Wiley-Interscience publication."
    Bibliography: p.
    Includes index.
    1. Social surveys—Atlantic States. 2. Regional
planning—Atlantic States. 3. Community power.
4. Environmental policy—Atlantic States. I. Title.

HT392.5.A8M54   1975   301.15   74-22395
ISBN 0-471-60519-0

Printed in the United States of America

10 9 8 7 6 5 4 3 2 1

For
Blair
and
Nancy Bower

THE WILEY SERIES IN URBAN RESEARCH

Cities, especially American cities, are attracting more public attention and scholarly concern than at perhaps any other time in history. Traditional structures have been seriously questioned and sweeping changes proposed; simultaneously, efforts are being made to penetrate the fundamental processes by which cities operate. This effort calls for marshaling knowledge from a number of substantive areas. Sociologists, political scientists, economists, geographers, planners, historians, anthropologists, and others have turned to urban questions; interdisciplinary projects involving scholars and activists are groping with fundamental issues.

The Wiley Series in Urban Research has been created to encourage the publication of works bearing on urban questions. It seeks to publish studies from different fields that help to illuminate urban processes. It is addressed to scholars as well as to planners, administrators, and others concerned with a more analytical understanding of things urban.

TERRY N. CLARK

PREFACE

The research described in this book was undertaken with the encouragement and funding of Resources for the Future, Inc., and with the assistance of Allen V. Kneese and Blair T. Bower of RFF's Quality of the Environment Program.* Recognition was mutually shared by the researchers and corporation officials that the region as a basis for study and administrative action was growing increasingly important in the treatment of many urban problems. Environmental quality in particular does not respect political boundaries. Air pollution control districts established under the requirements of federal law reveal the regional attack on air quality. The Delaware River Basin Commission provided a base of experience to demonstrate how the Federal Government and the states of Pennsylvania, New York, New Jersey, and Delaware have worked together in a large watershed area to effect water management. These administrative actions raise the question of the nature of a region. Can a region that is undoubtedly a common geographic and economic area also serve as a sociological community? In other words, can men think in terms of a region as they would of a city—or state identifying with it and accepting it as a natural unit for political and governmental action? Will they in the future tackle their urban and environmental quality problems on a regional basis? Can sociological techniques of community power analysis be applied to find the answers to these questions?

These were the initial inquiries that sparked the research program. Eastern Megalopolis (Boston to Washington) was selected because it seemed on many counts the appropriate "region" for study. It had a network of economic and social ties and it had massive urban and environmental quality problems. A major decision was made to conduct parallel investigations of influence networks among leaders and or-

* Blair T. Bower is now a private consultant and lecturer.

ganizations in Megalopolis affecting urban problems in general and environmental quality problems specifically. It was believed that this strategy was important to a thorough understanding of the way in which quality problems fit the priorities and administrative contexts of all competing urban problems. It was decided that after these two separate investigations were completed by independent sociological researches a study of the linkage of leaders and organizations of the two problem areas would be carried out.

The research that followed spans the four-year period, 1968 to 1972. This period in American history was turbulent and urban problems were of high concern. In 1968 the research team was composed of Delbert C. Miller as principal investigator and James L. Barfoot, Jr., and Paul D. Planchon as research associates. Our first activities covered a nine-month period of field research. We began in Washington to identify powerful Eastern leaders and organizations engaged in urban and environmental problems and to determine the issues that were common to Megalopolis. Subsequently the team moved to New York, Philadelphia, and Boston. Baltimore was reached from our Washington base. The field research entailed extensive interviewing and documentary searches. Numerous recording instruments were devised to collect data on leader roles and organizational structure (see Appendix B).

In 1969 the researchers divided responsibilities. Miller focused on urban-oriented leaders and organizations; Planchon and Barfoot concentrated on environmental leaders and organizations in Megalopolis and each conducted special studies on the Delaware River Basin to test various hypotheses relative to decision making in water quality management in a subregion. Three questionnaires were prepared and sent to selected respondents during April and May. These may be examined in Appendix A as the Leadership Interaction and Urban Problem Inventory, the Megalopolis Environmental Quality Inventory, and the Delaware River Basin Questionnaire. James Barfoot also interviewed 40 environmental leaders active in a water quality issue in the Delaware River Basin. His interview schedule is in Appendix C.

The second phase involved analysis and a written report to Resources for the Future on the regional aspects of environmental problems.*

Phase 3 involved a resurvey of the 400 key and top leaders of Megalopolis during July 1970 to ascertain stability or change in urban problem interest and activity. This resurvey was conducted 14 months after the initial investigation. Environmental problems received heightened interest between May 1969 and July 1970. A report of findings is presented in Chapter 4.†

The final research activity was aimed at discovering more knowledge of decision-making processes as key and top leaders engaged in regional issues common

* Delbert C. Miller, James L. Barfoot, Jr., and Paul D. Planchon, *Power and Decision Making in Megalopolis, with Special Reference to Environmental Quality Problems,* Resources for the Future, Washington, D.C., 1970 (copies available on request.)

† For a more detailed report see the author's paper "The Allocation of Priorities to Urban and Environmental Problems by Powerful Leaders and Organizations" in William R. Burch, Jr., Neil H. Cheek, Jr., and Lee Taylor, *Social Behavior, Natural Resources, and the Environment,* Harper and Row, New York, 1972, 306–331. The most complete statement on research design may be found in the author's chapter, "Power Structure Studies and Environmental Management" in *Environmental Quality Analysis: Theory and Method in the Social Sciences,* Allan Kneese and Blair T. Bower (eds.), John Hopkins Press, 1972, 345–395.

to the major cities of Megalopolis. The interactional data collected enabled us to identify those leaders who demonstrated the highest interaction between leaders in different cities of megalopolis. These have been labeled "MEGA-leaders" to contrast with those leaders whose interaction tends to be confined to their local cities. The inventory of Mega-leaders shown in Appendix A was sent on June 1, 1971. The results of that survey are found in Chapter 6, titled MEGA-leaders, Regional Issues, and Patterned Strategies of Decision Making.

The collected body of data promised to open new research frontiers in regional sociology. During the summer of 1971 Lloyd Temme, a computer specialist in sociology, was engaged to make a sociometric analysis of leadership cliques with data collected in the Leadership Interaction Inventory of Key and Top Leaders and in which a new computer program was applied. The results of this pioneering effort are reported in Chapter 10, the Measurement of Contact and Clique Structures. At this time, the writer was exploring a new field that might be called the sociology of associations. The data collected on government agencies and private associations lent itself to an examination of this area of interaction. Chapter 11 attempts to outline organizational interaction and its measurement.

A final chapter on the widening of social consciousness is a reflection on the significance of the research results. The concept of a regional community rests on the inexorable demands for governmental integration and the imaginative capacity of a wider public to form new social identities. This book is addressed to social scientists, political leaders, city planners, social workers, and intelligent laymen everywhere who are seeking to understand how leadership and organizational coalitions are developed and how they function to promote social objectives in a regional setting.

We are indebted to a large number of people: all of the "judges" who helped us in rating the power and influence of leaders and organizations in Boston, New York, Philadelphia, Baltimore, and Washington and the hundreds of selected respondents who answered our four questionnaires on urban and environmental problems in Megalopolis.

Three foundations offered us accommodation. We want to thank Resources for the Future for our work space in Washington from September 1 to December 1, 1968, the Russell Sage Foundation for space in New York from December 1, 1968, to March 1, 1969, and the Fels Institute of Local and State Government (University of Pennsylvania) from March 1, 1969, to June 1, 1969.

A special debt is owed to our wives who packed bag and baggage and made homes away from home as we moved from city to city. In addition, Wing Barfoot and Susan Planchon served as traveling secretaries, research assistants, and janes of all trades for our peripatetic research team. At home base in Bloomington we are indebted to Jane Wellman, Carol Stevenson, Melva Myers, and Carol Sue Lester for secretarial service. The Institute of Social Research at Indiana University also provided valuable assistance.

DELBERT C. MILLER

Department of Sociology, Indiana University
Bloomington, Indiana
January 1975

CONTENTS

TABLES

PART FIVE

PART SIX

APPENDICES

FIGURES

PART SIX

LEADERSHIP
AND POWER
IN THE
BOS-WASH
MEGALOPOLIS

INTRODUCTION

The Search for an Interactional Net of Leaders and Organizations in Megalopolis: Pragmatic and Scientific Considerations

This study had as its central theme the identification of powerful leaders and organizations and their working relationships on urban and environmental problems along the axis from Boston to Washington, D. C., known as "Megalopolis." It was clear at the outset that the search for an interactional net across Megalopolis would involve risk and an act of faith. The risk would rest in the possibility that the highly localized nature of administration on city and state levels would nullify high rates of interaction beyond such bounds. Perhaps Megalopolis was not a sociological entity at all. The faith required would entail a research decision to move toward an understanding of leadership and organizational interaction because this was consonant with trends in regional planning. There were many indications that increased activity of government was drawing leaders into wider spheres of contact. A growing need for knowledge of regional organization was apparent.

The Trend Toward Regional Integration

Megalopolis, like other areas of the United States, has vigorously resisted any fundamental restructuring of its traditional units of local government to provide for growing economic, political, and social interdependence and integration. Adaptations have occurred, however, which have filled Megalopolis with a multitude of governmental and private organizations that assume responsibility for wider areas of concern. The principal trends exhibit the movement of community decision-making powers to higher echelons of public authority and the increasing emphasis on cooperative devices as an alternative to formal restructuring of the governmental pattern.

The governmental mixture usually consists of a county government of rising importance, a network of small and large districts, and growing state and national

1

programs. Contacts between local units, mutual aid agreements, and the creation of metropolitan regional councils and interstate compacts represent governmental adaptations.[1]

Problems of water quality and water supply in the Delaware Basin led as early as 1936 to the creation of the Interstate Commission on the Delaware River Basin, which brought together the states of New York, Pennsylvania, New Jersey, and Delaware in an attempt to coordinate plans for future use. The Commission drew up the Delaware River Basin Compact which in 1961, after many difficulties, was adopted by joint legislation of the United States government and the four member states. These states now have 38 years of experience in interstate cooperation.

In 1965 the Water Quality Act authorized a concerted nationwide attack on water pollution in river basins. This law required the establishment and enforcement of water-quality standards on interstate and coastal waters by the separate states. In 1967 all states proposed standards and programs to achieve them. The Potomac River Basin Advisory Committee secured agreement for a compact involving the interstate cooperation of Maryland, Virginia, West Virginia, Pennsylvania, and the District of Columbia. The final draft released in November 1968 now waits on ratification by the separate states.

Active interstate cooperation is also taking place in air quality. The Air Quality Act of 1967 authorized the Federal Government to establish air quality control regions based on technical considerations and to place responsibility on the state or states within the region to set quality standards. At the end of 1968 air quality control regions had been designated for Washington, New York, Philadelphia, and the Boston metropolitan area. Environmental quality administration promises to be a pace setter in forging regional relationships.

Other regional efforts have also strengthened interstate relations. The most important administrative bodies are the Tri-State Transportation Agency (created in March 1965 by New York, Connecticut, and New Jersey), New York Metropolitan Regional Council (New York, New Jersey, and Connecticut, 1956), Washington Metropolitan Council of Government (District of Columbia, Virginia, and Maryland, 1957), and Port Authority of New York (New York and New Jersey). The Federal Government has been encouraging the growth of regional bodies by legislation and with financial assistance. The New England Regional Commission, one such active body, was established by the Congress in 1965 and directed by it to develop a comprehensive plan of economic projects for the region by 1967. In 1965 federal aid was extended to metropolitan area councils of government; in 1966 the Demonstration Cities Act required that applications for federal loans or grants for certain projects in metropolitan areas be reviewed by an area-wide planning agency responsible to elected local officials. By presidential order in 1969 new regional headquarters were established in Boston, New York, and Philadelphia staffed by the U. S. Department of Health, Education and Welfare, the U. S. Office of Economic Opportunity, the U. S. Department of Labor, U. S. Housing and Urban Development, and the U. S. Small Business Administration. The order called for the creation of regional coordinating councils manned by representatives from the five separate agencies. The efforts at integration on broader geographic levels suggest that numerous integrating forces are at work and that if Megalopolis is not yet the focus of political activity interstate problems are demanding more attention by leaders. The environmental quality problems by federal law are compelling the formation of new interstate administrative bodies. Moreover, the mounting pressures of urban problems are stimulating common representations from leaders of Megalopolis on the national government and national associations. All of this indicates that leaders and organizations are being drawn into wider urban interest and activity patterns.

The long-standing assumption that the Eastern Establishment is a real and viable sociological entity has been another spur to the researcher.

The Eastern Establishment

Probably no one knows who coined the term, Eastern Establishment, but it has been used a thousand times since its inception. Somewhere in every national organization the cry has been raised that the "Easterners run the show." To my knowledge no one has ever fully studied the "Eastern Establishment," but its structure has been variously identified as the upper class families centered in Boston, New York, and Philadelphia; the business aristocracy that controls the great corporations, banks, and insurance companies headquartered largely in New York City; the trustees of the largest (Eastern) foundations, Ford, Rockefeller, and Carnegie; the political and governmental leaders of the Eastern states and cities; the presidents, professors, and graduates of the Ivy League universities; the military leaders centered at the Pentagon; the top (Eastern) administrators of the Federal Government; the national labor leaders headquartered in Washington; the civil rights leaders of New York City, and so on.[2] The reputation of the Eastern Establishment can be traced in part to its megalopolitan base in which is crowded "an extremely distinguished population—a population that is, *on the average,* the richest, best educated, best housed, and best serviced group of similar size in the world."[3]

A high interaction between leaders is often posited. Mills claims that the dominant national leaders are from big business, big government, and the military establishment and that these leaders are acquainted with one another and interact together. The inner core, he states, consists of those who interchange commanding roles at the top of one dominant institutional order with those in another.[4] He recognizes the dominance of the East in which New York is the financial capital and Washington is the political capital of the United States. He also points to a high interaction of upper social class members in the major cities.[5]

An analysis of the Eastern Establishment is not the function of this study.[6] It is referred to because the oft-repeated claim of its power dominance does imply that high interaction rates between leaders and organizations exist in Megalopolis.

Megalopolis as a Regional Community

Jean Gottman in his 20-year study of Megalopolis gives strong assurances that the North Atlantic Seaboard region is closely integrated as one system and that the people and institutions are geographically and functionally related to one another by links of neighborhood.[7] He marshals numerous flow maps to show the region's high degree of integration.[8] He claims that the Eastern Seaboard area has a unique regional economy and that each of the major cities, Boston, New York, Philadelphia, Baltimore, and Washington, is linked like a chain and that the weakening of any of these central hubs would necessarily affect all the others and all the areas around them.[9]

Here, then, were three social foundations for the study: the accelerating trend toward regional integration, the alleged interaction of leaders in the Eastern Establishment, and Gottman's claim for an integrated region. These were promising bases, but there were serious problems to solve.

The size of the region would make it impossible to do more than achieve an approximation of the structures of power and influence. The research resources themselves were limited for such a task, but the stakes were promising. If the most powerful leaders and organizations engaged in urban problems could be identified and the interactions shown, the important dimensions of the structures could be revealed. A decision was made to proceed, but the research design was not fixed until Megalopolis was examined more fully as a regional system. Chapter 1 treats of this subject.

Notes

1. John C. Bollens and Henry J. Schmandt, *The Metropolis*, Harper & Row, New York, 1965, p. 582.

2. G. William Domhoff, *Who Rules America*, Prentice-Hall, Englewood Cliffs, N. J., 1967, and *The Higher Circles*, Vintage, Random House, New York, 1971. C. Wright Mills, *The Power Elite*, Oxford University Press, New York, 1956. R. Joseph Monsen, Jr., and Mark W. Cannon, *The Makers of Public Policy: American Power Groups and Their Ideologies*, McGraw-Hill, New York, 1965.

3. Jean Gottman, *Megalopolis, The Urbanized Northeastern Seaboard of the United States*, Twentieth Century Fund, New York, 1961, p. 15.

4. Mills, *op. cit.*, p. 288.

5. *Ibid.*, p. 47. "In Boston and in New York, in Philadelphia, in Baltimore, and in San Francisco, there exists a solid core of older, wealthy families who look first of all to one another."

6. John Franklin Campbell, "The Death Rattle of the Eastern Establishment," *New York* 4 (September 20, 1971), 47–51.

7. *Ibid*, pp. 691 and 693.

8. *Ibid.*, p. 741.

9. *Ibid.*, p. 750.

PART ONE

The Region
Called Megalopolis

CHAPTER ONE

System Characteristics of Megalopolis

The central research question is whether Megalopolis is a regional community with high rates of common social interaction within its boundaries. Because the proposed search is based on the premise that a network of interaction will be found between leaders and organizations in its major cities, it is important to discover the degree of regional integration. Ideally, it would be desirable to determine whether such integration has been increasing and whether the prognosis is for more rapid advances. The major specialists working on problems of regional integration have been geographers, economists, sociologists, and various city and regional planners. In substance, geographers have looked at the extent to which there are geographic features that give form to a common area, economists have sought economic indices of integration, and sociologists have searched for social indicators. Each has sought integration in his own terms. Moreover, the current interest in regional research has generally centered on the spatially narrower, more intensive, metropolitan area base study.[1]

It is widely recognized that cities are extending their influence more and more beyond their immediate environs and that the flow of goods and services has become interurban as well as rural-urban. Cities have become linked to one another in ever greater degree. Functional hierarchies between cities link them in exchange relations. Systems of cities can be studied by observing how changes in the characteristics of one city can influence the characteristics of others. Because of the paucity of data, however, this aspect of urbanization has not received extensive consideration.[2] Urban geographers and regional science scholars have been active in formulating theoretical bases and a new impetus is underway.

In summary, the knowledge base is limited and the findings reported for regional integration rest on different indicators and often specify different regional boundaries for the same general area. Many researchers, are concerned with the problem of regional integration and their work will be examined to see what consensus exists as an answer to the question: What is Megalopolis?

What Is Megalopolis?

Megalopolis ("large city") as a term was first applied by Jean Gottman in his study of the urbanized Northeastern Seaboard of the United States (1961)[3] in which he gave new identity to what has often been called the "East Coast" or just "the East." He describes a region stretching north of Boston to south of Washington and points out that 38 million persons (1960) populate the central cities, suburbs, and satellite areas lying along an axis about 600 miles long and 30 to 100 miles deep—more the size of a nation than a metropolis. A close look at the area shows that the axis of Megalopolis crosses the boundaries of 10 states and the District of Columbia. Thus Megalopolis is administered by 10 state governments plus the committees of the Congress which control the District of Columbia. On the local level the administrative map includes 117 counties and 32 major cities of more than 50,000 population, and the counties are subdivided into many more townships and boroughs.[4] Figure 1.1 shows the urban axis stretching through a network of sea-trading towns that sprang up along the coast from Boston to New York and then along the fall line from New York to Washington.

Gottman stresses the economic integration of Megalopolis as the major index of regionalism. He describes Megalopolis as a grouping of the main seaports, commercial and financial centers, and manufacturing activities in the United States. He points also to the function of cultural leadership expressed in its universities, laboratories, and libraries, periodicals and publishing houses, theater, music, and art.

Speaking of Megalopolis as a community, Gottman concludes that

> even though we do not feel justified in considering this region as one
> community, much less, of course, as one city, we have found enough
> integration in the whole and enough interplay between its various
> parts to indicate strongly that all those thirty-seven million inhabitants
> counted in Megalopolis by the 1960 Census are close neighbors.[5]

Lewis M. Alexander, the geographer, divides the Boston-Washington axis into four subregions: Southern New England, Metropolitan New York, the Delaware Valley, and the Baltimore-Washington conurbation.[6] In each of the four subregions the urbanized areas focus on the principal cities: Boston, New York, Philadelphia, Baltimore-Washington. The proximity of Baltimore and Washington brings them into a tight regional configuration. In contrast, Southern New England is focused on Boston and its satellite cities of Brookline, Cambridge, and Somerville. Its subregion includes such metropolitan districts as Worcester, Providence-Pawtucket, Fall River, and Lawrence-Haverhill. In Southwestern New England there is not one large urban center but rather a series of cities in the Connecticut River Valley and along the shore of Long Island Sound. Starting

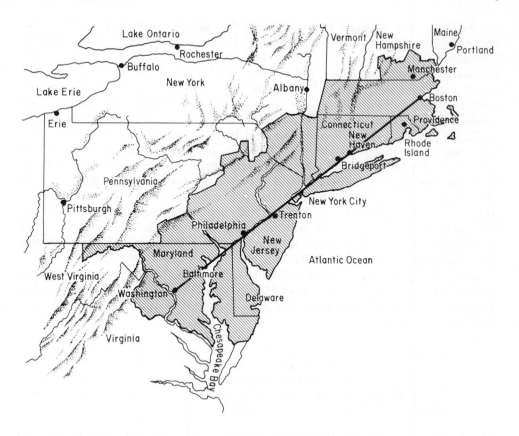

Figure 1.1 Megalopolis: a very special region. Wolf von Eckhardt, *The Challenge of Megalopolis,* based on the original study of Jean Gottman, © 1965 by the Twentieth Century Fund, New York. Some two thousand years before the Pilgrims reached our shores a group of ancient Greeks planned a new city-state in the Peloponnesus. They called it Megalopolis, or "very large city," because they dreamed that it would become the biggest and greatest of all the cities of Greece. A few hundred years later the Jewish philosopher Philo of Alexandria applied the name Megalopolis to his concept of a city of ideas which would rule our material world. Ancient Megalopolis still exists but only as an insignificant town. It never became really large, nor great, but the dream, it seems, has become true in our country today.

with Springfield, Massachusetts, this area contains Hartford, New Haven, Bridgeport, and Stamford.

The New York and Philadelphia metropolitan areas sit in the center of the Bos-Wash axis. With 15 million people in the New York subregion and close to 5 million in the combined Philadelphia-Wilmington region, or 20 million all told, these two subgroups contain almost half the population of Megalopolis.

The Regional Plan Association examined Megalopolis and chose to call it the Atlantic Urban Region.[7] It found that a number of issues, especially high-speed ground transportation, air travel and airport location, water supply, major parks for day-long and weekend recreation, and freeway location, were pulling the region together. They found little evidence, however, that Megalopolis could be considered a single community. In a recent report they say that even with continuous urbanization between Boston and Washington "this whole urban belt would consist of somewhat self-contained communities, both local and metropolitan—strung together one by one like beads."[8] They base the probability that communities can remain separate and self-contained on a mapping of commuter-sheds for each of the metropolitan areas of more than 250,000 (see Figure 1.2). The map shows that even today's older cities in the Atlantic Urban Seaboard have distinct commuter areas with little overlapping. The Regional Plan Association recommends that new metropolitan centers be encouraged to grow around older regional centers—New York, Philadelphia, Boston, Washington, Baltimore, Hartford, and Providence, "Organizing the population into metropolitan community by strengthening urban centers should clarify and strengthen the sense of community and the process of self-government even as population increases along the Atlantic Urban Seaboard."

In the face of this evidence of differentiated communities there is also a strong case for an underlying integration of Megalopolis. The economic intergration has been noted, the social intercourse has been documented. Gottman has done both and he points out that

> the emphasis on flow especially of people, demonstrates graphically the vast web of variegated and often abstract relationships that unite the different cities and counties of megalopolis in one regional system. Beyond the limits we have outlined for this region the intensity of all these flows slackens, the density of interconnections weakens.[9]

The five major cities lie close to one another: Washington to Baltimore is 39 miles, Baltimore to Philadelphia, 98 miles, Philadelphia to New York, 87 miles, and New York to Boston, 231 miles, a total of 455 miles. By automobile the most distant of the cities can be reached in one day's drive over high-speed freeways. The four cities, New York, Philadelphia, Baltimore, and Washington, are situated within a maximum of 224 miles. By train, New York and Philadelphia are 1 hour and 36 minutes apart; New York and Baltimore, 3 hours and 50 minutes. The train and air schedules for the five major cities are shown in Table 1.1. The long Boston-to-Washington leg is an 8-hour and 55-minute trip by train.

The new Metroliners are high-speed trains in service between New York and Washington (with stops at Newark, Trenton, Philadelphia, Wilmington, and Baltimore). The initial trains (1969) are running from New York to Washington in just under three hours. The railroad plans more than 20 Metroliners a day over the route with hourly service between New York and Washington and half-hourly service between Philadelphia and New York. An improved roadbed could cut running time substantially. We can see Philadelphia and New York becoming less than one hour apart—downtown to downtown. The modern train is proving to be competitive with air travel on the basis of time even on the older roadbed. The *Washington Post* ran contests in 1969 that pitted travelers going by Metroliner and by air, departing from the Washington Post Building in Washington and arriving at Times Square, New York. These contests resulted in ties.

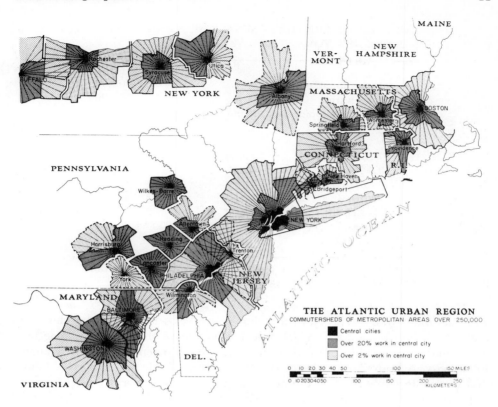

Figure 1.2   Commutersheds of Megalopolis in Atlantic Urban Region.
SOURCE: Draft, *Second Regional Plan*, Regional Plan Association, New York.

TABLE 1.1 TRAIN AND AIR TRAVEL TIME BETWEEN THE FIVE MAJOR CITIES
OF MEGALOPOLIS*

	Boston		New York		Philadelphia		Baltimore		Washington	
	Train	Air	Train	Air	Train	Air	Train	Air	Train	Air
Boston			4.30	0.50	6.30	1.00	7.53	1.15	8.55	1.15
New York	4.30	0.50			1.39	0.35	3.15	0.48	3.50	0.50
Philadelphia	6.29	1.00	1.39	0.35			1.34	0.30	2.14	0.40
Baltimore	7.53	1.15	3.09	0.48	1.34	0.30			0.40	0.15
Washington	8.55	1.15	3.50	0.50	2.14	0.40	0.40	0.15		

*As shown on Penn Central Schedule for April 27, 1969. These are the regular trains and
times are for leaving and arrival at downtown stations. All air travel schedules refer to
airport destinations only.

The air schedule (Table 1.1) (based on airport destinations and not counting
"on the ground time") shows that the airline is still the fastest when compared

TABLE 1.2 INTERNAL VERSUS OUTSIDE DAILY TRIPS
FOR THE NEW YORK STUDY AREA*

Internal trips for all purposes	35,000,000
Internal work trips	13,500,000
Trips to and from points outside the Study Area	260,000

PHILADELPHIA	20,000
BOSTON	12,000
WASHINGTON	11,000
Chicago	4,500
Los Angeles	2,000
Overseas	17,000
All others	193,000

*Source.   *The Region's Growth*, Regional Plan Association,
New York, May 1967, p. 35.

with the older trains. The cities are drawn ever closer together by the rapid
movement of air passengers. Megalopolis is everywhere only more than one hour
away, more or less. This means that all its leadership potential is easily available
to any city. A Bostonian can reach the Washington Municipal Airport in 1 hour
and 15 minutes, only 25 minutes more than it takes a New Yorker to get from his
airport to Washington. If physical proximity facilitates community, Megalopolis
has that requisite.

The physical movement of persons in Megalopolis can be partly estimated
from the volume of daily trips recorded in the New York metropolitan area in
the estimates of the Regional Plan Association for 1965. (See Table 1.2.)

Table 1.2 shows that a resident of the New York metropolitan area is most
likely to travel about each day within that area. If he visits any other city in
Megalopolis, it is most likely to be Philadelphia. Boston and Washington run a
close second. Travel up and down the North Atlantic Seaboard is considerable
and is known to be greater for business and professional leaders of all kinds.

All the evidence indicates that an economic and social base exists in which
there is growing integration of the megalopolitan region.

Urban geographers have been searching for measures to reveal the integration
of urban systems of cities. Ekistics, the science of human settlements (served by
a journal of that name), represents the scale of settlements in 15 classifications in
order of population size and following a logarithmic scale. This list includes,
successively, man, room, dwelling, dwelling group, small neighborhood, neighborhood, small town, town, large city, metropolis, conurbation, megalopolis, urban
region, urbanized continent, ecumenopolis. This all-embracing list envisions an
ever greater growth and concentration of urban populations when at the end
(about A.D. 2100) all the megalopolises of the world will be interconnected as
one huge city which Constantinos Doxiadis calls the "ecumenic city" or ecumenopolis. The rate, distribution, and character of urban interconnection becomes
a principal object of study. Network analysis focuses on public utility, transpor-

tation, communication, and computer and information systems. Much effort is being made to find meaningful boundaries, not an easy task. Gottman avoided defining a concrete boundary for Eastern Megalopolis and geographers today use his maps to represent study areas rather than actual boundary definitions.[10] The ways of bounding a region are arbitrary. The urban region may be viewed as an integrated pattern of activities, or a focus for the consideration of problems developing from these activities, and for the formulation of policy goals and strategies to deal with these problems.[11] The criteria selected will therefore give varying bounds for the region. Brian Berry has pointed out that the city and the continuously built up urbanized area had already been superseded by commuting areas which Doxiadis has named daily urban systems, where in 1960 all but 5 percent of the nation's population lived. If one calls the zones beyond these commuting areas the interurban periphery and then traces out combinations of commuter sheds and boundaries between television viewing areas, a fairly distinct regionalism of the country can be seen. Regular gradients traced within each region demonstrate that identical systems characterize a broad range of social and economic phenomena. Figure 1.3 shows the gradients of urban influence, New York to Boston. Note that as the degree of commuting declines so does the median income, but the proportion of the population below the poverty line increases. The peripheral zones of poverty are the zones of emigration.[12]

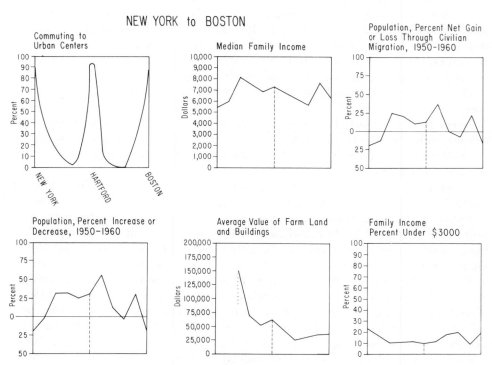

Figure 1.3   Gradients of urban influence. New York to Boston.
SOURCE: Brewton Berry, *Ekistics*, 20, No. 174 (May 1970), p. 343. Reproduced by permission of *Ekistics* (and the author), Athens Center of Ekistics, Athens, Greece.

This kind of search for links between cities becomes an intriguing challenge and is regarded as the key to the understanding of complex patterns of megalopolitan clusters of cities. Clusters assume the existence of strong interconnecting physical strips between the settlements of the cluster. Clusters tend to form along axes or corridors.[13] It has been generally considered that one of the main characteristics of a true megalopolis is that it constitutes a number of large centers strongly interacting with one another.[14] It is widely believed that the creation of a megalopolis relates to the development of a strong, high-speed transportation axis.

The urban geographer seeks to determine the strength (S) of the pull on a unit lying between two large centers in such a way that if this strength were great enough we would speak of a megalopolis: if it were weak, we would not. Papaioannou has developed a formula, based on a gravity model, for determining the strength of urban links. The variables include the population of the two centers, the distance separating the centers, the number and size distribution of the intervening units between them, and a transportation factor.[15]

It has been found that S varies from 0 to slightly more than 8 and that a critical value of $S = 4$ could be assumed to constitute the characteristic of the true megalopolitan nature of a link. An exhaustive world-wide survey has been made of all megalopolitan links likely to have reached a strength $S = 4$ or more as well as of a considerable number of other links with weaker strength but likely to become megalopolitan in the near future. Table 1.3 shows the 1960 links by decreasing strength and provides also other data for each link; upward from $S = 4$, the list is exhaustive; downward from $S = 4$, the list is selective. Note that Washington to Baltimore and New York to Philadelphia have about the highest link strength of any centers ($S = 7.14$ and 7.06, respectively). New York to Boston and Philadelphia to Baltimore are shown with S values of 5.50 and 5.13, respectively, and are described as moderately strong.

These determinations indicate that a geographic base exists for interaction between the four centers of Eastern Megalopolis as specified by their S values. It does not prove that social interaction takes place as specified. Indeed, we show subsequently that Baltimore which has a very high rank on the population gravity model occupies a low rank in the interaction of its leaders with other leaders of Megalopolis.

Geographic and economic indicators establish only that conditions exist for interaction. Usually geographers are more interested in the growth and concentration of population along main axes. An interesting economic indicator is a pull index described by Sheather, which is calculated from the difference between a city's total retail sales and its daily subsistence sales to its population.[16] He has applied this index to cities in the Great Lakes area but not, unfortunately, to Eastern Megalopolis. He does demonstrate that the potential (attractiveness) of a population field shows strong correlations with the flows and spatial patterns of certain features, such as telephone calls, telegrams, mail, bank checks, bus, railway, and airline passengers, visitors to fairs, hotel registrations, marriage licences, obituary notices, college attendance, areas of cities, rural population densities, land values, highway and railway network densities and alignment, bank deposits and velocity of money, information flows and decision making, administrative areas, taxes, patients, business failures, alcoholism, mental health, farm sizes, and commodity prices.[17]

Walter Isard, an eminent regional science researcher, describes an urban metropolitan region as a hierarchy of strategic nodal sites classifiable by order and degree of dominance. He specifies first-, second-, third-, and fourth-order nodes. Input-output analysis is used to determine the direct requirements by national, regional, and local sectors. Isard has not applied his instruments to the study of Eastern Megalopolis but has ventured an expert opinion:

> I do think you are dealing with a big region which has some hierarchical structure centered on New York, if we can leave aside the national policy areas. Boston, Philadelphia, Baltimore, and Washington are then just second-order nodes and in turn are focal points for still lower order nodes in their jurisdictional areas.[18]

Isard has sought to model the spatial pattern of decision making. He describes a concept of participation potential and specifies an interaction coefficient that might be applied in terms of the "degree" of participation of any individual (or population) in a given decision. He suggests that the measure could be ascertained in terms of the number of telephone calls the individual made to affect a decision or the number of letters written, telegrams sent, meetings attended, or some other act of communication.[19] He demonstrates how participational potentials for various spatial patterns of decision-making authority could be computed, but unfortunately there is no empirical test reported for Megalopolis or anywhere else.

This survey of the Eastern Megalopolis shows that empirical data are still limited and almost nothing exists on the interaction of its social variables. Theory is increasing, however, and efforts at boundary setting is certainly putting to the test many demographic and economic variables that are significant in defining fields of interaction. Vournas and Drymiotis have applied formal mathematical methods to boundary setting for the Great Lakes and Eastern megalopolises by using principal component and similarity analyses. Factor analysis of various input variables in an early study revealed three components: an index of urban concentration, an index of suburbanization, and an index of agricultural character. Later, 40 variables were separated into seven categories: demographic size and structure, demographic change, economic conditions, educational and occupational status, housing conditions, volume of sales and employment, and transportation indices. The Great Lakes Megalopolis and the Eastern Megalopolis which have 467 and 253 counties, respectively, were studied with the same set of input variables. A separate principal component analysis was then performed in each subarea and followed by comparisons of all the steps taken, from the behavior of initial variables to the final mapping results. The picture drawn on the basis of these conclusions shows a continuous megalopolitan formation in the Eastern Megalopolis which has already reached a level of maturity in its urban development, although its present growth still maintains dynamic rates.[20]

Projections of growth and spatial distribution of the population for the year 2000 indicate that the United States will have three gargantuan megalopolises which Kahn and Wiener have called "Boswash," "Chipitts," and "Sansan." Boswash is expected to contain almost one quarter of the population of the United States (perhaps about 80 million people). The extension of Boswash is variously estimated. One estimate places its northern boundary at Portland, Maine, and its

TABLE 1.3 MEGALOPOLITAN LINKS CLASSIFIED BY DECREASING STRENGTH b.f.*

Date: 1960, when not otherwise mentioned
For $S > 4.00$ the list is exclusive; for $S < 4.00$ it is selective

Link (in italics: composite settlements except metropolises)	Strength S	Distance D (km)	N unit factor	T transportation factor	$P = \sqrt{P_1 P_2}$ equivalent population (million)	Strength range
Manchester-Birmingham	8.25	56	4.50	1	4.10	Over 8 Very strong
Washington-Baltimore	7.14	56	0	1	1.96	
New York-Philadelphia	7.06	130	0.50	1	8.39	
(*Shenyang-Anshan*)	(6.55)	(90)	(1.25)	(1)	(2.18)	6-8 Strong
Frankfurt-Mannheim	6.45	70	0	1	1.89	
Randstadt-Ruhr	6.38	170	1			
Peking-Tientsin	6.26	120	0.25	1	4.46	
Hong Kong-Canton	6.11	125	0	0.75	2.50	
Lille-Brussels	5.96	103	0.50	1	2.45	
London-Birmingham	5.94	166	1	1	5.30	
Shanghai-Nanking	5.78	270	4.25	1	3.60	
Osaka-Nagoya	5.70	140	0.5	1	3.76	
Ruhr-Frankfurt	5.65	190	1.25	1	5.20	
Tokyo-Nagoya	5.61	270	3.25	1.	5.06	
Djakarta-Bandoeng	5.60	115	0.50	0.75	1.96	
Stuttgart-Mannheim	5.59	100	1	1	1.50	
New York-Boston	5.50	300	2.75	1	6.95	
Manchester-Newcastle	5.32	170	1.25	1	3.30	
Ruhr-Hamburg	5.28	310	3.50	1	4.93	4-6 Moderately strong
Pittsburgh-Cleveland	5.22	180	2.50	1	2.24	

City pair						
Philadelphia-Baltimore	5.13	145	0.50	1	2.74	
Chicago-Milwaukee	5.11	135	0	1	2.79	
Ruhr-Berlin	5.07	447	4.0	1	7.41	
Detroit-Cleveland	4.93	160	0.5	1	2.89	
Randstadt-Brussels	4.89	172	1.5	1	2.30	
Berlin-Leipzig	4.76	148	0	1	2.63	
Shenyang-Dairen	4.67	360	4.5	1	3.10	
Milan-Turin	4.53	126	0	1	1.62	
Paris-Lille	4.34	198	0	1	3.55	
Los Angeles-San Diego	4.22	180	0	1	2.68	
Cairo-Alexandria	4.20	180	0.50	1	2.21	
Osaka-Yahata (1966)	4.10	420	3.50	0.75	4.34	
Wuhan-Nanking (1972)	4.05	450	3.75	0.75	3.85	
Chicago-Detroit (1965)	4.00	375	1.50	1	5.95	(megalopolitan)
Chicago-Detroit	3.86	375	1.50	1	5.40	(nonmegalopolitan)
Detroit-Toronto	3.57	340	2.25	1	2.79	
Osaka-Yahata	3.53			0.75	3.78	
Manchester-Glasgow	3.51	300	0.75	1	3.50	
Stuttgart-Munich	3.49	190	0.5	1	1.51	
Buenos Aires-Montevideo	3.23	210	0	0	2.60	
Rio de Janeiro-S. Paulo	3.15	340	0	1	4.53	Weak
(Dairen-Anshan)	(2.86)	(270)	(1.25)	(1)	(1.51)	2-4
Seoul-Pusan	2.82	325	1.25	0.75	2.33	
Shenyang-Changchun	2.78	280	0.50	0.75	2.19	
Harbin-Changchun	2.76	230	1	0.75	1.23	
Delhi-Kanpur	2.76	390	2.50	1	1.92	
Chungking-Chengtu	2.60	270	0.50	0.75	1.79	
Los Angeles-Bengalore	2.53	300	0.25	0.75	2.30	
Wuhan-Nanking	2.20	450	2.25	0.5	2.25	
Harbin-Tsitshihar	1.83	275	0	0.75	1.29	
Toronto-Montreal	1.07	500	0.50	1	1.94	0-2 Very weak

Source: J. G. Papaioannou, "Megalopolis: A First Definition," *Ekistics*, 26, No. 152 (July 1968) p. 45.

southern at Portsmouth, Virginia.[21] Another prediction is that the Eastern Megalopolis at a megalopolitan level is expected to reach Norfolk around 1972,
Greensboro-Salem around 1980, Portland (Maine) around 1990, and Atlanta
(Georgia) around 2000.[22] Chipitts, another developing megalopolis, is concentrated around the Great Lakes, which may stretch from Chicago to Pittsburgh,
north to the Toronto region of Canada, and along a corridor that will include
Detroit, Toledo, Cleveland, Akron, Buffalo, and Rochester. Projections indicate
that extensions by 1990 will reach southern and southwestern clusters thrusting
to St. Louis, Louisville, and Cincinnati. The Mohawk Bridge (Buffalo/Hamilton/
Toronto cluster) will link the Great Lakes Megalopolis with the Eastern Megalopolis to form a real "megalopolitan network" within which a "key proportion
of the Northern American population, wealth, business, and culture will be concentrated, making it into the Heart of English America.[23] The economic base of
these two interconnected megalopolises is already in place. Figure 1.4 shows
clearly how the old manufacturing belt and the midwest manufacturing belt
interrelate with the Eastern Megalopolis.

Figure 1.5 shows the formation of megalopolitan systems for the United States
and Southern Canada for A.D. 1965–2000. Note the vast interconnected network
formed by the Eastern and Great Lakes megalopolises projected for A.D. 2000.
"Sansan," the third megalopolis and the smallest of the three units, stretches from
San Francisco to San Diego. It will have a larger income than all but five or six
nations of the world. The predictions for these three megalopolises coincide to a
remarkable degree with studies of the same areas by other authors.[24]

The answer to the question: "What is Megalopolis?" can now be given fuller
meaning. The urban geographer and economist have demonstrated that larger
and denser urban areas are interconnected. The base for wider interactions is
constantly being formed and extended. Urban regions, as they are emerging, are
neither separate nor clearly definable, for they in turn are interlocked in an ever
larger urban system of amazing complexity.[25] The question whether a regional
community exists remains elusive. The sociologist must recognize that allied dis-
ciplines cannot help him much. He is on his own and he must develop his own
bases for a sociological determination of a region. We turn now to the central
question, "Is Megalopolis a community?"

Is Megalopolis a Community?

There are five possible answers to this question:

1. Megalopolis is a regional community united by common sentiments and
identity. It is a psychosocial concept that exists in the thinking of the inhabitants
and leaders as the community to which they belong.

2. Large subregions (such as Southern New England, Metropolitan New York,
the Delaware Valley, and the Baltimore-Washington conurbation) are unified
communities but Megalopolis is not.

3. Megalopolis is a regional system of interrelated metropolitan areas that
contains a network of leaders and organizations who interact with concerns that
are local, state, interstate, regional, and national in character. This network indi-

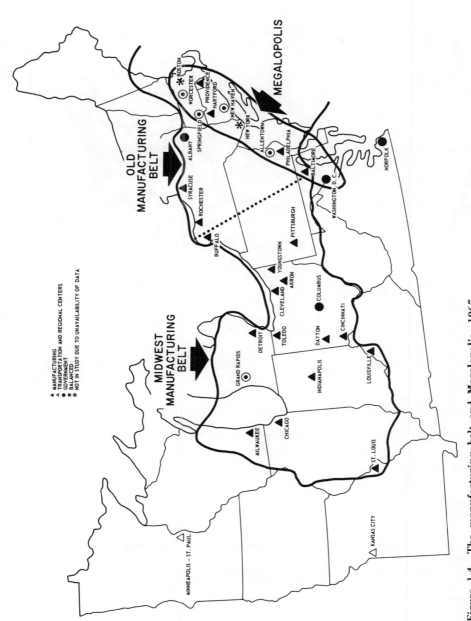

Figure 1.4 The manufacturing belt and Megalopolis, 1965.
SOURCE: U.S. Bureau of the Census, The Conference Board. Reprinted with permission of The Conference Board, New York from Juan de Torres, *Economic Dimensions of Major Metropolitan Areas.* March, 1967, p. 8.

19

0 miles   500   1000   1500   2000   2500   3000

Megalopolitan Network
▬ 1965
▨ 1980
☐ 2000
☐ connective branches

Figure 1.5   Formation of Megalopolitan systems, United States and southern Canada, 1965-2000.
SOURCE: Constantinos A. Doxiadis, Emergence and Growth of an Urban Region, Vol. 3, *A Concept for Future Development,* The Detroit Edison Co., Detroit, 1970, p. 169. Reproduced by permission of Athens Institute of Ekistics, Athens, Greece.

cates the presence of an incipient power base for a regional unit but does not provide its inhabitants with a full sense of community.

4. Distinct regional groups organized around specific functions (such as water supply and highways) have communal significance in Megalopolis, but a regional subcommunity does not function as a meaningful sociological unit.

5. Megalopolis exists as a congeries of metropolitan centers. No evidence of an overall communal base can be found.

Operating Definitions of Megalopolis for Research Study

An examination of the five possibilities of community in Megalopolis shows that in one sense all are useful definitions. For different functions they are all literally true because Megalopolis is a macroscopic concept within whose boundaries are numerous overlapping subcommunities. Our research tasks have led us to employ differing concepts. For the study of urban-oriented leaders and organizations the concept of best fit seems to be that which conceives of Megalopolis as interrelated major metropolitan areas with a network of leaders and organizations interacting across the region (option 3).[26]

It is known that business and professional leaders assemble in their own associations and that the Eastern regional component in all national associations is large and vigorous. Some national organizations have leaders from many walks of life, and Eastern leaders active in business, politics, and religious, labor, and civic groups are often reported meeting together. Meanwhile the movement of people and the flow of telephone calls and letters indicates that a tremendous web of contacts binds the residents of Megalopolis.[27]

Faced with this evidence, we turned to the concept of linkage. Charles P. Loomis defines systemic linkage as "the process whereby the elements of at least two social systems come to be articulated so that in some ways and on some occasions they may be viewed as a single system."[28] In Megalopolis the major problem is how systemic linkage relates members of the five principal metropolitan areas to one another. The research problem is to discover the kinds of activity and the degree of interaction between leaders and organizations of the major cities.

Systemic Linkage in Megalopolis

LINKAGE OF EASTERN LEADERS TO NATIONAL ASSOCIATIONS IN MEGALOPOLIS

Many national associations establish bases from and to which residents and leaders of Megalopolis move or communicate in pursuit of their professional or civic duties. There are 13,600 national associations of trade, professional, labor, fraternal, and patriotic affiliation in the United States. The number in major cities lying along the Bos-Wash axis is given in Table 1.4. Note that the national headquarters of 5606 of them (42%) are located in Megalopolis. Percentages are computed for each city on the basis of this number.

Table 1.4 shows that New York with more than 67 percent has the largest share. Washington is second with about one-fourth (23.2%), Boston and Philadelphia can muster only 4.5 and 3.4 percent, respectively, and Baltimore has less than 1 percent. A study of national associations most influential in urban problems is a part of this research and is described in detail in Chapter 7. It is important here to report that among the 37 national associations identified as most

TABLE 1.4 THE NUMBER AND PERCENT OF NATIONAL
ASSOCIATIONS LOCATED IN THE BOSTON TO
WASHINGTON AXIS

	Number	Percent
Boston	249	4.5
Providence	13	0.2
Hartford	10	0.2
New York	3777	67.3
Newark	14	0.2
Philadelphia	191	3.4
Wilmington	6	0.1
Baltimore	45	0.8
Washington	1301	23.2
Total	5606	99.9

Source.   National Trade, professional, labor, fraternal, and patri-
otic organizations; Encyclopedia of National Associations, 5th ed.,
Vol. II, Geographic and Executive Index, Gale Research Co.,
Detroit, Michigan, 1968.

powerful in dealing with urban problems 29 (80%) are located in Washington,
seven (19%) are located in New York, and only two, the U. S. Junior Chamber
of Commerce and the Council of State Governments, are located outside
Megalopolis.[29]

At these national headquarters people can meet and discuss their common
problems. The most influential organizations are active communication centers
that keep in constant touch with members and government and other association
officials by telephone, letter, or literature, in an effort to persuade them to support their goals. Some also operate government lobbies. Washington is a major
hub of political action, and many strong New York-based business, professional,
labor, and civil rights associations maintain large Washington offices.

A matrix of major organizations which shows the interaction of members in
and between national and regional organizations would reveal a large part of the
policy participation network in Megalopolis. It is this network that weaves the
growing fabric of regional ties and it is this network that is so little known.

The locus of leadership participation can be identified. It is known, for example, that powerful business leaders can be found in the Business Council, on
the National Industrial Conference Board and the Committee on Economic Development, in the National Alliance of Businessmen, and in the National Urban
Coalition. Table 1.5 is a compilation of the membership in the cities of Megalopolis of each of these five organizations.

The Business Council is one of the most prestigious bodies of businessmen in
the United States. It is composed of men in private industry, chosen as broadly
representative of a geographical as well as a product point of view and for their
own characters, ability, and sense of public responsibility. The Council stands

TABLE 1.5 BUSINESS LEADERS OF MEGALOPOLIS IN POWERFUL AND PRESTIGOUS ASSOCIATIONS SHOWING REPRESENTATION BY NINE CITIES OF MEGALOPOLIS

Major associations and proportion represented in Megalopolis and the United States

Eastern cities represented	Business Council Members (1968)		Members of National Industrial Conference Board (1968)		Research and Policy Group of the Committee on Economic Development (1968)		Chairman and members at large of National Alliance of Businessmen (1968)		Steering Committee of National Urban Coalition (1968)	
	N	Percent	N	Percent	N	Percent	N	Percent	N	Percent
Boston	7	9.7	8	8.6	2	7.7	2	18.2	1	5.0
Providence	0	0.0	0	0.0	0	0.0	1	9.1	0	0.0
Hartford/Bridgeport	2	2.9	4	4.3	2	7.7	0	0.0	0	0.0
New York	48	66.6	67	72.0	16	61.5	3	27.2	12	60.0
Jersey City/Newark	0	0.0	2	2.2	1	3.9	1	9.1	0	0.0
Philadelphia/Camden	5	7.0	6	6.4	3	11.5	2	18.2	1	5.0
Wilmington	1	1.4	5	5.4	0	0.0	0	0.0	0	0.0
Baltimore	1	1.4	0	0.0	1	3.8	1	9.1	1	5.0
Washington	8	11.0	1	1.1	1	3.8	1	9.1	5	25.0
Total for nine cities of Megalopolis	72	100.0	93	100.0	26	100.0	11	100.0	20	100.0
Total for the United States	191		250		49		49		38	
Megalopolis representation in the United States	38%		37%		53%		23%		53%	

23

ready on request to provide advice to all departments of government. The Council's active membership is limited under the bylaws to 65. A small number may be reappointed to graduate or honorary membership after completing service as active members. All members are appointed by the Council's nominating committee and are given final approval by the Executive Committee. In April 1968 there were 191 active, graduate, and honorary members, 72 of whom lived in Megalopolis (see Table 1.5). This distribution is an indication of the concentration of top business leaders in the New York area. Two out of three are found there. Washington has 8, Boston 7, Philadelphia 5, Hartford 2, Wilmington 1, and Baltimore 1. These leaders of Megalopolis are able to communicate with one another through this organization. Note that Megalopolis provides 38 percent of the Business Council members on the nation.

The National Industrial Conference Board was founded in 1916 to provide information on the experience of companies in the management of their enterprises. It brings leaders together in committees and councils and in seminars, conferences, and training sessions. A group of 250 regular members are distinguished business leaders who are officers or directors of firms that support the Conference Board. New York has 67, Boston 8, Wilmington 5, Philadelphia and Camden 6, Hartford and Bridgeport 4, Newark 2, and Washington 1. Megalopolis claims 37 percent of the leaders in the NICB.

The Committee on Economic Development was formed in 1942 to bring businessmen and industrialists into a close working alliance with outstanding economists and social scientists for the development of new ideas. In the World War II years the Committee worked on postwar planning. Today 183 members from all over the United States are on the Board of Trustees. The Research and Policy Group, which provides major direction, has 49 members, 26, or 53 percent, of whom come from the cities of Megalopolis. Megalopolis also supplies 53 percent of the steering committee members.

The National Alliance of Businessmen received its charter following on President Johnson's manpower message to the Congress on January 23, 1968. The President asked business to find jobs for the hard-core unemployed. The Department of Labor was enjoined to work closely with the Alliance, whose chairmanship was assumed by Henry Ford II, Chairman of the Ford Motor Company, and who appointed a vice chairman, an executive vice chairman, and five members-at-large. A national office was opened in Washington. The United States was divided into eight regions and major cities were designated. Top businessmen were recruited to serve without compensation as a public responsibility. A regional chairman was appointed and appointees were named in 49 cities. Boston, New York, Philadelphia, Jersey City, Newark, Baltimore, and Washington, D. C., were named in Eastern Megalopolis. Various top posts were filled by Roger P. Sonnabend and Louis W. Cabot of Boston, G. William Miller of Providence, Harold S. Geneen, A. L. Nickerson and Floyd D. Hall of New York, Thomas J. Stanton of Jersey City, Orville E. Beal of Newark, Stuart T. Sanders of Philadelphia, Jerold C. Hoffberger of Baltimore, and Stephen Ailes of Washington. By their membership, often multiple, on such organizations business leaders in Megalopolis maintain a network of contacts.

All of these links stress the ties of business leaders. The National Association of Manufacturers, the U. S. Chamber of Commerce, the American Management

Association, and numerous trade associations based in Megalopolis multiply the opportunities for communication. It would be of interest to know how top business leaders interact with labor, political, religious, civic, and civil rights leaders in Megalopolis. If one seeks organizational contexts, it is necessary to examine those private associations and governmental commissions and committees that bring leaders together from different walks of life.

Some government commissions and private associations demand wide representation.[30] The National Urban Coalition was born in the midst of the violent urban crisis of 1967. National leaders in business, labor, religion, government, and civic rights were assembled and organization plans were developed. The Urban Coalition became a nonprofit corporation with John Gardner as its chairman and chief executive officer. A steering committee of 38 members was selected, 20, or 53 percent, of whom were residents of Megalopolis. As Table 1.5 shows, 12 are from New York, 5 from Washington, and 1 each from Boston, Philadelphia, and Baltimore. Powerful business leaders, such as David Rockefeller (Chase Manhattan Bank), James F. Oates (Equitable Life Insurance Co.), Theodore Schlesinger (Allied Stores Corp.), Joseph H. Allen (McGraw-Hill Book Co.), and James Rouse (The Rouse Co.), met with powerful leaders from government, labor, religion, and civil rights—men like John V. Lindsay, Roy Wilkins, James H. J. Tate, George Meany, Rabbi Jacob P. Rudin, Dr. Ellen G. Hawkins, A. Philip Randolph, John F. Collins, Andrew Heiskell, I. W. Abel, the Reverend George H. Guilfoyle, and others.[31]

This kind of interoccupational communication is encouraged for many more leaders of Megalopolis in the Boston, New York, Philadelphia, Baltimore, and Washington urban coalitions.[32] It is difficult to estimate how many have been brought together.

The examination of this overlapping, multiple participation became an important part of the process of identifying influential leaders of Megalopolis active in urban problems. Patterns of multiple participation are presented in Chapter 10. At this point it is our purpose to sketch the bases of leadership linkage by occupational groupings. We want to know if leaders in Megalopolis make contacts and establish working relations. We could determine the intensity of interaction as Megalopolis labor leaders interact with national labor officials in Washington, where the AFL-CIO and other major labor organizations have headquarters. Washington is the labor center for making national policy and initiating programs for exerting influence on Congress. Political and government leaders of Megalopolis come to Washington to engage in the activities of such organizations as the National League of Cities, National League of Counties, the U. S. Conference of Mayors, the National Council of State Governments, and the U. S. Governor's Conference. Religious leaders meet in New York at the National Council of Churches, the Catholic Federations, and the American Jewish Congress. As the home of the National Association for the Advancement of Colored People, the Urban League, and the Congress of Racial Equality, New York is also the civic rights center of the nation.

Professionals go to New York and Washington to visit their national and regional organizations. Teachers, lawyers, doctors, professors, architects, bankers, planners, broadcasters—all are drawn into common contact in one of these two centers. Boston, Philadelphia, and Baltimore serve as important regional centers and hold many annual meetings of the numerous national organizations.

Civic leaders belong to myriad organizations. Politically active women gather at the National headquarters for the League of Women Voters or the National Federation of Business and Professional Women's Clubs. Civic leaders active in environmental problems may be found at the Conservation Foundation, the Sierra Club, the National Parks Association, the Izaak Walton League of America, the Wildlife Management Institute, the National Audubon Society, and the National Wildlife Federation.

The channels in which leaders of different institutional segments of the region can meet have special interest because interoccupational contacts widen the scope of relationships. Government commissions and government advisory or fact-finding committees provide outlets for such acquaintance.

The roster of boards, committees, and commissions attached to the executive and legislative branches of government is long. The executive branch calls largely on lay personnel outside the Federal Government. In 1968 there were 68 bodies variously called board, committee, advisory committee, study commission, commission, council, or conference, three of which were especially important to the study of urban problems—the National Commission on Urban Problems, the National Advisory Commission on Civil Disorders, and the National Advisory Council on Economic Opportunity. All provide examples of an effort to represent business, labor, government, religion, and civil rights.

The National Commission on Urban Problems was appointed by President Lyndon B. Johnson on January 12, 1967, and charged with seeking ways to increase the supply of decent housing for low-income families. Among the 16 members appointed seven were residents of Megalopolis: Mrs. Cloethiel W. Smith and Paul H. Douglas, Washington, D. C.; Lews Davis, Richard O'Neil, and Richard Ravitch, New York; Alex Feinberg, Camden, New Jersey; and Jeh V. Johnson, Poughkeepsie, New York.

Leaders of Megalopolis were brought together in the National Advisory Commission on Civil Disorders which was formed in 1967 to make a full investigation of the large-scale riots in Detroit, Washington, and many other American cities in that year. A national crisis was recognized and the Commission was asked to get the facts and make recommendations with all haste. Goevrnor Otto Kerner of Illinois was appointed chairman and 10 other members represented business, labor, government, and civil rights groups. Megalopolis provided Edward W. Brooke, U. S. Senator from Massachusetts, John V. Lindsay, Mayor of New York, and Roy Wilkins, Executive Director of NAACP, all of whom as powerful and influential leaders and were well known in Megalopolis and the nation.

The National Advisory Council on Economic Opportunity was established on March 31, 1968, to deal with the problems of employment and opportunity. In this 19-member council were five lawyers, two physicians, two religious leaders, two educators, three government officials (one federal, one state, and one city), one television official, one civic leader, one labor leader, one civil rights leader, and one American Indian leader. All the major metropolitan sections of Megalopolis except Philadelphia had one or more members. The Washington area was represented by Mrs. Robert McNamara, civic leader, George R. Davis, Sr., religious leader, James A. Suffridge, labor leader, and Horace Busby, governmental aide to President Johnson. Theodore McKeldin, attorney and former governor of Maryland and former Mayor of Baltimore was a member, as were New York's Morris Abram, attorney, Donald H. McGannon, broadcasting official, and the late Whitney Young, civic rights leader. Otto Eckstein, professor at Harvard, represented the Boston area.

Other sources of interoccupational communication are the boards, of the various foundations. Generally the stress is on wide leadership representation. Because most of the large foundations and many associations are headquartered in Megalopolis, many Eastern leaders meet at such intersections.

Summary of Documentary Search for Systematic Linkage of Leaders

This documentary search for links among leaders of Megalopolis is now ended, not because the survey has been exhaustive but because the case for extensive linkage has been delineated. We can see that the opportunities for communication between top leaders are many, both by leaders within and between the five principal metropolitan areas of Megalopolis. We can assume that these records are more than mere formal entries. Acceptance for membership in most of the commissions and policy-making boards carries with it a strong obligation to participate. In some, failure to attend one or two meetings is sufficient basis for being dropped from the group. The documentary search does not make it clear whether leaders in all the principal cities receive proportionate recognition and are drawn into interaction. New York and Washington always loom large. Philadelphia, Boston, and especially Baltimore seem to be underrepresented; hence leadership links to these cities appear to be weaker. This premise was subjected to research and will be reported. The role of the separate cities would appear worthy of some study. How do they produce leaders? What function do the cities serve in Megalopolis? Are there reciprocal, systemic functional relations between the cities? We turn to a brief examination of these questions with an initial look at the five principal cities of Megalopolis.

Notes

1. John M. Mattila and Wilbur R. Thompson, "The Measurement of the Economic Base of the Metropolitan Area," in Jack P. Gibbs, *Urban Research Methods*, Van Nostrand, New York, 1961, p. 329.

2. Gibbs, *Urban Research Methods, ibid.*, p. 397.

3. Jean Gottman, *Megalopolis, The Urbanized Northeastern Seaboard of the United States*, The Twentieth Century Fund, New York, 1961.

4. *Ibid.*, p. 740. The U. S. Department of Commerce, commenting on the 450 miles of seacoast extending immediately from Boston to Washington, D. C., reports an overall population increase of 11.2 percent between 1960 and 1970. Less than 1 percent of the nation's land is occupied by Megalopolis, but 18 percent of all residents of the United States are now found in this region. *Washington Post*, September 29, 1970.

5. *Ibid.*, p. 692.

6. Lewis M. Alexander, *The Northeastern United States*, Van Nostrand, Princeton, N. J., 1967, p. 15.

7 Regional Plan Association, *The Region's Growth*, Bulletin No. 105, New York, May 1967.

8. The Regional Plan Association, *The Second Regional Plan, A Draft for Discussion,* Bulletin No. 100, New York, November 1968, p. 30.

9. Gottman, *op. cit.,* pp. 691-692.

10. Theodoros Vournas and Andreas Drymiotis, "The Great Lakes Megalopolis: Principal Component and Similarity Analyses," *Ekistics,* **26** (July 1968), p. 82.

11. Donald Foley and Derek Senior in *The Regional City,* Derek Senior, Ed., Longmans, Green, London, 1966, p. 18.

12. Brian Berry, "The Geography of the United States in the Year 2000," *Ekistics,* **29** (May 1970), 341. Other gradients have been plotted: St. Louis to Memphis, Des Moines to Lincoln, Des Moines to Peoria, and San Francisco to San Diego.

13. J. G. Papaioannou, "Megalopolis: A First Definition," *Ekistics,* **26** (July 1968), 41. That the chain has an oblong string or band form has been confirmed by the study of more than 100 present or future megalopolises; cf. Myrte Bogdanou, "Great Lakes Megalopolis: General Considerations on National Transportation Axes," *Ekistics,* **27** (June 1969), 429–433.

14. *Ibid.,* p. 41.

15. *Ibid.,* p. 42.

16. See Graeme Sheather, "North and Central Great Lakes Study Region: A System Analysis," *Ekistics,* **27,** No. 163 (June 1969), 413.

17. *Ibid.,* p. 423.

18. Letter from Walter Isard to writer—February 25, 1971.

19. Walter Isard, *General Theory,* M.I.T. Press, Cambridge, Mass., 1969, p. 60, suggests that if the individual participated in 4 percent of all communication acts taken by all individuals his degree of participation in that decision mght be 4 percent. Collecting data would be difficult and validity of the measure is unknown.

20. Theodoros Vournas and Andreas Drymiotis, "The Great Lakes Megalopolis: Principal Component and Similarity Analyses," *Ekistics,* **26** (July 1968), 74.

21. Herman Kahn and Anthony J. Wiener, *The Year 2000,* Macmillan, New York, 1968, p. 61.

22. Vournas and Drymiotis, *op. cit.,* 78.

23. *Ibid.,* p. 78.

24. Richard L. Meier, *Megalopolis Formation in the Midwest,* University of Michigan, December 1965; Jerome P. Pickard, *Metropolitanization in the United States,* Urban Land Institute Research Monographs; Office for Regional Development of New York State, *Change, Challenge, Response:* A Development Policy for New York State, State of New York, Albany, 1964.

25. John Friedmann, "The Spatial Organization of Power in the Development of Urban Systems," Comparative Urban Research, **1** (December 1972), 5–42; Terry N. Clark, *Community Power and Policy Outputs, A Review of Urban Research,* Sage Publications, Beverly Hills, Calif., 1973.

26. For our studies of environmental quality leaders and organizations we chose options 3 and 4 and examined the interaction in Megalopolis and regional interest groups. For tests of decision-making processes studies were designed for the specific subregion, the Delaware River Basin, and issues involving water quality and trust of leaders were examined.

27. Gottman concluded that, "As the vast region of Megalopolis grows, regional integration into one interwoven system is bound to progress. The first evolution must be achieved in the minds of the people, and many signs indicate it is already occurring. . . . The people of Megalopolis must first realize fully the implications of the region's present structure and the assets and liabilities involved in the present tighter neighborhood on a large scale." Gottman, *op. cit.,* 738.

28. Charles P. Loomis and Zona K. Loomis, *Modern Social Theories,* Van Nostrand, New York, 1961, p. 16.

29. The Council of State Governments has a sizable Washington office and an Eastern regional office in New York in addition to its national headquarters in Chicago.

30. These two organizations have now merged.
31. The late Whitney Young was a member of the Steering Committee.
32. A roster of Urban Coalitions in the five major cities shows the following: Boston, Small Organizing and Development Committee. New York, 33 on Board of Directors; 22 on Economic Development Task Force; 27 on Education Task Force; 23 on Housing Task Force; 44 on Education Task Force. Philadelphia, 21 on Board of Directors and numerous persons on various task forces to study economic development, education, housing, and manpower. Baltimore, Three major committees: Business in the Ghetto Committee, 12 members; Committee on Racism, 7 members; Legislative Committee, 8 members. Washington, 84 members of which 22 are blacks and 62 are white.

CHAPTER TWO

The Five Big Cities of Megalopolis

New York, Philadelphia, Washington, Boston, and Baltimore are five of America's 11 largest cities. Figure 1.1 showed how they form an urban axis. More than 60 percent of the people of the Northeast live in the urbanized belt surrounding this axis,[1] on or near which rests other cities such as Providence, Rhode Island; Hartford, New Haven, and Bridgeport, Connecticut; Newark, Camden, and Trenton, New Jersey; and Wilmington, Delaware.

As centers of manufacturing, communication, transport, finance, retailing, wholesaling, recreation, education, and science, the five major cities serve to organize and administer the functions that move the life of Megalopolis—and much of the United States and the world. Their size is best portrayed by examining their positions among the top metropolitan areas of the United States. (See Table 2.1.) In 1970 the New York metropolitan area, with a population of nearly 12 million, was easily the largest urbanized region in the United States. The Philadelphia-New Jersey area ranked fourth, Washington seventh, Boston eighth, and Baltimore eleventh. These are positions within the 66 major metropolitan areas (population of 500,000 or more) of the country.[2]

The New York consolidated area constitutes the City of New York and Northeastern New Jersey in which are such large centers as Newark, Jersey City, Patterson, Passaic, and Elizabeth; altogether more than 16 million people, or approximately one-third of the total population of the Northeast, live in this area. The growth of suburban areas since the late 1930s has been extremely high.

Philadelphia, with more than 2 million people, is surrounded by a metropolitan district which adds another 2.75 million who live in cities like Camden, Chester, and a number of smaller towns. To the southwest on the Delaware river is Wilmington; more than 5 million people live and work in the combined Philadelphia-Wilmington area.

TABLE 2.1   MAJOR METROPOLITAN AREAS OF THE
UNITED STATES, 1970

		1970 Census (thousands)	1960 rank
1.	New York	11,529	1
2.	Los Angeles-Long Beach	7,032	3
3.	Chicago	6,979	2
4.	Philadelphia	4,818	4
5.	Detroit	4,200	5
6.	San Francisco-Oakland	3,110	6
7.	Washington, D.C.-Maryland-Virginia	2,861	10
8.	Boston	2,754	7
9.	Pittsburgh	2,401	8
10.	St. Louis, Mo.-Illinois	2,363	9
11.	Baltimore	2,071	12
12.	Cleveland	2,064	11
13.	Houston	1,985	15
14.	Newark	1,857	13
15.	Minneapolis-St. Paul	1,814	14

Source.   U.S. Bureau of the Census.

Washington has well under a million but it has one of the most rapidly growing metropolitan areas. Alexandria and Falls Church, Virginia and Chevy Chase
and Silver Spring, Maryland, are among the towns that are growing into cities.
The Washington area has risen from tenth to seventh place in the size of metropolitan areas in the 1960–1970 decade.

Boston, which has an inner city population of about 700,000, is surrounded by
a metropolitan district that supports a population of more than 2 million in such
centers as Brookline, Cambridge, and Sommerville. A pronounced population
movement away from Boston itself has been evident in the last two decades, and
the Boston metropolitan area has dropped from seventh to eighth in size in the
last 10 years.

Baltimore is almost a twin city of Washington. Between the two, along the
Baltimore-Washington Parkway, are located Baltimore Friendship Airport, College Park, the home of the University of Maryland, the new town of Columbia,
and a growing agglomeration of bedroom communities. As yet there is no continuous string of suburbs between Baltimore and Washington, but they are building
toward one another and the vacant space between them is fast disappearing.
Columbia, Maryland, a newly planned community, with a future population estimated at 75,000, is indicative of the rapid growth expected. Baltimore itself has
a central city of 1 million but its metropolitan district is the smallest of the five.
However, its rise from twelfth to eleventh position in the last decade indicates a
continuous growth pattern.

As we look at the urban axis from north to south and examine the population bases from which megalopolis leaders come a number of things become clearer. First, it is obvious that Boston, as the northern anchor, lacks the population strength of the middle and southern nodes. It is also removed in distance. A population of more than 21 million is concentrated in New York and Philadelphia, and Washington and Baltimore at the southern end combine almost 5 million. The New York area is so large that it can be expected to hold a reservoir of leaders. To understand the interactional base from which regional leaders operate, it is necessary to establish functional relations between the cities.

Functional Interdependence of the Major Metropolitan Areas

THE ECONOMIC GOODS AND SERVICES OF THE MAJOR AREAS

The five principal cities of Eastern Megalopolis have many characteristics in common. All take pride in their modernity and culture, their universities, their art, and their music. All are large centers of wholesale and retail trade. Boston, New York, Philadelphia, and Baltimore have excellent ports and are heavily engaged in world trade. Each of these major cities is located at or near the estuary of one or more rivers, and each is a financial and real estate center for a wide market area surrounding it. Because these cities service highly populated metropolitan districts, transportation, construction, and services of all kinds occupy a high proportion of the work force. Table 2.2 shows the percentage distribution of employment in the Boston, New York, Philadelphia, Baltimore, and Washington metropolitan areas. The general impression received from this table is the high similarity between the cities. There are distinct differences, however. Note that the number circled in each column is the highest statistic in each category for the five metropolitan areas, the number that expresses the greater predominance of employment in the given category for one of the five major cities. The high proportion of employees in the Washington area in government jobs (38.6%) is no surprise. It is, however, the only statistic that appears to signal a truly significant difference in the economic life of the various cities. If the data on mining and manufacturing were available for the Washington area (see Table 2.2 for further information), it would undoubtedly show the significant low level that obtains in comparison with the other cities. All metropolitan areas except Washington rely most heavily on manufacturing for their major source of employment. Philadelphia, with 34.4 percent, has the largest proportion in that category.

These statistics offer clues to the kind of economic contribution each city can make as well as to the wider national and international market each of them can serve.

The location of the headquarters of the largest industrial corporations, banks, life insurance and retail companies, transportation facilities, and utilities reveals even more sharply the focus of economic power and decision making as it is distributed in Eastern Megalopolis. The power of a business leader is highly correlated with the importance of the corporate base from which he operates. The next section shows how New York dominates Megalopolis by economic function.

TABLE 2.2   PERCENTAGE DISTRIBUTION OF EMPLOYMENT IN METROPOLITAN AREAS BY INDUSTRY, MARCH 1967

	Total number of employees (1)	Mining, manufacturing (2)	Contract construction (3)	Transportation, and public utilities (4)	Wholesale and retail trade (5)	Finance, insurance and real estate (6)	Service and miscellaneous (7)	Government (8)
Boston (SEA)	100.0	n.a.	3.7	5.6	21.9	6.8	n.a.	14.8
New York (NY-NJ)	100.0	28.4	3.5	7.9	20.6	8.2	17.5	13.8
Philadelphia (Pa-NJ)	100.0	34.3	4.2	6.6	19.5	5.2	15.8	14.3
Baltimore	100.0	28.3	5.4	7.4	21.2	5.1	15.7	16.9
Washington (Md-Va)	100.0	n.a.	6.4	5.4	18.7	6.2	n.a.	38.6

n.a.: not available

Source.   Bureau of Labor Statistics, *Employment and Earnings*. Analyzed and assembled by Juan de Torres, *Economic Dimensions of Major Metropolitan Urban Areas*, National Industrial Conference Board, New York, 1968, p. 39.

33

New York is the headquarters for 25 percent of the 500 largest industrial corporations in the United States. Those situated in Megalopolis in 1969 were distributed as follows:

	Number	Percentage of Top 500
New York	125	25.0
Philadelphia	10	2.0
Boston	4	0.8
Baltimore	1	0.2
Washington	0	0.0
Total	140	28.0

Source. The Fortune Directory of the Five Hundred Largest Industrial Corporations, *Fortune* (May 1970), 184–194.

New York not only leads in the number of corporate headquarters in Megalopolis and in the United States but also has a concentration of the giants (See Table 2.3). Seven of the first top 12 are located in New York: Standard Oil of New Jersey (2), General Electric (4), Mobil Oil (7), Texaco (8), International Telephone and Telegraph (9), Western Electric (11), and U. S. Steel (12); 118 other top corporations are located in New York and many others are in the vicinity. Philadelphia has limited representation with such large corporations as Sun Oil (42) Scott Paper (154), International Utilities (156), and six others in the 200 to 500 rank. Boston, the only other metropolitan center to hold the headquarters of any members of the top 500, has four corporations; Gillette (ranking 182) is the largest.

The dominance of New York as the center of economic decision making is clearly shown by these statistics. It is further reinforced by the city's position in banking, life insurance, retailing, and utilities. This preponderance can be quickly noted by looking across Table 2.3.

New York is also the headquarters of 10 of the country's top 50 banks: First National City (2), Chase Manhattan (3), Manufacturers Hanover Trust (4), Morgan Guaranty Trust (5), Chemical, New York (6), Bankers Trust (7), and others. Philadelphia has four of the largest: First Pennsylvania Banking and Trust (20), Philadelphia National (24), Girard Trust (30), and Fidelity (43). Boston has the First National Bank of Boston (17) and the Shawmut Association (46). Baltimore and Washington, D.C., are not represented.

In life insurance Philadelphia, Boston, and Washington are the headquarters of six large companies but altogether they cannot match the seven that do business in New York.

In retailing New York holds a commanding lead with 13 of the top 50 retail establishments. Philadelphia with three, Boston with one, and Baltimore and Washington with none are no match for the giant. The story is repeated in utilities except that Baltimore and Washington are represented by one utility in the top 50.

TABLE 2.3 THE DISTRIBUTION BY RANK OF LARGEST INDUSTRIAL CORPORATIONS, BANKS, LIFE INSURANCE, RETAIL, AND UTILITY CORPORATIONS AMONG THE FIVE MAJOR CITIES OF MEGALOPOLIS

	500 top industrial corporations	50 top banks	50 top life insurance companies	50 top retail companies	50 top utilities
New York	Standard Oil, N.J. (2) General Electric (4) Mobil Oil (7) Texaco (8) IT&T (9) Western Electric (11) U.S. Steel (12) Shell Oil (16) General Telephone & Electron (19) RCA (21) Union Carbide (24) Atlantic-Richfield (29) 113 others	First National City Chase Manhattan Manufacturers Hanover Morgan Guaranty Chemical New York Bankers Trust Charter New York Franklin New York Bank of New York National Bank of North America	Metropolitan (2) Equitable (3) New York Life (4) Mutual of NY (5) Teachers Insurance & Annuity (7) Guardian of America (13) Home Life (21) (22) (38)	A. & P. (2) J. C. Penney (4) F. W. Woolworth (7) W. T. Grant (16) Allied Stores (17) Spartana Industries (22) R. H. Macy (24) Associated Dry Goods (28) Gimbel Brothers (30) Interstate Department Stores (31) Pueblo International (42) J. J. Newberry (46) City Stores (47)	AT&T (1) Consolidated Edison (2) American Electric Power (6) Columbia Gas System (10) General Public Utilities (11) Consolidated National Gas (29) Allegheny Power System (33) Western Union (46)
Philadelphia	Sun Oil (42) Scott Paper (154) International Utilities (156) Rohm & Haas (233) Pennwalt (246) Crown Cork & Seal (264) Smith, Kline & French (297) ITE Imperial (328) ESB (388)	First Penn PNB Girard Trust Fidelity	Penn Mutual (23) Provident Mutual (25) Fidelity Mutual (30) (48)	Food Fair Stores (10) Acme Markets (11) ARA Services (38)	Philadelphia Electric (13)
Boston	Gillette (182) USM (271) Eastern Gas & Fuel (407) Cabot (439)	First National Shawmut	John Hancock Mutual (5) New England Life (12) (18) (46)	Stop & Shop (29)	
Baltimore	Easco (448)				Baltimore Gas & Electric (40)
Washington			Acacia Mutual (43)		Potomac Electric Power (39)

Source. Fortune, The Fortune Directory (May 1970), 184-213.

35

In transportant Penn Central of Philadelphia ranks first, but New York holds the dominant position as the headquarters of air and steamship lines.

The economic dominance of New York is all the more impressive in historical perspective when the substantial movement of industry from the Northeastern industrial belt to the West and South in the 1940s and early 1950s is considered:

> This represented a decentralization of economic activity—but not of economic power. It consists mainly of the establishment of branch plants in new communities or the purchase of locally owned small industries by major national concerns. Capital and control continued to be concentrated in the great Northeastern cities, from New York to Chicago. *The concentration of control in the New York* area was even intensified, as companies which had previously maintained their headquarters in other cities of the Northeast and Great Lakes area, in order to be near their plants, found that they could relocate in or near the "Empire City" and rely on modern communications facilities to maintain contact with an even wider network of field operations.[3]

Raymond Vernon has described the external economies that have resulted in the concentration of office activity in New York. He points out that the problem of the central office of a giant corporation is to maintain two links in the chain of communication: an easy flow of facts and decisions from headquarters to branch plants, warehouses, and regional sales offices and an easy interchange of ideas among headquarters personnel and their outside advisors. Vernon says that

> the most probable outcome of the increased freedom offered by swifter air travel will be the further concentration of the office elite at a few headquarter cities. This tendency will be fortified by the use of high speed electronic data-processing machines. For these machines will contribute to the centralization of data-processing and decision making at fewer points in the structure of the giant company. . . . There is typically a preference for locating them in some degree of proximity to the decision makers.[4]

In the context of economic structure New York functions as a primary node around which the other cities of Megalopolis seem to revolve. This concentration of industry, business, and finance creates a large reservoir of business leaders. In New York the chief executive officer may preside over a corporation with immense assets. Table 2.4 shows the top 38 industrial corporations, life insurance, retail, and utility companies ranked by assets. *Fortune* calls this the *Top of the Top*. Any corporation with headquarters in one of the five major cities of Megalopolis has been noted. The assets of each corporation are shown and the chief executive (in 1968) is given. It will be noted that New York (with 21 of the 38 places, Philadelphia (1), and Boston (1) occupy 61 percent of the top spots. This was the year in which our Eastern Leadership Survey was undertaken, and those business leaders from the list who were chosen by expert judges as most powerful in the shaping of urban policy and program for the region are listed. Eleven of the 23 chief executives (recorded in the last column of Table 2.4) of the top corporations in Megalopolis were chosen for the survey as described in Chapter 4.

Examination of the regional organization of Megalopolis brings out the question of reciprocal relations among the major cities. This question invites the broader concern of functional interdependence of all levels of life: social, cultural, recreation, educational, health, political, and economic.

FUNCTIONAL BASES OF CONTACT AND INTERDEPENDENCE

In the six states of New England there are more than 240 colleges and universities that grant higher degrees. Some 52 colleges and universities concentrated in the Greater Boston area include such institutions as Harvard, M.I.T., Radcliffe, Brandeis, Tufts, Wellesley, Boston University, Northeastern University, Emmanuel, Regis, University of Massachusetts, and Wentworth Institute. This complex constitutes a major industry. Thousands of young men and women come from the other cities of Megalopolis to be admitted to these excellent schools.

The concentration of scientific talent along the Charles River is a valuable resource which has helped to spawn many industries. More than 500 producers of electrical machinery are located in the Boston area alone, many of them along Route 128, the "electronics highway," where the research facilities of Harvard and M.I.T. have made heavy contributions. Nearly 90,000 people are employed in this industry in Massachusetts. To Megalopolis Boston offers liberal, scientific, and engineering training. The manufacture of machinery, tools, and instruments are significant industries, as are aircraft, brass, and typewriters. Advances in modern medicine and surgery have been made in the medical schools and hospitals. As a tourist center Boston and environs offer numerous historic sites and proximity to seashore, mountains, and resorts.

New York has already been shown to hold great attraction for management and finance and to have achieved first place as a center of economic decision making. New York is also noted as an art center. Lincoln Center of the Performing Arts, the Metropolitan and Guggenheim museums, the Museum of Modern Art, the Museum of Natural History, Broadway and Off Broadway theaters—all are immensely popular among residents of Megalopolis. New York's educational institutions which include Columbia and New York universities among a large number of private and public colleges and universities are the goal of many students from Megalopolis, and millions of people come to New York every year to participate in educational and cultural activities. Others rely on New York for their books, magazines, and newspapers and many use the city as the source of their television viewing. Advertising is a speciality, and to others New York is the center of the fashion world. New York is therefore a supplier of goods and services to all of Megalopolis and a symbol of leadership in various fields. It is often admired for the best in urban life, yet is also sometimes held up as a model of what is worst in metropolitan living.

Philadelphia, the second largest city of Megalopolis, is only 87 miles from New York. It gains and loses from this proximity. Perhaps, more than any other city, it takes advantage of New York's cultural services but it loses by its magnetic attraction for industrial and managerial talent. Yet Philadelphia makes its own distinctive contribution. It is an old city with deep historic roots to which Americans come by the millions to visit Independence Hall and other historic sites. It offers most of the advantages of a large center but at a slower pace than demanded by

TABLE 2.4 THE TOP 38 OF THE RANKING INDUSTRIAL CORPORATIONS, BANKS, LIFE INSURANCE, RETAIL, AND UTILITY CORPORATIONS (RANKED BY ASSETS) IN THE UNITED STATES, SHOWING ASSETS AND CHIEF EXECUTIVE OFFICERS

Company	Headquarters in Megalopolis	Assets	Chief executive officer	Selected for Eastern leadership survey
1. American Telephone & Telegraph	New York	$37,607,901,000	Haakon I. Romnes	x
2. Prudential	New York	25,111,192,000	Orville E. Beal	x
3. Metropolitan Life	New York	24,600,589,000	Gilbert W. Fitzhugh	x
4. Bank of America	New York	21,267,639,000	Rudolf A. Peterson	
5. Chase Manhattan	New York	17,770,525,000	George Champion	x
			David Rockefeller	x
6. First National City	New York	17,497,373,000	George S. Moore	
			Walter B. Wriston	
7. Standard Oil of New Jersey	New York	15,197,439,000	Michael L. Haider	
8. General Motors	New York	13,273,083,000	James M. Roche	
9. Equitable Life	New York	13,093,110,000	James F. Oates, Jr.	x
10. New York Life	New York	9,579,215,000	Richard K. Paynter, Jr.	
11. Manufacturers Hanover	New York	9,171,603,000	Robert E. McNeill, Jr.	
12. Morgan Guaranty	New York	9,168,394,000	Thomas S. Gates	
13. John Hancock Mutual Life	Boston	8,865,318,000	Robert E. Slater	x
14. Chemical Bank N. Y.	New York	8,365,693,000	William S. Renchard	
15. Ford	New York	7,966,800,000	Henry Ford II	
16. Texaco	New York	7,162,830,000	J. Howard Rambin, Jr.	
17. Bankers Trust	New York	6,850,864,000	William H. Moore	

18. Gulf Oil		6,457,954,000	Ernest D. Brockett	
19. Penn Central	Philadelphia	6,264,316,000	Stuart T. Saunders	x
20. Aetna		6,244,477,000	Olcott D. Smith	
21. Mobil Oil	New York	6,223,861,000	Albert L. Nickerson	
22. Continental Ill. National		6,173,138,000	David M. Kennedy	
23. Sears, Roebuck		6,006,825,000	George M. Metcalf	
24. First National Bank of Chicago		5,956,875,000	Homer J. Livingston	
25. Security First National		5,617,800,000	Frederick G. Larkin, Jr.	
26. United States Steel	New York	5,606,311,000	Roger M. Blough	x
27. International Business Machines	New York	5,598,670,000	Thomas J. Watson, Jr.	x
28. Northwestern Mutual Life	New York	5,475,938,000	Robert Dineen	
29. General Telephone & Electronics	New York	5,430,576,000	Leslie H. Warner	
30. General Electric	New York	5,347,189,000	Fred J. Borch	x
31. Standard Oil of California		5,309,748,000	Otto N. Miller	
32. Wells Fargo		$4,693,301,000	Richard P. Cooley	
33. Crocker-Citizens National		4,304,889,000	Emmett G. Solomon	
34. Travelers		4,147,935,000	Sterling T. Tooker	
35. United California		4,082,582,000	Frank L. King	
36. Irving Trust	New York	4,076,354,000	George A. Murphy	
37. Standard Oil of Indiana		4,058,071,000	John E. Swearingen	
38. Connecticut General Life		4,033,397,000	Henry R. Roberts	

Source: *Fortune* (June 15, 1968), 319. Reprinted from the June 15, 1968 issue of Fortune Magazine by special permission; © 1968 Time Inc.

New Yorkers. It has established itself as a center of music and art which supports orchestras, museums, and schools of art and music. Its educational system paced by the University of Pennsylvania is a complex that includes Swarthmore, Haverford, Temple, and Drexel. It has also built a good reputation in medical science and has pioneered in urban planning. It substantiates its claim by pointing to the newly created city center, and a science center is now under construction, also near the University of Pennsylvania, on another planned area of 200 acres.

As a rail center Philadelphia holds a strategic position between New York and Washington, and the new fast Metroliners promise increased travel to and from other centers of Megalopolis. Because of the shortened travel time to New York, some people are calling it a coming dormitory city that will serve a growing number of New York commuters.

Baltimore is the home of Johns Hopkins University, a manufacturing center and port, and a satellite of Washington. It is the Pittsburgh of the eastern seaboard because of its leadership in primary metal industries. It now has the largest steel plant in the United States and from its steel production have developed various steel fabricating industries such as shipbuilding, machinery, and machine tools. New York, Philadelphia, and Boston provide the light manufacturing and finished products; Baltimore's distinctive contribution to Megalopolis is heavy industry and the primary materials for fabrication.

Washington is the political center of the United States, a fact that dwarfs all others. It is, in addition, an important airline, retail trade, and tourist and convention center. It is also a center of education and the arts. Because of governmental requirements for managerial and technical talent, it attracts a large number of highly trained people.[5] A recent report showed that among 30 selected regions the Washington-Maryland-Virginia area has the highest proportion of adults who have completed four years or more of college; 25 percent were listed as college graduates.[6] Washington, as shown earlier, houses a large number of national associations. We shall show that the District of Columbia is the headquarters for almost all the most influential organizations that deal with urban problems.

Washington is also the labor center of the United States. Labor has an enormous stake in capital affairs and the presence of a large number of union headquarters is no coincidence. Several stand near the White House; others are clustered in the Capital Hill area. Six of the 10 largest unions in the country are Washington based. Among the 190 (129 AFL-CIO and 61 independent) national and international unions 56 have their headquarters in Washington; 41 are AFL-CIO affiliates, and 15 are independent unions. In addition, the national headquarters of the AFL-CIO and the National Federation of Independent Unions are located in the District.

These characteristics mark out the broad contours of the five cities and delineate them as bases of contact and interdependence in the life of Megalopolis.

The Urban Problems of the Major Cities of Megalopolis

The major cities of Megalopolis all have the same urban problems, but they vary in intensity. An inventory includes jobs for the unemployed, low-cost housing, better schools, control of lawlessness and crime, race relations (especially in jobs, education, housing, and police-community relations), traffic and parking, environmental quality of all kinds, including air, water, and the disposal of solid wastes, noise reduction, and recreational needs. Welfare costs are rising sharply and are causing heavy financial drains on public budgets. Crime has become a growing concern in all segments of urban metropolitan areas, and planning and zoning problems are more demanding than ever.

New York is a miniature urban nation, a microcosm of the problems facing modern man. The Regional Plan Association found that large numbers of people were dissatisfied with the prospects of the New York metropolitan area. In meetings, conversations, and a formal public response project based on the replies of 5600 volunteers the association identified eight major concerns:

1. Uncontrolled urbanization—failure to save enough green space and the crowding together of too many people.

2. A segregated society—growing separation of rich and poor, Negro and white.

3. Lengthening work trips—growing separation of worker and work place.

4. Inadequate shelter—tight housing market, low replacement rate of obsolete housing, and limited choice of new housing.

5. Few urban advantages—lack of big city advantages outside the core, and for almost all trips no alternative to driving.

6. Low transportation standards—overcrowded subways, poor trains, infrequent off-peak service, congested highways, and local traffic jams.

7. Lack of community focus in many parts of the area.

8. A general tawdriness in new building; a system of development that encourages mediocre design, from the individual structures to the regional pattern and an indifference to natural beauty and the function of nature.[7]

Other cities of Megalopolis report similar concerns. Similarity in urban problems may be assumed, but what discriminant factors produce important differences among the cities?

Richard L. Forstall presents a new social and economic grouping of 1761 cities in the United States of 10,000 or more population, based on a multivariate analysis of 97 variables. Fourteen principal factors emerge from a factor analysis, of which the most significant clusters of correlations are associated with size of community, population growth, nonwhite population, and socioeconomic status.[8] (Socioeconomic status relates to median income, percentage of families with incomes under 3000 dollars, median years of education, percentage of persons in white collar jobs, percentage of persons who have graduated from high school, and median years of school completed). Other principal factors are stage in family cycle, proportion of foreign-born population, proportion of manufacturing and mining, and presence of a college, university, or military installation. Important discriminant factors to be illustrated for the five cities of Megalopolis are (a) size, growth, and density of the city; (b) proportion of black population; and (c) personal income and costs of living.

Important Differences Among the Cities Affecting Urban Problems

SIZE, GROWTH, AND DENSITY OF THE CITY

Sheer size, the rate of growth, and density (inhabitants per square mile) compound the problem of providing services, especially transport and parking, refuse collection and disposal, street maintenance, and the furnishing of utilities. Air pollution is worsened by engine exhaust, incinerators, and household heating. Housing costs pyramid as demand exceeds supply. Table 2.5 shows the population, area, annual growth rate, and density of the metropolitan areas of the five principal cities.

The size of the New York metropolitan area and its density indicate the tremendous problem of maintenance and supply that faces the city daily. It has learned to deal with these problems, but growth increases the pressure. The annual growth rate between 1960 and 1965 was 1.4 percent, which has little meaning until it is translated into a population that rose from 14,759,000 in 1960 to 15,821,000 in 1965—an increase of more than a million. Given a density that is the highest in any city (9810 per square mile), this added population put more pressure on housing. New York now reports low vacancy rates and rising rents. In such massed congregations of people strikes against public services and utilities often produce physical hardship and health hazards. Good cases in point are the garbage and fuel strikes of 1968. Air pollution is a constant hazard in the congested city as incinerators and combustion engines add their fumes to industrial gases. Garbage and waste removal can be a mountainous task if the sanitation service is interrupted. The crime rate is high (first among the top 11 cities in 1970).

Philadelphia shares these difficulties with New York, and its high density (9379 inhabitants per square mile), the second highest among American cities, produces similar service and maintenance problems. Street surfaces are particularly in need of repair, and air pollution, heightened by its large oil refineries, is ever present.

Boston, Washington, and Baltimore all have the advantage of lower populations, smaller areas to maintain, and lower densities than New York and Philadelphia. The Washington metropolitan area, however, shows the largest annual rate of growth for any of the five cities. Its increase in population from 1,989,000 in 1960 to 2,861,000 in 1970 has put a severe strain on services, especially police

TABLE 2.5   POPULATION, AREA, ANNUAL GROWTH RATE, AND DENSITY OF PRINCIPAL CITIES OF MEGALOPOLIS

	Population 1965 (thousands)	Urban area 1950 (sq mi)	Annual growth rate 1960-1965	Density 1950 (persons/sq mi)
New York (N.Y.-N.J.)	15,821	1253	1.4	9810
Philadelphia (Pa.-N.J.)	4,664	312	1.4	9379
Boston	3,205	345	0.6	6478
Washington (D.C.-Md.-Va.)	2,408	178	3.9	7216
Baltimore	1,854	152	1.4	7654

Source.   U.S. Bureau of the Census, Current Population Reports, Series P-25, No. 371.

protection. However, because of the exodus of the white population, middle-class housing in the inner city is available, and the absence of heavy and light industry has minimized air pollution.

Table 2.6 shows the cost of maintaining the public life of the five major cities. The first column lists general expenditures for all functions. New York's budget of almost 6 billion dollars speaks of the immensity of that city. More than one million residents were on welfare in 1970 and the New York City Human Resources Administration requested a 2.1 billion budget for welfare and Medicaid.[9] The next columns (b) and (c) report on the number of police and firemen employed. Column (d) is a report on the number of persons served by the sewer treatment plants. The final columns, (e) and (f), set out expenditures in thousands of dollars for utilities and highways. The enormity of New York's public expense dwarfs the other cities. Mayor John Lindsay's request for a national city charter to give New York the status of a state had many sound bases of consideration. The other major cities may be smaller, but the time and effort that city officials must give to maintenance functions alone is testimony of the difficulty of improving the quality of life. Dealing with rapidly rising crime rates is only one example.

Crime rates for the 11 largest cities are given in Figure 2.1a. Note that New York, Baltimore, and Washington, which rank first, fourth, and fifth, all have high rates. Philadelphia has the lowest. Boston has had a rising crime rate and the

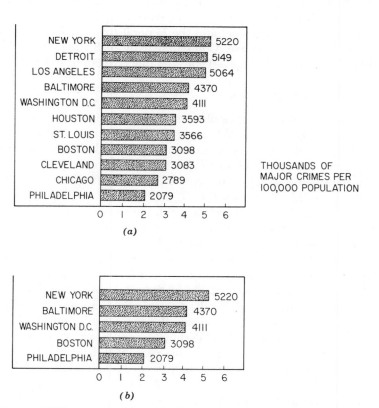

Figure 2.1 (a) 1970 crime rates in 11 largest cities. Thousands of major crimes per 100,000 population; (b) 1970 crime rates for the five major cities of Megalopolis. SOURCE: Uniform Crime Report, 1970.

TABLE 2.6   THE GENERAL EXPENDITURES AND PUBLIC SERVICE REQUIREMENTS OF THE
FIVE MAJOR CITIES OF MEGALOPOLIS (data for 1967-1968-1969)

The five major cities	General expenditures (in thousands) all functions except utilities (a)	Number of public safety employees (b)	Number of firemen (c)	People served by sewer treatment plants (in thousands) (d)	Utilities expenditures for water, gas, electricity, transit in thousands) (e)	Highways expenditures (in thousands of dollars) (f)
New York	$5,877,823	49,731	14,882	7,750	$799,693	$79,597
Philadelphia	504,138	10,707	3,078	2,003	23,414	14,815
Washington	527,008	6,280	1,490	810	11,391	14,642
Baltimore	412,841	6,049	2,232	911	14,134	9,464
Boston	384,252	4,975	2,094	not given	5,669	6,924

Source.   Municipal Year Book 1971: (a) Data for 1968-1969, p. 255; (b) January 1970 data, pp. 202-203;
(c) January 1970 data, pp. 202-203; (e) data for 1968-1969, pp. 203-204; Municipal Year Book 1970: (d)
data for 1967-1968, p. 358; (f) data for 1967-1968, p. 231.

dubious distinction of having reached eighth place in thousands of major crimes
per 100,000 population. Figure 2.1b separates the five Eastern cities, and the dif-
ferentials in their crime rates can be clearly seen. Philadelphia has secured a rate
that is less than half that of New York and Baltimore, but every city has added
substantially to its safety personnel and the Federal Government has contributed
heavily to the fight against crime. Compared with 1968 rates, New York, Baltimore, and Washington have achieved considerable reductions in their crime rates.

PROPORTION OF BLACK POPULATION

The proportion of blacks in the populations of the principal cities is a serious factor in their problem orientation. Wherever blacks have migrated rapidly in large
numbers there are new problems of accommodation and change. In size of black
population among the central cities Washington easily ranks first (71% in 1970),
followed by Baltimore (46%), Philadelphia (34%), New York City (21%), and
Boston (16%),[10] Table 2.7 ranks the 50 cities in the United States with the
largest number of blacks in 1970 and shows the proportions in each of them. This
table indicates that in total numbers New York leads with almost 1.7 million.
Boston has the lowest black population of the five cities of Megalopolis and is
significantly outranked by the others. However, its black population did increase
more rapidly between 1960 and 1970 than in the preceding decade. Table 2.8
lists the black population as percentages of the total population, 1950, 1960, and
1970, and the percentage change in the five principal cities of Megalopolis. The
20-year 1950–1970 change pattern reveals the rapid transition of blacks from a
minority to a majority population in Washington and nearing that status in Baltimore. The trend pattern forecasts that in the year 2000 there will be black majorities or near majorities in Washington, Baltimore, Philadelphia, and New York.[11]
Washington and Baltimore are currently the best examples of what is required to
make new accommodations and new changes. In these cities almost all the major
urban problems are intensified by the higher proportion of blacks; jobs, education, housing, crime and lawlessness, waste, police-community relations, and

recreational demands. This is not to say that blacks necessarily cause these problems, but they certainly are the result of accommodations to the rising numbers and new requirements of black people.

PERSONAL INCOME AND COSTS OF LIVING

The quality of urban life depends to a great extent on the property and income of its citizens and what they, in turn, must pay for private and public services. From property and income come taxes to provide needed public services and the capacity of government units to respond to local urban problems. Table 2.9, which reports on the median family income in the five principal cities, shows that in size of family income Washington leads with $12,933 dollars followed by Boston, New York, Philadelphia, and Baltimore. This ranking pattern has been maintained since 1960.[12]

It can be said that Washington should be in the best position to provide private and public support for urban programs, but many factors intrude. Washington is under the direction of a Board of Commissioners controlled by the Congress. Federal and local distinctions are blurred. Washington, Boston, and New York complain of the amount of nontaxable property (between 35 and 40 percent of all real estate), and each city supports a large number of nonprofit organizations. All we can say about the family median income statistics is that they point out the potential of each metropolitan area.[13]

The capacity to pay has been explored, but the cost of living in the cities of Megalopolis is a necessary counterpart to the problem of sustaining and improving personal and public life. The U. S. Bureau of Labor Statistics has released findings for the cost of living in 40 metropolitan areas in the United States based on a four-person family in 1970. According to the Bureau, national urban averages indicate that an annual income of 10,664 dollars was needed by a city worker's four-person family to maintain a "moderate" standard of living. The same family required an income of 6960 dollars to maintain an "austere" standard. For a fuller, more expansive life an income of 15,511 dollars was needed.[14] Each city required different amounts based on costs. Table 2.10 shows these costs for the 40 cities studied. The relative ranking of each city based on requirements for a moderate budget reveal that New York leads all major cities in Megalopolis. Boston, Washington, Philadelphia, and Baltimore follow. In fact, it costs more to achieve a moderate or high standard of living in New York than in any other city in the 50 states, but a low standard is cheaper than in 11 other cities. The low cost of a low standard of living is the result of cheaper public transportation and rent-controlled housing.

A careful scrutiny of Table 2.10 shows that in spite of differences New York and Boston actually have similar living costs. New York is only slightly higher.[15] Baltimore and Philadelphia are lower. It is interesting that it costs more for the low-income family to live in Boston than in any of the other four principal cities of Megalopolis. Philadelphia offers the lowest costs for the low-budget family.

What is pertinent to the urban dwellers is the change in costs. New York has experienced price rises greater than those in other cities. The consumer price index issued by the Bureau of Labor Statistics measures the changes in prices and goods bought for family living. Figure 2.2 shows the rise in prices from 1959 to

TABLE 2.7   RANKING OF THE 50 CITIES OF THE UNITED STATES
WITH THE LARGEST NUMBERS OF BLACKS IN 1970

City	Rank	Black population	Black Percentage
New York City	1	1,666,636	21.2
Chicago	2	1,102,620	32.7
Detroit	3	660,428	43.7
Philadelphia	4	653,791	33.6
Washington	5	537,712	71.1
Los Angeles	6	503,606	17.9
Baltimore	7	420,210	46.4
Cleveland	9	287,841	38.3
New Orleans	10	267,308	45.0
Atlanta	11	255,051	51.3
St. Louis	12	254,191	40.9
Memphis	13	242,513	38.9
Dallas	14	210,238	24.9
Newark	15	207,458	54.2
Indianapolis	16	134,320	18.0
Birmingham	17	126,388	42.0
Cincinnati	18	152,070	27.6
Oakland	19	124,710	34.5
Jacksonville	20	118,158	22.3
Kansas City, Mo.	21	112,005	22.1
Milwaukee	22	105,088	14.7
Pittsburgh	23	104,904	20.2
Richmond	24	104,766	42.0
Boston	25	104,707	16.3
Columbus	26	99,627	18.5
San Francisco	27	96,078	13.4
Buffalo	28	94,329	20.4
Gary	29	92,625	52.8
Nashville-Davidson	30	87,851	19.6
Norfolk	31	87,261	28.3
Louisville	32	86,040	32.8
Fort Worth	33	78,324	19.9
Miami	34	76,156	22.7
Dayton	35	74,284	30.5
Charlotte	36	72,972	30.3
Mobile	37	67,356	34.5
Sheveport	38	62,162	34.1
Jackson	39	61,063	39.7
Compton Calif.	40	55,781	71.0
Tampa	41	54,720	19.7
Jersey City	42	54,595	21.0
Flint	43	54,237	28.1
Savannah	44	53,111	44.9
San Diego	45	52,971	7.6
Toledo	46	52,915	13.8
Oklahoma City	47	50,103	13.7
San Antonio	48	50,041	7.6
Rochester	49	49,647	16.8
East St. Louis	50	48,368	69.1

Source.   U.S. Census

46

TABLE 2.8   BLACK POPULATION AS A PERCENTAGE OF THE TOTAL
POPULATION, 1950, 1960, and 1970: PERCENT CHANGE IN THE BLACK
POPULATION 1950-1960, 1960-1970 IN THE FIVE PRINCIPAL CITIES OF
MEGALOPOLIS

	Percent			Percent increase in proportion of population		
	1950	1960	1970	1950-1960	1960-1970	Total 1950-1970
Washington	35.4	54.8	71.1	19.4	16.3	35.7
Baltimore	23.8	35.0	46.4	11.2	11.4	22.6
Philadelphia	18.3	26.7	33.6	8.4	6.9	15.3
New York	9.8	14.7	21.2	4.9	6.5	11.4
Boston	5.3	9.8	16.3	4.5	6.5	11.0

Source.   U.S. Census

TABLE 2.9   MEDIAN FAMILY INCOME
(1969), RANKED BY SIZE, IN THE STAND-
ARD METROPOLITAN AREAS OF THE FIVE
PRINCIPAL CITIES OF MEGALOPOLIS

	Median family income (dollars)
Washington	12,933
Boston	11,449
New York	10,870
Philadelphia	10,783
Baltimore	10,577

Source.   U.S. Bureau of the Census, Census of
Population and Housing: 1970 Census Tracts,
Final Report. U.S. Government Printing Office,
Washington, D.C., 1972

1966 in the average worker's family budget in the United States and its 10 largest
metropolitan areas. Note that New York also has the dubious honor of leading
this category with a 71 percent increase and Boston is not far behind with 61
percent. Philadelphia and Washington are just slightly above the national urban
average of 51 percent.[16]
    Taken together these factors, size, growth, density proportion of black popula-
tion, personal income, and cost of living explain many of the differences in the
problem difficulties of megalopolitan cities. At first glance they seem to be what
they truly are: modern cities of the twentieth century with skyscrapers, shops,
apartments, and slums. Most of the problems are not visible. The observer is
aware that millions of people are constantly moving—going to work or school,

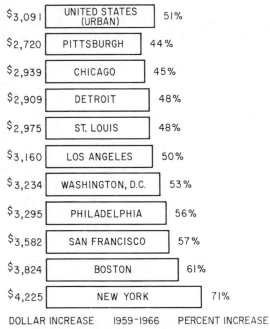

DOLLAR INCREASE   1959-1966   PERCENT INCREASE

Figure 2.2   Rise in the average city worker's family budget in the United States and 10 largest metropolitan areas from 1959 to 1966.
SOURCE: Consumer Price Index of U.S. Bureau of Labor Statistics.

going home, shopping, playing, and worshiping. Life goes on and the maintenance of the facilities for these activities absorbs the greater amount of human energy. Quality of life must be achieved as a lower priority requirement. The city is more often a machine that processes the goods for a given level of living. When cities find leaders and citizens who have the willingness and ability to grapple with urban problems or to adorn the quality of life, they add something beyond a given level of maintenance. Where obstacles are greater, the difficulties are compounded. New York has been called "ungovernable," but it is governed. Washington has had to make a vast transition as the black population increased. Each of the mayors in the cities of Megalopolis agrees that there are common problems, but each is also quick to point out that his city is different. Environmental quality problems represent a good example of these urban differences.

The Environmental Quality Problems in Major Metropolitan Areas

If urban problems in general were found to be large in magnitude and severity in the principal cities of Megalopolis, there was reason to believe that environmental quality problems would also be a major concern. What we need to know is the extent of these problems and what priorities are given to them in the context of others equally pressing. In Part Two these considerations are examined in detail. Here we evaluate Megalopolis as a field site for an environmental study.

TABLE 2.10   THREE BUDGET STANDARDS FOR METROPOLITAN AREAS, 1970: THE ANNUAL COST OF LIVING IN 40 CITIES AND METROPOLITAN AREAS IN THE SPRING OF 1970, BASED ON BUDGETS FOR FOUR-PERSON FAMILIES

		Lower Budget	Intermediate Budget	Higher Budget
	National average	$ 6,960	$10,664	$15,511
1.	Achorage	10,783	14,535	20,301
2.	Honolulu	8,597	12,776	19,311
3.	San Francisco	7,686	11,381	16,526
4.	Seattle	7,630	11,012	15,626
5.	Hartford	7,577	11,584	16,312
6.	Los Angeles	7,507	10,770	15,989
7.	Boston	7,351	12,037	17,819
8.	Chicago	7,273	11,120	16,019
9.	Washington	7,242	11,047	16,125
10.	Champaign-Urbana, Ill.	7,235	10,864	15,769
11.	New York	7,183	12,134	18,545
12.	San Diego	7,166	10,467	15,309
13.	Minneapolis-St. Paul	7,140	10,897	15,808
14.	Portland, Me.	7,130	10,835	15,088
15.	Indianapolis	7,101	10,892	15,620
16.	Cleveland	7,080	11,184	15,897
17.	Milwaukee	7,079	11,405	16,575
18.	Buffalo	7,022	11,425	16,424
19.	Baltimore	7,018	10,580	15,590
20.	St. Louis	6,987	10,546	15,125
21.	Kansas City, Mo.	6,981	10,599	15,575
22.	Philadelphia	6,958	10,587	15,845
23.	Detroit	6,931	10,588	15,460
24.	Bakersfield	6,910	10,040	14,283
25.	Cedar Rapids	6,873	10,614	15,390
26.	Durham	6,771	10,187	14,630
27.	Green Bay	6,769	10,596	15,582
28.	Wichita	6,722	10,105	14,536
29.	Dayton	6,712	10,094	14,724
30.	Pittsburgh	6,701	10,236	14,876
31.	Lancaster	6,698	10,301	14,711
32.	Denver	6,697	10,326	15,005
33.	Dallas	6,683	9,894	14,471
34.	Cincinnati	6,611	10,220	14,329
35.	Orlando	6,562	9,469	13,679
36.	Houston	6,481	9,645	13,917
37.	Atlanta	6,424	9,523	13,765
38.	Baton Rouge	6,411	9,704	14,379
39.	Nashville	6,326	9,665	13,930
40.	Austin	6,197	9,212	13,337

Source. U. S. Census.

Specifically, there is the question of the type, extent, and priority of environmental problems in the five principal cities. There is also the question of the extent to which their demands for solution create and establish bonds of community in Megalopolis. Environmental quality problems have the special quality of demanding regional solutions. Water and air do not respect political boundaries.

Water control in the major cities presents two interrelated situations: the demands of supply and quality are continuous. All five cities are located on or near the estuary of one or more large rivers. Boston has the Charles and the Mystic; New York, the Hudson and the East, the Hackensack and Passaic; Philadelphia, the Delaware and the Schuylkill; Baltimore, the Patapsco and the nearby Susquehanna; and Washington, the Potomac. Rivers and bays are integral parts of these urban areas.

New York, by far the greatest withdrawer of water in the Northeast, not only has tapped water supplies in nearby Westchester and Putnam counties but has constructed reservoirs in the Catskills and beyond in the upper basin of the Delaware River, more than 100 miles from Manhattan Island. Its use of the upper waters of the Delaware River has brought repercussions from cities downstream on the Delaware such as Trenton and Philadelphia.

Boston reaches 60 miles westward beyond Worchester and close to Springfield in its search for water supply, and Philadelphia draws water from the Delaware and Schuylkill rivers. In drawing water from the Potomac, Washington must consider the fact that the river flows through Maryland, Virginia, and West Virginia. Batlimore is perhaps in the most fortunate position, but it must reckon with Pennsylvania and suburban areas of Washington if it draws large amounts of water from the Susquehanna.

For the great cities the need for new water supply continues—a need that requires setting aside woodlands, farmlands, and other areas for eventual use as reservoir sites. In most of the northeastern states voters are asked every election year to approve bond issues to create future reservoirs and other water facilities to serve increasing metropolitan demands. The various supply systems are coming closer together and the necessity for joint planning and legislative action both in and between states is increasing.

Water quality deterioration or water quality management is the companion problem to water supply. Boston, New York, Philadelphia, and Baltimore have great ports which have not only brought shipping and commerce but also industry, with multiple types of waste. Philadelphia is situated at the juncture of the Delaware and Schuylkill Rivers; directly across the Delaware is the satellite city of Camden, New Jersey. For 30 miles southwest of Philadelphia and Camden the Delaware River is lined on its western shore with industries, oil refineries, chemical plants, and cities and towns like Chester, Wilmington, and New Castle.

The growth of cities in the drainage basin of the rivers in the Northeast is so great that each river and stream faces immediate or incipient problems of water quality. The death of plant and fish life in the rivers is only one of the consequences that announce the deterioration of water quality.

The recreational needs of the principal cities send millions of persons into every section of Megalopolis. Open space is being reduced by the desire to reach a beach, a park, a resort, a campground, or an isolated retreat. Each weekend the exodus begins and bumper to bumper traffic ends only as the remaining open space is occupied. The problems of waste that plague the cities are carried to the hinterlands.

Environmental quality problems can include water and air pollution, solid wastes, noise, excessive illumination, billboards, destruction of open space, lack of planning and zoning of lands for buildings, landscape disfiguration, and ugliness of any kind. The five major cities of Megalopolis and their metropolitan areas are subject to all of these blots on urban environments. A quick survey showed us that Megalopolis was perhaps the best of all possible field sites for a study of environmental quality problems. The prospect for studying regional planning seemed equally promising.

A number of "problem sheds" were identified for water pollution as situses in which Eastern leaders may be active. They include the Connecticut, Delaware, Susquehanna, and Potomac river basins and the Northeastern urban region and the nation in general. Problem sheds for air pollution and solid-waste disposal were recognized as the Boston, New York, Philadelphia, and Baltimore-Washington metropolitan regions and the Northeastern urban region and the nation in general.

It is known that leaders may be active on water, air, or solid-waste problems on local, state, regional-interstate, or national levels. Our major interest was to be focused on regional-interstate and national activity.

However, urban and environmental problems press on citizens and their leaders at all levels of government. How to identify, relate, and compare activity in the local community and distinguish it from the wider activity across Megalopolis became a crucial part of the research effort.

Notes

1. Gottman's designation of Megalopolis as a continuous urbanized area was first demonstrated in 1950 when the Census introduced the definitions urbanized areas, standard metropolitan areas, and metropolitan state economic areas. When the latter were mapped on a county basis, they showed an impressive and continuous stretch of counties, from Hillsborough in southern New Hampshire to Fairfax in northern Virginia, classified as having a metropolitan-type economy. *Megalopolis*, p. 21.

2. A Standard Metropolitan Statistical Area refers to a county or group of counties containing at least one city (or twin cities) with 50,000 inhabitants or more plus adjacent counties economically and socially integrated with the core of the central city.

3. Daniel J. Glazer, "Megalopolis and the New Sectionalism," *The Public Interest*, No. 11 (Spring 1968), 68–69.

4. Raymond Vernon, *Metropolis, 1985*, Doubleday, Anchor, New York, 1963, p. 118.

5. A study of *Who's Who* showed that Washington has 25 percent of the listings for the five cities of Megalopolis. The five cities appear in the following order, based on 9458 listings in 1940: New York, 54%; Washington, 25%; Boston, 9%; Philadelphia, 8%, and Boston 4%. See Digby Baltzell, *The Philadelphia Gentleman*, Free Press, Glencoe, 1958, p. 29.

6. U. S. Department of Commerce Report, "Educational Attainment in 30 Selected Standard Metropolitan Statistical Areas: 1968," Series P-20, No. 214, March 3, 1971, U. S. Government Printing Office, Washington, D. C.

7. Regional Plan Association, *The Second Regional Plan—A Draft for Discussion*, 230 West 41st St., New York, New York, 1968, pp. 8–9.

8. Richard L. Forstall, "A New Social and Economic Grouping of Cities," *The Municipal Year Book, 1970*, International City Managers Association, Washington, D. C., 1970, pp. 102–135.

9. National Civic Review, **60,** No. 2 (February), 105.

10. Released by the U.S. Bureau of the Census and reported in *The New York Times,* May 19, 1971.

11. *U.S. News and World Report,* February 21, 1966, gives estimates for the year 2000: Washington, 75 percent black; Baltimore, 56 percent black; Philadelphia, 50 percent black; New York, 50 percent black; Boston, no estimate but probably less than 50 percent.

12. Ben J. Wattenberg and Richard M. Scammon, *This U.S.A.,* Doubleday, New York, 1965, pp. 462–464.

13. A high correlation between level of formal education and income is expected in the five principal cities. These data are not available, but the high level of education in Washington has been established.

14. By 1972 these budgets continued to climb; the high family budget was set at $16,558 dollars, the moderate budget at $11,446, and the low budget of $7386.

15. Boston was inching ahead of New York in 1972 in the intermediate and low budget categories.

16. These price movements continued into 1972. Boston and New York are still the highest priced cities in which to live. Philadelphia, Washington, and Baltimore rank lower and have almost similar costs. See Jean Brackett, Urban Family Budgets Updated to Autumn 1972, *Monthly Labor Review,* **96,** No. 8 (August 1973), 72–75.

PART TWO

Theoretical Positions,
Operating
Assumptions, and
Methodological
Decisions

CHAPTER THREE

Theory and Method Guiding Regional Study

Community power researchers can draw on a wide range of theoretical ideas and methodological techniques. As an empirical area of study, however, this specialized field is scarcely 20 years old. During that time sociologists and political scientists have been giving almost equal time to testing and contesting. The controversy over method is one of the most vehement in the general field of social science. There are constant demands that researchers reformulate their definitions of power, influence, authority, leadership, and other basic concepts in the field. Critics often complain that the research has missed a vital part of the power structure or distorted it by the method employed. No one ever seems fully satisfied that closure has been achieved—and they are probably right!

Large macroscopic systems of power are especially difficult to deal with. C. Wright Mills has been criticized severely by a host of critics for his description of the power structure in the United States, but his *The Power Elite* has had wide influence. Sociologists and political scientists reject the methodology but use the book and often say there is nothing better.[1] Floyd Hunter studied the power structure of the United States with the same techniques he used in his community power studies. Yet *Top Leadership, U.S.A.* is seldom read or referred to.[2] It has been dismissed as biased toward business dominance and not getting at the complex web of decision-making processes. Arnold Rose tried to strike a more balanced treatment in *The Power Structure* but has not convinced readers that he has written a definitive account.[3] Mills was never so sure of his conclusions as some of his readers imputed to him. He was careful to point out that the power elite in the United States was "a sprawling and controversial topic" and pleaded for a chance to reason together. He stated that "we cannot allow the impossibility of rigorous proof to keep us from studying whatever we believe to be important. We must expect fumbles. . . ."[4]

The Methodological Background

A quick review shows that community power research has progressed through three identifiable stages. The first was characterized by case studies of relatively small or middle-sized American communities and the various uses of positional, reputational, and issue-decisional methods of identifying influential leaders and decision-making processes. Stage two began with the appearance of comparative studies, both intranational and international. In both stages emphasis was on the structure and functioning of the community *qua community*. It was marked especially in stage two by the combined use of two or more methods of identifying influential leaders and associations. Usually the reputational and issue-decisional methods were selected. The issues were those considered by community judges as the most important. It mattered little what they were. The researcher simply wanted salient points that would identify community leaders and the contours of community decision-making processes.

Stage three has emerged in recent years and is characterized by a focus on power relations as centered on a specific problem or a community decision organization. The issue is now one that arrests the specific attention of the researcher because of its *nature*. Stage three can be illustrated by the work of current researchers. Terry N. Clark of the University of Chicago has published his study of the relation between community structure, decision making, budget expenditures, and urban renewal in 51 American communities.[5] Roland L. Warren of Brandeis University is conducting research on community decision organizations (urban renewal authority, health and welfare council, board of education, antipoverty organization, mental health planning board, and the city demonstration agency of the Model Cities Program) in nine cities extending from Oakland, California, to Boston, Massachusetts.[6] Peter Rossi, Robert Crain, James L. Venecho, and Laura Horlock, all of Johns Hopkins University, are studying school desegregation and power in 91 cities of the United States.[7] Robert R. Alford and Michael Aiken of the University of Wisconsin have investigated political orientation and public policy on urban renewal, poverty, and public housing programs based on their statistical archive of 200 American cities. Harold Wolman of the University of Pennsylvania, in his study of how federal housing policy is made, interviewed 68 top influentials in the Congress, the White House, Housing and Urban Redevelopment, the Bureau of the Budget, and various professional organizations and lobbies representing housing.[8] Ray E. Johnston of Wayne State University has sought the relationship between holders of reputed power or influence and the political demand-articulation processes by which priorities and allocation of resources are determined for urban problems.[9]

This inventory could be extended at length and a fuller list may indeed be examined in the Newsletters of the Committee for Comparability in Community Research.[10] The list of current studies underway reveals a number of characteristics in the emergent stage of community research. The distinctive emphasis on a specific problem and the inclusion of large samples of communities can also be noted. There is often a search for statistical relationships between community factors and the problem investigated. Path analysis, factor analysis as well as simple, multiple, and partial correlation analysis are making their appearance. It can probably be said that interest in patterned relationships and policy outputs is dominating over concern for processes and qualitative analysis. Most recently, Clark has been stressing that linkages to state and national systems are essential to the understanding of local decision making. Federalism and its counter, local autonomy, are setting the context for local decisions.[11]

Many researchers active on urban problems use community power methodologies, but a dearth of research effort is focused on the region and on environmental quality specifically. When my associates, James Barfoot and Paul Planchon and I began work on this study there was almost nothing in the literature to serve as a guide. No one had ever undertaken a regional power structure. Roscoe Martin, Guthrie S. Birkhead, Jesse Birkhead, and Frank Munger, in their book *River Basin Administration and the Delaware* (Syracuse University Press, 1960), had identified working relations between environmental organizations active in the Delaware Basin. This was a useful start and was suggestive of much of the organizational analysis that we were to carry out. Martin and his associates stopped, however, with a simple tally of mentions given to organizations that respondents said were those with which his organization most often cooperated.[12] Mathew Crenson has recently made a pioneer effort in a study of power relations and air pollution problems in a sample of American cities.[13]

Diversity in Concepts Significant for the Shaping of the Research Design

To proceed on a study of power structures across a region and especially to an attack on environmental quality was to compound difficulty. The situation was to prove especially difficult because of the lack of consensus on Megalopolis as a region, on the nature of the power structures within a region, on methodological techniques, and on the outcomes desired from the study. The researcher found himself in the center of the schema shown in Figure 3.1.

Competing Concepts of Megalopolis

This schema tries to convey the competing varieties of concepts and problems that require decisions in research design. Note that the concepts of Megalopolis, described in Chapter 1, range from the definition of a true regional community to a geographic area fractionated into separate metropolitan centers. In between these two poles are notions of Megalopolis as a congeries of subregions, an agglomeration of regional interest groups, or an interlinked part of the nation. The selection of any one of these concepts is destined to set the design in one of five different directions.

Competing Concepts of Power Structure and Influence Systems

Similarly, the differing concepts of power structure and influence systems not only move the study toward different data but also different methodological choices. The use of positional, reputational, and issue analysis each develops dif-

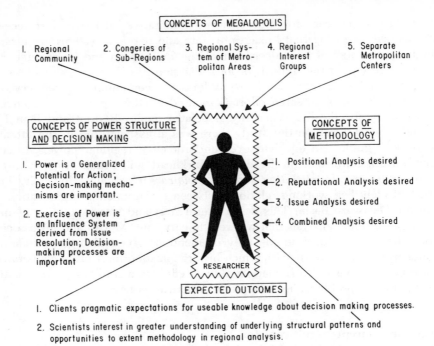

Figure 3.1 Schema showing four principal substantive and methodological areas characterized by competing varieties of concept.

ferent bodies of data and quite different investments of time and money. The researcher must make decisions that depend on explicit formulation of goals. He must understand the sharp difference between a power structure and an influence system. Terry Clark has pointed out this distinction with clarity. *Power is the potential ability* of an actor or actors to select, change, and attain the goals of a social system. *Influence is the exercise of power* that brings about change in a social system. It follows then that a *power structure* is a patterned distribution of power in a social system distinguished from a *decision-making structure* which is the patterned distribution of influence in a social system. Clark continues,

> To study a power structure it is necessary to measure the distribution
> of resources and the potential ability of actors to bring about change
> in the system. Implied is a strategy for analyzing the system at one
> point in time. A decision making structure, on the other hand, is best
> analyzed by studying actual processes of influence as exercised over
> time.[14]

In our research program we have found it useful to study both power and decision-making structures. In studies in which the region is the geographic entity *power structures* have been our major focus. In studies made in a subregion, such as the Delaware River Basin, the *decision-making structure* has become the principal focus. It is important to be aware of these differences, for the differing concepts of method relate directly to whether a power structure or a decision-making structure is under study.

Competing Concepts of Methodology

In general, positional, and reputational analysis is utilized on power structure studies and issue analysis, on decision-making structures. Table 3.1 shows these methodological distinctions, the techniques employed, and principal products derived from each type of analysis. A combination of these analyses is often possible and is desirable for checking the validity of findings. Positional and reputed leaders and organizations can be asked what issues they have participated in and' what stands they took. Issue leaders can be ranked for their reputed standing and their official positions can be analyzed for the potential authority they may wield.[15]

Both decision-making mechanisms and decision-making processes can be analyzed. A decision-making mechanism refers to modes and patterns of decision making, such as working with powerful persons on an informal basis or working with organizations in formal channels. A decision-making process refers to the actual progress of issue resolution from inception to decision. The roles of actors and decision-making mechanisms are described as they actually occur in time.

The impetus to alter behavior may be a compound of power, influence, and authority with stimuli so subtly interminged that it is impossible to separate them. After all, powerful leaders are often influential and vice versa. Power and influence are generated in many different ways and occasionally these terms are used interchangeably. Research versatility requires an ability to move through the range of technical skills available and to make applications to appropriate situations

Competing Concepts of Expected Outcome

A final consideration was of major importance in shaping the research design. Our client expected us to come up with useful knowledge about decision-making processes centered around roles of decision makers engaged in environmental quality management. Problems of interest included power struggles over the setting of air and water quality standards, the decision-making orientations of environmental quality commissioners, the forces impinging on authorities in establishing and maintaining standards, and the power struggles centered around the securing of new legislation and regulations. Client and investigator found a strong common interest in regional power structures focused on urban problems in general and environmental quality problems in particular. It was believed that the true priority given to environmental quality problems could not be ascertained except as they were examined within the competing claims of other urban problems. The proposal to study power structures and decision-making processes at various levels within the region provided a common ground for agreement. Both basic and applied research goals could be pursued.

The gain for scientific research lay in the effort to apply community power techniques to a regional system of cities. This would be a pioneer effort because the techniques had hitherto been used only on independent cities. The study of leadership interaction is not new, but the chance to look at leadership as a problem in interaction among leaders in business, labor, politics, religion, civic action, and civil rights has not been extensively carried out. Contemporary demands for

TABLE 3.1   POSITIONAL, REPUTATIONAL, AND ISSUE ANALYSIS AND THE
ACCOMPANYING RESEARCH TECHNIQUES TO INVESTIGATE POWER AND
DECISION-MAKING STRUCTURES

Type of analysis	Conception of power or influence	Research operations	Techniques employed	Principal products of research
Positional (structural)	Power that can be mobilized if available resources are used; ordinarily employed in private decisions	Identification of the institutions, organizations, and offices in the community that have potential power	Documents Informants	List of persons in the most influential offices; resources of persons and organizations; records of results achieved
Reputational (sociometric)	Power that is imputed to persons and organizations and institutions; employed variously in both private and public decision making	(1) Identification by judges of the most influential leaders, organizations, and institutions; (2) description of roles played by influential leaders	Interviews with panel of judges, informants, and influential leaders	List of leaders considered most important and their participation patterns
Issue (issue-relevant)	Influence that can be assigned to persons, organizations, and institutions in the debate of public issues or promotion of public projects; employed mainly in decisions on public matters	(1) Identification of recent issues that are considered most important in the life of the community; (2) identification of the persons and their parts taken in resolving issues or projects	Interviews with persons associated with issues or projects during decision making; attendance and recording of decision-making meetings	List of most influential leaders in recent issues; analyses of roles played

representative leadership in social action agencies and commissions give importance to this approach. The search for patterns of organizational interaction also sets new goals for research development.

On these bases decisions were reached and the research design was developed. Theoretical formulations follow.

THEORETICAL POSITIONS

1. Premise. *Urban oriented and environmental quality leaders and organizations are linked in supportive patterns.*

The first major decision involved the theoretical assumption that the urban oriented leaders and associations were influential in initiating, supporting, or vetoing actions taken by environmental quality leaders and organizations. It was believed that a high degree of supportive relations was necessary to increase the attention, resources, and personnel directed to environmental quality problems and that such maximum support would originate with powerful urban oriented leaders and associations. Little was known about the ties between the two groups. Theoretical leaps were taken to bring these parts into an integrated study design.

2. Operating Assumption. *A regional power structure can be identified.*

A network of economic and social concerns ties the region together and regional (or national) leaders and organizations emerge and can be identified On this proposition rests the premise that a number of power structures exist in this region and that decisions with respect to policy, programs, and institutional organization are influenced by these structures. Within a generalized urban-problem-oriented structure there may be "substructures" derived from regional interest groups focused on such problems as environmental quality, transportation, and housing; for example, the "birth" of the Delaware River Basin Commission would have been impossible without the support of top influentials in Pennsylvania, New York, New Jersey, and Delaware.

3. Theoretical Base. *Coalition decision model of a complex social system.*

A region such as the Eastern Seaboard or a subregion such as a river basin is a complex social system. It encloses a decision-making network composed of persons and groups in interrelated governments and public agencies woven in a net of influence generated by persons and organizations in the private sector. This network functions in formal and informal channels. The units in the complex social system are heterogeneous and interdependent. The power base is wide and large and diverse coalitions are formed to exercise policy making. In spite of wide distribution of power in the coalitions central figures frequently hold considerable power. Policy decisions affecting innovation, control, and order are not something generally achieved by an administrator or lay groups at any one unit or level but is a process that links persons and groups at local, state, regional, and national levels. Therefore administration is not process that flows down from one level to the next but is related to the interaction of levels and component groups.

Final Design of the Study

These theoretical positions point to a design that contains three networks of influence: a general urban influence network of leaders and organizations in Megalopolis, an environmental quality regional network of leaders and organizations in Megalopolis, and a Delaware River Basin environmental subregional network of leaders and organizations, all of which are believed to interlock and interact in policy-making and other decision-making processes affecting environmental quality problems. Key concepts for analysis are power elements, linkage, and coalition. *Power elements* refer to the identifiable units regarded as important. They are divided into two classes: powerful leaders and powerful organizations. Equal attention is given to each so that collective structure and individual leadership will be carefully considered. *Linkage* refers to those bonds that tie the urban, environmental quality, and subregional network together in policy and decision making. These bonds may be discovered in shared problem interests, acquaintance and contact, and working relationships on committees, boards, and commissions. *Coalition* refers to the uniting of interest and shared support of issues. Such coalitions can be observed when parties at interest appear at various public and governmental hearings.

A heuristic model of the three networks is shown as Figure 3.2. Some 15 intra- and interlinkage patterns are represented. The central connections are (a) the intralinkages between leaders in the influence networks (1, 4, 7); (b) the intralinkages between organizations in the networks (3, 6, 9); (c) the intralinkages between leaders and organizations in the networks (2, 5, 8); and (d) the interlinkages to all similar connections between leaders and organizations in the three networks (10, 11, 12, 13, 14, 15). The model demonstrates that the interactional matrix is complex and points to the necessity of identifying the leadership and organizational structures before attempting to characterize decision making in the influence networks. Obviously no one study could map all these interactions except by long and laborious effort!

A selection was made to provide for the study of the intralinkage between the most powerful leaders and organizations in each of the three influence networks and the interlinkage between them. Attention was thus focused on six structures:

1. Powerful urban-oriented leaders in Megalopolis.
2. Powerful urban-oriented organizations in Megalopolis.
3. Powerful environmental quality leaders in Megalopolis.
4. Powerful environmental quality organizations in Megalopolis.
5. Powerful environmental quality leaders in the Delaware River Basin.
6. Powerful environmental quality organizations in the Delaware River Basin.

The search for linkages and coalitions has followed on the identification of these required power elements.

In the beginning it was not recognized that the sociometric data found in acquaintance and working relations among leaders would offer an opportunity to apply new computer programs and enable us to find clique relations among a large leader population. Nor did we recognize that the search for interactional patterns among organizations was to lead into an unexplored field of study—that of associational sociology. These opportunities have been recognized and crystallized in two theoretical and methodological contributions reported in Chapter 10, The Measurement of Contact and Clique Structures, and Chapter 11, The Measurement of Organizational Interaction: Toward a Sociology of Associations. It is hoped that these research probes will challenge future scholars to move forward with greater interest in regional sociology.

Prospectus

We have posited that Megalopolis is an integrated economic unit in which powerful leaders and organizations wield influence on national, state, interstate,

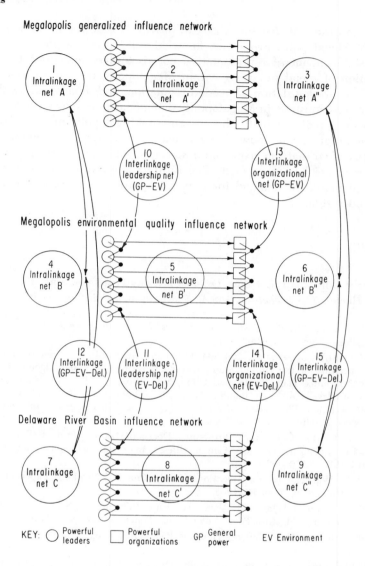

Figure 3.2 **A heuristic model of three influence networks centered on urban and environmental quality problems.**

and local problems as representatives within the region. A regional power structure is expected to present itself as differentiated by many constituent networks interrelated within it.

It is anticipated that a megalopolitan power structure will consist primarily in common interactional contacts made by the overlapping patterns of leadership and organizational activity among the traditional units of government—city, state, interstate, and federal—and local, state, and national associations. Powerful leaders and organizations know one another well and will have worked together, participating in decisions on boards, committees, and commissions. If this can be demonstrated by research, it can be said that the region has an incipient leadership and organizational structure that can provide a base for social action on the problems of Megalopolis. From such knowledge it would be possible to achieve a better establishment of representative boards and commissions for study or administration of social programs within Megalopolis, the use of more efficient channels to secure legislation or needed regulation, and, finally, an awakening of community consciousness in Megalopolis. If regional problems are ever to be administered on a regional basis, the citizens of Megalopolis must be aware that they live in a region. They now have no clear sense of regional community. Gottman demonstrated that the economic base exists; this study should show that the elements of a social base do exist. The future should validate the social trends that forecast increased demand for regional approaches to problems embedded in urbanized systems.

Notes

1. C. Wright Mills, *The Power Elite,* Oxford University Press, New York, 1956.
2. Floyd Hunter, *Top Leadership, U.S.A.,* University of North Carolina Press, Chapel Hill, 1952.
3. Arnold M. Rose, *The Power Structure: Political Process in American Society,* Oxford University Press, New York, 1967.
4. C. Wright Mills, *op. cit.,* pp. 363–364. Other important efforts to determine the national power structure of the United States include those of G. William Domhoff, *Who Rules America?* Prentice Hall, Englewood Cliffs, N.J., 1967, and his *The Higher Circles: The Governing Class in America,* Random House, New York, 1970; R. Joseph Monsen, Jr., and Mark W. Cannon, *The Makers of Public Policy: American Power Groups and their Ideologies,* McGraw-Hill, New York, 1965.
5. Terry N. Clark, "Community Structure, Decision-Making, Budget Expenditures, and Urban Renewal in 51 American Communities," *American Sociological Review,* **33,** No. 4 (August 1968), 576–593.
6. Roland L. Warren, "Interorganizational Study Project," Working Paper of the Project, Brandeis University, April 18, 1968.
7. Robert R. Crain and James J. Vanecko, "Elite Influence in School Desegregation," in James Q. Wilson, Ed., *City Politics and Public Policy,* Wiley, New York, pp. 127–148.
8. Harold Wolman, "How Federal Housing Policy is Made," *Journal of Housing,* **4,** 69, 188–191.
9. Ray E. Johnston, "Levels of Community Demand—Articulation and Indices of Power," *Proceedings,* Indiana Academy of Sciences, **II** (April 1968), 74–98.
10. Newsletter of the Committee for Comparability in Community Research. April 1969 and October 1969, Terry N. Clark, Chairman, University of Chicago. Continuing inventories of on-going research now appear in the new journal, *Comparative Urban Research.* This is a "mini-journal" devoted to rapid communication among scholars and others interested in the comparative study of urban areas throughout the world. For further information write *Comparative Urban Research,* 33 West 42 Street, New York, New York, 10036.
11. Terry N. Clark, *Community Power and Policy Outputs: A Review of Urban Research.* Sage Publication, Beverly Hills, Calif., 1973.
12. Roscoe Martin et al., *op. cit.,* p. 56. One nugget of truth, especially, was to challenge us. They reported, "In this as in all attempts to analyze power relations among groups, the most difficult problem is the attribution of influence to groups not ordinarily concerned with water problems, but capable of exercising great influence when they do feel an interest. The Pennsylvania Manufacturing Association, a very small circle on the chart

(based on number of mentions) but extremely influential within its state, is an obvious illustration (see Figure 9.4).

13. Crenson found that perceived influence of industry in a community tends to thwart the rise of dirty air as an issue. Even when industry enjoys no reputation for power in the pollution field it may affect the course of pollution politics through power reputations that it has established in other issue areas. See Mathew Crenson, *The Un-Politics of Air Pollution, A Study of Nondecision-making in the Cities,* Johns Hopkins, Baltimore, 1971.

14. Terry N. Clark, *Community Structure and Decision Making: Comparative Analysis,* Chandler, San Francisco, 1968, p. 47.

15. For a fuller discussion see Delbert C. Miller, *International Community Power Structures,* Indiana University Press, Bloomington, 1970, pp. 3–21.

PART THREE

Powerful Urban
Oriented Leaders
and Organizations
of Megalopolis
and Their Civic
Relationships

CHAPTER FOUR

The Identification of
Key and Top Leaders
of Megalopolis
and Their Linkage
Patterns

The search for systemic linkage has involved the examination of the functional dependence and interaction among the cities of Megalopolis; the inquiry now leads to the identification and analysis of working relationships among the most powerful urban oriented leaders and organizations of the region. This chapter describes network characteristics of leaders of Megalopolis. Chapter 5 focuses on the Top of the Top, those sociometric leaders who are the shakers and movers of the region and the nation. Chapter 6 reviews the regional issues and patterned strategies of decision making of the most powerful leaders. The concluding chapter in this section describes the organizations, the bases of their power, and their working interrelations.

The desire to learn about the network characteristics of leaders rises from the following questions:

What are the urban problem interests of the influential leaders? What problems are they actually working on? What priority do problems of environmental quality receive?

Do leaders of business, labor, government, religion, and civic organizations know one another in their own cities? In various major cities of the region?

Are the various groups of leaders working together on urban problems across the major cities: Boston, New York, Philadelphia, Baltimore, and Washington?

Who are the key sociometric leaders that top leaders of Megalopolis consider as those who could best represent the Boston to Washington axis in the shaping of urban policy and programming for the region?

What modes of decision making do key and top leaders employ?

Macro Versus Micro Power Systems

The acceptance of a regional chain of cities as a unit for study opens up a number of distinctive considerations. Large, macroscopic social systems are not simply a number of local community power structures studied separately or a comparative analysis of independent cities. Contacts between powerful leaders and organizations occur on local, state, intercity, interstate, subregional, and national levels. These contacts are overlapping and varied. Leaders meet one another in pursuit of occupational, social, and civic matters. Lehman has specified a number of ways in which power in macroscopic social systems can be differentiated from micro systems. He says power in the macro-system has a generalized capacity; that is, a given power leader at specified and recurrent intervals acts in such a way that members are able to anticipate his power behavior with a relatively high degree of predictability. This is because the major "power centers" in the macro systems contain certain positions and collectivities that have a *legitimate right* to exercise power as well as to have *stable, regularly patterned access to certain resources.*

In contrast, on the micro level, power is more likely to be relatively specific, that is, less likely to be institutionalized and more likely to operate outside formalized positions.[1] Power rests on interpersonal and idiosyncratic factors. The power wielder in the micro system depends heavily on personal qualities of leadership. He is the man who can mobilize normative resources—by the skillful use of praise, ridicule, and encouragement to build cooperative relationships.

A distinctive characteristic of macro power wielders is that they operate from multiple resource bases. A number of writers have developed inventories of resources.[2] One list includes *money and credit; control over jobs; control of mass media; high social status; knowledge and specialized technical skills; popularity and esteemed personal qualities; legality; subsystem solidarity; the right to vote; social access to community leaders; commitments of followers; manpower and control of organizations; and control over the interpretation of values.*[3] The availability of these resources provides the macro power leader with a range of persuasions and constraints over others. He may mix different kinds of resource to bring different types of power to bear on persons or groups to induce, constrain, or persuade them. The leader's reputation for power derives more from the acceptance by other leaders and followers of shared cultural values and common perceptions. Lehman emphasizes that "a macro power leader on the basis of a relatively stable attribution of power can frequently obtain acquiescence without spending actual resources." By merely making threats or promises that seem credible he can often neutralize the resistance of other system members because they emanate from an institutionalized power center.[4]

Finally, because macro social systems often have different structural levels—such as city, state, region, or nation,—structural differentiation takes place and allows for extensive *vertical* exercise of power by telephone, telegraph, or letter as a secondary means of communication. Many macro leaders also travel extensively to make short and numerous contacts. Macro systems, with their vertical structuring, enlarge the capacity of a social system to set, pursue, and implement collective goals. Micro systems, in contrast, emphasize local intermember relations. Sustained face-to-face contact is more important. It is in these primary group contacts that leaders convert their personal power into political power, but there are limitations on the range of influence under these more constraining demands.[5]

We have discovered that the most powerful Eastern leaders have learned to operate in both kinds of power system by utilizing position, reputation, and personality traits in local groups and institutions and often almost simultaneously in far-flung state, regional, and national organizations. They move back and forth from micro to macro systems as easily as they interrupt an office interview with a local leader to respond to a long distance telephone call.

The Formulation of Hypotheses

Science is a search for constancies, for invariants. Kaplan has said, "the basic scientific question is 'What the devil is going on around here?' "[6]

We knew at the beginning we should never fully explain Megalopolis as a power structure phenomenon. The difficulties of tracing decision making in a macro social system were clearly recognized, but certain goals could be specified with good chances of attainment. It seemed feasible to undertake the identification of important leaders and to discover their urban problem interests and activity. Acquaintance and contact patterns could be revealed if leaders were willing to respond to questions about their relation with other Megalopolis leaders. A next step could then be taken. Relations between leaders' acquaintance and contacts and their ranking among different leadership groups in Megalopolis could be determined. Finally, leadership behavior could be probed to ascertain various modes of decision making in dealing with civic problems.

Eight hypotheses were formulated to study these matters and findings are reported in this chapter. The first hypothesis deals with urban problem interest and activity. The next three are concerned with acquaintance and contact patterns as exhibited between leadership groups, occupational groupings, and cities. Correlations reflecting on the nature of leadership power rankings and the relations of different leadership groups are treated in hypotheses five and six. The final two include an assembly of test suppositions relating to the decision-making perspectives and mechanisms used by key and top leaders in civic behavior. The concluding summary indicates that we have learned a good deal about "what is going on" among leaders in Megalopolis.

Test Hypotheses

URBAN PROBLEM INTEREST AND ACTIVITY

I.   Influential urban-oriented leaders will place their highest priorities of personal interest and activity on race relations, crime, and unemployment (in that order) and their lowest priorities on environmental problems of air and water pollution and waste. These priorities remain relatively constant in a given setting because ever-growing urbanization does not permit rapid amelioration of urban problems.

These hypotheses rest on the belief that a vigorous competition exists among urban problems for the attention, funds, time, and energy of leaders. Influential leaders must choose among demands on their time for allocations of personal effort to the many needs of public life. Even a minimal list must include air pollution, control of lawlessness and crime, improvement of public education, water pollution, transport, traffic, and parking, wastes, housing and urban renewal, roads and streets, planning for land and preservation of open spaces, un-employment and poverty, and race relations. Many leaders are busy with other problems of improving local government and governmental relations, family welfare, drug addiction, student protests, juvenile delinquency, and mental health. Race relations, crime, and unemployment seem to be most visible and most damaging to private property and public order. For these reasons it is hypothesized that leaders will place their highest priority on them. Almost by default environmental quality problems will suffer low attention because of energies drawn off to higher priorities. Moreover, environmental problems are not so visible and do not thrust themselves on public recognition as immediately damaging.

The interest and activity given to environmental quality by influential leaders is important for this study because it is assumed that the interest and support of the most powerful urban-oriented leaders are vital to the progress of environmental quality. Roughly, the equation may be: the higher the interest and activity of key influentials in environmental problems, the greater the legislation, funding, and activity given to environmental quality efforts. As long as other urban problems command high priority, environmental problems will suffer relative neglect.

How stable these interests are is another matter of importance. There are charges that the current attention focused on environment is transitory and that concern with race relations is cooling off. Our task was clear: find the priorities and discover the stability or change of major leaders in their urban problem interests and activity.

Four hundred of the most powerful leaders from Boston to Washington active in urban affairs were identified by stratified sample, interview, and reputational techniques during a nine-month search.[7] Leaders were sought from business, labor, political and governmental, religious, educational, civil rights, and welfare sectors. *Key* leaders were identified as those having the greatest influence in urban decision making related to urban problems. Two hundred leaders constitute this group. Another 200 leaders of somewhat lesser influence are called *top* leaders. Ten-page questionnaires were sent to these groups in May 1969 and 178 responded (a 45 percent return). In July 1970, 14 months later, a shorter resurvey of the same leaders was made by using the urban problem interest and activity format of the first survey.[8] A copy of the shorter questionnaire sent in July 1970 is shown as Figure 4.1. It is identical to that part of the earlier questionnaire except for questions added on changes of interest and activity. Note that it lists 11 major problems (with space for OTHER PROBLEMS) and provides checks for both "most interest in" and "working hardest on." Inquiries about changes in interest and activity are directed to each respondent with a request for reasons when changes are indicated.

Findings of the Surveys

INTEREST PATTERNS OF LEADERS

The profile of urban problem interest among key and top leaders is shown in Figure 4.2. This profile reveals the interests of 178 key and top leaders in May

1969 and compares them with a resurvey in July 1970. Note that major attention in both 1969 and 1970 was concentrated in *race relations, housing, unemployment and poverty, public education, and crime.* Air pollution, water pollution, and waste ranked in sixth, ninth, and tenth positions among the 11 problems. Minor shifts do occur, but we may conclude that *no significant change in interest patterns occurred in the 14-month interval.* The increase in a variety of other interests develops some significance, as the survey of activities subsequently reveals in Figure 4.3. The results shown here are based on the answers to the instruction: "Mark the *one* problem on which you are currently working hardest."[9] They again indicate *a high similarity of activity in the 14-month period.* The big five remain but in different order: housing, race relations, unemployment and poverty, public education, and crime. In the interval there is slippage in race relations and unemployment and poverty, but activity in housing and crime increased. Activity in environmental problems remains low, with water pollution, air pollution, and waste in eighth, ninth, and tenth places. Note the large rise in *other problems* and that the list shown at the bottom of Figure 3.5 is a long one. There is evidence that this intrusion of other problems has weakened activity in many of the earlier problem areas as can be observed by the declines.

STABILITY AND CHANGE IN URBAN PROBLEM PRIORITIES

When asked if they changed their interests and activities during the last year, 83 percent said no, 17 percent, yes. This conforms to the corollary hypothesis that states that priorities remain relatively constant. Respondents who explained their reasons for maintaining their priority patterns gave such reasons as, "My position requires constant attention to all major urban problems"; "My job stabilizes attention on those problems for which I have responsibilities"; and "My interests are stabilized on national priorities which I perceive as relatively constant."

These reasons can be illustrated with some of the replies. A business leader writes of concern with all urban problems:

> As a large corporation, we are working with the local, state, and federal governments in all phases of urban problems.

A labor leader who has been working hardest on unemployment and poverty says he has developed increased interest in housing needs and solutions but he writes:

> As a Labor Union official my major activity in poverty and unemployment is most time consuming and my time does not allow for major activity in other areas.

An executive director says:

> Running a Chamber of Commerce as I do, all of these urban problems have been major interests for several years. They don't change—they intensify.

EASTERN LEADERSHIP AND ENVIRONMENTAL QUALITY STUDY

DEPARTMENT OF SOCIOLOGY – INDIANA UNIVERSITY
BLOOMINGTON, INDIANA 47401

URBAN PROBLEM INTEREST AND ACTIVITY PATTERN OF CIVIC
LEADERS IN THE BOSTON TO WASHINGTON URBAN REGION

(1)   Check problems in which you have the highest personal interest.
(2)   Mark the _one_ problem on which you are currently working most intensively.

(Note.   The researcher is seeking to estimate the degree of interest and current
activity pattern of civic leaders engaged in urban problems. All information is
confidential and each person will be recorded by code number.)

I have most interest in	I am currently working hardest on		Urban problems
		1.	Air pollution
		2.	Control of lawlessness and crime
		3.	Improvement of public education
		4.	Water pollution
		5.	Improvement of transport, traffic movement, and parking
		6.	Waste (garbage, litter, and dumps)
		7.	Improvement or elimination of Poor housing; rebuilding of cities
		8.	Improvement and maintenance of roads and streets
		9.	Planning and zoning of land; preservation (or improvement) of park and other natural areas; beautification
		10.	Unemployment and poverty
		11.	Race Relations

Figure 4.1   Urban Problems Resurvey Questionnaire (July, 1970).

12.   Other (please specify)

Have you changed your interests and activity in urban problems during the last year?   [ ] yes   [ ] no

If yes, what interests and activity have changed?

INTEREST CHANGES   ACTIVITY CHANGES
(indicate by number of problem
as shown above)

_____   _____
_____   _____
_____   _____

How would you account for these changes?

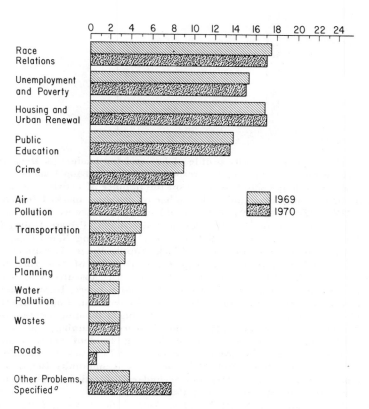

Figure 4.2 **Urban problem interest profile of key and top leaders (N = 178) of Megalopolis in May 1969 compared with the resurvey of key and top leaders (N = 167) in
July 1970. Each percentage is based on the number of interests marked for each problem over the total number of interests for all problems (in 1969 N = 561; in 1970 N =
505).**
SOURCE: Delbert C. Miller, in *Social Behavior, Natural Resources and the Environment,*
William R. Burch, Jr. et al., Harper & Row, New York, 1972.

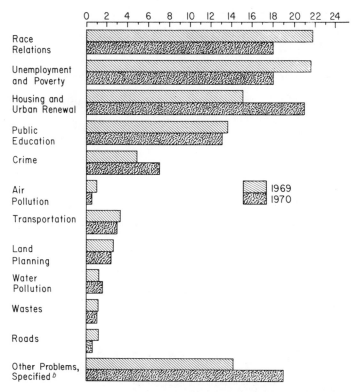

Figure 4.3   Urban problem activity profile of key and top leaders of Megalopolis, May 1969 ($N = 178$) compared with resurvey responses of key and top leaders in July 1970 ($N = 167$). Each percentage shown is based on the number of activity checks (problem I am working hardest on) over the total number of activities marked for all problems (1969, $N = 277$; 1970, $N = 239$). Other problems specified were Reduction of Drug Abuse, Family Planning, Economic Development of Ghetto, Private University Education, Child Welfare, Creation of New Value System, Developing New Cities, Black Participation in Decision Making, Educating Black Youth, Peace, Consumer Education, Guaranteed Work and Income, Alienation of Youth, Revision of New York State Social Service Law, Police Brutality, Preparation of Cities for Absentee Ownership, Black Liberation by Any Means Necessary, Structure of Social Services, Improvement of Education for Government Services, Improving Urban Government, Improvement of Philadelphia and Pennsylvania Political Climate, Establishing a Reading Center for a Public Elementary School, Health Problems, Recreation Research, Planning, and Programming, Civil Legal Assistance to Indigents, Status of Women, Student Activism and Judicial Process in the University, Legalization of Abortion, Civil Liberties, Court Administration and Judicial Practices, Vocational Rehabilitation, Police-Community Relations, Training for Prison Inmates, Private Elementary and Secondary Education, Labor Relations, and Regional Organization for Air, Water, and Mass Transit.
SOURCE: Delbert C. Miller, In *Social Behavior, Natural Resources and the Environment*, William R. Burch, Jr. et al., Harper and Row, New York, 1972.

A labor leader writes that his interests have been stabilized on public education, housing, and jobs because "national priorities should be education, housing, and jobs. I see no reason to change."

Those relatively few leaders who said that their interests and activity had changed during the last year were asked to account for these changes. Their answers reveal six different reasons:

1. Appointment to positions that arouse and focus new interest and activity.

2. Search for a different, more comprehensive approach rather than specific concentration on a given "project."

3. Disenchantment, frustration, and blockage induce shifts of interest.

4. Awareness of new problems and a shift of interests to them.

5. Increase of intensity in the listed problems which arouses new interest but not necessarily activity.

6. New activity aroused in the listed problems due to change of public attitudes and support.[10]

Examples and discussions of each of these reasons for change are set forth. They are important, for if changes in priorities are to occur these reasons for change provide an understanding of how priority shifts come about.

APPOINTMENT TO POSITIONS

This reason seems to dominate all others. A growing number of professional full-time and lay voluntary positions now draw more persons directly into contact with responsibilities for urban problems. A professional who takes a full-time position cannot duck his new responsibility. Nor can lay persons do so, even though they work only part-time. The following illustrations all show that involvement arouses new interests and commitments.

> My interest and activity changed with my appointment to the Justice Coordinating Board last year. That has focused my efforts on control of lawlessness and crime.

A respondent who has shifted from activity on urban health problems to civic legal assistance for indigents says:

> [I] left law practice where I was chairman of the board of Municipal Hospital to become Dean of University Law School.

A respondent describes his addition of housing and crime to his activity in race relations:

> I received an opportunity to participate in a specific housing project in my immediate area. This has motivated my addition of housing. And awareness of local crime has added control of lawlessness and crime.

Another respondent reports that he changed his interests to water pollution and race relations.

> I became interested in water pollution because it is business-related. I became involved as a speaker bringing about government changes. My work in race relations began when I accepted a regional chairmanship for the National Alliance of Businessmen. The immediate demand is to find a meaningful program and result.

And still other respondents:

> My interest and activity was changed to court administration and
> judicial practices when I became professionally employed to study the
> criminal courts. My interest had been previously aroused by newspaper
> investigations of poor and illegal judicial procedures.

> As I learn more through my activity as chairman of the League of
> Women Voters in my city, I have become more interested in transpor-
> tation. Transportation is the main two-year program item of the
> League, continuing now into its second year.

SEARCH FOR A DIFFERENT, MORE COMPREHENSIVE APPROACH

A number of leaders report changes or shifts in emphasis based on a desire for
more effective answers to urban problems. Many report their discoveries of overlap and interrelatedness and want to find more effective ways to get to root
causes. The illustrations express this common yearning and searching.

A respondent who has shifted to economic development of low-income areas
says:

> I have been searching for a more comprehensive and effective solu-
> tion to economic problems. I am working more intensively now and
> seeking wider understanding and acceptance of this approach.

A religious leader writes that he has shifted his interest on the housing problem
from being most active in discrimination to working for an increased supply. He
says:

> As a white activist, I feel that nondiscrimination in housing and race
> relations will proceed on its own, if minorities take a more militant role
> and improve their income earning and if housing supply increases for
> low-income groups and for the elderly. The indifference of the white
> middle class to damage and dangers of excessive suffering and hard-
> ship requires intensive united action for planning and massive federal
> and state investment in housing as a public utility.

Another respondent reports that he is working hardest on the structure of regional
government.

> I feel that one of the greatest needs in this region is the establishment
> of area-wide governments, and an objective analysis of entities, the
> taxes imposed, and, based on this analysis, an approach to an improved
> system of government operation, services, and taxes. If environmental
> problems are to be licked, we better know what level of government
> would be responsible for "what" and the funds needed to support
> them.

> I believe there has been some change in the quality of my interests—
> but no shift in checking the listed categories. I am more interested now

in the interrelationship of problems and how citizens can grasp and express the wider implications of the immediate concrete issue presented. My growing interest in environmental quality turns not to listed items, but to how we can clarify and simplify our values so that we use less of the valuable, natural resources and thus have less to clean up."

I have changed from working directly on urban problems to political activity as the way to bring about social reform.

A religious leader writes:

My interests have not changed substantially; however, a greater interest is now being shown by us in dealing with problems of our own people in urban areas (that is, control of lawlessness and crime) and, as well, a new interest in the white ethnic American working class. In essence, there is less focus on black problems specifically, and greater focus on a broader range of problems and for other minority groups as well.

DISENCHANTMENT, FRUSTRATION, AND BLOCKAGE

These three psychological causes are well described, one by one, in the following excerpts.

My faith in the system responding to the needs of black people is drastically changing. I have real fears regarding police repression and genocide of black people.

This respondent is working hardest on unemployment and poverty, race relations, and public education but reports most interest in police-community relations.

Another respondent reports that he has shifted from a direct agency attack on housing in the Model Cities program to a college position in which he will develop new nonprofit, modular housing and delivery systems and assist in changing the "exploitative housing market."

I left the Model Cities program. I found the city political system impossibly rigged by putrid, political interests.

Another respondent switched to work on race relations.

"I am less active in the problems of unemployment and poverty because of restrictions inherent in the recession.

AWARENESS OF NEW PROBLEMS

The rise of new problems (or old problems and a new public awareness) has been cited as one of the compelling drains of time and energy from the list of "major" problems. A few illustrations indicate how shifts to these new problems produce new concentrations of interest.

> My interest has shifted from crime and race relations to drug abuse.
> I believe that the drug situation, which has moved from the ghetto to
> the colleges and now to the secondary schools, is the most serious
> threat to the country.

A respondent writes:

> Abortion has become a "hot" issue in D.C. and I am involved in it
> actively.

INTENSIFICATION OF LISTED PROBLEMS

A few leaders express new interests in many of the listed problems but do not
indicate activity. Environmental problems tend to fall in this category. New interest is reported most commonly in air pollution, water pollution, and waste—in
that order—but activity does not follow.

> "I have increased interest in air pollution." But respondent reports:
> "I am currently retiring early from present jobs to work full time on
> housing."

Another respondent, who is working hardest on improvement of public education,
says he has added control of lawlessness and crime to his list of interests: Other
interests are unemployment and poverty and race relations.

> I have added control of crime because of the increase in lawlessness
> and crime.

A respondent who is working hardest on unemployment and poverty says that he
has a new interest in air and water pollution. When asked to account for these
changes, he writes, "Improving knowledge about pollution."

NEW ACTIVITY IN LISTED PROBLEMS

It is hoped that broad public encouragement would increase awareness and support. Only one leader mentions this point as a cause for his change. Perhaps
others are influenced by this factor more than they realize.

A leader writes that he has shifted his interests from purely local issues to
problems of overall environment. When asked how he accounts for this change,
he writes, "Greater public support of environmental problems."

Summary of Reasons for Change

The six reasons for change suggest that personal interest and activity is aroused
in many different ways. Some hypotheses may be proposed to account for them.

1. Interest arousal precedes activity investments.
2. Position responsibilities at the professional or lay level greatly increase interest and subsequent activity in urban problems.

3. The psychological states of disenchantment, frustration, and blockage induce shifts of interest.

4. Individual efforts to solve urban problems will often result in shifts from concentrated attention on "projects" to a search for a broader, more comprehensive approach to a solution as time elapses and experience is gained.

5. New problems as they intensify will drain efforts away from earlier high priority problems even though they are neither solved nor remedied.

Conclusion and Report on Hypothesis I

These findings now provide a central point for the ensuing research. The initial hypothesis must be slightly modified. We now know that powerful leaders of Megalopolis are actively and consistently concentrating their major efforts on *housing, race relations, unemployment and poverty, public education, and crime* (1970). Interest and activity in housing and public education is more commanding than once appreciated. Both problems have impinged more directly on the middle and upper classes than was realized. The priority pattern must, however, be considered as relatively constant. We can also see clearly that environmental problems have not achieved high priority and only a few key leaders are actively involved,[11] but that these few may have substantial impact. This point of view is explored carefully in Chapter 8 in which the roles of key and top leaders and powerful urban oriented organizations are examined and related to environmental leaders and organizations. The task now is to discover patterns of working relations as leaders act on local, state, regional, and national levels.

Acquaintance and Contact Patterns

ACQUAINTANCE AND CONTACT PATTERNS BETWEEN LEADERSHIP GROUPINGS

The acquaintance and contact pattern has three dimensions:

1. Lateral A, the extent to which a leader's acquaintance and contacts extend across the local community through all leadership groups.

2. Vertical B, represented by a leader's acquaintance and contacts in his own occupational group, from Boston to Washington.

3. Oblique C, the residual dimension which includes all other acquaintance and contacts that a leader has with other leaders outside his *own occupational group* and his *local community*. If he is truly a citizen of Megalopolis, the most convincing dimension is this residual gradient.

These three dimensions are heuristically described for a Boston business leader in Figure 4.4. Note how the acquaintance and contact vectors extend along all three dimensions. He is the ideal personification of the regional leader who usually begins his career as a representative of his own occupational group and over time extends his acquaintance and contacts in that group. These activities induce him to expand his contacts to other leadership groups in his community. If, simultaneously, he is making advances in his own career, he enlarges his ver-

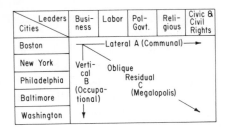

Leaders Cities	Busi-ness	Labor	Pol-Govt.	Reli-gious	Civic & Civil Rights
Boston					
New York					
Philadelphia					
Baltimore					
Washington					

Lateral A (Communal) →
Vertical B (Occupa-tional)
Oblique Residual C (Megalopolis)

Figure 4.4   The three dimensions of leader acquaintance and contact in Megalopolis (a heuristic diagram drawn to represent a Boston business leader).

tical contacts with like occupational leaders in other cities of Megalopolis as well as with leaders of other capacities across the region.

II.   It is hypothesized, therefore, that activity on any one of the three dimensions of acquaintance and contact tends toward interdependence and enlargement of activities on the other two. This theory of leadership growth was tested by examining the scores received by key leaders and top leaders as they checked the leadership acquaintance and working relationship scale. Figure 4.5 shows that part of the questionnaire and the instructions given to the leaders.[12] Note that the sample part shown includes five business leaders in the Boston area and that all leaders are asked to check their *degree of acquaintance* from don't know, have heard of, know little, know well, and know socially. *Contact* may also be checked for business, civic, or social contacts during the last three years and/or for working on a committee or project dealing with urban problems during the last three years with the specified leader. An acquaintance score, derived from 0 to 4 as shown, ranged from don't know to know socially; business, social, or civic contact is given a score of 3, which is also given to an urban committee or project contact. Thus a given leader may secure a maximum score of 10 from any leader who knows him well and has both kinds of contact with him.[13]

Because the questionnaire contained 200 names, any key leader could make a score of (199 × 10) 1990. Actually a score of such magnitude is almost beyond human attainments. The largest score obtained was 795. The leader with this score has a background history as a top government official, having served in many capacities, including a major Cabinet post, before assuming his present position as a college president. An interest in leaders' total acquaintance and contact scores derives from a desire to know the intensity of the activity pattern of different occupational groups. It is believed that such scores are gross indices of decision-making participation in urban problems. They also provide initial indications of the nature of social networks that exist in Megalopolis.

In the following analysis key and top leaders are first compared by using their mean acquaintance and contact scores in their local communities and in the rest of Megalopolis. Thus the two scores separate the "Local" and "Megalopolis" dimensions. An analysis of the relationship between the two dimensions shows a Pearsonian correlation of .33 for key leaders,[14] which indicates that their Megalopolis Acquaintance-Contact scores bear a low but definite relation to their Local Acquaintance-Contact scores. Replicating for top leaders, a lower correlation of .17 occurs.[15] These two correlations, although low, indicate that the two dimensions are somewhat interdependent. Admittedly, different social forces are also

Please look at the leaders listed. All live and work in the Boston to Washington urban region. Please indicate (√) your acquaintance and civic activity with each. All information is confidential and each person will be recorded by code number.

(*Note.* The researcher is trying to discover the degree of acquaintance and contact within and between such leadership groups as business, labor, political, religious, and civic leaders in the metropolitan area and the Atlantic urban region.)

	Acquaintance					Contacts	
	0	1	2	3	4	I have had business, civic, or social contacts during last three years	Worked with him on a committee or project dealing with urban problems during last three years
Name of leader	Don't know	Have heard of	Know little (reading or contact)	Know well (reading or contact)	Know socially (visit at home or personal contact)		
Boston Leaders (business)							
1. Robert Slater							
2. Paul C. Cabot							
3. Eli Goldstone							
4. John M. Fox							
5. Roger P. Sonnabend							

Figure 4.5   Partial exhibit of leadership acquaintance and working relationship scale.

operating to concentrate participation in either Local or Megalopolis areas of interest.

Table 4.1 shows clearly the difference between the local and megalopolis acquaintance-contact scores of key and top leaders. Key leaders consistently outscore top leaders in both (with one exception), which is expected for it provides additional evidence to support the hypotheses that states that dimensions of ac-

TABLE 4.1   MEAN LOCAL COMMUNITY AND MEGALOPOLIS ACQUAINTANCE AND CONTACT SCORES FOR BUSINESS, POLITICAL, RELIGIOUS, AND CIVIC LEADERS AS REPORTED BY KEY LEADERS, TOP LEADERS, AND COMBINED KEY AND TOP LEADERS

Leaders scores on local and Megalopolis acquaintance & contact	Mean local community acquaintance-contact scores			Mean Megalopolis acquaintance-contact scores		
	Key leaders	Top leaders	Key and top	Key leaders	Top leaders	Key and top
Civic	174	158	166	177	158	165
Political	170	155	164	160	83	133
Business	169	159	165	129	112	123
Labor	163	147	132	137	150	148
Religious	138	114	128	125	83	109

quaintance and contact tend toward interdependence and enlargement. Because of the findings, the key leader population is regarded as representing broader megalopolis contacts. The top leaders constitute a control sample and are used to determine whether similar patterns are replicated by the two samples. The combined sample presents a further possibility of checking results as sample size is increased by combining the two populations. The advantage of this design can be utilized to test the second hypothesis of occupational differentiation in leadership.

PATTERNS AND OCCUPATIONAL GROUPINGS

III. It is hypothesized that key business, labor, government, religious, and civic leaders in Megalopolis will differ markedly in their acquaintance and contact with one another. *Highest acquaintance and contact scores will be registered by business leaders* and followed succesively by *civic, political, religious,* and *labor leaders.*

This hypothesis is derived from observations of the character of leader behavior in the community. Business leaders have more personal income, enjoy corporate expense accounts and corporate policy support for time spent in civic affairs, and more freedom of movement away from their offices. It was believed that these facts would predispose those business leaders who seek civic participation to engage in it more actively than all other leaders. Civic leaders are ranked second because of the broad scope of their contacts which are encouraged by their jobs and the nature of democratic participation in community organizations. Political, religious, and labor leaders are believed to be restricted to limited areas of movement because of many factors characterized by their jobs and the cultural definitions of their roles.

By referring again to Table 4.1 the mean *local* and *megalopolis* acquaintance and contact scores for the different occupational leaders may be examined.

These results demonstrate that the hypothesis on the rank ordering of leaders from business, civic affairs, politics, religion, and labor is *not* appropriate. On the contrary, the new ranking of key leaders shows two different orders. See Figure 4.6; local community mean scores are shown on the left and megalopolis mean scores on the right.

It can be noted that civic leaders place first and religious leaders last, as shown by their scores on both local and megalopolitan dimensions. Business, political, and labor leaders occupy intermediate positions on both dimensions. If there is a "problem" group in terms of community and regional isolation, it resides in the religious leaders who consistently occupy the bottom rung in all tests. Key and top religious leaders combined show a mean of 128 for local community acquaintance-contacts and 109 for their megalopolis scores.[16] These are the lowest scores registered by any leadership group. A surprising finding is the uneven ranking of business leaders who have among the highest scores for local community acquaintance and contacts but who drop to fourth place in Megalopolis acquaintance-contact. Civic, political, and labor leaders exhibit higher average scores,[17] which indicates that key and top business leaders are more closely tied to their local urban areas than is imagined. The hypothesis must be rejected and reformulated to order ranking of key leaders in megalopolis acquaintance and contact as *civic, political, labor, business,* and *religious.*

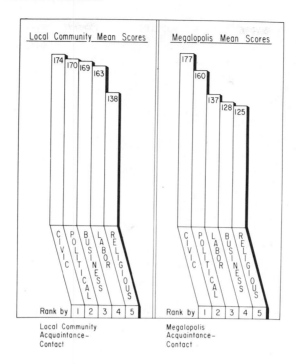

Figure 4.6   Rank ordering of key leaders on local community and Megalopolis dimensions of acquaintance and contact.

ACQUAINTANCE AND CONTACT PATTERNS BETWEEN LEADERS
IN THE MAJOR CITIES OF MEGALOPOLIS

IV.   A significant variation occurs in acquaintance and contact between leaders in the major urban areas, with the greatest to least ranging from New York to Washington, Philadelphia, Boston, and Baltimore.

This hypothesis focuses attention on the acquaintance and contacts of leaders between cities. There is reason to believe that New York, the largest city, with its high remunerative opportunities, has a selective influence in attracting key leaders. Moreover, leaders from other cities frequently visit these leaders in New York. Washington, as the national capital, is the center in which political and labor leaders of high repute are located. Philadelphia is believed to be in the third position because of its size and its nearness to both New York and Washington. Boston is thought to rank fourth as a contact point because of its relative geographic isolation. It lies to the north, 231 miles from any other major city in Megalopolis. Baltimore, whose position is advantageous, lacks the historic, political, cultural, and even the economic attractions that would enable it to inspire a key leader movement. In spite of its industrial prominence, it places fifth.

The nature and extent of these intercity ties is crucial to the determination of bonds by which we can affirm or reject the existence of a network of influence. The questionnaire has sought to discover the ties among the 200 key leaders

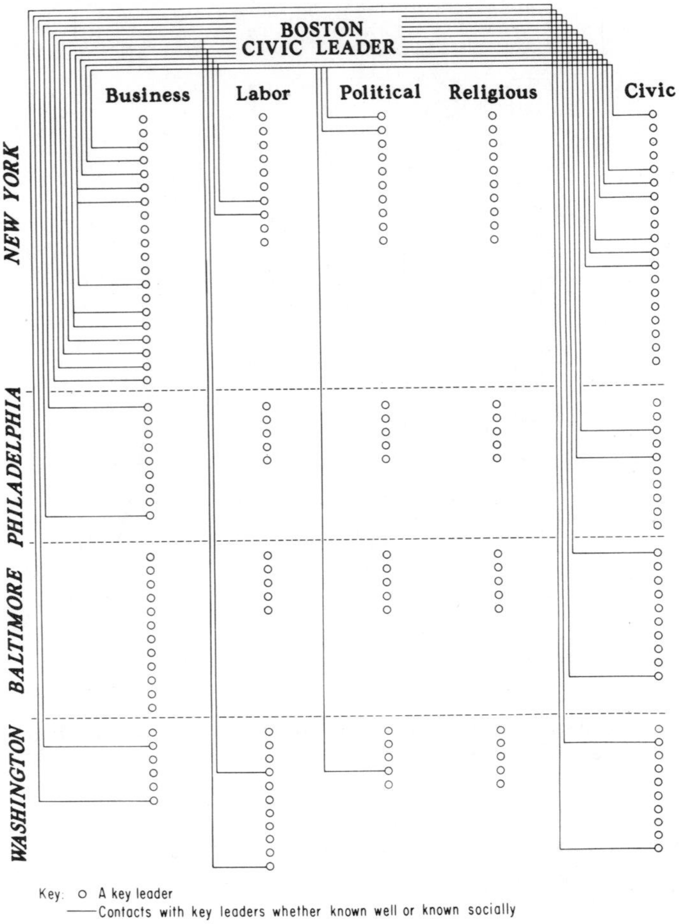

Figure 4.7   Net of acquaintance and contact of a Boston civic leader with other key leaders in New York, Philadelphia, Baltimore, and Washington.
SOURCE: Delbert C. Miller in *Environmental Quality Analysis,* edited by Allen V. Kneese and Blair T. Bower c 1972 for Resources for the Future, Inc., by Johns Hopkins Press, Baltimore.

themselves and their ties with the 200 top leaders. Each of the 178 respondents has an individual web of connections. Some individual and group networks are examined for evidence of acceptance or rejection of the hypothesis. Figure 4.7 illustrates a Boston civic leader's net of acquaintance and contacts with other key leaders in New York, Philadelphia, Baltimore, and Washington. The various lines refer to a record made by the respondent to show key leaders whom he "knew well" or "socially" and with whom the "has had business, social, or civic contacts." His local community contacts, although extensive (acquaintance and contact score is 169), are not shown. What is set forth are the ties between business, labor, political, religious, and civic leaders in the cities outside his own community; in other words, the Megalopolis dimension. The Boston civic leader's net shows the highest incidence of contact with business (16), civic (12), labor (4), and political leaders (3), in that order. No outside connections with key religious leaders are recorded.

The diagram in Figure 4.7 can be likened to a closed telephone exchange. Each station represents a potential and accessible contact. If this Boston leader wanted advice or assistance for a problem involving decision making in Megalopolis, it is predicted that the most likely contacts would be made in his personal network of acquaintance. There is no question that this leader, with his 35 ties to other key leaders in Megalopolis, is a part of the larger megalopolitan network which is our major object of study. His total Megalopolis acquaintance and contact score is 302, an outstanding record but not unique. One New York civic leader has a score of 473. The sociograms of the top 10 regional leaders are presented in the next chapter. These individual networks demonstrate that there are true citizens of "Megalopolis," leaders who move in and through the leadership net of other major urban areas which constitute the Atlantic urban region. This fact can be more effectively illustrated by the group configurations.

The acquaintanceships of all 100 key leaders were examined. Reciprocal markings of leaders who answered "know well" or "know socially" were identified and appear as Figure 4.8. This chart makes clear the nature of acquaintanceships in local metropolitan areas and among the five major cities.[18] Baltimore, Philadelphia, and Boston reveal high intensities of local acquaintance,[19] and 78 intercity reciprocations with strong flow lines are indicated between New York and Washington, Philadelphia and Washington, Boston and New York, and Philadelphia and New York. In order to impose a more rigorous criterion a similar analysis of reciprocal response was made on the checking of "I have had business, civic, or social contacts during the last three years." Figure 4.9 reveals these patterns. Baltimore's strong local interaction stands out; the intercity nets emphasize the New York-Philadelphia and the Boston-New York connectiveness. Note also the ties between Boston, New York, and Philadelphia with Washington.

A search for a net of megalopolitan ties was made between leaders who expressed an interest in or named environmental quality (air, water, or solid waste) as a working activity. Figure 4.10 is an exhibit of these data that shows those leaders who have first indicated general contacts with one another and have also said environmental quality was an interest or activity. Twenty environmental leaders are listed. It is obvious that an intercity network exists which suggests that a regional approach to environmental problems based on the availability of interested and powerful urban-oriented leaders is possible. It is believed that a board or commission of such leaders could generate maximum influence in pressing for more vigorous efforts in improving environmental quality.

Further insight into leader acquaintance can be discerned from the different approach taken when the leaders were asked to make a general response to the following statement:

> *My best to poorest knowledge of leaders and organizations in the major cities of the Atlantic urban region can be ranked 1 through 5 as* (1 = best knowledge)
> __Boston, __New York, __Philadelphia, __Baltimore, __Washington.

It should be noted that this statement asks the leader to think about his knowledge of all the leaders and organizations in the five major cities. It differs from

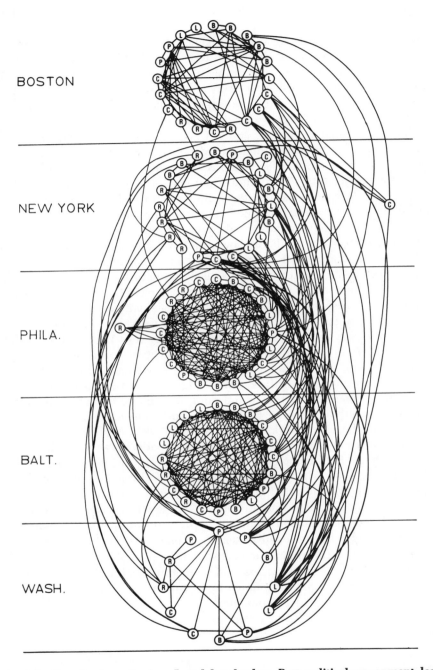

BOSTON

NEW YORK

PHILA.

BALT.

WASH.

Figure 4.8 B = business leader; L = labor leader; P = political-government leader; R = religious leader; C = civic leader. Reciprocal relations of key leaders in Megalopolis who identified one another as "know well" or "know socially."

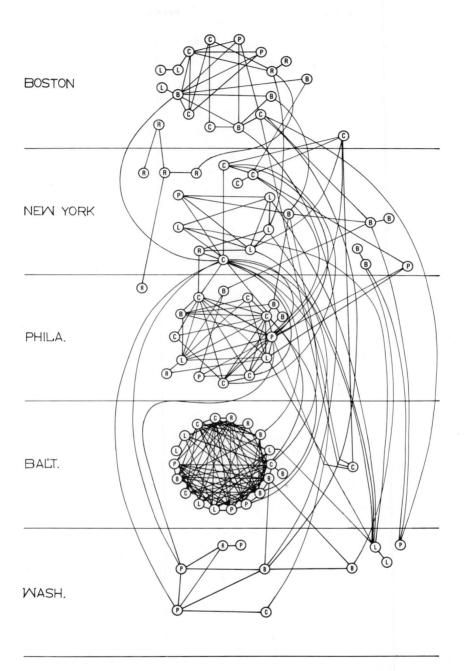

BOSTON

NEW YORK

PHILA.

BALT.

WASH.

Figure 4.9 Reciprocal relations of key leaders in Megalopolis who identified one another as "having business, civic, or social contacts during the last three years."

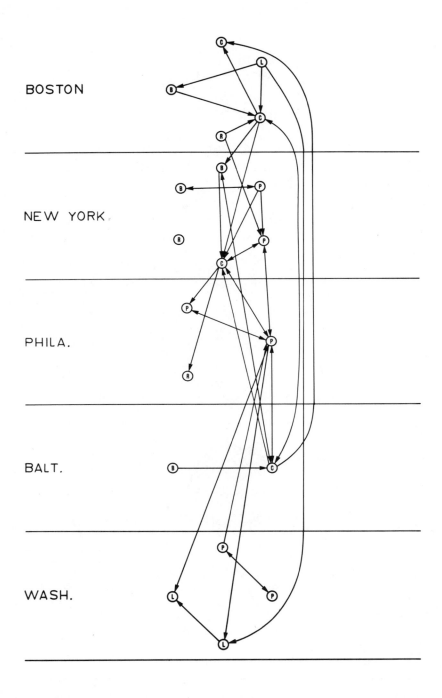

BOSTON

NEW YORK

PHILA.

BALT.

WASH.

Figure 4.10 Reciprocal relations of key leaders in Megalopolis who identified one another as having general contacts and who shared common interests in environmental quality problems.

TABLE 4.2   BEST TO POOREST KNOWLEDGE OF LEADERS AND
ORGANIZATIONS IN THE MAJOR CITIES OF MEGALOPOLIS

Percent of leaders responding "know least well" of the leaders and organizations
residing in the five cities

Baltimore	38%
Boston	23
Philadelphia	17
Washington	11
New York	3

his own acquaintance-contact scores because they were based on designated leaders. Here he is asked to respond more widely to leaders and organizations as he
defines them. A rank of 5, *"know least well,"* was singled out for analysis. The
results are shown in Table 4.2. Note that Baltimore and Boston leaders and organizations remain least known and New York and Washington are best known.
What explains this order? Baltimore is least known probably because it does not
occupy an economic, social, and cultural position that attracts other leaders.
Washington is such a close neighbor (39 miles to the south) that Baltimore is
overshadowed by the nation's capital city. Philadelphia in the mid-position shares
Baltimore's problem. It has a giant city as its closest neighbor. The awesome size
and dominance of New York is a real fact of collective life. Some even call Philadelphia a dormitory suburb of New York. Boston does not have to worry about
the immediate competition of powerful competing cities and is often called the
hub of New England. It seems, however, to suffer from isolation because of its
removal from the other four major metropolitan areas. Its location places it like
an extended thumb separated from the four finger cities that lie below it, yet
geographical disadvantage does not prevent it from attaining the fourth position
among the Big Five.

These findings move understanding of leadership contact one step forward.
Directionality of focus is fairly well established. New York and Washington are
the poles around which leadership contacts are concentrated. Patterns of
acquaintance and contact depend to a significant degree, however, on the extent
to which leaders do free or can free themselves from the demands of local problems. It is also noted subsequently from the evidence derived from Hypotheses V
that at the very top of the megalopolitan leadership structure there are "stars"
that are concentrated heavily in the New York area.

Leadership Power Ranking and Leadership Groups

V.   *Top policy-making leaders and their institutional identifications.*   The policy-
making ranking of leaders chosen for their ability and influence in shaping urban
policy will reflect *a patterned institutional power ranking in which business, government, labor, civic,* and *religious sectors* are exhibited in the order named.

This hypothesis follows the contours of a study of a national power structure
which describes business and government as powerful in national decision mak-

ing, followed by labor, education, and religion in that order. In this leadership study 25 leaders are nominated by each respondent as his choices for those best able to represent the Boston-to-Washington urban region in the shaping of urban policy and programming. He made his choices by choosing freely among the 200 key business, labor, government, religious, and civic leaders. It is from these nominees that the hypothesis is put to the test. The nomination ranking is secured by a tally of votes received from the item on the questionnaire which reads as follows:

NOW PLEASE LOOK OVER THE LIST OF 200 LEADERS AND NOMI-NATE 25 LEADERS THAT COULD BEST REPRESENT THE BOSTON TO WASHINGTON URBAN REGION IN THE SHAPING OF URBAN POLICY AND PROGRAMMING FOR THE REGION.

Simply put the NUMBER of your nominee here. See list. The order is not important. (All information is confidential and each person will be recorded by code number. This information is for research purposes only.)

_____

_____

Place other names, not on the list, to which you would give higher priority. (Please do not name U.S. Senators, Congressmen, or Cabinet members. They have been omitted.)

_____

_____

The city of residence and occupational identity of the 178 leaders who made the nominations are shown in Table 4.3, which lists a fairly even distribution of nominators by city and occupational identity. Certainly the distribution is sufficiently representative to permit the nomination of any outstanding leaders, wherever they might live. The importance of this representation becomes clear when the 26 nominees have been examined.

The top 26 policy-making representations actually chosen are shown on the facing page. (The ordering is by city and has no reference to the number of votes received.)

Table 4.4 shows the distribution of these top policy makers by occupation and city of residence.

Unlike the identity of the nominators, the distribution of top ranking nominees is uneven. The order of occupational representation shows _civic_ with 42 percent, _political-governmental_ with 27 percent, _business_ with 15 percent, and _labor_ and _religious_ with 8 percent. The hypothesis does not predict this ranking, but the findings must be seriously viewed as a rough approximation of institutional power as it impinges on urban problems and the issues underlying their resolution. It may be noted that black leaders occupy a high position among those chosen: Bayard Rustin, Whitney Young, Roy Wilkins, Kenneth B. Clark, Leon Sullivan, Walter Washington, and Robert C. Weaver, most of whom are regarded as civil rights leaders. Perhaps civil rights should now be recognized as a separate institutional sector and included in any institutional view of power structure. New

Leader nominated*	Leader type	Urban area
John K. Galbraith	Civic	Boston
John Collins	Political	Boston
Kingman Brewster	Civic	New Haven-New York
Nelson A. Rockefeller	Political	Albany-New York
John V. Lindsay	Political	New York
Bayard Rustin	Civic	New York
Whitney Young (deceased)	Civic	New York
Arthur J. Goldberg	Political-Civic	New York
David Rockefeller	Business	New York
Terrence, Cardinal Cooke	Religious	New York
Cornelius W. Owens	Business	New York
Robert C. Weaver	Civic-Political	New York
Roy Wilkins	Civic	New York
A. Philip Randolph	Labor	New York
Kenneth B. Clark	Civic	New York
Andrew Heiskell	Business	New York
McGeorge Bundy	Civic	New York
Paul N. Ylvisaker	Civic-Political	New Jersey-New York
Richard J. Hughes	Political-Civic	New Jersey-New York
Richardson Dilworth	Political	Philadelphia
The Reverend Leon Sullivan	Religious	Philadelphia
Joseph Clark	Political	Philadelphia
James Rouse	Business	Baltimore
Milton Eisenhower	Civic	Baltimore
Walter E. Washington	Political	Washington
George Meany	Labor	Washington

*Twenty-six are listed because positions 25 and 26 resulted in a tie vote.

York, by virtue of its civic, political, business, and, to some extent, labor and religious dominance, offers a high concentration of policy-making leaders (61%). The first nine to rank in nomination are all from the New York area. This predominance of New York leaders cannot be explained by a predominance of New York raters. It will be remembered that those who made the nominations were fairly equally divided among the cities. As Table 4.3 shows, 138 or 78 percent of the nominating leaders came from urban areas outside New York.

We must conclude that the institutional power ranking in urban problems in Megalopolis places the *civic, political-governmental, business, labor,* and *religious sectors* in that order of influence. These conclusions are made with the reservation that federal administrators and legislators are not included. The leaders treated in this study are those who are in a position to influence federal officials. Federal officials are viewed as formulaters and executers of policy and therefore the targets of influence. For this reason the study concentrates, as the various urban coalitions do, on leaders who can exert influence on decisions made in Washington or in local and state governments.

The original hypothesis must be rejected and reformulated to rank institutional power as *civic, political-governmental, business, labor,* and *religious.*

TABLE 4.3   MATRIX OF 178 NOMINATORS OF INFLUENTIAL POLICY MAKERS

City leaders	Business	Labor	Political	Religious	Civic	Totals
Boston	6	5	3	6	8	28
New York	10	7	3	11	9	40
Philadelphia	10	6	3	7	14	40
Baltimore	7	9	7	6	13	42
Washington	2	9	4	4	9	28
Totals	35	36	20	34	53	178

TABLE 4.4   IDENTITY OF 26 TOP POLICY-MAKING NOMINEES FOR MEGALOPOLIS BY OCCUPATION AND CITY OF RESIDENCE

	Business	Labor	Political-government	Religious	Civic	Totals
Boston			1		2	3
New York	3	1	3	1	8	16
Philadelphia			2	1		3
Baltimore	1				1	2
Washington		1	1			2
Totals	N %	N %	N %	N %	N %	
	4 15	2 8	7 27	2 8	11 42	26

ACQUAINTANCE AND CONTACT BACKGROUNDS OF ALL LEADERS
NOMINATED FOR REGIONAL POLICY MAKING

An emergent question is how such sociometric leaders are chosen by other key and top leaders. What factors bring these leaders forward?

VI. It is hypothesized that these *regional board nominees* establish high *acquaintance and contacts with other leaders.*

This hypothesis suggests that in order to receive recognition and backing for any appointment a leader must be known to others. It is believed that his degree of acquaintance and contact is an index of his willingness to engage in civic activity and his acceptance by others as a leader.

The question is whether a definite relationship between a leader's acquaintance and contact and the nomination ranking he receives as a policy maker can be established. Table 4.5 demonstrates that this relationship exists and that it can be demonstrated repeatedly. The nominations received by each leader were recorded and correlations established between the number of nominations each received and the local acquaintance-contact scores.

The first set of correlations relates the leaders local acquaintance-contact scores to the number of nominations received. These range from $r = .19$ to $r = .23$ for the three nominating groups. The standard errors indicate that these correlations are all statistically significant for the 178 key and top leaders combined, 100 key leaders only, and 78 top leaders only. The correlations between Megalopolis acquaintance-contact scores and nomination rankings range from .33 to .45. There is no question of the statistical significance of this dimension. It is now believed that those leaders who have achieved wide acquaintance and contacts in Megalopolis become better known and more active and that this base of acquaintance and contacts is essential to the highest attainments of leadership. The correlations support the hypothesis but do not explain fully the reason some leaders achieve nomination. Certainly the acquaintance and contact of a leader explains a minor part of the variance, yet the matter of visibility is a moot point in understanding how a leader becomes prominent in a wider circle. It is obvious that to achieve visibility in a large metropolitan area is not easy. It is still more difficult to obtain recognition as a broad gauged leader in whom others may have confidence. To maintain the visibility of leaders across Megalopolis requires almost national prominence, but perhaps we should conclude that prominence in Megalopolis is tantamount to national prominence.

These problems are treated in detail in Chapter 5, where the top regional nominees are studied for their participation in organizations and their roles in regional and national life. In this chapter we continue to examine certain characteristics of the total leader population. A question of much interest is whether top leaders consider the power structures in which they operate to be monolithic or pluralist in character.

TABLE 4.5   THE RELATIONSHIP OF LEADERSHIP ACQUAINTANCE AND CONTACT AND THE NUMBER OF NOMINATIONS RECEIVED AS A POLICY-MAKING POLICY REPRESENTATIVE

Nominating ranking as received by	Local community acquaintance and contact scores of key leaders		Megalopolis acquaintance and contact scores of key leaders	
	r	sd	r	sd
All nominations from 100 key and 78 top leaders	.23	$\sigma_r = .07$	.41	$\sigma_r = .06$
Nominations from key leaders only	.19	$\sigma_r = .09$	.33	$\sigma_r = .09$
Nominations from top leaders only	.23	$\sigma_r = .11$	.45	$\sigma_r = .09$

Decision-Making Perceptions and Mechanisms

TOP LEADER PERCEPTIONS OF THE POWER STRUCTURES IN WHICH THEY OPERATE

VII.   There is a relationship between the *degree of acquaintance and contact of leaders and their perception of decision making as monolithic or pluralistic.*

This hypothesis rests on the belief that the more a person is aware of the many influences generated by many different people the more likely he is to see decision making as pluralistic.

The following statement was presented to each respondent:

> As you watch different issues of high importance arise in urban life, would you say that leaders generally change according to the issue or that the same crowd generally makes the decisions regardless of the issue.
>
> ___Leaders generally change with the issue at stake.
>
> ___Same crowd of leaders generally makes the decisions regardless of the issue.

COMMENTS

The respondent did one of three things: he marked one of the two statements and nothing else; he marked one of the two statements and made comments; he marked neither but wrote in a response and made comments. When the write-in response was used, a common reply was *"both, depending on the circumstances."* One leader explained:

> Can't answer categorically—if I had to choose one I would say #2—but in public education more and more leadership is changing with broad issues that arise—in taxing problems, for example, #1 would apply.

Another wise and experienced political leader warned:

> Please don't throw all of these answers into a computer and think you can come out with anything useful. It's all a question of very personal human relations. The most foolish question ever asked public figures is: "If you had to choose one action which would it be?"

Another respondent echoed the same thought with the succinct statement that a "questionnaire can't handle the important but elusive variables."
Still another was stimulated to write out a philosophic reply:

> If you want creative solutions you have to avoid all those who have participated in planning in the immediate past, since they have only succeeded in creating pipe dreams and setting up smoke screens, be-cause in reality all the programs have been a total failure. The schools don't educate; urban renewal tears down, but can't build; welfare begets illegitimacy; militants produce polarization and perhaps even

civil war; churchmen have budgets and building programs but no religion; businessmen have economy but no ethic; civic leaders know the
problems but have no answers. One answer is a job for everybody,
including welfare mothers and the so-called unemployable—not a
minimum income but a real, live job. Another answer is food for
everybody and easily available so that there are full bellies.

A definitive comment was made by one respondent who said, "In my city
almost everything is controlled by questionable persons both black and white.
In my opinion, there is no hope for the poor." A more hopeful leader wrote:

> The most important issue of our times is the need to democratize the
> decision-making process in all levels of government, particularly on the
> city level. To achieve true citizen participation you need an educated
> (in the practical sense) electorate. The untapped reservoirs of leader-
> ship in our streets is one of America's greatest resources.

Leaders who tried to explain the structure of leadership as it was revealed on
issues saw both rigidity and fluidity, agreeing with the earlier respondent who
said that the statement could not be answered categorically. Some of their replies
show their individual perceptions.

> Leaders generally change with the issue at stake but this must be
> qualified; in most cities some of the same crowd of leaders are fre-
> quently encountered on many issues. NEW YORK CIVIC LEADER.

> "Same Crowd" make many, or perhaps even a majority of decisions
> but on a substantial number of issues they make it with a special con-
> tact with a particular group. In a reasonable number of issues their
> part in the decision is nominal or non-existent. PHILADELPHIA CIVIC
> LEADER

> The same groups—not necessarily the same individuals—make the
> major decisions concerning politics, economic development, legislative
> policy, and minorities. A growing but far from decisive force is the in-
> creased organization and assertiveness of the black community on mat-
> ters touching it deeply, but not on general issues which it does not
> recognize as bearing on its needs. A shift is taking place in that politi-
> cal and economic power is increasingly shared by Catholics (Italian
> as well as the earlier Irish Catholics). Labor is mostly influential on
> political candidates." PHILADELPHIA CIVIC LEADER

With a specific admonition not to put the data into a computer the researcher
hesitated but decided to proceed anyway. It is well indeed to recognize that a
categorical answer is a simplification of a complex process, and it is important to
recognize that in accepting categorical answers the results must be viewed tentatively. Yet the search here is not for the reality of the process so much as the
psychological perspective. How do leaders view the leadership structure as relatively rigid (same crowd) or relatively flexible (many persons involved)?

The frequencies of response show that 48 leaders, or 27 percent, saw leaders
generally changing with the issue at stake; 101, or 57%, reported that the same

crowd generally makes the decisions (five leaders said both and 24 either did not report or could not be assigned.) By a more than 2 to 1 majority, therefore, leaders generally perceive that the "same crowd" makes the decisions.

The hypothesis seeks to determine whether increased acquaintance and contacts make any difference in the perception. First the combined key and top leaders were examined; then the analysis was completed for key leaders and top leaders separately. Point biserial correlation was used to determine coefficients. Table 4.6 shows the findings.

This table indicates that little, if any, relation is indicated between the two variables. The negative sign signifies increased acquaintance-contact with a pluralistic perspective of leaders changing with the issue. The fact that the highest coefficient, $-.15$. appears for key leaders with higher Megalopolis acquaintance-contact scores is in the supportive direction of the hypothesis, because it is the key leader with the greatest knowledge of other leaders who is responding more frequently to the pluralist perspective. However, point biserial ranges from 0 to 1, and this correlation is so low that it is almost nonexistent. The fact that it fails to hold up for the top leaders by swinging from .06 on local acquaintance scores to $-.06$ on megalopolis acquaintance-contact scores suggests a firm report of no correlation and rejection of the hypothesis. It seems likely that the clue to the lack of correlation can be found in the remarks of the respondents. Leaders vary greatly in their perception of the leadership decision-making structure. Many indicate that they see an overlapping between monolithic and pluralistic conceptions. If this is truly the situation, it might be concluded that we have a happy and realistic picture of a democracy in action.

DECISION-MAKING MECHANISMS USED BY KEY AND TOP LEADERS

VIIIa. Business, labor, government, religious, and civic leaders will differ greatly in their contact patterns with governmental and voluntary organizations but will demonstrate particular patterns. It is expected that *business, labor, and government leaders will have their closest ties to governmental agencies* and that *religious and civic organizations will have their closest ties to voluntary organizations.*

This hypothesis is directed toward the identification of organizational contacts made by different occupational groups of leaders. Therefore an initial determination involves the nature of organizations approached in civic activity. Leaders were asked the following questions:

> In your civic activity on urban problems do you work mainly with leaders associated with (rank in order of the amount of activity):
>
> ___ Private voluntary organizations
>
> ___ City government agencies
>
> ___ State government agencies
>
> ___ National government agencies

TABLE 4.6   THE RELATIONSHIP OF LEADER ACQUAINTANCE AND CONTACT AND PERCEPTION OF THE LEADERSHIP STRUCTURE AS MONOLITHIC OR PLURALISTIC

Community acquaintance and contact	Combined population of key and top leaders point biserial r	Key leaders only point biserial r	Top leaders only point biserial r
Local community acquaintance-contact scores	−.12	−.14	.06
Megalopolis acquaintance-contact scores	−.13	−.15	−.06

___ Business organizations

___ Your own firm or organization

___ Universities

___ Independent professionals

This was not easy for most respondents. Some did not answer at all; others marked a few of the options with a 1 and 2, then stopped; some put a check before some of the organizations. However, at least one-half of the 178 leaders rated most of the organizations. Table 4.7 shows the percentage for each of the eight ranks by occupational groups that might be given to any of the organizations, and important differences in contact patterns can be discerned. Stars show the largest percentage (mode) recorded by each occupational group for a given organization. An evaluation of response patterns reveals the order of ranking for the various leader groups. Leaders are associated with organizations in civic life (see p. 102).

The order of these ranks permits a number of conclusions that may be used in evaluating the hypothesis:

1. Each occupational group of leaders has a distinctive pattern of organizational contacts, although considerable variation occurs around any given pattern (supportive of the hypothesis).
2. Business leaders have a high frequency of contacts with city governmental agencies but low levels of contact with state and national governmental agencies (supportive of the hypothesis). Business has a high concentration of contacts with private voluntary organizations, other business organizations, and universities (unexpected and not supportive of hypothesis).
3. Labor leaders record a high ranking of contacts with city and national governmental agencies, higher than any other group of leaders (supportive). Its

TABLE 4.7   PERCENTAGE OF RESPONSE BY TYPE OF KEY AND TOP LEADERS RANKING THE EIGHT ORGANIZATIONS (FROM ONE TO EIGHT) WITH WHICH THEY WORK MOST ACTIVELY IN CIVIC MATTERS

Rank	In civic activity I work mainly with Leaders associated with								Not ascertained	Total N	Total %
	(1)	(2)	(3)	(4)	(5)	(6)	(7)	(8)			
Private voluntary organizations											
Business	25.7*	14.3	17.1	5.7	14.3	0.0	0.0	0.0	22.9	35	100
Labor	30.6*	16.7	8.3	2.8	2.8	0.0	2.8	0.0	36.1	36	100
Government	20.0*	20.0	15.0	10.0	15.0	10.0	0.0	0.0	17.6	34	100
Religious	44.1*	29.4	5.9	2.9	0.0	0.0	0.0	0.0	17.6	34	100
Civic	41.5*	15.1	7.5	9.4	3.8	5.7	0.0	0.0	17.0	53	100
City government agencies											
Business	11.4	28.6*	17.1	5.7	0.0	0.0	0.0	0.0	37.1	35	100
Labor	27.8*	8.3	11.4	2.8	2.8	0.0	0.0	0.0	47.2	36	100
Government	25.0*	25.0	25.0	10.0	5.0	0.0	0.0	5.0	5.0	20	100
Religious	20.6*	14.7	17.6	5.9	2.9	2.9	5.9	0.0	29.4	34	100
Civic	20.8	26.4*	20.8	3.8	3.8	3.8	0.0	0.0	20.8	53	100
State government agencies											
Business	2.9	2.9	8.6	14.3*	8.6	8.6	0.0	0.0	54.3	35	100
Labor	5.6	2.8	8.3*	8.3	5.6	0.0	0.0	2.8	66.7	36	100
Government	0.0	15.0	10.0	25.0*	10.0	10.0	10.0	5.0	25.0	20	100
Religious	2.9	5.9	0.0	14.7*	5.9	2.9	0.0	5.9	61.8	34	100
Civic	1.9	9.4*	9.4	7.5	9.4	9.4	5.7	3.8	43.4	53	100
National government agencies											
Business	2.9	8.6	8.6	8.6*	8.6	5.7	8.6	0.0	48.6	35	100
Labor	22.2*	8.3	2.8	2.8	5.6	8.3	0.0	5.6	44.4	36	100
Government	10.0	15.0	5.0	10.0	25.0*	20.0	5.0	0.0	10.0	20	100
Religious	8.8	2.9	8.8	8.8	14.7*	5.9	5.9	0.0	44.1	34	100
Civic	5.7	5.7	18.9*	15.1	7.5	1.9	9.4	3.8	32.1	53	100

Business organizations

Business	25.7*	17.1	22.9	5.7	5.7	0.0	2.9	0.0	20.0	35	100
Labor	13.9*	2.8	8.3	8.3	2.8	0.0	5.6	5.6	52.8	36	100
Government	5.0	5.0	15.0	10.0	5.0	25.0*	15.0	5.0	15.0	20	100
Religious	8.8	0.0	14.7*	0.0	5.9	8.8	2.9	8.8	50.0	34	100
Civic	3.8	7.5	3.8	9.4	18.9*	7.5	0.0	1.9	47.2	53	100

Own firm or organization

Business	31.4*	11.4	5.7	5.7	0.0	0.0	0.0	0.0	45.7	35	100
Labor	27.8*	8.3	2.8	0.0	0.0	0.0	5.6	0.0	55.6	36	100
Government	40.0*	5.0	5.0	0.0	5.0	0.0	5.0	5.0	35.0	20	100
Religious	38.2*	11.8	11.8	0.0	2.9	0.0	2.9	0.0	32.4	34	100
Civic	20.8*	9.4	2.9	3.8	1.9	1.9	5.7	0.0	54.7	53	100

Universities

Business	14.3†	2.9	2.9	8.6	0.0	11.4	0.0†	14.3†	45.7	35	100
Labor	8.3†	0.0	2.8	0.0	5.6	8.3†	8.3†	5.6	61.1	36	100
Government	10.0	5.0	10.0	5.0	10.0	10.0	20.0*	10.0	20.0	20	100
Religious	5.9	5.9	2.9	5.9	2.9	5.9	14.7*	0.0	55.9	34	100
Civic	9.4†	7.5	9.4	7.5	5.7	9.4†	7.5	7.5	35.8	53	100

Independent professionals

Business	5.7	2.9	2.9	5.7	0.0	5.7	5.7	2.9	68.6	35	100
Labor	0.0	5.6	0.0	8.3	2.8	8.3	2.8	5.6	66.7	36	100
Government	5.0	10.0*	0.0	15.0*	10.0	10.0	15.0	20.0	15.0	20	100
Religious	8.8*	0.0	0.0	11.8*	2.9	8.8	2.9	8.8	55.9	34	100
Civic	5.7	3.8	9.4	5.7	3.8	5.7	5.7	9.4	50.9	53	100

* Indicates the largest percentage recorded (mode) by each occupational group for a given organization.
† Ties for highest percentage.

Business	Labor	Government	Religious	Civic
Own firm	Private voluntary	Own organizations	Private voluntary	Private voluntary
Private voluntary organizations	Own organization	City government	Own organization	City government
Business organizations	City government	Private voluntary	City government	Own organization
City government	Business organizations	National government	National government	Independent professionals
Universities	National government	Universities	Universities	Business organizations
National government	State government	Business organizations	Business organizations	National government
State government	Universities	State government	Independent professionals	Universities
Independent professionals	Independent professionals	Independent professionals	State government	State government

greatest organizational contacts are recorded for private voluntary organizations (unexpected and not supportive of hypothesis).

4. Government leaders do concentrate their contacts in city, state, and national governmental agencies (supportive).

5. Religious and civic leaders have their highest ranking of contacts with private voluntary agencies (supportive).

The weight of the evidence is supportive of the hypothesis, but additional findings were discovered.

Leaders have a large number of contacts in all occupational groups within their own firms or organizations. In their dealings with governmental agencies city governments lead; national and state agencies are in second and third position. Their lowest levels of contact are with independent professions, state governments, and universities.

VIIIb. Business, labor, government, religious, and civic leaders will differ greatly in the level of activity they find the most rewarding:

> In civic activity do you personally find it most rewarding to work at the local level _____; state level _____; national level _____; all three _____?

One hundred fifty-eight responded, as shown in Table 4.8.

It can be seen that the largest number of respondents chose the local level (42.8%). This seems to indicate that most of them believe that they can exert their influence most effectively in the local community and perhaps sustain a more continuous application of their efforts. In contrast, it is significant how few say that the state level is most rewarding (2%), and this response is not raised much by such combinations as local and state (2%) or state and national (0.5%). The national level with all its prestige secures a response of only 7.6 percent, but a local and national combination adds 6.5 percent. A sizable group (39.2%) stated that they find work at local, state, and national levels most rewarding.

In the perspective of regional development these findings have a pronounced significance that indicates that leaders are motivated to reach out and engage in extralocal levels of activity. At the same time they reveal the high degree of concentration on local activity which also dominates much of the effort on urban problems. These opposing motivations raise interesting questions why some leaders concentrate problem activity at the local level and why other leaders extend their activity to the state and national. The nature of the attractions of work at the regional level remains even more problematic

VIIIc. *Contact patterns of key and top leaders demonstrate high intraoccupational contacts and widely varying patterns with other occupational leaders.*

To ascertain the frequency of contact between leaders the following statement was put before the key and top leaders.

TABLE 4.8   LEADER IDENTIFICATION OF MOST REWARDING LEVEL OF ACTIVITY (158 Key and Top Leaders Responding)

Local	State	National	All three (local, state, and national)
42.4% (N = 67)	2.0% (N = 3)	7.6% (N = 12)	39.2% (N = 62)
	Local and state	Local and national	State and national
	2.0% (N = 3)	6.3% (N = 10)	0.5% (N = 1)

> In regard to contacts I have established with leaders my most frequent
> to least frequent contacts with various groups of leaders can be ranked
> 1 through 5 as (1 equals most frequent)
>
> ___ business, ___ labor, ___ political-governmental, ___ religious, ___ civic.

These data were regarded as important in establishing the basis on which leaders come to know and perhaps understand one another. In attempts to secure representative or coalitional efforts a knowledge of leader patterns is useful in predicting problems of communication and participation in decision making. Frequency of contact is important in building common understanding. The findings show that business leaders rank frequency of contact with other business leaders very high. Their next most frequent contact is with political leaders, followed by civic, labor, and religious leaders in that order. Other patterns may be delineated for other groups. Table 4.9 demonstrates patterns of intercontact for each of the occupational groups.

A number of conclusions can be drawn from these contact patterns, all of which confirm the hypothesis.

1. All leaders have a preponderance of contacts with other leaders in their same occupational groups, but, depending on their occupational identity, there is wide variation in frequency of contact with other leader groups.

2. Outside their own groups political and civic leaders are most frequently approached by all groups.

3. Leaders approached least are labor and religious leaders.

Any efforts to put coalitions of leaders together must come to grips with such patterns. A more profound question is the meaning of such facts for American life in general. If business, political, and civic leaders are isolated from labor and religious leaders, a fragmentation of urban policy making and concensus may be an expected outcome. Value concensus is much more likely when different groups can be brought together face-to-face and communication channels are accessible.

TABLE 4.9   PATTERNS OF INTER-CONTACT FREQUENCY FOR BUSINESS, LABOR, POLITICAL, RELIGIOUS, AND CIVIC LEADERS

Leadership group	Highest frequency				Lowest frequency
	(1)	(2)	(3)	(4)	(5)
Business → leaders	Business →	Political →	Civic →	Labor →	Religious
Labor → leaders	Labor →	Political →	Business →	Civic →	Religious
Political → leaders	Political →	Civic →	Business →	Religious →	Labor
Religious → leaders	Religious →	Civic →	Political →	Business →	Labor
Civic → leaders	Civic →	Political →	Business →	Religious →	Labor

VIIId.   *Key and top leaders will regard their political contacts as their most valuable in civic affairs and policy making; labor and religious contacts will be assessed as least valuable.*

This hypothesis is based on the belief that legislation or governmental action is necessary for the improvement of urban problems

The low ranking for value of contacts involving labor and religious leaders is based on a predicted similarity to frequency of contact patterns already demonstrated.

Key and top leaders were asked to answer the following statement by ranking their responses:

> *For me the most valuable contacts in civic affairs and policy making dealing with urban problems have generally been with leaders from (rank 1 through 5)*

> ___ business, ___ labor, ___ political-governmental, ___ religious, ___ civic.

The attempt here is to probe still further the various dimensions of contact. Its frequency does not tell us what motivates the leader to seek or avoid it. An estimate of its value is an index of the utility assigned to it by different groups of leaders. Modal patterns can be identified from the findings and these are shown in Table 4.10.

A number of conclusions can be examined in relation to the hypothesis.

1. As the rankings are traced from highest value (1) to lowest (5) it can be seen that the highest is always given to a leader's own occupational group (unanticipated).

2. Most value assigned to a leader outside his own group is given to the political. Only political leaders choose civic leaders (supportive of hypothesis).

TABLE 4.10   VALUE PATTERNS OF CONTACT FOR BUSINESS, LABOR, POLITICAL, RELIGIOUS, AND CIVIC LEADERS

Key and top leaders responding	Highest value (1)	(2)	(3)	(4)	Lowest value (5)
Business →	Business →	Political →	Civic →	Religious →	Labor
Labor →	Labor →	Political →	Civic →	Business →	Religious
Political →	Political →	Civic →	Business →	Religious →	Labor
Religious →	Religious →	Political →	Civic →	Business →	Labor
Civic →	Civic →	Political →	Business →	Religious →	Labor

3. Lowest value assigned to a leader outside his own group is given to labor and religion (supportive of hypothesis).

A high relationship exists between the rankings on frequency and value of contact. The same patterns tend to be replicated for all occupational groups except for variations among religious and labor leaders.

It is probably true that political leaders win high standing because they are at the center of political forces. They know what is going on politically and they are in position to get things done. Civic leaders seem to have won their place because of their knowledge and probably their considerable political savvy. The relatively low position of business is somewhat surprising. Business does not lack funds or leadership. Why does it not rank higher? It may be suggested that it often takes a status quo position and is ideologically in some conflict with many other leaders. (This finding is demonstrated in Chapter 11.) Labor may lack the leadership necessary for civic activity (as often shown in community power studies) or because to business and government they represent adverse viewpoints. The low rank of religious leaders is perhaps explained by an opinion similar to that held by a number of urban coalition officers who explained their absence on their boards. "Religious leaders don't work in well with other leaders. They always talk of changing *Man*; they don't want to change institutions."

The research hypothesis failed to anticipate that the highest value given to contacts would be accorded by each occupational group to leaders in the same group. The findings demand an interpretation. It can be assumed that much civic activity is conducted for the marshaling of opinion and the mobilization of people and resources. In American life effort tends to be directed to the development of public opinion before approaches to government are undertaken. That origination of action begins as leaders interact with other leaders of their own occupations in which the most frequent and probably the easiest access exists. Leaders are also more comfortable with their "own kind," with whom they share common cultural and ideological predilections. They can communicate and get things done.

VIIIe. *Regional policy-making leaders are chosen by other key and top leaders as their representatives because these sociometric leaders are able to work well with others and possess high reputed influence.*

After key and top leaders had chosen those leaders that could best represent the Boston-to-Washington urban region in the shaping of urban policy and programming they were asked the following:

In my choices I have given most weight to the criterion that states the following:

___ 1. A leader should be able to work with other business, labor, governmental, religious, and civic leaders.

___ 2. A leader should commit himself to the work required.

___ 3. A leader should be able and willing to influence others.

The responses of the leaders are shown in Table 4.11. Perhaps most significant is that the highest frequency goes to "able to work with others." This quality is always important if a democratic process is to be preserved. When urban coalition officials were asked what they did when they were under pressure to ask a militant leader who could not work with other leaders to serve with them, the response often given was that such a leader was not invited because "the first responsibility of an organization is to survive and it must get its work done and hold the loyalty of all members who wish to work together."

The importance of influence (in second rank) is expected because key and top leaders appreciate that the most influential leaders can reach wider circles and command greater attention. Leaders often reply, however, that many highly influential leaders do not work well on committees. The findings show that many of the responding leaders made commitment their first consideration. Other leaders responded that their judgment depended on all three critria, including commitment.

TABLE 4.11 RESPONSES OF THE KEY AND TOP LEADERS TO THE CHOICE CRITERION USED IN SELECTING REPRESENTATIVE POLICY-MAKING LEADERS

N	Percent	
58	40.0	Able to work with others
36	24.6	Able to influence others
23	15.7	Commit himself to the work required
23	15.7	All three critera above
6	4.0	Scattered responses
146	100.0	

VIIIf. *Key and top leaders are most effective in civic policy making in face-to-face contacts, by working in committees, or by talking to small informal groups.*

This hypothesis was formulated to permit primary means of communication to be compared with the secondary. To learn what key and top leaders of Megalopolis do leaders were asked to respond to the following item and check the most appropriate methods of contact:

> *I find that I can be most effective in civic policy making by*
>
> ___ face to face contact, ___ telephone calls, ___ letters, ___ committee activity, ___ talking to large groups, ___ talking with small groups of leaders meeting informally.

Table 4.12 reports the percentage responses of 157 leaders. It can be seen that most leaders employ different methods of communication and usually cite two or three of the most effective, which, according to them, are face-to-face contacts and small informal meetings. Committee activity and talking to large groups are useful. A minority checked telephone calls and letters as effective.

Obviously these questions are an oversimplification. Leaders use all of them as appropriate to the task. These methods vary in phases of the policy-making processes from initiation, marshaling support, resolving issues, to making a final decision. Although these processes are too complex to be reduced to simple fact finding, it was useful to learn that leaders still rely mainly on the most primary mode of contact—face-to-face between individuals and groups. All the modern technological devices of communication do not change this fact. The ease of using the telephone or the relative simplicity of writing a letter do not provide comparable advantages.

Summary

Two hundred key and as many top influential urban-oriented leaders were identified by a consensus of knowledgeable judges in Boston, New York, Philadelphia, Baltimore, and Washington; 178 responded to a 10-page questionnaire regarding the acquaintance and contacts of key leaders. All cities and all occupational groups were well represented by the respondents.[20]

TABLE 4.12   RESPONSES OF THE KEY AND TOP LEADERS TO THE MODES OF CONTACT USED BY THEM IN CIVIC POLICY MAKING

68.0%	Face to face contact with another person
64.3%	Talking with small groups of leaders meeting informally
38.2%	Committee activity
28.6%	Talking to large groups
17.8%	Telephone Calls
16.5%	Letters

1. Initial efforts were made to uncover interest and activity patterns and priorities assigned by leaders to major problems. The findings show that key and top leaders center their activity on *housing, race relations, unemployment and poverty, public education,* and *crime* (1970). Environmental quality, represented by air and water pollution and waste, rank low in the scale of interests. An increase in the number of different urban problems was recorded over a 14-month interval (May 1969 to July 1970), but priority patterns remained relatively stable; only 17 percent of the leaders changed their urban problem interests and activities within one year. The intrusion of other problems weakened activity on many of the earlier problems.

2. Three dimensions of acquaintance and contact may be distinguished: lateral, vertical, and oblique. Lateral refers to local acquaintance and contacts; vertical and oblique include all extralocal or megalopoli contacts. Correlations were discovered between "local" and "Megalopolis" dimensions. Key leaders consistently outscore top leaders in both local and Megalopolis acquaintance and contact scores. The weight of the evidence supports the hypothesis that the three dimensions tend toward interdependence and enlargement.

3. Key leaders vary in their Megalopolis acquaintance and contact scores. The ranking order shows that civic leaders are highest, followed by political, labor, business, and religious leaders.

4. Variations between mean acquaintance and contact scores are found for key and top leaders in the major cities. The ranking order here is Washington, New York, Philadelphia, Boston, and Baltimore, reading from highest to lowest in Megalopolis orientation. When asked about their relative knowledge of *all* leaders (rather than the 200 key leaders) in the five cities, those leaders "known least" are reported for Baltimore as first, followed by Philadelphia, Boston, Washington, and New York.

5. The institutional power ranking of urban problems in Megalopolis (as derived from the distribution of key leaders nominated to regional policy positions) places the civic, political-governmental, business, labor, and religious sectors in that order of influence.

6. Positive correlations support the hypothesis that "regional board nominees" establish high acquaintance and contact scores. It is believed that this base of acquaintance and contacts is essential to the highest leadership attainments.

7. No relationship is demonstrated between the leaders' degree of acquaintance and contacts and their perception of decision making as monolithic or pluralistic.

8. A number of findings on decision-making mechanisms used by key and top leaders include the following:

> (a) Leaders in labor and government have their closest organizational ties to government agencies. Religious and civic leaders maintain their closest ties with private voluntary agencies. Business leaders have a high frequency of contact with city government but low levels with state and national governments; business leaders demonstrate a high concentration of activity with private voluntary organizations, other business organizations, and universities.

(b) Most leaders choose the local community as their most rewarding level of activity. The second most rewarding choice is work at all three levels, local, state, and national. Work at state or national levels alone is not regarded as rewarding except by a small number of leaders.

(c) All leaders have a preponderance of contacts with other leaders in their own occupational groups. Beyond these groups political and civic leaders are the most frequently approached by all groups. Labor and religious leaders are approached least often.

(d) Key and top leaders regard the contacts made in their own occupational groups as most valuable; outside their own groups they say political contacts are also valuable; the lowest value is assigned to labor and religious leaders.

(e) Criteria used in nominating key leaders to the proposed regional policy board show that respondents stressed "able to work with others" as the most important criterion. Secondary criteria were "able to influence others" (second rank) and "commit himself to work required" (third rank).

(f) Key and top leaders report that in civic policy making the most effective methods of contact are face-to-face and in small, informal meetings. Committee activity and talking to large groups is considered useful. Letters and telephone calls are given a low rank of effectiveness.

Notes

1. Edward W. Lehman. "Toward a Macrosociology of Power," *American Sociological Review,* **34** (August 1969), 456.
2. Peter H. Rossi. "Theory, Research, and Practice in Community Organizations," in Charles R. Adrian, Ed., *Social Science and Community Action,* Institute for Community Development and Services, East Lansing, Mich., 1960, pp. 9–24. Floyd Hunter et al., *Community Organization,* University of North Carolina Press, Chapel Hill, 1956, pp. 37–39; Robert A. Dahl, *Who Governs?* Yale University Press, New Haven, Conn., 1961, pp. 266ff.
3. Terry N. Clark, *Community Structure and Decision Making,* Chandler, San Francisco, 1968, pp. 57–58.
4. E. W. Lehman, *op. cit.,* p. 458; cf. William A. Gamson, "Reputation and Resources in Community Politics," *American Journal of Sociology,* **72.** (September 1966), 122–123; Peter Bachrach and Morton S. Baratz, "Decisions and Nondecisions: An Analytical Framework," *American Political Science Review,* **57** (September 1963), 632–642.
5. *Op. cit.,* p. 461.
6. Abraham Kaplan, *The Conduct of Inquiry,* Chandler, San Francisco, 1964, p. 85.
7. See Appendix A for the Leadership Interaction and Urban Problem Inventory. Accompanying letters to respondents and analysis of questionnaire response are shown in this appendix. For detailed information about research design and decisions made in executing the research see Delbert C. Miller, "Power Structure Studies and Environmental Management: The Study of Powerful Urban-Oriented Leaders in Northeastern Megalopolis," in *Environmental Quality Analysis: Theory and Method in the Social Sciences* (Allen V. Kneese and Blair T. Bower, Eds., Johns Hopkins, Baltimore, 1972, pp. 345–395.
8. Final results show that 167, or 42 percent, responded. Among them more than 75 percent were respondents of the first survey. The responses of the repeaters have been carefully checked against the total sample and no significant deviations have been found.

9. In answering, some did not restrict their activities to one problem and named several problems on which they were active. This does not distort the results as the true focus of effort.

10. For a more complete report of these reasons for changes see Delbert C. Miller, "The Allocation of Priorities to Urban and Environmental Problems by Powerful Leaders and Organizations" in W. Burch et al., Eds., *Social Behavior, Natural Resources, and the Environment,* Harper and Row, New York, 1972, pp. 306–331.

11. Various opinion polls show that leaders conform to the wider American public in this low priority assigned to environmental problems. One month before the 1972 general election the Gallop Poll published its survey on the question: What do you think is the most important problem facing the country today? The results show the following:

Vietnam war	27%
Inflation, high cost of living	27
International problems (general)	10
Drug use abuse	9
Crime/lawlessness	8
Pollution/the environment	4
Poverty/welfare	3
Corruption in government	3
Lack of national unity/purpose	2
Problems of youth	2
Moral problems, lack of religion	2

George Gallop, Gallop Poll, October 8, 1972 (International Herald-Tribune) October 9, 1972.

12. See Appendix A for a complete list of 200 key leaders.

13. It is recognized that the most rigorous criteria are probably "know well or socially," "had contact" and "worked with him on a committee or project." These criteria are utilized in the sociometric analysis of the data.

14. Standard error of $r = .08$.

15. Standard error of $r = .10$.

16. Note that the means for top religious leaders reach a low of 114 for their local community scores and 83 for their megalopolis scores.

17. The top leader population tends to parallel the same patterns and the replication reinforces the ranking order.

18. A much more detailed examination of this data has been made and the computor program and its application to the acquaintance and contact data is explained in Chapter 10, The Measurement of Contact and Clique Structures.

19. This showing is magnified by high returns from these three cities.

20. See Appendix for additional information on returns from respondents.

CHAPTER FIVE

The Top of the Top:
Regional Shakers
and Movers in Action

At the top of the leadership structure of Megalopolis stands a remarkable group of men who command great respect and who wield political and organizational influence over a wide range of public problems. All have enormous influence in their respective Metropolitan areas; most exercise leadership in the region and the nation. Men like John Lindsay, Nelson Rockefeller, and George Meany are known by the average man and woman anywhere in the fifty states. Others like Arthur Goldberg, Philip Randolph, Roy Wilkins, Milton Eisenhower, Kingman Brewster, and John Galbraith have wide national reputations in special areas. Beyond Eastern Megalopolis such well-known regional names as Bayard Rustin, David Rockefeller, Kenneth Clark, Leon Sullivan, Walter Washington become less distinct. Even in the Eastern region such persons as James Rouse, John Collins, Cornelius Owens, and Andrew Heiskell have limited visibility. The top leaders of Megalopolis know them all and generally know them well either by reputation or by personal contact.

As shown in Chapter 4, 178 top leaders selected the "best representatives in the shaping of urban policy and programming in the Boston-to-Washington urban region." Although fewer than one-fourth of the top leaders who voted came from New York, 13 of the 26, or one-half, who received the highest votes operate directly from that city. These leaders included John Lindsay, Bayard Rustin, Whitney Young (deceased), Arthur Goldberg, David Rockefeller, Philip Randolph, Kenneth Clark, Roy Wilkins, McGeorge Bundy, Terrence, Cardinal Cooke, Robert Weaver, Andrew Heiskell, and Cornelius Owens. Another group living near or having major ties to New York included such persons as Nelson Rockefeller (office in Manhattan), Paul Ylvisaker (office in Princeton, N.J.), Richard Hughes (offices in Newark and Trenton, N.J.), and Kingman Brewster (office in New Haven, Conn.). It is significant that the top nine nominees were from New York or nearby.

To the north, Boston has provided such leaders as John Galbraith and John Collins. Probably Mayor White would have been on the list if voting were more recent. Philadelphia has the Reverend Leon Sullivan, Richardson Dilworth, and Joseph Clark; Baltimore, James Rouse and Milton Eisenhower; and Washington, George Meany and Walter Washington.[1]

The heavy concentration of leadership in New York and environs is surprising. Note that almost one-quarter of the top leaders who voted were from Baltimore, but they placed only two leaders from that city on the top list; Philadelphia with as many voters as New York (40) placed only three leaders from their city, and Boston and Washington, with substantial voting blocs, placed only two leaders each. It is true that the top leaders were asked to exclude all senators, representatives, and cabinet members from their voting, and it will be remembered that this decision was made in order to identify only those leaders who could bring political pressure to bear on national officials. All mayors and governors were eligible, however, and many did make the top list. It must be concluded that New York, because of its size and national prominence, does draw top leaders. We have pointed out that it is the economic center of the region and holds a major position as headquarters for Negro organizations, industrial and trade associations, corporations, cultural and religious organizations, and various civic groups.

A second characteristic of the top leadership group is the large black representation: Bayard Rustin, Whitney Young (deceased), Philip Randolph, Kenneth Clark, Roy Wilkins, the Reverend Leon Sullivan, Walter Washington, and Robert Weaver. Walter Washington, as the Mayor of Washington, wields direct political power. The others now function as leaders of influential organizations or as public servants who have built up their influence over a lifetime of service. The number of black leaders is testimony to their rising influence in urban life and their importance in solving urban problems.

In this chapter we propose to examine the 26 top leaders as the regional shakers and movers who can mobolize men and get things done. We shall refer to them as the regional board for specific identification. A number of questions must be answered about them:

> What ties have these regional board leaders among themselves and with organizations?
>
> What is their background? How did they achieve visibility? What are their regional and national channels of communication?
>
> In what issues have they been active?

Data have been gathered to provide partial answers to each of these questions.

Leadership Ties of Regional Board Nominees in Megalopolis

When key and top leaders were asked to vote for regional board members, they had the option of selecting any of the slate of 200 key leaders whose names were presented to them or of adding any names of their own choosing. They were also asked to indicate their acquaintance (don't know, have heard of, know little, know well, or know socially), their contacts (have had business, civic, or social communication during last three years), and their participation (worked with him on a committee or project that dealt with urban problems during the last three years). A scoring key of four possible points for acquaintance, three points for contacts, and three points for urban problem participation was employed. A maximum score could be attained by a leader when another key or top leader replied that he knew him socially (4 points), had contact with him in the last three years (3 points), and worked with him on an urban project or committee (3 points); 178 business, labor, religious, political, and civic leaders specified their respective acquaintance, contacts, and participation with the nominated regional board leaders. Table 5.1 shows the acquaintance, contact, and participation scores of the 26 regional board leaders in rank order. Note that the late Whitney Young received the largest score from leaders along the Bos-Wash axis. His untimely death looms as the more tragic against this background of influence won at the peak of his career. Other leaders with high scores (300 or more) include Bayard Rustin, John Lindsay, Roy Wilkins, Kenneth Clark, Arthur Goldberg, Nelson Rockefeller, Robert Weaver, and Joseph Clark. In some cases the scores resulted because these leaders are active in civic life, move about, and meet many people. In other cases people come to them wherever they are to seek counsel, to petition, or just to talk and get ideas. The most active among them

TABLE 5.1   TOTAL ACQUAINTANCE, CONTACT, AND PARTICIPATION SCORES FOR THE 26 REGIONAL BOARD NOMINEES

Regional board nominees	Boston score	New York score	Philadelphia score	Baltimore score	Washington score	Total Megalopolis score
1. Whitney Young	85	144	72	56	57	414
2. Bayard Rustin	69	123	71	51	56	370
3. John V. Lindsay	60	132	65	61	38	356
4. Roy Wilkins	81	98	63	46	54	342
5. Kenneth B. Clark	55	158	55	38	33	339
6. Arthur J. Goldberg	50	114	49	54	48	315
7. Nelson A. Rockefeller	59	106	61	53	30	309
8. Robert C. Weaver	68	81	60	55	43	307
9. Joseph Clark	44	68	111	35	36	304
10. McGeorge Bundy	69	101	41	44	33	288
11. Walter E. Washington	39	78	43	46	81	287
12. Richardson Dilworth	28	45	150	40	23	286
13. Andrew Heiskell	42	133	48	39	22	284
14. Reverend Leon Sullivan	27	70	117	47	17	278
15. David Rockefeller	52	89	47	57	30	275
16. John K. Galbraith	69	81	39	44	37	270
17. A. Philip Randolph	50	89	55	37	36	266
18. George Meany	38	85	39	41	43	246
19. Milton Eisenhower	45	49	50	65	29	238
20. James Rouse	9	38	49	108	31	235
21. Paul N. Ylvisaker	26	72	67	40	25	230
22. John Collins	115	35	27	34	12	223
23. Kingman Brewster	49	73	36	30	14	202
24. Terrence, Cardinal Cooke	24	77	28	26	17	172
25. Richard T. Hughes	15	72	23	23	21	154
26. Cornelius W. Owens	2	30	9			41

communicate in both ways. As a researcher who has sought interviews with them, I can testify that they are out of their offices as much as they are in. "Out of the office" just as frequently can mean "out of town." I have been asked by most of these men to put my request for an appointment in writing and to await a reply. An affirmative reply usually resulted in an appointment a month or two later. Generally I was urged to talk with the "second" or "third" in command who would be available on short notice and would "call the matter to the attention of the "top" man. The top of the top are neither snobbish nor brusque. They are just inordinately busy and their time must be protected so that they can devote much of it to making necessary contacts. When a top leader wants to get through the "office screen," he undoubtedly can. Researchers have lower priorities.

Sociometric Leaders Among Regional Board Nominees

Although a high correlation exists between the votes for regional leaders and their acquaintance-contact scores, the correlation is not perfect. Actually, the top 10 nominees were, in order, John V. Lindsay, Nelson A. Rockefeller, Bayard Rustin, Whitney Young, Arthur Goldberg, David Rockefeller, Richard J. Hughes, A. Philip Randolph, Kenneth B. Clark, and John K. Galbraith. If this board were to assemble to do business, there is a strong probability that they would elect John Lindsay or Nelson Rockefeller as chairman. To get a better picture of the leadership ties of the top 10 regional nominees, sociograms were made to describe those leaders (from the top 178) who said they knew both men well or socially and had had contacts or had worked on committees with them. Each sociogram is constructed to show the range and intensity of acquaintance and contact with key and top leaders in the five major cities.

Each number on the sociogram refers to a key or top leader. The outer ring specifies acquaintance, the inner ring refers to contacts or committee participation. Figures 5.1 to 5.10 show the top regional board nominees. It is interesting to observe that although John Lindsay and Nelson Rockefeller had a wide acquaintance in Megalopolis their activity was concentrated in New York. In contrast, Whitney Young, Bayard Rustin, and Kenneth Clark, three top black civil rights leaders, were both well acquainted and active in all the principal cities of Megalopolis. Arthur Goldberg, David Rockefeller, and John Galbraith represented wide acquaintance and participation but in varying intensities. The sociogram of Arthur Goldberg reflected his activities in Washington as general counsel to the AFL-CIO and the steel workers, as Secretary of Labor, and as Associate Justice of the Supreme Court; it reflected his life in New York as United States Representative to the United Nations, his race for governor of New York, and his many organizational contacts. He has built ties with all the major cities; only those to Boston are weak.

The New York banker, David Rockefeller, is a quiet, retiring man, but people come to him. Business and financial leaders are in touch with him constantly; only his ties to Philadelphia seem weak.

John Galbraith of Boston and Cambridge is a multifaceted person—writer, professor, political counselor, organizational leader, and diplomat. His sociogram re-

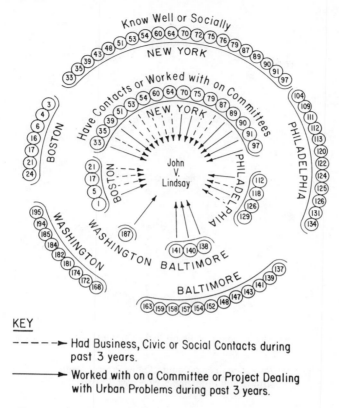

Figure 5.1 Acquaintance and participation sociogram of John V. Lindsay.

flects great scope but it demonstrates selected contacts based on the character of his daily life.

Richard Hughes and Philip Randolph are so different in background that they would appear to be inappropriate persons to compare, yet each possesses a leadership quality that is significant in any study of influential leaders. Philip Randolph is now in his eighties. He is a Negro civil rights and labor leader who has given a lifetime of service and is widely respected.

Richard Hughes is in his sixties. He has been in some kind of public service most of his life: district attorney, judge, and governor of New Jersey from 1961 to 1970. He is still active in many organizations but, like Philip Randolph, the peak of his political influence has past. Each man commands respect and their imputed influence is great. Perhaps each has attained the quality of veneration in the best sense of the term. Neither man is considered "retired." Both have life legacies of contacts; if a matter requiring mobilization of leaders were pressed on them, an answering cohort would follow. Their advice and counsel would always be sought. It is for these reasons that they won high votes as regional board policy makers.

It must be remembered that all the sociograms are based on responses of the 178 key and top leaders in our sample. Actually, if all potential leaders in the

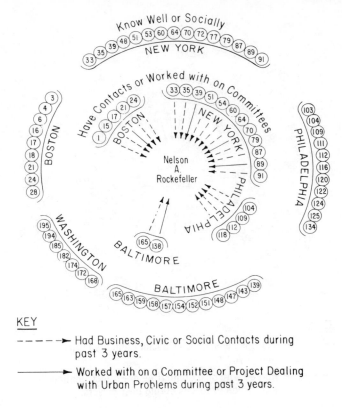

Figure 5.2   Acquaintance and participation sociogram of Nelson A. Rockefeller.

universe of their acquaintance and contact had responded, the lines would be multiplied by some factor that would have caused a blackened net. These leaders are the top of the top and their ties are numerous. We have looked carefully at the data on acquaintance and contact projected by a leader in comparison with similar data received by that leader. In general, the more influential leaders obtain greater acquaintance and contact response than they reciprocate from the same sample. This is understandable. Lesser leaders seek out and remember their contacts with the more important. If all potential lesser leaders had been given the opportunity to express themselves, the regional board leaders would have been amazed at the number of leaders who knew them and had had contact with them.

Organizational Ties of Regional Board Nominees in Megalopolis

A persistent question regarding the decision-making activity of leaders is whether top leaders know one another and work together on common problems. A major point of contact is the voluntary organization. Others include government boards, commissions, and committees. Social clubs cannot be discounted. It is not uncommon for a top leader to have at least 25 to 50 nominal contact points,

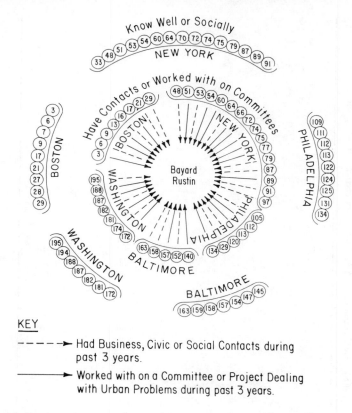

KEY

------→ Had Business, Civic or Social Contacts during
          past 3 years.

———————→ Worked with on a Committee or Project Dealing
          with Urban Problems during past 3 years.

Figure 5.3   Acquaintance and participation sociogram of Bayard Rustin.

but a full display for each leader would be extensive and not too useful. What is
needed is an identification of the most important contact points at which top
leaders meet and conduct public business. The participation matrix is the most
promising device. On such a matrix one affixes the leaders he wishes to study
and then selects the organizations and other contact points at which he expects
maximum joint participation.

The participation matrix shown in Table 5.2 was first developed by listing the
26 regional board leaders and then selecting those voluntary organizations
deemed most important because of the character of their work on urban problems. In some cases names of leaders were secured from membership lists of the
organization or at least their policy boards; in others documents like *Whos Who
in America* were used. This matrix, although admittedly incomplete, does show a
pattern of overlapping memberships that bring many of the leaders together.

It shows clearly how political leaders assemble at the *National League of
Cities or U.S. Conference of Mayors.* John Lindsay (New York), Walter Washington (Washington), Richardson Dilworth (Philadelphia), John Collins (Boston), and Joseph Clark (Philadelphia) are all current or past mayors of the
cities shown. Among them, John Lindsay has met another cadre of business,
labor, and civil rights leaders in such organizations as *National Urban Coalition,*

TABLE 5.2   ORGANIZATION PARTICIPATION MATRIX OF REGIONAL BOARD NOMINEES (1961-1971)

Regional board nominees	National League of Cities	U.S. Conference of Mayors	National Urban Coalition	Policy Committee Common Cause	Urban America (1968)	National Advisory Committee Civil Disorders	Executive Committee AFL-CIO	National Governors Conference	Federal City Club of Washington
John V. Lindsay	X	X	X	X		X			
Walter Washington	X	X							
Richardson Dilworth	X	X							
John Collins	X	X							
Joseph Clark	X								
James Rouse			X	X	X				
Andrew Heiskell			X	X	X				
Bayard Rustin				X					
Roy Wilkins			X			X			
Whitney Young			X		X				
David Rockefeller			X						
George Meany			X				X		
A. Philip Randolph			X				X		
Nelson Rockefeller								X	
Richard Hughes								X	
John Galbraith									X
Number of overlapping memberships	5	4	8	4	3	2	2	2	1

Grand total 31

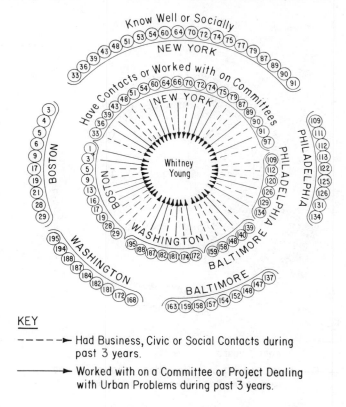

KEY

- - - - → Had Business, Civic or Social Contacts during past 3 years.

———→ Worked with on a Committee or Project Dealing with Urban Problems during past 3 years.

Figure 5.4   Acquaintance and participation sociogram of Whitney Young.

Common Cause, Urban America (now merged with National Urban Coalition), and *National Advisory Commission on Civil Disorders.* The participation matrix shows clusters of overlapping memberships: James Rouse (banker-builder), David Rockefeller (banker), Andrew Heiskell (publisher), John Lindsay (government), George Meany and Philip Randolph (labor), and Bayard Ruskin, Roy Wilkins, and Whitney Young (civil rights). The contacts here are made on policy boards, and there is no question that significant decisions are made by these men in the direction, leadership, and financing of these important organizations. A description of the influence ranking of the organizations appears in Chapter 7.

Nelson Rockefeller (Governor of New York) 1958–1973) and Richard Hughes (Governor of New Jersey, 1961–1970) made contacts in the *National Governors Conference.* Usually, the governors meet once a year for a week-long session at which they and their wives have an excellent opportunity to make political and social friendships.

The matrix indicates that John Galbraith and Walter Washington may meet at the Federal City Club of Washington.

What the matrix does not reveal is intriguing. John Galbraith, who has been most active in Americans for Democratic Action (ADA) and the Democratic Party, must certainly meet many of the regional board leaders who are members

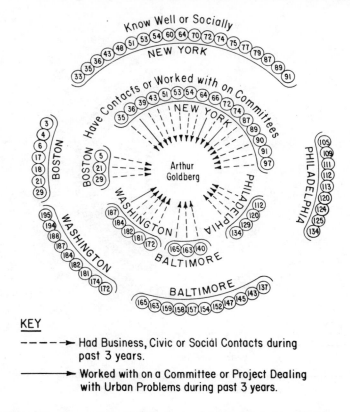

KEY

- - - - → Had Business, Civic or Social Contacts during
          past 3 years.

——————→ Worked with on a Committee or Project Dealing
          with Urban Problems during past 3 years.

Figure 5.5   Acquaintance and participation sociogram of Arthur Goldberg.

of that organization or have Democratic political affiliation. Almost all the board leaders belong to the National Association for the Advancement of Colored People (NAACP) or the Urban League (or both) and have had close connections with their executive directors, Roy Wilkins and Whitney Young (deceased), respectively. Regional board leaders meet at conferences and on government and organization boards that are too numerous to place in the matrix. Their political party affiliations and activities add to their contacts. It must be remembered also that all usually have numerous local contacts with regional leaders in their respective cities.

In order to secure additional data on participation I selected seven of the regional leaders whom I believed could best (and most willingly) give me information about places at which the top 26 regional leaders meet on various occasions.[2] The leaders selected included John F. Collins (M.I.T.), John Galbraith (Harvard), McGeorge Bundy (Ford Foundation, formerly of Harvard), Kenneth Clark (Metropolitan Applied Research Center and New York University), Paul Ylvisaker (Princeton University), and Milton Eisenhower (formerly of Johns Hopkins University). Former U.S. Senator Joseph S. Clark of Philadelphia completed the panel. A participation matrix schedule was sent to each (shown in Table 5.3) on which all 26 regional leaders were shown and their identifications

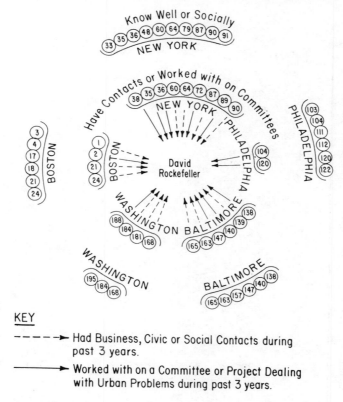

Figure 5.6 Acquaintance and participation sociogram of David Rockefeller.

with the various organizations described. The schedule added four columns that sought information about other organizational contacts, acquaintance with each of the leaders, and whether each had worked with other leaders on local or state problems and/or interstate or national problems. Comments were invited on how contacts were developed and whether the Boston-to-Washington area was looked upon as a community.

The responses received were most helpful in compiling the answers to many of these questions. Four leaders responded that they "knew well" more than half the other 22 leaders, and men like former Senator Joseph Clark and Milton Eisenhower replied that they had made numerous government contacts with them. Senator Clark listed the U.S. Senate as the place at which he had met 10 of the regional board leaders. In addition, meetings of the Democratic Party on various occasions in Philadelphia was the point of contact with four other regional leaders. He pointed out that Paul Ylvisaker had been his executive secretary in 1954–1955, when he was Mayor of Philadelphia, and that he had had contacts with David Rockefeller as each had served on the Board of Overseers at Harvard University. Dr. Eisenhower listed the government commissions on which he had met six leaders and educational business for three others.

McGeorge Bundy, President of the Ford Foundation, wrote me:

TABLE 5.3 PARTICIPATION MATRIX SCHEDULE 1961-1971 (AS SENT TO SEVEN KEY REGIONAL LEADERS FOR ADDITIONAL INFORMATION)

Regional leader nominee	ID	Area residence	National Urban Coalition	Urban America (1968)	U.S. Conference of Mayors	National League of Cities	National Governor's Conference
John K. Galbraith	Civic	Boston					
John Collins	Political	Boston			xx	xx	
Kingman Brewster	Civic	New Haven-New York					
Nelson A. Rockefeller	Political	Albany-New York					xx
John V. Lindsay	Political	New York	xx		xx	xx	
Bayard Rustin	Civic	New York					
Whitney Young (dec.)	Civic	New York	xx	xx			
Arthur J. Goldberg	Political-Civic	New York	xx				
David Rockefeller	Business	New York					
Terrence, Cardinal Cooke	Religious	New York					
Cornelius W. Owens	Business	New York					
Robert C. Weaver	Civic-Political	New York					
Roy Wilkins	Civic	New York	xx				
A. Philip Randolph	Labor	New York	xx				
Kenneth B. Clark	Civic	New York					
Andrew Heiskell	Business	New York	xx	xx			
McGeorge Bundy	Civic	New York				xx	
Paul N. Ylvisaker	Civic-Political	New Jersey-New York					
Richard J. Hughes	Political-Civic	New Jersey-New York					xx
Richardson Dilworth	Political	Philadelphia			xx	xx	
Rev. Leon Sullivan	Religious	Philadelphia					
Joseph Clark	Political	Philadelphia				xx	
James Rouse	Business	Baltimore	xx	xx			
Milton Eisenhower	Civic	Baltimore					
Walter E. Washington	Political	Washington			xx	xx	
George Meany	Labor	Washington	xx				

124

Regional leader nominee	Executive Board AFL-CIO	Policy Committee Common Cause	National Advisory Committee Civil Disorders	Federal City Club of Washington	Other	Know well	Worked with on local or state problems	Worked with on Interstate or national problems
John K. Galbraith								
John Collins				xx				
Kingman Brewster								
Nelson A. Rockefeller								
John V. Lindsay		xx	xx					
Bayard Rustin		xx						
Whitney Young (dec.)								
Arthur J. Goldberg								
David Rockefeller								
Terrence, Cardinal Cooke								
Cornelius W. Owens								
Robert C. Weaver								
Roy Wilkins			xx					
A. Philip Randolph	xx							
Kenneth B. Clark		xx						
Andrew Heiskell		xx						
McGeorge Bundy								
Paul N. Ylvisaker								
Richard J. Hughes								
Richardson Dilworth								
Rev. Leon Sullivan								
Joseph Clark								
James Rouse		xx						
Milton Eisenhower				xx				
Walter E. Washington								
George Meany	xx							

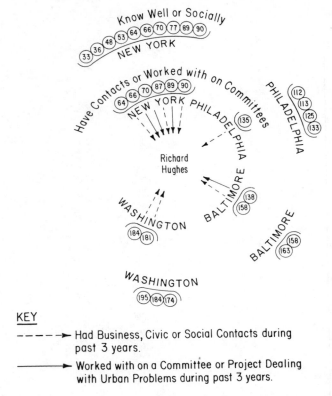

Figure 5.7   Acquaintance and participation sociogram of Richard Hughes.

I have worked with these men in a number of contexts and at a number of different times, and most of this work does not fall readily into
the categories marked at the end of your sheet. While my place of
business is here at the Ford Foundation, at least as often as not my
business with these gentlemen has been transacted in other locations
and under other auspices.[3]

Paul Ylvisaker reported that he knew 14 of the regional board leaders and
explained:

My network of contacts began slowly at Harvard (received M.P.A.
and PhD. there),[4] expanded slowly at Swarthmore (professor of political science), picked up rapidly in Philadelphia with Joe Clark (Executive Secretary to Mayor Clark), mushroomed at Ford Foundation
(executive), and intensified in New Jersey (Commissioner of New
Jersey Department of Community Affairs) . . . I've long and deliberately developed networks simultaneously in different planes and
dimensions. You might try a multi-dimensional model. Each, or most,
individuals you list do work in different planes—radiating out in 360°.
The more rounded the person, and the more multi-directional his networks, the more (seemingly, at least) his influence. Or maybe it's just
that he becomes a more active circuit-switcher and breaker.[5]

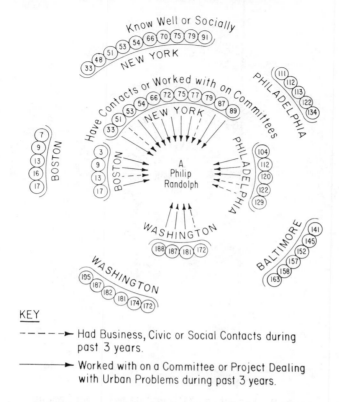

KEY

--- --- ► Had Business, Civic or Social Contacts during
past 3 years.

——————► Worked with on a Committee or Project Dealing
with Urban Problems during past 3 years.

Figure 5.8   Acquaintance and participation sociogram of A. Philip Randolph.

This description of a process of developing and expanding personal contacts validates the design used in this research. This design, as described in Chapter 4, postulates the extension of contacts on the local plane; it includes a variety of leaders in business, labor, politics, religion, and civic affairs and a simultaneous grouping along the Boston-Washington axis in vertical and oblique planes of top and key leaders in all occupational categories. The manner in which these contacts multiply and expand follows no uniform pattern. Professor Ylvisaker points out that he has "long and deliberately developed networks." This suggests a rational plan. Many career patterns demonstrate that contacts ensue almost automatically as the result of holding an important office. Thus Senator Clark described the bulk of his contacts with the regional board leaders as occurring in the U.S. Senate (or office) to which leaders came. Perhaps many leaders seek a succession of offices rationally guiding their careers and thus develop contacts as by-products of their career decisions. These questions are discussed more thoroughly as the career pattern of each regional leader is analyzed.

One of the questions for which I wanted answers concerned activity on local, state, interstate, or national problems. In an interview with Walter Phillips, a top civic leader of Philadelphia, I asked him:

"Is the Boston-to-Washington urban complex a region suitable for unified urban planning and administration?"

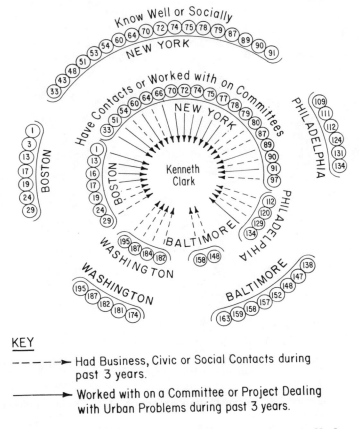

Figure 5.9 Acquaintance and participation sociogram of Kenneth Clark.

His answer was, "I believe that Megalopolis is more real as to economic and cultural activities than as to civic. Civic work is mostly local in character—at least that with which I have been involved."

This question of regional community continues to be a central hypothesis of this research. In asking the regional leader informants about their activities, it was assumed that concerns of a local or state character should be separated from those of interstate or national character. If these regional board leaders (the very top of the top) were identified as working on interstate and national problems, the case for regional bonds could be made. The findings show that there is abundant evidence for this conclusion based on the reports of the four informants, who show an average of 16 working contacts with the regional board leaders on interstate or regional problems and 13 on local or state problems. This means that each leader (if the sample results can be extended to the population of 26 leaders) has met in working contact with at least one-half the regional board leaders on both interstate or national and local or state problems. What Walter Phillips described as the heavy involvement of a top leader in local civic activity may not be entirely true for key and, in particular, regional board leaders. There

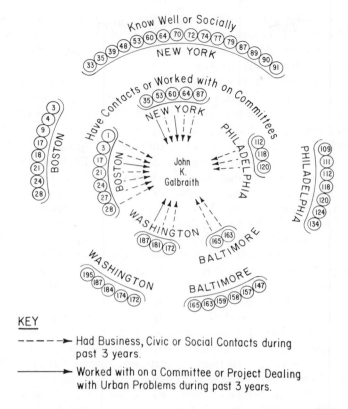

KEY

-----► Had Business, Civic or Social Contacts during
       past 3 years.

————► Worked with on a Committee or Project Dealing
       with Urban Problems during past 3 years.

Figure 5.10 Acquaintance and participation sociogram of John K. Galbraith.

is sufficient evidence from other leadership studies of community power structures to suggest that the most influential leaders are drawn progressively away from local activity into state, interstate, and national policy making. Leaders must become influential enough and also conscious of a larger community of interests to develop motivation, visibility, and recognition for extralocal activity. This problem is dealt with at length in Chapter 12, Megalopolis Growth and the Widening of Community Consciousness. The evidence presented here is one small research step in a continuing inquiry. Chapter 6, MEGA-Leaders, Regional Issues, and Patterned Strategies in Decision Making, and Chapter 10, The Measurement of Contact and Clique Structures, make further efforts to trace the social bonds of regional community. As announcers on television are accustomed to say, please stay tuned in!

Career Analysis of the Regional Board Nominees

How did these leaders who represent the very top in influence and acceptance among key leaders achieve their positions? To find an answer an analysis was made of their education, career channels, major positions from which they gained visibility, and their regional and national channels of communication. Table 5.4 lists these background data for each of the 26 nominees, beginning with the age of the leader when nominated and continuing through an examination of each of the listed characteristics.

A quick survey of the careers of these regional board nominees reveals that all are men who have attained high positions in their respective organizations; most commonly they hold the chief executive post. With a few exceptions, all are university graduates. Some hold advanced degrees and six have earned doctorates. All have climbed career ladders to get to their present positions and have spent a large part of their lives in attaining them. The two Rockefellers (Nelson and David) are the only exceptions. Both have reached their present prominence through the legacy of the family fortune and by holding positions that extended their visibility—Nelson in political life and David in the financial and business world. Both have reinforced their influence through many regional and national channels of communication, as Table 5.4 only partly indicates. Each was well educated, Nelson with an A.B. from Dartmouth and David with a B.S. from Harvard and a Ph.D. in economics from Chicago. Both have proved their high capability in the achievements they have demonstrated, but, as the colloquial phrase puts it, "they had everything going for them."

In contrast, the two labor leaders among the nominees "came up the hard way." George Meany and Philip Randolph climbed out of working-class backgrounds and found careers not as plumber and sleeping car porter but as leaders in the labor movement that embraced their occupations. George Meany never stepped across the threshold of any college until as president of the newly formed AFL-CIO he began collecting honorary doctorates at more than a dozen universities. George Meany was a plumber and a good one; he never lets anyone forget it. He began as an apprentice, attained journeyman status, and worked at the trade for 12 years. His entry as a labor official began as business representative for his local union in New York, and from there his rapid climb to the top job in labor was in state and national labor organizations.

Philip Randolph, now the beloved and venerated black labor and civil rights leader, won his position by organizing the Brotherhood of Sleeping Car Porters and serving in many executive positions in labor. He is remembered in the civil rights movement as the principal organizer of the March on Washington movement which in 1941 led President Roosevelt to establish the Commission on Fair Employment Practice.

If Nelson and David Rockefeller, on the one hand, and George Meany and Philip Randolph, on the other, represent the extreme patterns of career development, it is appropriate to ask what is an average or modal pattern. It is difficult to single out a given leader and identify him as the average of the group. An intriguing career pattern is that of a man of relatively low visibility. James Rouse is a Baltimore civic leader who is not well known outside the East. He is not especially prominent among the key and top leaders in his own region. As shown in Table 5.1, he ranks twentieth in total acquaintance, contact, and participation, but many regional board nominees know this man well and have worked with him on the policy boards of Urban America, National Urban Coalition, and Common Cause. He is a businessman who cares about the urban plight of the United States, and as a mortgage banker and builder has worked in various ways on the

Baltimore and national scene to improve neighborhood and community life. As the developer of the new city of Columbia, Maryland, he has concentrated attention on what private enterprise can do to build on sociological and aesthetic principles. As trustee for the Peale Museum, Union Memorial Hospital, chairman of American City Corporation, and founding member of the Business Commission for the Arts, he has reached out in many directions. As a coauthor of *No Slum in Ten Years* he has written as well as built. His education and experience reveal unusual variety and depth. He earned a law degree at the University of Maryland after undergraduate study at the University of Hawaii and the University of Virginia. His career began in the Federal Housing Administration in Baltimore during depression years. Then, as manager of the mortgage department for the Title Guarantee and Trust Company, he began to acquire financial knowledge. His interest in housing and community development continued to parallel his capacity as a mortgage banker. His own firm, James W. Rouse and Company, was incorporated in 1939. With this step he was subsequently able to follow his own inclinations and to move more fully into community life by serving on governmental commission and becoming involved with Urban America, Inc. This national organization was a central contact point for architects, city planners, housing specialists, both governmental and private, and latterly for those interested in all urban problems. The contacts that James Rouse made on the policy board were developed even more fully at the newer National Urban Coalition and later at Common Cause. He is one of the few men who have served as a policy maker for these three influential national organizations which seek amelioration and reconstruction of political and urban life. It seems entirely in conformity with his breadth of interests that he should serve at one time as president of the Maryland chapter of United World Federalists.

Occupational Portraits of the Regional Shakers and Movers

There may be no single leader that can be singled out as the average representative among our top regional board nominees but collective patterns can be discerned. It is these patterns that give a degree of permanence to a study of leaders. Leaders, at best, are short-lived. Few reach positions of top influence before age 50 and generally by age 65 they pass from the parade of leaders who continue to emerge from the younger, more energetic and eager bidders for power and influence. Leaders change but leadership patterns remain, especially if they are analyzed for the respective occupational groupings that develop within them. Table 5.4 is an analysis of the regional board nominees by their occupational identities as business, labor, political-governmental, religious, civic, and civil rights leaders. Note that the business leaders have an average age of 55 years, that all are college graduates with training in business and law, and that their visibility has been won by working in civic organizations. Their regional and national channels of communication are based on business directorships, university trusteeships, and activity in social and civic organizations.

The leaders of labor are extraordinarily old: George Meany and Philip Randolph were an average 78 at the year of nomination (1969). Their leadership knowledge was gained through experience and their ties to urban problems were

TABLE 5.4   CAREER ANALYSIS OF THE REGIONAL BOARD NOMINEES

Regional board nominees (business)	Age at nomination (1969)	University	Educational specialization	Career channels	Major positions of visibility	Regional and national channels of communication
Cornelius W. Owens (utilities executive)	56	A.B., Boston College	General education	Vice-president, 1959, New York Telephone Co.; 1965, president New York Telephone Co.; 1970, Executive vice-president A.T. &T.	Director: Economic Development Council New York United Fund, Greater New York ARC Campaign, Board of Governors Federal Hall Memorial Association	Director: bank; life insurance company; subway company; New York Chamber of Commerce Clubs and Associations: Newcomen Society Roman Catholic; Bankers; Economic; University
David Rockefeller (banker)	54	B.S., Ph.D.; Harvard University, University of Chicago	Economics	Vice-president to president to chairman and chief executive officer of Chase Manhattan Bank	Secretary to Mayor LaGuardia; chairman Downtown Lower Manhattan Association	Director: of large real estate holdings Rockefeller Center and Morningside Heights; Chase International Investment Company; Trustee: Chicago and Harvard, Rockefeller Universities Clubs: Harvard, University; Century; Links; Knickerbocker
Andrew Heiskell (magazine publisher)	54	Educated in Europe, Harvard Business School	Business Management	Reporter to top positions for *Time* and *Life*, Chief executive officer, Time, Inc.	Chairman of the board Urban America; cochairman, Urban Coalition	Trustee: University of Chicago, Bennington Inter-American Press Association; Atlantic Council

Name	Age	Education			
James Rouse (mortgage banker-builder)	55	L.L.B., University of Maryland	Law	From manager of mortgage Department to president of James W. Rouse & Co.; developer of new city, Columbia, Maryland	President American Council to Improve Our Neighborhoods; Greater Baltimore Commission; Baltimore Urban Coalition; National Urban Coalition	Trustee: Peale Museum; Union Memorial Hospital; Chairman American City Corporation; Business Commission for the Arts Coauthor No Slum in Ten Years; Lieutenant Commander (USNR)
Regional board nominees (labor)					
George Meany (president, AFL-CIO with Democratic Party power base)	75	New York City grade and high schools; holder of many honorary degrees	General education	Apprentice plumber local business agent to president of State Federation of Labor to highest national labor office	Member of National War Labor Board; spokesman for labor in general	State and national labor federations; National Urban Coalition; Roman Catholic; Democratic Party
Asa Philip Randolph (labor and civil rights activist)	80	CCNY; honorary degree from Howard University	General education	Organized Brotherhood of Sleeping Car Porters, the first black union vice-president of AFL-CIO	Organized March on Washington in 1941, which led to U.S. Commission on Fair Employment Practices	National Urban Commission and executive board AFL-CIO; Bayard Rustin speaks for him at A. Philip Randolph Institute

TABLE 5.4   CAREER ANALYSIS OF THE REGIONAL BOARD NOMINEES   (*Continued*)

Regional board nominees (business)	Age at nomination (1969)	University	Educational specialization	Career channels	Major positions of visibility	Regional and national channels of communication
Regional board nominees (political-government)						
John F. Collins (professor and Democratic Party leader)	50	LL.B., Suffolk University	Law	Practicing lawyer; state representative; councilman; Mayor of Boston; professor of M.I.T.	Mayor of Boston, 1960-1965	American Legion; American Bar Association; Boston Bar Association; U.S. Conference of Mayors; League of Cities
Nelson Rockefeller (governor and republican party leader)	61	A.B., Dartmouth	General education	Director, Rockefeller Center to numerous positions in State Department and Health, Education and Welfare	Assistant Secretary of State and member of special commissions for the President in Latin American Affairs	National Governors' Conference; Museum of Modern Art Clubs: Century; University; Dartmouth; Knickerbocker; Cosmos; Metropolitan
John V. Lindsay (former Mayor and, since late 1971, Democratic Party leader)	48	A.B., LL.B., Yale	Law	Private practice to representative at 86, 87, 88, 89th sessions of the Congress to Mayor of New York, 1965-1973	Congressman, Mayor of New York	National League of Cities; Freedom House; New York Bar Association; National Urban Coalition; Common Cause

Name	Age	Education	Field	Career	Positions	Affiliations
Arthur Goldberg (lawyer-diplomat)	61	B.S., J.D., Northwestern University	Law	Private practice to general counsel to steelworkers, AFL-CIO, Secretary of Labor, Supreme Court Justice, U.N. Representative	Secretary of Labor Supreme Court Justice, U.N. Representative	Labor Association; Democratic Party; Jewish Congress; United Nations

Regional board nominees (political-government)

Name	Age	Education	Field	Career	Positions	Affiliations
Richard J. Hughes (governor and Democratic Party leader)	60	LL.B., New Jersey Law School	Law	Assistant U.S. attorney, New Jersey; private practice; judge, Governor of New Jersey 1961-1970; senior partner in private law practice	Governor of New Jersey, 1961-1970	Bar Association; Democratic Party
Richardson Dilworth (Democratic Party and civic leader)	71	A.B., LL.B., Yale	Law	Private practice to district attorney to candidate for governor to Mayor of Philadelphia to President of Board of Education	Mayor of Philadelphia, 1956-1962, Democratic gubernatorial candidate, 1962	Clubs: Philadelphia and Racquet Clubs (Philadelphia); Racket and Tennis, (New York); Colonel, (retired) U.S. Army; Democratic Party
Joseph Clark (Democratic Party leader and organization executive)	68	B.S., LL.B., Harvard University University of Penn. numerous honorary degrees	Law	Private practice to city controller (Philadelphia) to Mayor of Philadelphia to U.S. Senator to President, United World Federalists	Mayor of Philadelphia, 1952-1956, U.S. Senator (Pa.) 1957-1968	Democratic Party Colonel (retired), U.S. Army Senate contacts Philadelphia Club

TABLE 5.4   CAREER ANALYSIS OF THE REGIONAL BOARD NOMINEES   (*Continued*).

Regional board nominees (business)	Age at nomination (1969)	University	Educational specialization	Career channels	Major positions of visibility	Regional and national channels of communication
Walter E. Washington (Mayor of Washington, D.C.)	54	A.B., LL.D., Howard University, Howard University Law School	Law	Private practice to executive director, national capitol housing to public housing chief, New York, to Mayor of Washington	Mayor of Washington	Urban League; U.S. Conference of Mayors; National League of Cities Clubs: Federal City Club of Washington; City Club of New York; National Lawyers Club; Cosmos Club
Regional board nominees (religion)						
Terrence, Cardinal Cooke (major Catholic religious leader)	58	B.A., St. Joseph Seminary, M.A., Catholic University	Religion and social work	Ordained priest, 1945; assistant pastor to archbishop and cardinal	Secretary to Cardinal Spellman, vicar, general, titular bishop	Central communication to Catholic Church and civic leaders in New York and Megalopolis in general; board member of New York Public Library and Metropolitan Museum of Art. Office: 451 Madison Avenue, New York
The Reverend Leon Sullivan (minister and civil rights leader)	47	B.A. West Virginia University, Union Theological student, Union Theological Seminary; M.A. in religion, Columbia University; numerous honorary degrees	Liberal arts and religion	Ordained Baptist minister to pastor of Zion Baptist Church of Philadelphia, 1950–	Founder, chairman of the board Opportunities Industrialization Centers; many national awards for outstanding service; chairman of the board of Progress Aerospace	Has religious, educational, business and civic contacts because of the multiple base of his acquaintance; regarded as civil rights leader with workable programs

Regional board nominees (Civic and Civil Rights)

Name	Age	Field	Degrees	Career	Position	Affiliations
Whitney M. Young, Jr. (deceased, March 11, 1971); social work administrator	48	Sociology	B.S., M.A.; Kentucky State College; Student M.I.T., University of Minnesota, Harvard University; numerous honorary degrees	Urban League executive St. Paul and Omaha to Dean at Atlanta University and executive director of National Urban League	Executive director of National Urban League and author of five books; developed community action programs for black leaders; syndicated newspaper writer	Member of many federal commissions and advisory counsels; worked closely with Presidents Kennedy and Johnson; established relations with business leaders in Community Action Assembly; Domestic Marshall Plan and Street Academy Program
John K. Galbraith (economist, author, and Democratic political leader)	61	Economics	B.S., M.S., Ph.D., University of Toronto, University of California, student Cambridge University, numerous honorary degrees	Instructor to professor of economics at Harvard University; campaigner for Adlai Stevenson, John F. Kennedy, and Eugene McCarthy; Ambassador to India	Administrator U.S. Office of Price Administration; Board of editors at Fortune Magazine; U.S. Ambassador to India; well-known writer	Chairman, 1967—, Americans for Democratic Action; Century Association; political and educational ties in Megalopolis
Kingman Brewster (college president)	50	Law	A.B., LL.B.; Yale University Harvard University numerous honorary degrees	Assistant professor of law to professor of law, Harvard University; provost to president of Yale University	President of Yale University	Clubs: Tavern (Boston); Vineyard Haven (Mass.) Yacht; Yale (New York) Century (New York) Association; has Washington ties as consultant and member of various commissions; great speaker

TABLE 5.4   CAREER ANALYSIS OF THE REGIONAL BOARD NOMINEES   (*Continued*)

Regional board nominees (business)	Age at nomination (1969)	University	Educational specialization	Career channels	Major positions of visibility	Regional and national channels of communication
Bayard Rustin (civil rights and labor activist)	59	Student at Wilberforce, Cheney (Pa.) State Teachers College, CCNY; honorary LL.D., New School for Social Research	General education	Race relations director to director of A. Philip Randolph Institute	Organizer of March on Washington, 1963; shares power with A. Philip Randolph; known for his articulate writing and speaking	Writer and leader in labor and civil rights groups; policy committee of Common Cause
Kenneth B. Clark (educator and psychologist)	55	A.B., M.S., Ph.D.; Howard University, and Columbia University; numerous honorary degrees	Psychology	Instructor to professor of psychology at CCNY to president of Metropolitan Applied Research Center, Inc., of New York	Numerous government commissions; author of four books; past president of American Psychology Association	Educational and political ties on local, state, regional, and national levels; board of trustees, Howard University and University of Chicago; New York State Board of Regents
McGeorge Bundy (foundation executive)	50	A.B, Yale and Junior Fellow at Harvard University; numerous honorary degrees	Government	Military career, private to captain during WWII and later lecturer to professor of government at Harvard University and	Special assistant to Presidents Kennedy and Johnson for national security affairs	Governmental and education ties throughout Megalopolis and nation; brother is editor of *Foreign Affairs* of Council on Foreign Relations

Name	Age	Degrees	Field	Positions	Government/Other	Ties
Milton S. Eisenhower (retired university president and governmental consultant)	70	B.S., Kansas State University; 31 honorary degrees	General education	Dean of Arts and Sciences; special assistant to Presidents Kennedy and Johnson; president, Ford Foundation	American vice-consul, Edinburgh, Scotland; director of Information, U.S. Department of Agriculture and other government assignments; President Kansas State University, Pennsylvania State University, John Hopkins University	Brother of President Eisenhower; served on numerous government commissions; active in UNESCO and as consultant to President Eisenhower	Director of numerous financial and industrial corporations; widespread educational and governmental ties
Paul N. Ylvisaker (professor of public affairs and urban planning, Princeton University)	48	A.A., Bethany Lutheran College, B.S., Mankato State College, M.P.A., Ph.D., Harvard University	Government	Instructor to professor (Harvard, Swarthmore, Princeton); executive secretary to Mayor of Philadelphia; U.N. appointments	Director of Public Affairs of Ford Foundation, 1954-1967; commissioner of New Jersey Department of Community Affairs 1967-1971		Educational, governmental, and foundation ties in Megalopolis

TABLE 5.4   CAREER ANALYSIS OF THE REGIONAL BOARD NOMINEES   (Continued)

Regional board nominees (business)	Age at nomination (1969)	University	Educational specialization	Career channels	Major positions of visibility	Regional and national channels of communication
Robert C. Weaver (housing administrator; college president)	62	B.S., M.A., Ph.D., Harvard University Temple University numerous honorary degrees	Economics	From advisor on Negro affairs U.S. Department of the Interior to numerous housing administrative assignments to U.S. Secretary of Housing and Urban Development; President of Bernard M. Baruch College, New York; currently Professor of Urban Affairs at Hunter College	Secretary of Department of Housing and Urban Development 1966-1968; author of four books	Eleven years of top government assignments for New York State and 17 years in top Federal Government positions in Washington; former chairman, NAACP.
Roy Wilkins (social welfare executive)	68	A.B., University of Minnesota; numerous honorary degrees	General education	Managing editor, *Kansas City Call* to various assignments in NAACP to executive director	Executive director, NAACP	Integrationist policy of NAACP, largest black organization; relates to business, labor, political, religious, and civic leaders

created by the interests of the labor organizations in which they rose to prominence. The power of labor is such that top leaders are drawn into the political, social, and economic problems of the nation, whether they like it or not. The cry of governmental and urban organizations is a plea for labor representation.

The National Urban Coalition and Federal Pay Boards are just two examples in which labor support was strongly sought. Needless to say, both political parties want labor's backing in votes and money and is courted by most local, state, and national candidates for office. It is interesting to contemplate the kind of labor leadership that will replace men like Meany and Randolph. Walter Reuther, who wanted labor to be an aggressive social movement, tried to displace Meany but lost. Today white collar workers and professionals are forming new unions and becoming stronger forces in the AFL-CIO. Many labor members are earning middle-class incomes and in many respects becoming more conservative as they increase their stakes in the property system. The kind of leader who will be able to maintain a compromising position in this variety of forces is problematic.

The political-governmental nominees averaged 59 years of age (1969). All graduated from college and seven out of the eight have law degrees. It seems that either a law degree is required for acceptance as a political officeholder or that lawyers by motivation form the greatest reservoir of potential candidates. The advantages of a background in law in public office are analyzed in detail in the following section which describes the career patterns of the regional board nominees. At this point it can be shown that the visibility of these leaders is generally attained by election to such offices as mayor of a major city or governor of a state. It should be said again that all senators, congressmen, and cabinet officials have been omitted from this study. Those political officials in this study who have not attained elective office have found an alternate route to visibility. If they have been appointed to major governmental administrative posts, they can achieve a commensurate visibility. Arthur Goldberg is a good example of this alternate route. Never elected to any public office, he achieved visibility and influence by his appointments as Secretary of Labor, Associate Justice of the U.S. Supreme Court, and United States Representative to the United Nations (see Table 5.4). All the other political nominees, Collins, Rockefeller, Lindsay, Hughes, Dilworth, Clark, and Washington, won their positions by the traditional election route.

The two top religious leaders are studies in contrasts. Terrence, Cardinal Cooke, the successor to Cardinal Spellman, stands at the top of the Roman Catholic Church in the United States. He climbed the hierarchical ladder as priest, assistant pastor, director of the Catholic Youth Organization, Procurator of St. Joseph's Seminary, Secretary to Cardinal Spellman, Papal Chamberlain and Vice Chancellor of the Archdiocese of New York, domestic prelate and chancellor, vicar general, titular bishop, archbishop, and cardinal. Cardinal Cooke lives and works on Madison Avenue in New York. His fellow nominee is a black Baptist minister and civil rights leader, the Reverend Leon Sullivan of Philadelphia, who lives and works in the heart of the Negro district in his city. He has literally pursued two careers simultaneously since 1964. Appointed to the pastorate at Zion Baptist Church in Philadelphia in 1950, he began to look for ways to improve the economic lot as well as the spiritual life of the blacks. He pioneered new vocational training programs and in 1964 became founder and chairman of the board of Opportunities Industrialization Centers. So began his twin career. Money was raised from private sources and federal funds were secured. His success at this effort led him to found two companies, and in 1968 he became chairman of the board of Progress Aerospace Enterprise, Inc., and Progress Garment Manufacturing Co. He has written two books about his work, *Build, Brother, Build* and *Alternatives to Despair*. His achievements have been used as models for more than 100 cities which have developed centers for job training minority workers.

It is difficult to find a common pattern for these two contrasting religious careers. With only two cases no social scientist should try. It is interesting to note, however, that each had an education that opened new avenues of activity. Cardinal Cooke received an M.A. in Social Work at Catholic University, the Reverend Sullivan, a liberal arts degree and an M.A. in religion at Columbia. Two years at the liberal Union Theological Seminary in New York must have had a formative influence on the social outlook of this minister. Both religious leaders had abundant opportunities to work with young adults and to become motivated to improve opportunities for youth. Both also have used their religious offices as a base for multiple contacts in education, business, and civic affairs.

That civic and civil rights leaders have the widest scope of activity is borne out by the list of occupations for the 10 regional nominees in this classification. It includes two professors, three educators, a director of education, a research director, a foundation director, and two organization executives. Their average age was 57 (1969). All are college graduates, three have Ph.D.'s and all have numerous honorary degrees, centered in the social sciences. They have achieved visibility in four different ways: by appointment as presidents of universities, by writing, by consulting for presidents of the United States, or by serving as organizational spokesmen for large racial or ethnic blocs. Their channels of communication range widely among educational, civic, and organizational contacts. In some countries they would be called leaders of the *intelligentsia*—men who develop new ideas and activate new programs to reconstruct social and political life. They are certainly leaders who have multiple contacts with American universities and the professional personnel within them. Most of them accept invitations to lecture and stay in close contact with young people both in and outside the academic world. It is concern with social and intellectual ideas that provides a common denominator for all these regional leaders, most of whom also seek outlets for social action. It is not surprising that they are committed to working within the established system of government. The top and key leaders who voted for them and invested their confidence in them expect this kind of behavior. It is not our purpose to question the appropriateness of their leadership or the values that motivate it. This study is devoted to the research findings. These leaders are those whom other top leaders believe are influential, who can cooperate with one another and get things done. Confidence has been affirmed in the ability of these nominees to plan policy and programs for urban problems besetting the region. Other leaders may "shake harder" and "run faster" in their search for more rapid social change. They may have significant social impact but they are not among the regional board nominees because they have neither gained visibility nor the acceptance of top leaders.

A Comparative Career Analysis of the Regional
Board Leaders by Age and Education

Looking at all 26 leaders together highlights career patterns in sharper outline. The average age of all regional nominees was 59 years, which suggests the peak of a leader's influence, influence won by older men in spite of the emphasis on youth in our culture. In general, college graduation is a necessary educational base in order for leaders to mature, grasp ideas, and learn to articulate and act on them. The confidence bred from educational attainment cannot be underestimated. It is discounted by those who have it and overestimated by those who have not, but it is almost always a personal factor in the ego of the individual. The findings show that all regional nominees have an earned college degree except the labor leaders. The civic and civil rights leaders are the "best" (formally) educated" group. There is much graduate education in many of their backgrounds and they lead in honorary degrees.

The educational specialization of the 26 leaders is diverse. The law was the chosen field of nine, liberal arts the educational background of four and business and economics of four others. Two specialized in sociology and social work, two in political science, two in the ministry, and one in psychology. Two benefitted from high school and on the job vocational training.

TYPES OF CAREER CHANNEL

Career channels may be conventional single, conventional multiple, dual, or fluctuating.

Convential Single Channel. This channel develops along the hierarchy or on the job ladder of a given occupation. Business leaders are good examples, for they commonly progress from low-rung business positions to management in a 20-to-30-year span of advancement. The ladder of progression is clearly marked for the business leader, and all the regional nominees followed the conventional single channel (although David Rockefeller had a short climb that resembled a single bounce).

Labor leaders also reflected this type of career channel as they moved into higher positions, starting first as labor members, then becoming union officers business agents, international union labor organizers, and state and national officers. This channel is not so clearly defined and there are many options and variations, but a hierarchical skeleton always exists.

Organizational executives like Roy Wilkins, Bayard Rustin, and Whitney Young generally follow conventional single channels as they move from the lower rungs to the higher rungs of their organizations.

Conventional Multiple Channel. The conventional multiple channel is characterized by the presence of two hierarchies of ascent which are marked out by tradition and can be utilized in a career progression according to an informal time sequence. Some political leaders exhibit conventional multiple channels first as they secure a law degree, establish their early careers in private practice, and then seek political positions by moving progressively to more prestigious and influential elective or appointive posts in a second career. John Lindsay, Joseph Clark, and Walter Washington are examples of this kind of progression.

Dual Channel. The dual channel has many variations, but it is always characterized by the utilization of two or more hierarchies in building a career. It is not uncommon for political leaders to maintain their law practice or at least an associate position in a law firm while holding political office. This is so prevalent that Common Cause is mounting a campaign against six senators and 53 congressmen who continue to practice law in some form. The concern of the members of *Common Cause* is that dual participation in law practice and law making often involves a conflict of interests and that no member of Congress should engage in the practice of law or retain association with a law firm while in office.[6] The number of regional board nominees who have followed dual careers is not known to this researcher. It will be remembered that seven of the eight political leaders among them established themselves in the private practice of law early in their careers (see Table 5.4).

Top religious leaders generally establish dual patterns to command visibility and opportunity for wider social or public service. The position of the church is used as a base from which the religious leader reaches out to establish or lead organizations that have secular or quasi-religious functions—work centers, drug rehabilitation, street academies, and antiwar campaigns. The political effectiveness of the Reverend Adam Clayton Powell and the Reverend Martin Luther King is well remembered. Among our regional nominees the Reverend Leon Sullivan is a good example of a religious leader fulfilling a dual role as educational and business leader Terrence, Cardinal Cooke established himself as an effective leader in the education of youth and now carries this dual interpretation of the church into his administrative policy.

Fluctuating Channel. The fluctuating channel is characterized by intermittent career movement between two or more career bases or hierarchies. When the political leader does not follow the conventional multiple channel, he will employ the fluctuating channel by using his law practice as a base to initiate a political campaign or as a refuge following the termination of his political tenure. The practice of law is a form of security, something to fall back on when political life is ended either temporarily or permanently. In many cases it is used intermittently in a fluctuating political career. The most famous example is that of President Nixon who used his law practice in New York as a base between the vice presidency (and his unsuccessful bid for the governorship of California) and the office of president of the United States in 1968. He was following the much used path of a political leader who wants to stay in public life and who particularly wants to build an ascending political career. Most of the political leaders among the regional nominees have been successful in building and maintaining political or governmental careers. Most, however, keep law practice as a reserve; for example, Richard Hughes returned to the practice of law after the termination of his tenure as governor of New Jersey.

Educators and professors generally exhibit the conventional multiple channel or the fluctuating pattern. Kingman Brewster is an example of the conventional multiple career as he established himself in the professional hierarchy by moving from assistant professor to professor of law at Harvard and then moving to the administrative channel in which he became president of Yale University. More commonly the fluctuating pattern is utilized as they move back and forth from education to political office or governmental appointments. Thus John Galbraith left his professorship at Harvard to serve as U.S. Ambassador to India or to campaign for Adlai Stevenson, John F. Kennedy, Eugene McCarthy, and George McGovern. Short- and long-term leaves of absence provide the security of a university post for the itinerant. Paul Ylvisaker, in his varied career as professor at Swarthmore, secretary to the mayor of Philadelphia, Ford Foundation executive, New Jersey state office, and now a professor at Princeton, exhibits a large circular run in the fluctuating pattern. Because Professor Ylvisaker is a young man, he is "ripe" as a candidate for an important governmental appointment if he should want it.

Career Orientations of Top Leaders

The combining of career channels is as often the result of accident as of planning. Most of the top leaders are highly ambitious men. They reach out for interesting opportunities that provide prestige and growth. Whether they admit it or not, they are status climbers and as such they must acquire increased visibility. They will often make moves according to the kind of opportunity that presents itself rather than adhere to the strict definition of a given career hierarchy. This is why there is a predominance of multiple, dual, and fluctuating channels. An opportunity orientation will facilitate movement in three or more hierarchies. An example is that of an educator who distinguishes himself in university administration and is then called on to serve in a distinguished federal or state appointment and ends his career as a foundation or organizational executive. McGeorge Bundy, military officer, professor, university dean, special assistant to Presidents Kennedy and Johnson, and now president of the Ford Foundation, is a good example of this opportunity-oriented movement. Robert Weaver is another of the regional board nominees who has enjoyed a multiple career. He had accumulated three degrees from Harvard and his Ph.D. in economics at the age of 27. He then began a career in public service that included 10 different state and federal government posts before his final appointement as Secretary of Department of Housing and Urban Development. At that time it was the highest and most significant federal administrative post ever assigned to a black man. In 1969 he was appointed President of Bernard M. Baruch College in New York. This began a new career which later changed to the professorial ladder. He is currently Distinguished Professor of Urban Affairs at Hunter College in New York as well as director of its Urban Affairs Research Center. He is an active member of 13 boards of prestigious organizations (including New York's Mt. Sinai Hospital and the Metropolitan Life Insurance Company) and is working with a group of young black executives who are pushing for integration at the management level in the business world.

Milton Eisenhower can match this kind of multiple-career history with his record as president of Kansas State, Pennsylvania State, and Johns Hopkins Universities. Interspersed is a career as diplomat (Vice Consul to Edinburgh, Scotland) and as governmental official (assistant to the Secretary of Agriculture, director of information in the Department of Agriculture, Associate Director of OWI, numerous governmental commissions, UNESCO, and consultant to President Dwight Eisenhower, his brother). He is also a director of a half dozen or more industrial and transportation companies. His ties are therefore spread out along educational, governmental, and industrial lines that represent a simultaneous development of his career.

Another career orientation is that of *media outreach*. Many organizational executives and professors establish supplementary careers by using writing or lecturing as a way of increasing their public visibility and as another step in commanding positions of greater importance. Another kind of career can develop as these opportunities develop into lucrative outlets. In some cases book and magazine royalties or lecturing and television fees provide more income than the salary received for their regular jobs. Many senators and congressmen have found this to be true and the same opportunity exists for many educational and organizational leaders.

Attaining Visibility and a Power Reputation as a Regional Board Nominee

The research process by which the regional nominees were identified was a long one. The choice of more than 2500 names of leaders who were believed to be influential in urban affairs was the first step. In New York alone some 400 top business leaders were identified as having great potential influence. "Judges" were asked at the second step to make their selections and thus the lists were reduced. Finally, a list of 200 key leaders was prepared to represent the major cities, based on the votes of expert judges. A second list of 200 top leaders was prepared (based on the number of votes received). From the votes of all respondents the 26 regional nominees were identified. The potential number of influential urban-oriented leaders in the heavily populated Eastern Seaboard of the United States is enormous. It is therefore especially appropriate to ask how 26 leaders finally become selected as the top of the top—the regional shakers and movers of Eastern Megalopolis. The question focuses on the manner in which these regional leaders became visible to other leaders throughout the region. Visibility in a large city is difficult; visibility in a region requires much greater attainment.

The study of the careers of the regional nominees demonstrates that visibility is achieved in many different ways. For a prominent urban leader it generally depends first on a formally established career coupled with a reputation as a concerned and active leader in urban or social problems. Literally thousands qualify for positions of leadership based on their attainment of high posts in their occupational and organizational lives, but reputations for competent civic leadership are won by a limited number. Many potential leaders are simply not interested; others claim that the pressure of their work precludes civic activity. One top leader explained:

> Most leaders have no background or training in civic affairs. They
> bring no social philosophy and sometimes very little commitment. The
> top rung people are usually the large corporation presidents who are

not really secure. They are organization men who refuse to take chances. This is in contrast to the days of home-owned industry when the top men were owners and like the professional came out of wealth and background.

This explanation stresses the kind of risk taking that urban social leadership requires. The urban social leader is often embarking on new and untried courses of action in programs that are often controversial, and his identification with these programs may effect his organization (or he fears that it may) or his own career. Obviously, the regional nominees are men who have been willing and able to take risks and live with controversy in their commitments to the solution of urban problems. Men and women who do so win visibility among their peers, in the press, and throughout the region.

They must also make commitments to a larger entity than the satelite city or suburban community in which most key leaders live and raise their families. Suburban civic activity must be relegated to others, perhaps to the wife of the top leader. The top leader identifies with the metropolitan area in which he works and undergoes an informal training experience in urban affairs. Walter Phillips of Philadelphia sees the ideal training in three stages: apprentice, journeyman, and master craftsman. One path follows the organization of civic leadership mobilized at City Hall. The politically active person begins by working for a political party and holding an elective or appointive office. An alternate path more widely used is civic leadership by private voluntary organizations. Participation as a member, officer, and board member in a number of urban-related organizations develops the neophyte in stages and with increasing visibility as a by-product. At many points leaders from the two training schools meet and become well acquainted. They work together on ctiy commissions, state boards, and federal bodies, in many private organizations like the Urban Coalition (city or national), environmental foundations, religious societies, conferences, and other common areas of contact.

There are many things to be learned in the informal leadership experience before a leader reaches the top of the top. He must learn which men and women are on their way up and which are on their way down. He must size up the old crowd and the new crowd and make correct choices among people and programs.

One top leader, in making his evaluations of leaders, demonstrated the insights that formed his judgments. The following are excerpts from his comments about various leaders:

> "This man is bright but unscrupulous. You can't trust him. He will take the side of the issue which is expedient for him."
>
> "This man is too old. He had power but it is gone."
>
> "This man is a bumbler. He is smart enough but you have to lead him by the hand."
>
> "This man works quietly behind the scenes. But he can raise money and get people to go along."
>
> "This man is decent and wouldn't hurt anybody. But he can't stand up and fight. He is one of the decent people—nice, good fellows but not leaders."

"Here is a powerful man, but he is in and out of town so much that he can't really make his influence felt."

"This is a young man. Oh, he is 45, I suppose, but he can't really be judged yet. I think he has real potential and you will probably hear from him."

"This man has no philosophy. He seems whimsical and fickle. Just moves the way something strikes him."

"This man is astute. He sizes up the situation, knows what is needed, and acts. Very effective—a smooth, quiet person."

"This man is good. Cool. Very rarely shows his hand. A comer."

"This man has no background for civic affairs. He was just shoved into civic responsibilities. He has fine qualities. He could have been one of the greatest men produced in this city."

"Here we have a dedicated man, committed to the public good."

"This man is senile. We just let him resign. He couldn't even follow what was going on."

"This man is not really identified with our city. He lives in a distant community and is out of it here."

It is this kind of judgment that top leaders learn to make in choosing candidates for committees, to back for offices, and to trust when they want to get things done. As they prove their competence, their leadership is increasingly sought and their visibility and reputations grow. They learn that the means of gathering support for civic leadership include running for and winning public office, identifying with civic organizations or programs, speaking and writing, accepting important governmental assignments, becoming organizational spokesmen, developing new programs, leading protest movements, winning important consulting positions with key political figures, and being on the programs at important conferences. These widening activities are supplemented by regional and national channels of communication. Circles are broadened as the leader advances in his occupation and in positions of local leadership. Both open new opportunities for travel and the initiation of state, regional, and national contacts. More prestige is achieved by securing business directorships, university or foundation trusteeships, social club memberships, state and national offices in professional, civic, or trade associations, identification with labor and religious organizations, and by utilizing wealth, friendship, or political influence to gain entry into the company of key civic and political leaders.

At least 25 years are required to reach the rank of "master craftsman" in this on-the-job leadership climb and only the most determined attain regional and national visibility. Among them, a select few win the acceptance of key and top leaders and finally stand at the top of the top.

At the peak of their careers all the regional nominees had developed a public image. This image is based on the type of leadership role and the issue-and-project history associated with each leader. Table 5.5 summarizes the kind of thumbnail descriptions that become the labels or stereotypes that are fixed on leaders. They color the thinking of others as they reflect on the man. They are the visible points of reference of both men and ideas, and thus together the 26 have the power to mold public opinion and influence it as they speak, write, and take positions on issues and work for projects. A search of Table 5.5 reveals the variety of roles and the diversity of the issue-and-project histories. In the next chapter underlying patterns are identified.

The question might be raised why no woman is among the top regional nominees. In fact, only four women are listed among the 200 key leaders. This paucity of women is to be explained by the social definitions that have made it so difficult for women to advance to commensurate positions in the occupational world of men. It can be predicted that the names of more women will appear on subsequent lists and that they will generally be found where the first women were; that is, as civic and civil rights leaders. Women are beginning to appear as political leaders. The last channels to be opened would seem to be in the business, labor, and religious bureaucracies.

It has been emphasized that the road to top regional leadership is "rough." No one can make it unless he can take the "heat." The greatest number of potential leaders are eliminated because of this inadequacy. No body of scientific knowledge exists to describe how motivation is heightened to prepare the leader and what social experiences will sharpen the mental acumen and fortify the body for endurance to social stress. At the moment, combinations of birth and social experience dispatch a parade of potential leaders into a society that exorts, "May the best man win!"

In the next chapter we examine a larger group of leaders whose activity is characterized by a high proportion of contact across Megalopolis. They include many of the top leaders that have been analyzed in this chapter, but the focus on decision making is intensified. There are many questions of involvement, opposition, and the resolution of issues that await answers. To provide more detailed data about decision making another supplementary study was carried out and Chapter 6 reports the findings.

Notes

1. Some of these leaders, like John Lindsay and Nelson Rockefeller have shifted to other positions in recent months. Other key leaders will either die, retire, or change positions in the near future. This is not significant for leadership analysis because the vital data are found in the roles these leaders played and the relationships they developed. Any key leader must establish a leadership role and pattern. The sociological problem is understanding these roles (apart from the leader who occupied a given position at a specific time). Any future variation should be encompassed in the population of this study.

2. Six leaders are professors or are identified with education as former teachers or administrators. The choice of such informants seemed expedient because key leaders are very busy and most reluctant to answer mailed questionnaires. Aides of John Lindsay and Nelson Rockefeller wrote me that both men have a policy of answering no questionnaires because their busy schedules did not permit it.

3. Letter of November 8, 1971.

4. All parenthesis material added by author.

5. Letter of October 15, 1971.

6. *Common Cause*, Report from Washington, **2** (August 1972), 6–7. This report also names 34 members of the House of Representatives who are directors of one or more banks.

TABLE 5.5 BRIEF ISSUE AND PROJECT HISTORY OF REGIONAL BOARD NOMINEES

Regional leader	Issue and project history of each leader who has shaped his public image
John K. Galbraith Role type: action-oriented intellectual, spokesman for liberals on the left.	Has taken strong stand on Vietnam war; has opposed the military-industrial complex in public speeches and in his books, especially *The New Industrial State*: activities in ADA placed him in conflict with the organization and with public authorities; urges strong federal support of public services
John Collins Role type: liberal urban administrator of intellectual bent	Well-respected and popular mayor of Boston, 1960-1968; fought vigorously for urban renewal, honest government, tax reduction, urban planning, and integrated schools
Kingman Brewster Role type: progressive, resilient educator	Has supported increased student participation in decision making at Yale University and provided support for student protest against the Vietnam war; his position has incurred considerable conflict with some Yale alumni and others who supported a hard line; his diplomacy has been regarded generally as successful and his resilency is regarded as adaptive
Nelson A. Rockefeller Role type: liberal Republican politician and effective administrator	Four-term Governor of New York, 1959 to 1973; fought for federal revenue sharing with the states, a decentralization plan for administration of New York public schools; supported a federal family assistance welfare plan and is strong proponent of environment controls
John V. Lindsay Role type: liberal charismatic leader; spokesman for big city mayors	Was a leading opponent of the Vietnam war; fought for a plan to decentralize public schools and is a strong supporter of greater federal spending in support of cities by direct and categorical grants; has been urging national charter for New York City to operate with the authority of a state; recently identified with Democratic Party and a supporter of Democratic candidates

Bayard Rustin

Role type: moderate labor and civil rights integrationist; an independent, liaison leader; outstanding speaker

Identified as a black moderate who serves as a bridge between blacks and liberals in the labor movement and religious groups; joins Philip Randolph in support of common goals; an integrationist, he is also thought to lack support of large part of black community; has a record as organizer of epoch-making march on Washington in 1963; is credited with helping to bring about the reconciliation of New York's United Federation of Teachers and the black leaders in the bitter 1968 school decentralization conflict; alienated from the militants and lacking a strong power base, he is called a strategist without a movement

Whitney Young

Role type: militant integrationist, social action leader, contact man between business, intellectuals and black leaders

Became identified as a militant integrationist who was able to retain currency in the black militant community and the integrationist elements; established effective cooperation (and monetary contributions) with corporate executives, the foundations, and the business community in general; secured strong federal support for blacks through domestic Marshall Plan; an organizer of the historic march on Washington (1963); developed on-the-job training programs in the ghetto communities; organized Community Action Assembly of black and top political leaders

Arthur Goldberg

Role type: multiple based leader of labor, Jewish, and liberal Democratic political elements

Identified as a fighter for liberal causes based on his career as labor lawyer; Supreme Court Justice, U.N. Ambassador, leader in Jewish circles, and strong supporter of Democratic Party; ran on democratic ticket for Governor of New York in 1970

David Rockefeller

Role type: banker with a liberal outlook; intellectual in orientation.

Has assumed leadership in using the influence of the Chase Manhattan Bank in support of housing and business programs for low income and disadvantaged groups

Terrence, Cardinal Cooke

Role type: major Catholic leader with social outlook

Maintains policy of supporting Catholic parishes and schools in depressed areas of New York; enlarged a program by which Catholic personnel study Spanish and local mores in Puerto Rico so that they may serve Catholic schools and colleges throughout the city

151

TABLE 5.5   BRIEF ISSUE AND PROJECT HISTORY OF REGIONAL BOARD NOMINEES   (*Continued*)

Regional leader	Issue and project history of each leader who has shaped his public image
Cornelius W. Owens Role type: active business leader, good fund raiser	Active civic leader in various fund-raising activities for civic needs; active in economic development
Robert C. Weaver Role type: housing authority and administrator	A lifelong career in state and federal housing assignments as consultant and administrator: a black leader who has commanded respect for his administrative skill and has developed extensive acquaintance and contact; former president of Bernard Baruch College of New York, now distinguished professor of Urban Affairs at Hunter College
A. Philip Randolph Role type: aged but respected labor and civil rights leader	Respected as the wise old counselor and social philosopher based on a lifetime in labor leadership (president of the Brotherhood of Sleeping Car Porters) and as an active civil rights advocate; organized 1963 march on Washington (with Bayard Rustin and Martin Luther King); influenced Leon Sullivan who served as president of first march on Washington in 1944 under Randolph's general direction
Roy Wilkins Role type: major civil rights integrationist leader	Head of largest and richest civil rights organization in the country; strong advocate of cooperation with white power structure; has a leadership style which binds adherents to NAACP; is considered a leader in securing legal rights for blacks but is called laggard in innovative social action
Kenneth B. Clark Role type: action-oriented intellectual	Credited with brief to U.S. Supreme Court that evoked landmark decision of 1954 which stated that segregated schooling was unconstitutional; active on local level in New York — studying, setting up, and working on civil rights and antipoverty programs

Andrew Heiskel

Role type: mass media leader and urban activist

Has participated actively in Urban America and National Urban Coalition; as chief executive officer of Time, Inc., he can focus attention of mass media on urban problems

Milton Eisenhower

Role type: educator and government consultant

Known as a liberal Republican, has served in numerous government posts of wide ranging character; established himself as expert in agriculture and then as a government consultant, diplomat, and administrator; confidant to his brother, President Eisenhower; known in educational circles as President of Kansas State, Penn State, and John Hopkins; chairman of the National Commission on the Causes and Prevention of Violence (1968); a final report issued in December 1969 urged a reordering of national priorities and called on the nation to commit at least 20 billion dollars a year to the solution of urban social problems

Walter E. Washington

Role type: energetic black mayor of a black city

Has developed background of experience in housing and administration; as mayor of Washington he has acted to bring about the transition of the city from a white majority to a black majority; faced acute problems in the schools, crime, and urban violence; his success in bridging militant and integrationist elements is widely recognized; acceptable to white community and has confidence of both Democrats and Republicans

George Meany

Role type: indomitable, durable national labor leader and Democratic political power

Has led AFL-CIO in support of a strong program of legislative action in such areas as job training, housing, medical care, education, race relations, poverty, and unemployment; AFL-CIO supports candidates and incumbents who take a stand on the side of public services; Meany recently persuaded President Nixon to give wage-price board (1971) autonomy of action; often regarded as lagging in reorganizing AFL-CIO for more rapid internal changes in structure and policy; his neutral position (actually favoring re-election of President Nixon) was significant in 1972 presidential election

The Reverend Leon Sullivan

Role type: minister and social activist

Created community-sponsored, self-help, job-training program known as Opportunities Industrialization Center, opened in Philadelphia in 1964; more than 100 cities have developed similar centers for training minority workers for jobs; developed 10-36 investment plan ($10 dollars a month for 36 months) to *create* job opportunities for blacks, giving rise to Zion Gardens Apartments complex, Progress Plaza (shopping center in North Philadelphia), and Progress Aerospace Industries, Inc.

TABLE 5.5   BRIEF ISSUE AND PROJECT HISTORY OF REGIONAL BOARD NOMINEES   (Continued)

Regional leader	Issue and project history of each leader who has shaped his public image
Joseph Clark Role type: Democratic Party leader, former Mayor of Philadelphia, and senator from Pennsylvania.	Active in urban and national problems as Mayor of Philadelphia (1951-1954) and senator from Pennsylvania, 1956-1968; worked consistently for international cooperation and reduction of military expenditures; played key role in establishment of Delaware River Compact and strong advocate of environmental control
James Rouse Role type: builder-banker, urban planner	Known as the builder-financier of the new town, Columbia, Maryland; active in National Urban Coalition, Baltimore Urban Coalition; interested in neighborhood improvement, urban planning, and public housing
McGeorge Bundy Role type: foundation and urban policy maker	Has insisted that foundations should not avoid controversial issues but fill various roles, including positions, as the Ford Foundation does in the field of educational television, population control, and equal opportunity; it was the grant for a demonstration project on school decentralization that thrust the Ford Foundation into the center of a bitter controversy in New York in 1968; wealthiest of the private foundations, the president plays a crucial policy role as new emphasis is placed on urban and environmental problems
Paul V. Ylvisaker Role type: urban knowledgeable and intellectual leader	Twelve years as associate director of the Ford Foundation gave him an opportunity to direct influence and money in problems of law, government, justice, poverty, and prejudice; has added administrative experience to his career as Commissioner of the Department of Community Affairs; combines trained intelligence (Ph.D., Harvard), governmental experience, and broad policy decision on urban problems

Richard J. Hughes	Dominated New Jersey government as governor from 1961-1970; pressed for reforms and strengthening of education, housing, employment, welfare, law enforcement, and narcotics control; supported Delaware River Compact and strong environmental controls
Role type: Democratic Party leader and state governor	
Richardson Dilworth	Mayor of Philadelphia (1955-1962); has had a long career as a Democratic Party leader; as president of the Board of Education in Philadelphia, initiated decentralized practices and reforms
Role type: urban administrator with political acumen; education policy maker	

155

CHAPTER SIX

MEGA-Leaders,
Regional Issues, and
Patterned Strategies
in Decision Making

Megalopolis offers a representative sample of the urban ills that afflict modern industrialized societies. Not only does the region provide the usual number of problems (as presented in Chapter 4) but they exist in high intensity. In comparison with other industrialized societies Megalopolis is characterized by the greater severity of its racial and ethnic issues, the high rate of its unemployment, and the extent of its welfare list.

Every problem is a potential source of issues. Issues can and do develop over the definition of the problem, over the ways of dealing with it, and the implementation of a policy that seeks an alleviation. The selection of issues for study must be guided by some principle or the multiplicity would make the task nearly impossible.

Personalities and issues in the headlines today are not of interest here except as they exemplify the working of political processes and provide generalizations that extend over time and in a variety of cases. Current issues are utilized only to reveal the relatively unchanging features of political systems in various cities.[1]

The principle applied in this research is that of the underlying importance of the ideological cleavage represented by the collective policies selected to deal with urban problems. Four cleavages of this character emerge.

1. Metropolitan area government or planning with the cleavage: (a) support of central city needs versus (b) support of suburban needs.

2. Revenue sharing by Federal Government with the cleavage: (a) bloc grants to states versus (b) categorical grants to cities.

3. Community participation and control of public organizations and institutions with the cleavage: (a) centralized versus (b) decentralized control of schools, poverty programs, etc.

4. Executive control of organizations by direct line control or representative coalition of community members with the cleavage: (a) agency-directed versus (b)

coalition-directed policy formulation and administration (exemplified in National Alliance of Businessmen (business directed) and Urban Coalition (directed by representatives of business, labor, government, religion, and civil rights).

Each of these cleavages tends to divide citizens into ideological and vested interest groups and to generate the maximum in emotional and personal involvement. Thus the busing of school children widens the cleavage between interests of central cities and suburbs (Issue 1). The denial of cities of funds supplied directly by the Federal Government for housing and education which requires them to apply to the state government sets up an issue that divides city from state (Issue 2). The struggles experienced by community groups to gain stronger control over their local schools brings them into direct confrontation with teachers and school administrators who have fought for professional standards that require the protection of a centralized administration (Issue 3). The establishment of authority within an organization presents an issue between those who urge that the governing board be filled with the best qualified candidates and those who seek to establish a proportionate (quota) representation of racial, ethnic, religious, or occupational composition of the community as the primary requirement (Issue 4).

The Activity of MEGA-Leaders in Major Urban Issues

A supplementary study of decision-making processes was designed to gain greater understanding of regional shakers and movers engaged in issue activity. Eighty leaders with the highest "megalopolis scores" were selected from the total sample of respondents.[2] Megalopolis scores derive from the number of acquaintances and contacts that key and top leaders assign to other key and top leaders in major cities of Megalopolis *outside their own communities*. Because of this attribute, the leaders of this supplementary study are called MEGA-leaders. A number of inquiries were directed to them about their roles and contacts in decision making centered about problems and issues along the Bos-Wash axis. First they were asked to identify the issues related to the major ideological cleavages in which they had participated. Their answers are given in Table 6.1. The reports of leadership activity demonstrate that the issue of agency-directed versus coalition-directed policy formulation and administration engages 91 percent of all MEGA-leaders. This indicates that the issue must be pressing in many of their civic associations, which is not surprising, for quotas for representative policy groups are mandated in all federally assisted Community Action and Model City Housing Programs and the demand for representation by racial, ethnic, community, women's, and social-class groups is widely felt in organizational life in general.

It is interesting that 84 percent of the leaders were concerned with the closely related problem of community participation and control of public organizations. It is on this issue that the most active leadership is concentrated, undoubtedly because of the heightened interest in the administration of and teaching in the public schools.

Seventy-seven percent reported activity in the central city-suburb cleavage and 54 percent dealt with the issue of revenue sharing. The central city-suburb

TABLE 6.1   PERCENTAGE OF MEGA-LEADERS WHO REPORT THEMSELVES AS
VERY ACTIVE, ACTIVE, OR NOT INVOLVED IN FOUR MAJOR IDEOLOGICAL
ISSUE AREAS

Major ideological cleavages	Very active (%)	Active (%)	Not involved (%)
Metropolitan area government or planning with the issue: strong support of central city versus strong support of suburbs	54	23	23
Revenue sharing by Federal Government with the issue: bloc grants to states versus specific program (categorical) grants to cities	8	46	46
Community participation and control of public organizations and institutions with the issue: centralized versus decentralized control of schools, poverty programs, etc.	56	28	16
Executive control of organizations by direct line control or representative coalition of community members with the issue: agency-directed versus coalition-directed policy formulation and administration [agency direction is exemplified in National Alliance of Businessmen (business-directed), whereas coalition direction is demonstrated by the Urban Coalition (policy direction by representatives of business, labor, government, religion, and civil rights leaders)].	46	45	9

conflict engaged those whose loyalties are caught between the need for metropolitan planning and the desire to maintain a chosen way of community life. The
issue of revenue sharing tends to become the acute concern of urban political
leaders who seek control over categorical federal grants and those state-wide
leaders who want federal bloc grants to help finance the ever-increasing cost of
state government.

Some illustrations of the leadership role played by MEGA-leaders in the resolution of each of these four types of issue[3] will document the decision-making processes involved. The example presented in each case is taken from a given city,
but the challenge is similar to that faced by every other major city in the region.
For this reason leaders look up and down the Bos-Wash axis and compare their
problems and the behavior of their counterparts. Although the problems are
locally oriented, they serve to generate leadership communication of a regional
character. This chapter introduces research to demonstrate this point.

ISSUE: Metropolitan Area Planning

The conflict between inner cities and suburbs is both a social and a class struggle.
The National Commission on Urban Problems said that in 1967 metropolitan

areas in the United States were served by 20,745 local governments, or an average of 48 for each metropolitan county. In the suburbs, despite civil rights laws and the good intentions of many, municipal zoning restrictions "keep out the lower income groups, and especially large families which require significant public expenditures in education, public health and welfare, open space, recreational facilities, police and fire protection."[4] The end result is tension between central city and suburbs, rich and poor, and especially black and white. Any needs that conflict with the central city and the suburbs tend to raise issues which are invariably emotionally charged and just as often difficult to resolve. The range of these needs may be placed in counterpositions as follows:

Support of Central City Needs Versus Support of Suburban Needs

Need for rapid transit in central city and a minimum of freeway disruption of city life.	Need for freeways to commute from suburbs to and through central city.
Need for low-cost public housing in central city and suburbs.	Need to protect property values and middle-income or upper-income way of life.
Need for equality of opportunity in schools which requires busing to suburbs (or suburbs to central city).	Need to protect quality of schools attained by local control and local taxation.
Need to secure a larger tax base by annexation and/or metropolitan government.	Need to protect tax resources to support services of high qualtiy and efficiency.
Republicans (predominantly) desire voting strength of suburbs. Blacks may resist suburban annexation, fearing loss of recently achieved political power.	Suburbanites are torn by desire to have some control over central city and their strong desire to maintain racial and political independence.

No mayor in Megalopolis has escaped being drawn into all these points of conflict, and key leaders have played roles commensurate with their commitments. In Boston busing was a central issue in the last two local elections. In Baltimore and Washington the construction of freeways has opened up a torrent of opposing views and political forces. Public housing in the suburbs has been an explosive and political issue. Metropolitan area government has made little headway, although government planning has been going on with the financial encouragement of the Federal Government. The stubborn character of these problems can be illustrated by the freeway-subway controversy in Washington. Almost constantly during the last 12 years, since a congressionally funded study recommended both freeways and a subway, the city has been in an uproar over one, the other, or both. The city has tried to block a freeway program that requires the immediate construction of four projects, including the Three Sisters Bridge near Georgetown. Mayor Walter E. Washington and the City Council asked President Johnson to veto this legislation in 1968. The President refused and instructed the city to adopt a comprehensive road plan. At the end of 1971 both freeway and subway projects were stalled. Pressure from the suburban area for freeways grows as population increases and traffic congestion in Washington becomes more acute. The inner-city residents want no more high-speed roads, calling them pollution traps and neighborhood wreckers. Vice Chairman Walter E. Fauntroy of the City Council, an outspoken opponent, supported the Mayor in rejecting the freeway plan. Blacks facing destruction of their neighborhoods have often raised the issue into crisis proportions. The city has insisted on the completion of the subway, a multibillion dollar project, stalled because the Chairman of the House Appropriations Sub-Committee, Representative William H. Natcher, refuses to release funds until the freeway appropriated program is adopted and started.

At the end of 1971 the controversy over the Three Sisters Bridge halted the freeway program, and Representative Natcher continued to refuse to release funds for the 98-mile, 3-billion-dollar subway system. Contracts for slightly more than 10 percent of the subway project have been awarded in the last 12 years. Mayor Washington, although backed solidly by his council, is caught between the Congress, the National Capital Planning Commission, the black community, and the political pressures of Virginia and Maryland commuter groups.[5]

Nearby, the City of Baltimore has witnessed an almost identical situation. Arguments over the Baltimore freeway plans had persisted for nearly two decades. The "revolution" of city dwellers, particularly blacks and the poor, protested the spreading destruction of inner-city neighborhoods for suburban commuter routes and the loss of historically and esthetically valuable landmarks to freeway lanes. The original plan called for the condemnation and razing of much of the historic Federal Hill and Fells Point sections of the city, a massive low-level, 14-lane freeway bridge across the inner harbor, the destruction of hundreds of houses built before the Revolutionary War, and the dislocation of several thousand families. The original plan also threatened the destruction of Rosemont, a community of well-kept, lower middle-class black homes. An effective coalition of white and black freeway opponents has brought about a compromise plan that has been approved by the Federal Highway Commission.[6]

Boston and Philadelphia have had similar difficulties in freeway construction and the problem of saving neighborhood and historic sites has been troublesome. Each mayor has had to mediate between the protection of the inner city and pressures from suburbanites and business groups to build freeways in and through the city.

ISSUE: Federal Revenue Sharing

This issue raises questions of financing urban measures effectively and of control centers for the management of resources. It is essentially a problem in political organization and as such has brought governors and mayors into direct confrontation. In nearly every one of the industrial states the public witnesses an annual sparring match between governor and mayors. The mayors ask for state aid and find insufficient support. The reason is that the political base of the governor rests on rural and suburban voters, whereas the mayors represent inner-city residents. Although their political philosophies may be similar, aid to cities costs money and usually means higher taxes. If the mayors can no longer raise money through higher property taxes, neither can the governor go too far in urban aid lest he antagonize his suburban voters. The counterpositions may be set out as follows:

Federal Bloc Grants to States Versus Categorical Grants to Cities

Increase federal revenue sharing by block grants to states.	Maintain principles of categorical federal-aid grants to help cities by infusing large sums of federal money into relief of urban problems and rebuilding of cities.
State will apportion funds to cities for schools, health, welfare, manpower recruitment and training, unemployment, highways, and rapid transit.	
The desire of states to reduce or eliminate categorical grants is based on the ability of a state to plan and distribute more equitably state and federal funds to cities. Categorical grants commonly requiring state and local matching funds push government into new programs and expenditures often beyond their means.	Central city will petition and use funds for its problems of schools, health, welfare, manpower, unemployment, highways, and rapid transit.
	The defense of the more than 1000 categorical grants is a defense of local autonomy. A city administration knows best its own problems and needs.

The case for federal bloc grants has been waged by the Conference of Governors, the Council of State Governments, the U.S. Chamber of Commerce, the Republican Party, and President Nixon. All of these proponents consider the federal revenue-sharing plan basic to the "new Federalism." In Megalopolis Nelson Rockefeller was a major spokesman, urged the Congress to adopt a federal revenue-sharing program, effective July 1, 1971, that would return a minimum of 10 billion dollars of new money to state and local governments, nationwide—including a 1-billion-dollar approximate share for New York—to help support basic local services to the people.[7]

The case for direct aid to cities by categorical grants has been carried by the U.S. Conference of Mayors, the National League of Cities, the AFL-CIO, and the Democratic Party. Because most big city mayors are Democrats, the issue becomes intensely political. John Lindsay was especially vocal about his city's needs and the necessity for direct assistance. He expressed the general feeling that city problems are so critical that more direct federal grants are needed. Right down the roster of Megalopolis the mayors of the large cities have believed that state legislatures are dominated by rural and suburban interests and that as a result the cities do not receive their just share of revenues controlled by the states. This belief brought Nelson Rockefeller and John Lindsay into some severe personal confrontations. Perhaps no issue across Megalopolis so sharply divided governors and mayors and so completely mobilized Republican and Democratic loyalties.

ISSUE: Community Control

The issue of community control grows out of a widespread feeling that government—city, state, and national—is not responsive to the needs of citizens. As government has expanded and included more aspects of public life, the apparatus of bureaucracy has increased, authority has been centralized, communications lines have lengthened, and the people have come to feel that they are neither needed nor heard. This complaint has no specific bounds but it is more vocal when articulated by militant minorities in the black community. The cry for participation ranges from the demand to be consulted to near absolute community control of vital public functions. The fulcrum at which the issue pivots is the centralization of administrative authority. The counterpositions are set forth in the following statements:

ISSUE: Centralized Control of Public Organizations and Institutions Versus	Decentralized Control of Public Organizations and Institutions
There is a need to maintain standards within a system to plan more efficiently and to effect economies. This is exemplified by a centrally organized school or welfare system which sets professional standards under the control of qualified professionals.	There is a need to gain control in order to adapt organization to local needs and improve quality and efficiency by local participation. This is exemplified by a school or welfare system under local control which selects its own standards. It is claimed that better morale and more responsive officials can be attained, which will increase quality and service to clients. The advantages are often claimed for all urban services placed under decentralized direction.
Other areas of contest may be over housing administration, job training, health and drug programs, and police and fire administration.	Indeed, a challenge may be issued to all areas of administration, for example, when a section of a city threatens to secede (this has happened in New York, where some boroughs have made such threats).

Decentralized control should be distinguished from community control. Decentralization refers to a restructuring of authority from a central point to many different local units, but does not seriously alter the personnel or the abolition of a central coordinating organization and the controls useful for maintaining the standards and efficiency deemed necessary for all the decentralized units. Central boards of lay representatives continue to exert policy-making authority. In these terms decentralization is mainly an administrative change that permits somewhat more flexibility and responsiveness to local conditions.

On the other hand, community control projects the idea of indigenous representatives who will be granted complete control over the major functions of the local organization. The makeup of the governing board and the administrative personnel is subject to considerable variation. Election or appointment to the board may bring representatives who are chosen or appointed because of their qualifications. If boards are constituted by quotas to represent the racial, ethnic, or religious composition of the community, priority then shifts to "proportionate representation."

The issue of decentralization often becomes intertwined with the issue of the governing structure. In this chapter an attempt has been made to separate them. Decentralization and community control are used interchangeably, but the agency representation is discussed as a separate issue.

Greater citizen participation is now favored rhetorically by those who lead, or aspire to lead, virtually all our institutions. At the level of action, however, group participation conflicts at every turn with other ideals and well-entrenched interests. Every city of Megalopolis has had to grapple with the issues raised. The demands for greater participation by black spokesmen have included (a) placing as much authority as possible in the neighborhood communities; (b) direct representation of neighborhood communities on the city council, the board of education, the police commission, and other significant policy bodies; (c) black representation at all levels of the public service; (d) representation on the labor forces of government contractors; and (e) the use of public resources to develop black-controlled businesses.[8] New York's Ocean Hill-Brownsville experiment reveals the conflict of interests and the intensity with which such a conflict can be waged. Before the issue of community control of schools was resolved city school teachers were locked in three strikes with the city that kept a million pupils out of classes for most of the 1968 fall term. Mayor John Lindsay and McGeorge Bundy of the Ford Foundation became objects of villification. The harassment in Ocean Hill-Brownsville when unwanted teachers tried to return, exacerbated by remarks of a militant fringe that were taken as antisemitic and antiwhite, righted an entire city and mobilized massive white support for the teachers' cause. The dispute escalated to the level of a symbol of a city-wide power conflict between the dispossessed and the middle class, white, social order. The teachers, predominantly white and Jewish, aroused sympathetic support from the Jewish community and from whites in general.

The blacks believed that they were striving for better schools and for a control that they had been encouraged to seek. "Community control" became a magic word in the ghetto, the definition of which goes beyond schools, curricula, and teachers to life itself. To gain control of local institutions is to promise some control by blacks over their own lives and a defeat for the impersonal forces that seem to perpetuate the hopelessness that is experienced in places like Ocean Hill-Brownsville. So New York became a test case for the region and the nation.[9]

The Ocean Hill-Brownsville experiment had its roots in a school system that had been deteriorating for a long time. Six of the eight schools were outmoded structures with an average age of about 65 years. Until quite recently all the school buildings were drastically overcrowded, and pupil retardation in mathematics and reading was as great as five levels below grade.[10]

In the summer of 1966 the city school system had reached a crossroad. Whereas the white pupil population was declining rapidly, black and Puerto Rican enrollment was growing even faster. New York joined such cities of Megalopolis as Washington, Baltimore, and Philadelphia in which white pupils were in the minority.

A group of parents and others in the largely black and Puerto Rican East Harlem section made two optional demands in connection with the scheduled opening of Intermediate School 201. They demanded that the Board of Education integrate the school by bringing in white children or turn its control over to the community. The Board replied that neither integration nor local control was possible. The parents and their supporters took to the streets in protest. Now, seeking only control of the school, they demanded the right to replace the school's white principal with a black, asserting that a black administrator would provide a more suitable image for the pupils.

The demonstrators failed in their campaign, but they had raised a new battle cry—"community control." In the Spring of 1967 Mayor Lindsay pleaded with Albany for more state school aid. The legislature provided the money but, determined to force some changes in the city system, attached a proviso that the mayor submit a decentralization plan in the following year.

The Board of Education, seeking to develop its own decentralization plan to head off more drastic reforms, approved, in the summer of 1967, three experimental decentralized demonstration districts. Planning funds were provided by the Ford Foundation which had worked behind the scenes for the project.

McGeorge Bundy, president of the Ford Foundation, came into the school picture in late 1966 at the request of Mayor John V. Lindsay, who asked him to mediate the growing demand in black communities for local control of schools. Bundy and a Ford education expert, Dr. Mario Fantini, were drawn deeper and deeper into the issue. Bundy, in April 1967, accepted the chairmanship of a mayoral panel charged with drawing up a city-wide decentralization plan. The proposal, written largely by Fantini, favored a sweeping decentralization of the school system.[11]

Meanwhile Ford granted $135,000 in planning money for three experiments in decentralization which were approved by the Board of Education. One of the districts was Ocean Hill-Brownsville.[12]

The sentiment in favor of decentralization at this time was high. The state legislature wanted it, the mayor was highly in favor, and Albert Shanker, president of the United Federation of Teachers, approved. Mayor Lindsay said the schools were failing to educate. Parent teacher associations across New York complained of the lethargy at 110 Livingston Street, headquarters of the Central Board of Education facilities, and were demanding more flexible teaching methods and a modernization of archaic rules and procedures.[13]

Albert Shanker, speaking for the teachers, said decentralization was not a panacea and was educationally irrelevant, but teachers favored decentralization. They favored it because of the need for a large organization to delegate authority and because they believed in democratic participation.[14] Widespread approval by educators backed these propositions and the black community urged immediate action. The difficulties arose in the ensuing clash of interests.

Soon the New York Board was at odds with the elected boards in the three demonstation districts. The local boards demanded full authority, including power to hire and dismiss school personnel, to determine educational policy, and maintain control over school expenditures. The Central Board replied that it could not legally delegate this authority. In the spring of 1968 the Ocean Hill-Brownsville governing board tried to transfer unwanted union teachers; instead they set in motion the chain of events that was to lead to the serious and prolonged teacher strikes in the fall of 1968.[15]

A compromise plan was mandated by the state legislature in April 1969. The act replaced the New York school board appointed by the mayor with an interim board to be appointed by the presidents of the five boroughs. This board, in turn, was replaced in mid-1970 by one composed of two mayoral appointees and one elected representative of each borough. The bill also provided for the establishment of 30 to 33 "community school" districts in the city, each with no fewer than 20,000 pupils; it ensured that nearly all control would remain with the central board.

Thus a bitter conflict was accommodated. In effect, the teachers won the strike, but a thoroughly decentralized structure was not achieved. Leadership was required to mediate between the bitterly opposed factions. Civil rights leaders like Kenneth Clark, Roy Wilkins, and Whitney Young helped in relating black community interests to the teachers in a common search for an acceptable decentralization plan. Bayard Rustin, Executive Director of the A. Philip Randolph Institute, played a key role in bringing together Central Labor Council President Harry Van Arsdale, UFT President Albert Shanker, a group of black trade unionists, and other prominent members of the New York labor establishment. It was said that Bayard Rustin was just about the only man in New York who could call such a meeting and get it. Whitney Young said, "We all felt it important for Bayard to work on Shanker."[16]

A delegation headed by Van Arsdale and including Rustin then met with the UFT negotiating committee "to express the labor movement's concern about (black-white) polarization." Rustin spoke both of his support of the UFT's fight for teachers rights and of the growing hatred within the black community for the union. He made a strong plea for a reconciliation between black parents and unionized teachers. As a result Rustin has been credited with helping to bring about a nonpunitive settlement of the teachers strike. Said Shanker, "Bayard did help moderate the situation because we were aware of how he put his head upon the block."[17] Many other leaders spoke out against the polarization of the community and the growing antisemitic, antiwhite prejudice that emerged during the controversy. Meanwhile the other cities of Megalopolis watched and struggled with their own problems of school decentralization.

Philadelphia has experienced the same movement toward community control of the schools. In 1969 at least 13 full-blown "experiments in community control" were going on, some with the formal approval of the Board of Education, headed by Richardson Dilworth, the popular former mayor. Racial polarization has tended to develop with whites opposed and blacks in favor. The Board of Education appointed a decentralization commission to recommend guidelines, policies, and rules to direct the energy of the grass-roots movement for community control. The groups opposed to community control are the following:

The Philadelphia Federation of Teachers. The union is strongly opposed to local boards hiring and firing their own teachers and will fight formal evaluation of teachers by citizen groups. Frank Sullivan, president of the teachers' union, has said that the Philadelphia schools will be struck the day after the first teacher is "fired" by the first local "decentralized" board.[18]

The Philadelphia Principals Association is opposed to the selection, evaluation, or firing of principals by local citizens. Under community control principals fear, as do the teachers, that they will lose all authority and be subjected to harassment.

The Philadelphia Home and School Council is opposed because it fears that community control will weaken the quality of the schools and reject the community groups that compete for a spokesman's role.

Numerous citizens fear that dedicated militant community groups, once firmly entrenched, will reject any guidelines not considered to be in their best interests. Others fear that community control of the schools will be just the first step toward more direct community control of many governmental services and agencies.

Thus Philadelphia, like New York, grapples with the decentralization issue. The interested parties are almost identical. Philadelphia, however, has an "experiment" that is approaching decentralization differently and is being closely watched. A 21-member citizen committee was appointed to plan a school that opened in February 1970 in the mixed section of Germantown. The legislature announced that the principal of the school would be subject to annual review by the community board and that he alone would be responsible for hiring and evaluating teachers. This approach to decentralization contrasts with New York's Ocean Hill-Brownsville "experiment," in which Federal Judge Anthony J. Travia ruled that the community board was no more than "an unofficial body of citizen advisors" without power to transfer or dismiss teachers and supervisors.[19]

In Washington District School Superintendent William R. Manning calls for decentralization of Washington schools in "an equal partnership between educators and the community." He asserts that a centralized school system "with professionals solving the problems, is the old way, precooked in the administrative kitchens of the establishment."[20] The Congress has sought to develop greater participation of the District of Columbia community in local education by passing a law calling for a 10-member elected school board to replace a nine-member board appointed by District Court judges. Heralding broader community influence on school operations the new board took office on January 27, 1969. The city has been operating a decentralized program at an elementary school in the Adams Morgan district, a neighborhood of poor and middle-income blacks. The local governing board and the teaching staff, after much early bickering, reached mutual agreement on how the school should be operated. The central board has granted the 15-member community board substantial new powers and has prepared the way for expanding decentralization to 10 schools in Anacostia, one of the poorest sections of the city.[21]

Among all the cities of Megalopolis Washington may have the best opportunity to make decentralization work. More than 90 percent of the students and 80 percent of the teachers in the District of Columbia are black. There is almost no white blue-collar class and none of the white minority groups that in other cities fear black control of the schools. Thus racial tensions have not been a factor in the beginning of decentralization.

All the major cities of Megalopolis have felt the pressures of decentralization and the proponents have the ideals of grass-roots democratic participation on their side. Even trained professionals like Superintendent Mark Shedd of Philadelphia and Superintendent William Manning of Washington give it top priority in their personal philosophy and programming. The incipient polarization of black and white and the contest between professionalism and lay control are deep-seated. This is an issue of high saliency not only because it affects education but because it strikes at all public services of poor quality beyond citizen control. Closely related as an issue of widespread repercussions is the structuring of representation and control in any organization, whether centralized or decentralized.

ISSUE: Agency-Directed   Coalition-Directed
         Policy Formulation   Versus   Policy Formulation
         and Administration   and Administration

This issue involves a release of authority and control from a centralized body. It goes deeper than mere decentralization because it is organic populism in action. Coalition-directed policy formulation and administration is most commonly called "citizen participation." It grew into prominence with the urban crisis, but the ideological content of agency-directed versus coalition-directed organizations has been known for a long time and often debated. The counterpositions may be stated as follows:

The agency-directed organization claims that its executive board and officials are professional- and business-oriented and can provide better service at lower costs.

The coalition-directed organization claims it can represent the needs of a community more effectively and mobilize political power and resource by securing consensus of the factions or interests.

Agency-directed organizations claim a continuity of program and point to the instability and conflict of coalition-directed organizations.

Agency directed organizations are said to have lost touch with their clients and are unable to marshal the consensus needed to initiate and implement programs.

Private welfare agencies and community hospitals are often pointed to as models of efficiency and service.

Urban coalitions are models of city-wide representation; Boards of Community Action and Model Cities Programs and new models of neighborhood and community representation.

The roots of coalition-directed organizations can be found in such sources as the community chest movement, the Council of Social Agencies, community development councils, the New Town movement, and most conspicuously in the community action programs developed in 1964 by the Office of Economic Opportunity and the Model Cities program initiated in 1968 by the Department of Housing and Urban Development.[22] The formation of the National Urban Coalition in 1967 provided a dramatic capstone for the idea that important segments of the society must be welded together to achieve significant national action. Under its umbrella are leaders from five major segments of American society: business, labor, religion, racial minorities, and local government. John W. Gardner who became the first full-time chairman in March 1968 helped to create coalitions in most of the major cities of America. These organizations form themselves as they see fit. In Minneapolis the Urban Coalition is broadly based. Initially it was heavily business-sponsored, but in the search for a platform to connect the various power structures in the community labor, the church, and political and minority group representatives were invited. More than half the 60-man board is representative of various minority organizations. Stephen F. Keating president of Honeywell, Inc., and first president of the Minneapolis Urban Coalition said, "We threw open the doors and said, 'If you think you are leaders of some segment in Minneapolis that ought to be represented in this forum, come forward and we will put you on the board.' "[23] John Gardner has not been satisfied that national goals are being reached by the efforts of the urban coalitions and has taken the lead in organizing *Common Cause*, a mass coalition of interested citizens who number more than 200,000. The policy council is made up of 50 persons representated by the president of Americans for Indian Opportunity, the president of the National Council of Negro Women, and the president of the League of Women Voters in the United States. Six well-known key leaders on the board included in the Megalopolis study are Kenneth B. Clark, Andrew Heiskell, John V. Lindsay, James W. Rouse, Bayard Rustin, and John W. Gardner, chairman of Common Cause.

Two forces have combined to make cititzen participation a rapidly growing force in community and national planning. Federal legislation and, more telling, the demands of the citizens themselves have combined to make citizen participation an essential requirement in any urban project. Yet nothing in community planning to date has caused more contention. In city after city, program after program, citizen participation is the principal source of confusion and conflict.[24]

Walter Washington has defined citizen participation as essential to order in the streets. In a crisis-ridden city the streets are a new world, a hyped-up, frenetic, impatient, on-edge world. On the streets is the residue of decades of civic neglect. The once hopeful poverty program created unfulfilled expectations and left frustrations and bitterness. In 1967 and 1968 it was often said that a city was never more than 30 minutes from a riot. In such tenseness the problem of government is how to govern the streets. Table 6.2 is a representation of associations for maintaining order and improving human needs in cities. Note that they range from the established institutions to such newly emergent national, city, and community associations as the Urban Coalitions, National Alliance of Businessmen, and programs of the Office of Economic Opportunity and the Office of Housing and Urban Development. The streets are represented by those groups that organize, protest, and act. Many organizations are encouraging the development of neighborhood block associations. Others are organizing around local churches. The Community Actions Programs are aimed at community service.

TABLE 6.2 THE ESTABLISHED, EMERGENT, AND STREET ASSOCIATIONS FOR THE IMPROVEMENT OF HUMAN NEEDS IN THE CITY

Established institutions and associations	Emergent national and city-wide associations	The street
Established Institutions	National Associations	Leaders, gangs, and mass behavior
Business firms, government offices, unions, schools, churches, and welfare agencies	Urban coalitions National Alliance of Businessmen Office of Economic Opportunity Housing and Urban Development Small Business Administration	Organized Protest Group
		Black Panthers SNIC Unaffiliated groups
Established Associations	Emergent Community Oriented Associations	Organized Social Action Groups
Chamber of Commerce Labor union locals Local educational associations Federation of churches NAACP Urban League	Community action programs (CAP) Job Corps programs VISTA (Volunteers in Service to America) Pride	Neighborhood block associations Church parish groups Street academies

170

All these emergent activities are moving toward restructuring traditional forms. The establishment has been based on centralized authority and administration, agency-directed policy making, and programming for racial integration. Emergent institutions and community groups are experimenting with new forms of decentralized authority and administration, coalitional-directed policy making, and black autonomy and control in black communities.

Leaders must be prepared to play entirely new roles. Walter Washington explains his methods of governing the city of Washington in the following words:

> I put in a lot of time with a lot of people. That's the only way to bring them in. And what I try to do is try to involve all segments of the community.

> I do put some study to this, in an effort to bring people into a working format. These are efforts to bring segments of the community together in a concrete working relationship.[25]

Level of Issue-Relevant Activity of MEGA-Leaders

In order to get an estimate of the scope of their interests and activity each MEGA-leader was asked to specify the primary level of his activity in urban issues and problems. The 52 respondents of the issue questionnaire checked the level of their activity as follows:

Local	44%
State	6%
Interstate-regional	7%
National	14%
Activity at all levels	29%

A closer look at these figures shows that 44 percent of the activity is on the local level; 27 percent is definitely extralocal and 29 percent is on all levels. Local demands compel a high degree of activity among MEGA-leaders. Activity on this level joins leaders with others in Megalopolis because of the common character of the problems they confront in urban life. This is clearly shown in the similarity of ideological cleavages that create issues across the major cities. The out-of-community activity provides leaders with opportunities to approach other Megalopolis leaders, and their histories of acquaintance and contact with key and top leaders reaffirm this previously established network. It is interesting (and discouraging for a regionalist) to discover that only 7 percent of the reported activity is on an interstate or regional basis. Yet this fact is in conformity with the lack of regional consciousness and administrative machinery to grapple with problems at this level. What is most significant to this research is the fact that 27 percent of the activity is extralocal and 29 percent is pursued on all levels. Altogether, 56 percent of the problem activity is bringing regional leaders into joint participation.

Decision-Making Profiles of MEGA-Leaders:
The Training of a Decision-Making Process

Every research worker who has attempted to identify the roles of the influential in community decision making can testify that the task is long and difficult. There are such problems as naming the leaders who were most influential on both sides of an issue and the actions each took that were most effective in the outcome. There is then the problem of securing accurate information. Time will have elapsed and memories will have dimmed. Even the facts can be distorted by recall. If the researcher is disturbed by these difficulties in tracing an issue, he has but one alternative. He can employ a gatekeeper's method and try to secure an opportunity to observe the unfolding of a current issue and watch the key participants in action. This involves knowledge of and entry to decision-making arenas that may not be available to him. Even if successful, he will obtain data on only one issue which will limit the conclusions that he can draw.

Generally researchers elect to trace past decision making around a few crucial issues (3 to 5) and rely on interviews with the leaders who have been most active in the resolution of the selected issue within a relatively small community. With such data patterns of role behavior and decision-making processes are sought.

The problem faced in this research was even more demanding. It required the identification of leadership behavior and decision-making processes across a region, not just a single community. The region called Eastern Megalopolis has five giant cities, not small communities. In spite of the formidable obstacles the researcher determined to make the effort. It was reasoned that the venture would have to be made at a future date, and that knowledge of research techniques was also at stake.

The research design was focused on the use of an issue questionnaire as the principal tool, supplemented by selected interviews of top and key leaders. The selection of the MEGA-leaders previously described provided a wide sample of those believed to be most involved in issues across the region. The strategy developed in the questionnaire was based on a schema involving the following.[26]

1. Definition by the respondent of an urban problem and an issue on which he had been most active during the preceding three years.

2. Identification of top and key leaders of the region with which he had communicated on the problem or worked with on committees or projects during the

3. The goal of the leader—what he was trying to accomplish.
preceding three years.

4. Efforts to get things done. Specific activities including work with powerful organizations.

5. Nature of the opposition—leaders and groups involved and their activities.

6. Pattern of action taken by the leader.

7. Sources of power and influence considered most important for leaders who seek effectiveness in working on the problem illustrated by specific experiences.

8. Recommendations for assembling the strongest task force of influential top leaders and powerful organizations to deal with the problem.

The issue questionnaire was built on the research of the first leadership question-naire which identified the most powerful leaders and most powerful organizations that dealt with urban problems in the region. In asking the MEGA-leaders to make recommendations for the strongest task force to work on the urban problem on which the respondents were most active, a list of 200 key leaders and of the 36 most powerful organizations was attached. Each leader was asked to make his recommendations from this list or to add others that he deemed important. It was believed that an index of his knowledge and scope of regional leaders and organizations would thus be provided. If regional administration were a vital reality, then these task forces would have more than hypothetical significance. It was our purpose to find out if there were a need felt by key leaders to draw more than local personnel and resources into the struggle for improvement of urban problems.

Twelve interviews were held with key and top leaders across the region to explore in greater detail the reality of regional activity and some of the processes of decision making not covered in the questionnaire.

In the following sections five key leaders, one from each of the five major cities, represent typical profiles of decision making. Data are drawn from the issue questionnaire and a comparative view of the leaders is taken to illustrate impor-tant similarities and differences. This analysis is followed by a description of a pattern revealed by the total sample of MEGA-leaders. Both questionnaire and interview material are utilized to describe patterns of involvement, campaign strategies, and patterns of action that were followed.

Selected Case Studies of Decision-Making Profiles

KEY LEADER FROM BOSTON

A business leader from Boston reported that he has been most active in the hous-ing problem. The leaders he named as most influential and with whom he had been working included four in Boston whose contribution he described as follows:

ROBERT SLATER (business):	financial investment
JOHN F. COLLINS (Mayor, 1960-1968):	political muscle
KENNETH GUSCOTT (civic leader):	advice on minority problems
SALVATORE CAMILIO (labor leader):	keep labor unions quiet

The Boston respondent stated that he had been trying to increase the "stock of low- and middle-income housing" and that his efforts and those of others resulted in an increase of more than 3000 apartment units. Opposition had been expressed by "self-chosen minority group leaders." To be effective in working on the hous-ing problem it is most important to secure municipal and federal financing and a truce with ghetto militants. Work on this problem brought him face to face with the ideological issue of which revenue sharing is a part. He had been fighting for specific program grants to cities and believed that federal dollars should go to the states only if politically essential. He had been writing letters and serving on a committee to maintain this position. On his side of the issue he found Mayor

John Collins and "all the mayors" and the National League of Cities fighting the organizational battle. Opposition was defined as "mostly Republican and Rockefeller" (obviously Nelson).

For his strongest task force to work on housing on a regional basis he named the following key leaders:

Boston Leaders	New York Leaders
JOHN F. COLLINS (political)	NELSON R. ROCKEFELLER (political)
FRANK LICHT, Governor of	JACOB S. POTOFSKY (labor)
Rhode Island (political)	CHARLES F. LUCE (business)
	ANDREW HEISKELL (business)
Philadelphia Leaders	Baltimore Leader
JAMES H. J. TATE (political)	JAMES ROUSE (business)
REVEREND LEON SULLIVAN	
(religion)	

He chose the National Alliance of Businessmen and the American Bankers Association as the most powerful associations for backing the housing problem. It is clear that his choices included provision for support by business-oriented organizations.

KEY LEADER FROM NEW YORK

A civic leader who has been identified with the Federal Government during most of his life described urban development as the problem he had worked on most actively: "My main concern for eight years has been to develop a more viable and responsive program in housing and urban affairs." He named four leaders whom he believed have been most influential in major projects on which he has worked:

ELI GOLDSTONE (Boston business leader) "was a leader in a rehabilitation effort."

GILBERT FITZHUGH (New York business leader) "worked out a proposal for the creation of a billion-dollar insurance investment in ghetto housing and business."

ANDREW HEISKELL (New York business leader and publisher) "took leadership in ACTION and later in the Urban Coalition."

PAUL YLVISAKER (former Ford Foundation executive) "one of the most creative thinkers in urban affairs."

He indicated that his activities pulled him strongly into all the ideological cleavages described earlier. He specifically noted his stand on general revenue sharing.

I favor general revenue sharing with certain premises: that there be a specific pass through provision to protect cities; that it be specified that no cutback in vital local services and programs be permitted. Also I am opposed to so-called special revenue sharing, believing that it fails to recognize that special revenue sharing and categorical grants provide different types of problems.

The conflict over revenue sharing is "primarily in the political arena." Organizations that are considering general revenue sharing are the Committee on Economic Development and the National Academy of Public Administrations. Opposition to general revenue sharing and support of categorical grants to cities include NAACP and AFL-CIO.

This veteran leader has one of the highest MEGA-scores and from his federal position developed an extensive acquaintance and working contacts with key leaders of Megalopolis. He named the following key leaders and organizations as his strongest task force to deal with the housing problem:

New York Leaders	Philadelphia Leaders
THOMAS J. WATSON, JR. (business)	R. STEWART RAUCH (business)
ANDREW HEISKELL (business)	REVEREND LEON SULLIVAN
DAVID ROCKEFELLER (business)	(religious)
PAUL N. YLVISAKER (political and	WILLIAM L. RAFSKY (civic)
civic: New Jersey Commissioner	
of Community Affairs)	
BAYARD RUSTIN (civic)	

Baltimore Leader

JAMES ROUSE (business)

The most powerful organizations chosen were the National Association for the Advancement of Colored People, the Committee for Economic Development, the U.S. Department of Health, Education and Welfare, the U.S. Conferences of Mayors, the U.S. Department of Housing and Urban Development, the American Institute of Planners, and, his own addition, the National Association of Housebuilders.

It is interesting to compare the leader from Boston with the leader from New York. Each was concerned with housing but the Boston leader brought a businessman's perspective and the New York leader, the view of a longtime Federal Government official. In spite of some significant differences, note the overlap in their leader choices: three leaders were named on both lists: Heiskell, Sullivan, and Rouse. Each named three or more business leaders. The Boston leader was more concerned with a coalition of representation but relied heavily on business organization; the New York leader neglected labor and paid little attention to political leaders but gave high importance to U. S. government departments and to a wide variety of minority, research, planning, and housing organizations.

KEY LEADER FROM PHILADELPHIA

A veteran labor leader from Philadelphia described his urban problem activity as that "of helping to establish a viable system of public education; find answers to the problem of crime; and attempt approaches to improving racial attitudes." He litsed four leaders who have been most influential in his contacts:

RICHARDSON DILWORTH (political and civic leader) "has been able to arouse public opinion."

JAMES H. J. TATE (mayor) "has been able to contribute political know-how."

EDWARD F. TOOLEY (labor leader) "has been able to deliver labor support."

JOHN R. BUNTING (business leader) "has been influential with bankers and businessmen in working for the community."

He cited the ideological cleavage of centralization versus decentralization as producing the most controversial issue in which he had been involved. The union movement supported the Philadelphia Federation of Teachers in their fight against community control of the schools, about which the labor respondent said: "Decentralization would emphasize local political control rather than educational improvement. It would lessen central responsibiltiy for education and would increase costs at the time when the school system has serious deficits." He cited Mayor James H. J. Tate and political leader Paul D'Ortona as being on this side of the issue, but that opposition leaders Richardson Dilworth, Elizabeth Greenfield (Mrs. Albert M. Greenfield, civic leader) and Herman Wrice (civic leader) favored decentralization. In naming organizations backing decentralization he cited the National Urban League, the NAACP, and the Philadelphia Urban Coalition.

This issue, as described earlier, tends to divide the community into various interest groups: whites versus blacks; middle and upper classes versus working class; central city versus suburbs; liberals versus conservatives; teachers versus parent groups and sometimes school administrators; and well-meaning citizens versus other well-meaning citizens. In New York City it confronted the Jewish community (a high proportion of teachers are Jewish) with the black community (a high proportion of the pupils are black).

The labor leader from Philadelphia spoke of the difficulties and pointed out the slowness of change.

One example was the refusal of black school principals to join the Principals Organization which they claimed was white controlled. It took a long time (about a year) to get down to fundamental attitudes and blunt expression of mistrust, plus changes in organizational structure, to achieve unity.

When asked to name his most influential regional task force to work on the public school problem he gave the following:

Philadelphia Leaders

JOHN R. BUNTING (business)
GUSTAVE G. AMSTERDAM
  (business)
EDWARD F. TOOKEY (labor)
RICHARDSON DILWORTH (political
  and civic)
JAMES H. J. TATE (mayor)
PAUL D'ORTONA (political)
WILLIAM L. RAFSKY (civic)
CLARENCE FARMER (civic)
RAYMOND P. ALEXANDER (civic)

New York Leaders

HARRY VAN ARSDALE, JR. (labor)
ALBERT SHANKER (labor)
BAYARD RUSTIN (civic)

Washington Leader

GEORGE MEANY (labor)

He would summon the organizational support of the AFL-CIO, the National Educational Association, and the National Council of Churches.

The perspective of this leader is largely local and most labor leaders in the major cities have indicated that their civic participation is primarily local in character. The labor leader is drawn and held to local participation by the insistent demands of his labor-member constituents who elect and re-elect him only as he demonstrates visible results in his own commuunity.

KEY LEADER FROM BALTIMORE

A black religious leader reported that race relations and education have been the problem that have concerned him most. He has worked for a higher level of concern for peoples' problems by directly seeking a better welfare program and quality education for inner-city students. The leaders he named as those with whom he has worked and who he believes are most influential included the following:

> PARREN MITCHELL (civic) "has moved Baltimore into national prominence by his national activity and competence on all human issues."
>
> HOMER FAVOR (civic) "developed a new urban relations program at Morgan State University—creates a continuing ferment on urban problems."
>
> LAURENCE, CARDINAL SHEHAN (religious) "established with others an interfaith clergy board working together as religious institutions facing the urban crisis."
>
> JAMES ROUSE (business) "has developed a process for halting urban deterioration in Hartford, Connecticut, and contemplating a similar process for Baltimore. Developer of new town, Columbia, Maryland."

His activities have involved him in school lunch programs, a state coalition for a grant to raise the level of welfare in Baltimore, and the fight to use public funds for private education. He reported that these and other activities have taken him to the center of all four major ideological cleavages. He illustrated his fight to maintain strong support of the central city.

> Cities are being prepared for absentee ownership. Whites have moved to suburbia and are attempting to move the power of decision making with them so as to effectively continue control of the inner city.

He also said that he had raised the issue publicly, called for the establishment of metropolitan or regional government, and insisted that the strength of the central city be maintained in such issues as the home of "Baltimore Colts," location of an airport, and control of schools. Leaders and organizations on his side of the issues included Homer Favor, Parren Mitchell, and James Rouse and the Baltimore Urban Coalition, Morgan State University, and U. S. congressmen from Baltimore.

Opposition was attributed to Walter Sondheim, Jr. (business), among the key leaders of this study, and to such organizations as the Greater Baltimore Committee, the Ministerial Alliance, and the Masonic Order.

The strongest regional task force recommendation for this city versus suburb cleavage included the following:

Baltimore Leaders	Washington Leaders
JAMES ROUSE (business)	REVEREND CHANNING PHILLIPS
LAURENCE, CARDINAL SHEHAN	(religious)
(religious)	JOHN W. GARDNER (civic)
PARREN MITCHELL (civic)	
HOMER FAVOR (civic)	

Philadelphia Leader

REVEREND LEON SULLIVAN
(religious)

Organizations

National Association for the Advancement of Colored People
National Urban League
Ford Foundation
Congress on Racial Equality

This leader presents a different kind of cleavage in which the interests of the blacks are strongly felt. The perspective of a black leader and a religious leader is well illustrated. Names like James Rouse and the Reverend Leon Sullivan continue to reappear as nominees to the strongest task forces.

KEY LEADER FROM WASHINGTON

An outstanding black leader who represents both political and religious positions describes himself as most active on housing and his goals as

> production and rehabilitation of housing; housing advocacy for low-income families; and changes in FHA administration and housing legislation.

He cites the four most influential leaders with whom he has worked:

> WHITNEY YOUNG (civic) "provides leverage of natural stature where needed."

> McGEORGE BUNDY (civic) "grants resources where critical."

> WALTER WASHINGTON (political) "uses flexibility of government where justified and needed."

> GILBERT HAHN (political) "stands off pressure against the Mayor."

With the help of these leaders he brought about the building of 1800 dwelling units "or in pipeline" and produced changes in FHA administration that allowed for new flexibility in dealing with low-cost housing. These accomplishments have been made against opposition that included zoning opponents, FHA resistance, resistance of private finance to the high risks involved, and industry resistance to the nonprofit role of public housing. This leader's activity, like all of the other profiles described, has brought him into direct confrontation with the major ideological cleavages that generate most of the issues. He illustrates community participation and control as that in which he has become most deeply involved and has spoken and lobbied "for a decentralized form of municipal government that would institutionalize community control."

His strongest regional task force for housing included the following:

Washington Leaders

THORNTON W. OWEN (business)
JOSEPH D. KEENAN (labor)
GEORGE MEANY (labor)
SAMUEL JACKSON (political)
STERLING TUCKER (civic)

Baltimore Leader

JAMES ROUSE (business)

Philadelphia Leader

REVEREND LEON SULLIVAN
   (religious)

New York Leaders

DAVID ROCKEFELLER (business)
LUCIUS WALKER (religious)
McGEORGE BUNDY (civic)

Organizations

National Association for the Advancement of Colored People

National Urban League
Ford Foundation
U.S. Department of Housing and Urban Development
U.S. Office of Economic Opportunity

This repeated naming of Leon Sullivan, James Rouse, and David Rockefeller appeared in the recommendations of the three selected key leaders who reported housing as their area of greatest concern. Agreements on powerful organizations were reached as two of the three named the NAACP and the U.S. Department of Housing and Urban Development.

A Summary Review of the Five Leader Profiles

As all the selected leader profiles are examined a number of conclusions can be drawn. First, these leaders have almost uniformly been involved in all the major ideological cleavages, fighting for or against the issues. In a maximum of 20 (5 leaders $\times$ 4 major cleavages) involvements they said they were in the midst of 17. Only one reported that he had not encountered the community control and participation conflict and another said he had not been involved in metropolitan area government or revenue sharing.

Second, they named men with whom they have worked and those they would recommend for regional task forces from the list of key leaders identified in our initial study. In each case space was added in the decision-making inventory to encourage the additional names of any leaders they might elect to give. Only in a few cases were other names offered. This provides some evidence of the validation of the initial list.

Third, reliance on a wide variety of leaders was shown by their choices of leaders who have been most influential in the issues with which they have worked and in their regional task force recommend actions. Among the leaders they chose (62 in all) 27 percent were from business, 26 percent from civil affairs, 21 percent from politics and government, and 13 percent each from labor and religion. In all cases leaders were selected from at least three major cities to put together the strongest task forces.

Collective Patterns of Decision Making by MEGA-Leaders

INVOLVEMENT OF MEGA-LEADERS

The two dominant role patterns of leaders, *shakers* and *movers,* are vital in social change, whether it proceeds on local, state, interstate, or national levels. Shakers achieve by agitating and exciting for change, presenting ideas, and articulating goals. The movers work through well-defined power blocks, organizations, and friendship constellations. Shakers often serve as the goad or the civic conscience of the doers; the movers provide the will and the might to get things done. The shakers often get tagged as radicals and as not quite respectable. The movers, who play a more conservative role, validate the ideas of the shakers as sound and practical.

If social change is to occur, shakers and movers must work together. When they do, each group is content with its role in the power structure and each respects the other. They are mutually sustaining and interact to a point at which it is sometimes difficult to distinguish between them. Some leaders combine the two roles.

Among the regional board nominees who constitute a part of the MEGA-leader sample, "shakers" included John Lindsay, John K. Galbraith, Richardson Dilworth, Joseph Clark, Whitney Young, and Bayard Rustin. "Movers" included David Rockefeller, James Rouse, Cardinal Cooke, Robert Weaver, and Milton Eisenhower. Dual parts were taken by George Meany, Nelson Rockefeller, Walter Washington, Leon Sullivan, and McGeorge Bundy.

MEGA-leaders were asked the following question:

> What sources of power and influence do you consider most important for leaders who seek to be effective in working on the problem you have indicated?

The answers were various but most stressed personal attributes and bases of power. One leader asserted:

> . . . a man must be sufficiently secure in his own business or profession that he can take a stand on a controversial issue without worrying about the negative reactions from the organization in which he works or from clients. He must have money or access to money in order to move projects. Above all, he must be willing to commit his time and efforts. And he must be "hard." He cannot allow himself to be shouted down or shut up because of fear. Leaders get where they are because they have thick skins. This is why they get things done.

Another summarized his answer as "knowledge, political know-how, thick skin, energy, and administrative ability." Also stressed were "political influence and "financial contacts and resources"; "broad citizen support which can be translated into real political terms"; "national contacts and influence to ward off the 'hatchet' "; "control of the press"; "use of radio and TV"; and "good relations with government and nongovernment agencies."

Leaders who have been interviewed agree that the most important resource is men of business who are not content to work only "in" the city but "for" the city. One top leader said, "This civic work is like anything else. You can't sit around and wait for someone else to do it. There comes a time, too, when you either fight it out or quit."

A Philadelphia banker explained that involvement is a crescive process:

> You are asked to help on some specific problem because those concerned feel you have some special knowledge or ability that will help to put a project over. Then, you become involved in something else almost before you know it. Pretty soon you are up to your neck in civic activity."

Another businessman protects himself from the mounting requests for civic participation by turning down such invitations "unless I feel it's of real importance to the city and I can give it time. I don't become involved in things unless it looks like they will go somewhere in the next two to three years and achieve worthwhile results."

The Path to MEGA-Leadership

MEGA-leaders reach their positions by working their way upward, but there is no well-defined route. Generally, young executives go into the civic field with the idea of proving themselves more valuable to their employers. They find that the "heads" are involved or believe that their organization has an obligation to try to get things done in the community. One MEGA-leader tells his young executives that

> it is good business as well as good citizenship to work on civic projects. It keeps us in touch with the people and what they are doing. You will find that all of our top people are required to take leadership in some kind of social service. After all, what kind of a city would we have if everyone just did their day's work and then went home.

The aspiring young executive gets the message and begins with work in a service club, the chamber of commerce, the community chest, or a charity. Nothing too controversial.

Later, after "moving through the chairs" (offices) he may make the boards of lesser civic agencies. After 25 to 30 years he may join the civic elite that sits on the boards of top influence, provided he has what it takes to achieve a major position both in work and civic life.

This path to the top is repeated with variations by all leaders who achieve MEGA-leadership. Although there is no marked career progression, the strata within the power structure for progression to top leadership are well defined by informal norms of the community. What has not been so well known is how leaders achieve a regional position. It is understood that they must secure visibility and channels of participation and communication if they are to arrive at MEGA-leadership. This process was explained in Chapter 5 in which career patterns of regional nominees were presented as the Top of the Top, and they do represent the end-product of the most successful civic climbing to regional and national prominence.

Strategies in Issue Resolution

MEGA-leaders were asked a number of questions:

> What did you do to get things done?
> What was the nature of the opposition you encountered?
> What did you do to counteract this oppostion?

What have you accomplished?

How would you rate your accomplishments?

What was the pattern of action—the important events that influenced the outcome of your efforts?

Their answers reflect great variation, but some collective patterns can be discerned. In the mobilization of influence all leaders appreciate the importance of
"doing things that get people talking." It is essential to develop a climate in
which public opinion can be formed. A controversial issue will attract the newspapers. They will not print any matter in which they think readers are not interested, but if the issue develops a newsworthy climate they will cover the story.

Reaching out through radio and TV is important. Joseph Clark became known
to thousands for the first time by answering citizen complaints on television.
Later, he set up a complaint bureau. Many leaders have found that they begin to
get their messages on the grapevine by appointing blacks, women, or young
leaders to office.

Getting key leaders interested is crucial. Both "shakers" and "movers" are
needed. One Boston leader who was trying to get community action on unemployment and poverty tells of involving Whitney Young for "shaking up" the
establishment, Tom Atkins for local political organization, Sterling Tucker for
fund raising, and Kenneth Clark for shaping the problem and strategy to deal
with it.

When asked about patterns of action, direct contact with key government and
civic leaders emerged as most important. Table 6.3 shows that many different
efforts are enlisted. The activity is ordered by its degree. Note that contacts with
key government, civic, business, and labor) leaders rank highest, followed by
working with organizations, testifying before special committees or public hearings, raising money, communicating with religious leaders, organizing mass citizen support, and lobbying at state or federal levels.

It is of special interest to this research to examine closely the role of powerful
organizations. The MEGA-leaders have indicated (with 54% frequency) that they

TABLE 6.3 ACTIVITY PATTERNS OF MEGA-LEADERS IN PROJECT AND
ISSUE RESOLUTION

Frequency of mention (%)	Activity
83	Direct contact with key government leaders
75	Direct contact with key civic and civil rights leaders
57	Direct contact with key business leaders
56	Direct contact with key labor leaders
54	Working through organizations
44	Testifying before special committees or public hearings
33	Direct contact with key religious leaders
30	Organizing mass citizen support (radio, TV, telephone, newspapers, etc.)
29	Lobbying at state or federal levels

work with organizations. One question they were asked was: "If you worked with organizations, please check the attached list and note briefly their contribution." Table 6.4 is an ordered ranking of the frequency of mention for the top 12 organizations. The full list included 36 of the most powerful urban-oriented organizations identified by our research team.[27]

TABLE 6.4   TOP 12 URBAN-ORIENTED ORGANIZATIONS USED MOST OFTEN BY MEGA-LEADERS IN PROJECT AND ISSUE RESOLUTION

Frequency of mention (%)	Powerful urban-oriented organizations
42	National Association for the Advancement of Colored People
42	National Urban League
34	U.S. Department of Housing and Urban Development
33	U.S. Department of Health, Education and Welfare
33	U.S. Conference of Mayors
31	Ford Foundation
25	AFL-CIO
24	National Council of Churches
20	U.S. Office of Economic Opportunity
17	National Education Association
17	League of Women Voters
15	Congress of Racial Equality

What is immediately apparent from Table 6.4 is the role of the two largest organizations that represent black people and the importance of the two large departments of the Federal Government that provide support for housing, urban development, health, education, and welfare. When asked to discuss the value of these organizations, MEGA-leaders most commonly said that they turned to NAACP and the National Urban League because they exercised national leverage and political influence on such programs as housing and welfare. Others worked with these organizations to make contact with the black ghetto. Federal departments, including the U.S. Office of Economic Opportunity, were most often mentioned as the principal cources of funding. The Ford Foundation was also cited as the principal source of private funds, especially for special projects.

Both the U.S. Conference of Mayors and AFL-CIO were called on for their "political muscle." The remaining organizations on the list provided many different services. Mention was made of their "advocacy" roles by which they focused attention and political influence through research studies, conferences, lobbying, and testifying at public hearings.

The role of organizations can be summarized as threefold: sources of funds, origin of information and access to problem areas and leaders, and political influence. They provide useful and often clinical functions, but they are no substitute for direct contact with key leaders who are in immediate touch with the on-going process of issue conflict and resolution. The nature of the opposition and its counteractance make this very clear.

Opposition and Counteractance

When asked about the opposition they encountered, MEGA-leaders rather surprisingly tended to mention diffuse obstacles rather than specific groups or persons. Answers ranged from *apathy, city inaction, unwillingness to pay the price, and giving up privileged positions to real estate resistance, uptight middle-class resistance to racial integration, resistance of the suburbs,* and finally more definite targets such as the *right-wing Maryland lobby, F.H.A. resistance to liberalized funding of low-cost housing, and opposition by the Chamber of Commerce to Nixon's welfare reform proposals.*

Since many urban problems in housing, education, unemployment and welfare, crime, urban renewal, and even freeways all involve the black community so directly, most leaders have had to face "antiwhite" and "antiblack" opposition. Sometimes, it occurred simultaneously, and the activist was squeezed between the jaws of a vise. Many complain bitterly and often with pathos about the polarization of the races. Most leaders described specific attempts to deal with these problems; not many had a strategy. Those few leaders who reported their plans of attack had programs identified as Plans A, B, and C.

PLAN A

1. Try to identify leaders and isolate the problems.
2. Negotiate with them.
3. When negotiation fails, attempt behind-the-scenes pressure.
4. When all has failed, use media strength and organize citizen support.—(Outstanding black political and religious leader from Washington.)

PLAN B

1. Make personal contacts with people with power to affect decisions.
2. Organize large-group participation.
3. Collect names for petition and raise money.
4. Lobby at state level. Visit the Congressmen. (Civic leader from Baltimore.)

PLAN C

1. Study the problem and get the facts.
2. Educate and alert the public. Make speeches.
3. Mobilize public support for specific issues.
4. Put pressure on the pressure points: officials, administrative agencies, and civic leaders to press for favorable legislation, administrative policies and processes in government agencies, in business firms, among landlords, banks, etc. (Civic leader from New York.)

There are more similarities than differences in these three plans. All recognize the critical importance of key leaders and public support and putting on pressure where it counts. Other leaders describe their efforts to educate the participants. One leader said he dealt with opposition by appealing to the common interest people must think about when making compromises. Another speaks of the importance of presenting both sides of the issue in any attempt to educate. Still another leader reached the height of brevity with one word of advice: PERSISTENCE.

Admittedly, this sample of MEGA-leaders includes few, if any, militants. None has advocated violence. Some have strongly urged putting on the pressure and a few have described how they have used court suits to advantage. In one case an illegal referendum petition was removed from the ballot.

Accomplishment and Civic Satisfaction

Leaders were asked to rate their accomplishments in getting results. They replied: very effective, 8 percent; effective, 58 percent; somewhat, 34 percent; not effective at all, 0 percent. These results indicate that leaders feel they have made progress in their civic aspirations. However, when asked what they have accomplished, their answers were vague. One leader simply wrote, "? ? ." One leader said, "not much." Another said: "hard to say at the moment; will know in 10 years." One leader replied, "not nearly enough. Even when the parties were willing to cooperate it was slow motion." Some working in housing said, "2000 new low-cost housing units"; "3000 new low-cost housing units." A few said: "secured job placement and training programs," "a new expressway started," "integrated school system," "new environmental control legislation." The general conclusion is that top leaders are prepared to accept limited progress as a basis of sufficient civic satisfaction for their efforts. Nowhere does one find great expectations and certainly no great display of results. The general feeling is that this game is an uphill battle. No one who expects too much should play.

Rebuilding a City—Philadelphia: MEGA-Leaders in Joint Local Action

Leadership processes are best studied when leaders are engaged in joint efforts to "put over civic projects" or to "fight through crucial issues" that have large consequences for the community. The twentieth century has made the local community a natural center of action. Philadelphia like so many of the major cities has faced a major rebuilding effort—one that has required massive physical changes and extensive social rehabilitation. It is unique in that a fairly stable group of influential business and professional men form an "in-group" of interlocking directorates in which the same time-pressed men serve a number of causes. Many of the MEGA-leaders who have strong regional ties have distinguished themselves in local projects. The organizing centers of the shakers and movers include the Greater Philadelphia Movement, Old Philadelphia Development Corporation, and the Philadelphia Chamber of Commerce.[28]

At present the business elite's influence is exercised mainly in the Greater Philadelphia Movement (GPM). This is a nonprofit corporation established in 1949 and dominated by lawyers and bankers, most of them "old family." GPM limits membership to 35. Some of the founders wanted to limit the group to 10 decision makers. They said that a larger group would become nothing more than a debating society. Some felt so strongly about this that they refused to become part of GPM when the decision was made to include a representative of labor and other "minority members." There is no recruitment problem. When a vacancy occurs, the members discuss the prospects and decide who will be asked to join.

GPM has been particularly active in planning and renewal. Key leaders in our sample are R. Stewart Rauch, Jr., President, Philadelphia Saving Fund Society, Richard C. Bond, President, John Wanamaker, Inc., Dr. Gaylord P. Harnell, President, University of Pennsylvania (at time of study), and Stuart T. Saunders, Chairman of the Board, Pennsylvania Railroad, all of whom are representative of the movers of GPM which has helped to establish the Food Distribution Center, a 388-acre wholesale market used by 141 food-related firms. Mayor Richard Dilworth financed the center with a multimillion dollar loan over the objections of the city council.[29]

Interlocked with GPM is the Old Philadelphia Development Corporation composed of more than 50 presidents and board chairmen of banks and major business and industrial corporations or partners in prestige law firms. The OPDC is rebuilding "Old City," which includes Society Hill and the Penn Central. Meanwhile 17 men of OPDC are also active in the West Philadelphia Corporation and the University City Science Center.[30] These rebuilding efforts are aimed at renewing a large part of the inner city and restoring residential, commercial, and scientific vigor that had almost been lost.

The Chamber of Commerce of Greater Philadelphia is more generally representative of business; at any rate, it is not dominated by the GPM elite. Still, the Chamber operates somewhat at a disadvantage. GPM is thought of as a "group of civic leaders" and the Chamber as a "pressure group." The Chamber has increasingly attracted a mover bloc and made itself into an effective agency. Leaders like Richard Bond and Gustave Amsterdam (chairman of the board of Bankers Securities Corporation) have played leading roles in the revitalization of the Chamber. One of its accomplishments is the Philadelphia Industrial Corporation, a quasi-public body provided with a revolving fund by the city government to enable it to prepare land for the encouragement of new industry.[31]

Leaders like Walter Phillips have played important shaker roles. Phillips, a ninth-generation Philadelphian and a product of Episcopal Academy, Princeton, and Harvard Law School, has been active as a city representative in Joseph Clark's administration, a director of the Delaware River Port Authority, and a leader in numerous civic enterprises. During World War II he encouraged the creation of the City Planning Commission and has supported its current director, Edmund N. Bacon. He gathered around him a little band of shakers who got the movers interested—men like banker Edward Hopkinson, Jr., and the late Dr. Thomas S. Gates, President of the University of Pennsylvania.[32]

Today MEGA-leaders like the Reverend Leon Sullivan are shaking the attention of the civic elite on minority unemployment and poverty problems. Board chairman Thomas B. McCabe of the Scott Paper Company is providing leadership on environmental problems, and new leaders are rapidly coming on the scene. There is an especially deep involvement in civic affairs on the part of the city's big law firms. Major Dilworth's is a good example. Its people serve on the Old Philadelphia Development Corporation, Greater Philadelphia Industrial Development Corporation, West Philadelphia Corporation, University City Science Center, Community Leadership Seminar Program, Citizen's Charter Committee, Citizens Budget Committee, and Citizens Education Campaign Committee.

Other law firms that can provide matching lists of civic agency involvements are Drinker, Biddle, and Reath; Morgan, Lewis, and Bocklus; Fox Rothchild, O'Brien, and Frankel; Ballard, Spahr, Andrews, and Ingersoll; Dechert, Price, and Rhoads; and Duane, Morris, and Hecksher. One lawyer who came to Philadelphia from New York was surprised to learn that he was expected to be active in community affairs.

> I thought at first that it was a lot of nonsense, but I realize now that it is the best way to meet people outside the law. And this, of course, is the way you get clients.[33]

If there is anything approaching a seed bed of civic leadership, it is probably the United Fund. Many of the top movers and shakers have gained their first experience in the United Fund setup. A divisional chairman may eventually be asked to head the big drive and direct an organization far larger than that for which he works.

There is room at the top on the Committee of Seventy, a civic agency with a record of civic reforms dating back to 1904 and for many years alone in its field; in the Greater Philadelphia Chamber of Commerce with its officers and prestigious committees; on the Board of the Diagnostic and Relocation Center; in top jobs on the United Fund drive; the Old Philadelphia Development Corporation, and, at the summit, GPM.

Philadelphia has never looked to one family or one industry for civic leadership; rather it depends on an admittedly small but also relatively diversified elite for its leadership. In New York, the corporate web is so large that business leaders often move away before they ever have a chance to become part of the leadership of that city's civic group. These corporate shifts are not so extensive in Philadelphia, and the relative fixedness of men in banking and the law explains why so many rise to the top of the civic power bloc.

What does a city gain or lose if civic leadership draws in around a fairly fixed set of leaders? Philadelphia has gained a sustained and concerned leadership that has produced results. It is especially important, for it has a big and powerful competitor only miles away. It loses to the extent that labor, religious, minority, and educational groups are blocked out. The Philadelphia Urban Coalition, Community Action Boards, and Model Cities Boards are opening up new channels of leadership.

What is significant for this research is the pattern of interaction developed by a community like Philadelphia. It is a base of local civic action from which certain leaders rise to regional and national leadership. How do local bases become springboards to wider visibility and opportunities for service? We have some answers, but the contact communication channel is not yet clear. In Chapter 10 we search experimentally with new techniques for the contact and clique structures and new clues to the wider scope of civic interaction. At this point, however, it is important that the organizational bases of power be introduced, for both leaders and organizations are crucial agents of political action.

Notes

1. Cf. Edward C. Banfield, *Big City Politics,* Random House, 1965, p. 5.

2. Eighty leaders were selected from the 178 key and top leaders who responded in the major sociometric study. The questionnaire sent to this population received a 68 percent return. This questionnaire is shown in Appendix A with a mailing history and report of returns.

3. The data about the four major issues themselves are derived from documentary sources.

4. *The New York Times,* September 15, 1968, p. 70.

5. "Commuters, Environmentalists, and Lobbyists Vie for Three Sisters," *Louisville Courier,* November 17, 1971.

6. "U.S. Approves Modified Designs for Two Freeways," *The New York Times,* January 18, 1969.

7. Message to the Legislature of the State of New York, January 6, 1971, p. 55.

8. Alan A. Altshuler, *Community Control,* Pegasus, New York, 1970, p. 14.

9. Big-city school officials from around the nation visited New York's school system in late 1968 to profit from the experience of decentralization. William R. Manning, Superintendent of Schools in Washington, called it "the most potentially explosive issue in education today." *The New York Times,* January 9, 1969, p. 67.

10. Rhody A. McCoy, Administrator, Ocean Hill-Brownsville School District, *The New York Times,* January 9, 1969, p. 67.

11. Leroy F. Aarons, "Ford Foundation Attacked in New York Strike," *The Washington Post,* November 15, 1968.

12. The other two included a district around Intermediate School 201 and its four "feeder" elementary schools and a district established in the Two Bridge area on the lower east side of Manhattan.

13. *The New York Times,* January 9, 1969, p. 76.

14. *Ibid.,* p. 76.

15. Maurice R. Berube and Marilyn Gittell, Eds., *Confrontation at Ocean Hill-Brownsville: The New York School Strike of 1968,* Praeger, New York, 1969. Cf. Martin Mayer, *The Teachers Strike, New York, 1968,* Harper and Row, 1969, pp. 111–122.

16. Thomas R. Brooks, "A Strategist Without a Movement," *The New York Times Magazine,* February 16, 1969, p. 24.

17. *Ibid.,* p. 25.

18. John P. Corr, "Are Schools Heading for Trouble as Decentralization Spreads?" *The Philadelphia Inquirer,* April 6, 1969, Section 7, p. 1.

19. Martin Gansberg, "Courts Playing a Major Role," *The New York Times,* January 9, 1969, p. 69.

20. Carl Bernstein, "School Decentralization Supported by Manning," *The Washington Post,* December 4, 1968.

21. David E. Rosebaum, "A Capital Success Story," *The New York Times,* January 9, 1969, p. 68.

22. Severyn T. Bruyn, *Communities in Action,* College and University Press, 1963, p. 5–22.

23. Transcript of a Workshop, *Tell It Like It Is.* Chamber of Commerce of the United States, Washington, D.C., 1968. p. v-4.

24. Edmund M. Burke, "Citizen Participation Strategies," *American Institute of Planning Journal* (September 1968), p. 287.

25. "Mayor's First Year is Hectic," *The Washington Post,* November 3, 1968, D-15.

26. A careful study of the Decision-Making Inventory of MEGA-Leaders in Appendix A and is recommended for interested readers. Note also the Mailing History and Report of Returns.

27. See Chapter 7 for a full discussion of the organizations and their identification.

28. John G. McCullough, "Philadelphia's Movers and Shakers." A series of articles that appeared in *The Evening and Sunday Bulletin*, June, 1965. (In many ways Philadelphia demonstrates similarities to Floyd Hunter's Business Monolithic pattern found in Atlanta. Author's note.)

29. Edward C. Banfield, *Big City Politics*, Random House, 1965, p. 116.

30. Richardson Dilworth is a member of the Old Philadelphia Development Corporation and a member of the board of the West Philadelphia Corporation and the University City Science Center.

31. E. C. Banfield, *ibid.*, p. 116.

32. John G. McCullough, *ibid.*, p. 12.

33. McCullough, *op. cit.*, p. 16.

CHAPTER SEVEN

The Identification
of the Most Powerful
Urban-Oriented
Organizations and
Their Linkage Patterns

Leaders and organizations were selected as the two elements of the influence structure we elected to study intensively, both in the general area of urban-oriented activities and in the more specific environmental quality area. We had decided at the very beginning that whatever we might find applicable or not applicable to the regional concept of Megalopolis we should search for the nature of urban-problem-oriented activity in the Boston-to-Washington area. Leaders and organizations operating in that area were to be given equal attention.[1]

In the following discussion the role of urban-oriented organizations, governmental and voluntary, are examined. Leaders may come and go, but organizations provide a relatively stable base of power and influence. Professional staffs maintain the organizational structure, transmit policies, and build programs. The staff members interact with one another in both private and governmental agencies. They know what is going on in Washington and New York, where things are happening on the political and economic front. Many staff members of private associations have close working and friendship ties with federal and state officials. Some are professional lobbyists. All staff members learn who the influentials are that affect their jobs and their organizations. These influentials are often board members, committee members, or simply members of such prominence, prestige, and influence that the staff must be aware of their ideas as they affect the association and its aims.

Four Research Requirements

The search now focuses on four specific goals:

1. To locate the most powerful urban-oriented organizations from Boston to Washington.

2. To ascertain their problem interests and priorities.

3. To assess their bases of power.
4. To determine their working relations with other organizations.

The research steps required to complete these goals included an assembly of the most powerful organizations, a reduction of the list to a manageable size, and a rating of the final list. Finally, an inventory of problem interests had to be made, bases of power determined, and an assessment of the concluded working relations of the most powerful organizations. Findings for each of these steps are described.

Locating Powerful Urban-Oriented Organizations and Assessing Their Working Relations

A list of more than 70 voluntary and public organizations was assembled by documentary and informant techniques.[2] This list was reduced to 37 governmental and private associations by the ranking of five knowledgeable judges who were thoroughly familiar with these organizations.[3] The plan was to ask a wide-ranging panel of organizational officials to rate the influence of each organization and to indicate the degree of working relations and coalition formation between his own and the other 36 organizations. Figure 7.1 shows the rating code on the left: (1) most influential; (2) influential; and (3) less influential. The organizational acquaintance and working relations scale which follows describes a continuum of organizational activity leading to issue coalitions. The steps were specified as (1) know about their work in the urban field; (2) have approached or have been approached for information about urban programs; (3) have exchanged ideas about urban programs; (4) have worked together on program development (does not imply agreement or support of the organization); (5) have supported one another on issues (please name issue). Note that the schedule included the final list of 37 organizations rated by the knowledgeables as most powerful.

The organizational ratings of influence and the assessment of working relations were secured by interviewing 25 qualified officials who served in various capacities in the listed organizations. All were in positions of special knowledge and visibility that qualified them for competence[4] and all were promised anonymity.

Many raters pointed out that although they felt they knew the activities of their organizations well they did not have complete knowledge. Many asked other staff members to join them in making assessments. A few assembled a full staff in order to get complete information. Indeed, two officials said that this gave them a new idea for staff training and began to plan a training program on the spot. It became clear that to have the highest validity each organization should be rated by staff members who were able to provide full knowledge of staff activity within the matrix of relations of the 37 organizations. The requirement grew as the size of the organization increased, but assembling staffs is an expensive, time-consuming demand, and seldom feasible for research purposes. This makes the selection of the organizational rater all the more important. He must be able to represent the total staff as much as possible.

Instructions to Rater (1) Regardless of the positions they take or how you feel about them, which of the organizations listed below would you rate as most powerful in initiating, supporting, or vetoing activities affecting urban problems and policies in the Boston to Washington area or the nation in general; (2) check appropriate level of working relationship of your organization with the other

Rating	Name of organization*	1	2	3	4	5
1 = most influential		Know about their work in urban field	Have approached or have been approached for information about urban programs	Have exchanged ideas about urban program	Have worked together on program development	Have supported one another on issues (Please name the ISSUE)
2 = influential						
3 = less influential						

Figure 7.1 Organizational acquaintance and working relationship scale. The 37 organizations are Urban America, National Association of Colored People, National Association of Manufacturers, Business Council, Committee for Economic Development, National Industrial Conference Board, National Educational Association, U.S. Department of Health, Education and Welfare, U.S. Small Business Administration, National Council of Churches, U.S. Conference of Mayors, National Alliance of Businessmen, National League of Cities, International Association of City Managers, Ford Foundation, AFL-CIO, National Research Council and National Academy of Science, American Bankers Association, American Medical Association, U.S. Department of Housing and Urban Development, U.S. Office of Economic Opportunity, Chamber of Commerce of the U.S., Council of State Governments, American Bar Association, National Association of Broadcasters, National Urban Coalition, League of Women Voters, American Institute of Planners, National Federation of Business and Professional Women's Clubs, National Business League, National Commission on Urban Problems, U.S. Department of Labor, U.S. Junior Chamber of Commerce, National Association of Counties, Congress on Racial Equality, National Congress of Parents and Teachers, and National Urban League.

The raters were generally directors of urban affairs, public relations, or legislation. The executive director or his principal assistant was often solicited in smaller organizations where specialized urban program directors were not available.

THE TOP 20 MOST POWERFUL URBAN-ORIENTED ORGANIZATIONS

The top 20 urban-oriented organizations were selected by expert raters who judged them as "the most powerful in initiating, supporting, or vetoing activities affecting urban problems and policies in the Boston-to-Washington area or the nation generally." The listing is by order of ranking and shows whether the organization is governmental (G) or private (P):[5]

(G)	(1)	U.S. Office of Housing and Urban Development
(P)	(2)	U.S. Conference of Mayors
(G)	(3)	U.S. Office of Economic Opportunity
(P)	(4)	National Urban League
(G)	(5)	U.S. Department of Health, Education, and Welfare
(P)	(6)	AFL-CIO
(P)	(7)	Ford Foundation
(G)	(8)	U.S. Department of Labor
(P)	(9)	National Association for the Advancement of Colored People
(P)	(10)	National Urban Coalition
(P)	(11)	National Alliance of Businessmen
(P)	(12)	National League of Cities
(P)	(13)	Chamber of Commerce of the United States
(P)	(14)	International Association of City Managers
(P)	(15)	National Association of Manufacturers
(P)	(16)	National Association of Counties
(P)	(17)	League of Women Voters
(P)	(18)	Congress on Racial Equality
(P)	(19)	Urban America
(P)	(20)	Council of State Governments

As shown later, the most powerful urban-oriented organizations demonstrate a complex of government agencies and associations with close working relations as efforts are made to alleviate urban problems. At the center there are the big four of government: Department of Housing and Urban Development, Office of Economic Opportunity, Department of Health, Education and Welfare, and the Department of Labor. These centers represent reservoirs of money, technical staff, and authority to act.

The voluntary associations that are most influential have the closest ties with these giants of government: the U.S. Conference of Mayors, National League of Cities, International Association of City Managers, National Association of Counties, and Council of State Governments. These organizations are staffed by members who have direct contact with the programs as they are planned and implemented in municipality, county, state, and nation.

The civil rights organizations, such as NAACP, National Urban League, and CORE, have new importance in the programs of the inner city (employment, housing, education, welfare, and crime) because of the heavy involvement of blacks. Business and labor have large stakes and respond through their associations.

Organizational Structure and Programming of the Top 20

The list of the 20 most powerful urban-oriented organizations represents the best selection of sources of information about important policies and programs in the urban area. Anyone seeking to inform himself or set up working relations within the urban problem area should try to learn all he can about the work of the top 20. Although many other organizations carry out innovative and supportive programming that deserves inclusion in any search for fuller knowledge, time is restrictive and the top 20 represent the best selection for a survey of activity. A *Handbook of Organizations,* which contains descriptions of the organizational structure and programs of these most powerful urban-oriented organizations, is a useful guide for the social-action leader.[6]

Most of these organizations have their national headquarters in Washington. Contacts planned in that city will maximize your efforts. Perhaps a talk with your senator or congressman would be more efficient, and some would urge discussion with legislative members on key committees. For special problems like transportation officials at the Department of Transportation would be most helpful. Many conservation programs are being developed in the Department of Agriculture and the Department of the Interior. The Department of Justice is the source of programs on crime prevention and control and juvenile delinquency. Information on drug problems is best secured by talking with Justice and the Narcotics Bureau (Treasury Department). Employment problems are shared by the Office of Economic Opportunity, Department of Labor, and Department of Commerce. The Executive offices of the White House can explain the manner in which new programs are developed and approved, and the Budget Bureau can provide information on how the monies are finally awarded to a program.

Organizational Determinations of Problem Priorities, Problem Interests, and Current Activity

This specification of problem interests was carried out by the same organization officials who served as raters of influence of the most powerful organizations. They were provided with an urban-problem check list and asked to carry out the following instructions:

1. Indicate the order of importance or urgency that your organization assigns to the following 11 urban problems that prevail in Megalopolis (Boston–New York–Philadelphia–Baltimore–Washington urban complex).
2. Check the problems in which your organization has highest personal interest.
3. Mark those on which your organization is currently working.

Urgency ranking	Most interest in	Currently working on		
			1.	Air pollution
			2.	Control of lawlessness and crime
			3.	Improvement of public education
			4.	Water pollution
			5.	Improvement of transport, traffic movement and parking
			6.	Waste (garbage, litter, and dumps)
			7.	Improvement or elimination of poor housing; rebuilding of cities
			8.	Improvement and maintenance of roads and streets
			9.	Planning and zoning of land; preservation (or improvement) of park and other natural areas
			10.	Unemployment and poverty
			11.	Race relations

The data on such a measure are difficult to collate because the respondents exhibit many different patterns. An official of the National Alliance of Businessmen may check unemployment and poverty in all three columns (urgency, most interest in, and currently working on) and then decline to check any others as outside the scope of his association. On the other hand, the official at the National League of Cities or the League of Women Voters may insist that he puts a high priority on almost all the problems and that in his organization comprehensive efforts are being made by interested and responsible staff members. Between these two extremes are those who do rank all problems from 1 to 11 in priority and specify the interest and working activities of their organizations. An examination of all the data indicates that the 11 problems fall into five distinct priority levels or categories. These priority levels exhibit the following gradations:

LEVEL 1. Unemployment and poverty.
LEVEL 2. Education, housing and urban renewal, race relations.
LEVEL 3. Crime
LEVEL 4. Air pollution, water pollution, land planning and preservation, transport, traffic and parking.
LEVEL 5. Solid wastes, roads and streets.

TABLE 7.1   PRIORITY LEVELS ASSIGNED BY ORGANIZATIONAL RATERS
FOR INTEREST AND URBAN PROBLEM ACTIVITY

Level	Priority	Frequencies for most interest in		Frequencies for currently working hardest on	
		N	%	N	%
1	Unemployment and poverty	17	68	14	56
2	Education	13	52	11	44
	Housing and urban renewal	15	60	13	52
	Race relations	10	40	11	44
3	Crime	9	36	10	40
4	Air pollution	8	32	9	36
	Water pollution	8	32	10	40
	Land planning and preservation	6	24	8	32
	Transport, traffic, and parking	8	32	9	36
5	Solid wastes	6	24	8	32
	Roads and streets	4	16	3	10

Table 7.1 shows the frequency of "most interest in" and "currently working on" as the 25 organizational raters reported for their urban-oriented organizations.

This table also shows that interest and work patterns relate closely to the priority levels. Especially important to the interests of the study is the ranking of air pollution, water pollution, and solid wastes. These problems are at the bottom (levels 4 and 5) in priority. It will be recalled that key and top leaders were provided (see Chapter 4) with identical check lists and that they showed a similar pattern of priorities. However, organizations are devoting more interest and activity to environmental quality problems than are the key and top urban-oriented leaders. This is especially true for governmental organizations.

Bases of Organizational Power

A few of the organizational officials who made ratings of the most powerful organizations were later asked to specify the bases of power for the top 20. Their instructions were to examine each organization and to check the *principal bases* on which its power rests. Ten types of power or influence were specified:

1. *Political influence* (based on position with political organizations, voting strength, resources, and contacts).

2. *Economic power* (based on assets and operating budget or contacts with wealthy persons or organizations).
3. *Governmental authority* (based on formal authority derived from its place in government).
4. *Representative pressure or collective action* (based on representation of a group or organization as a lobby or pressure instrument or ability to mobilize large numbers of persons for protest, strike, and picketing).
5. *Means of communication* (control or access to mass communication).
6. *Social prestige* (composition of its members and officers and its standing among organizations).
7. *Personal qualities of leadership within the organization* (well-liked or esteemed, organizational ability or charisma of leaders).
8. *Specialized knowledge or skill* (trained expertise).
9. *Moral and religious persuasion.*
10. *Military influence* (direct or by access).

The Profiles of Three Private Associations with Distinctive Variations

When raters had completed their checking of the schedule, power profiles were constructed. Figure 7.2 is an exhibit of three organizational power profiles for the *AFL-CIO*, the *League of Women Voters*, and *Urban America*. These three private organizations show some interesting variations. Note that the AFL-CIO has received maximum rating (10 rating frequencies) for its political influence and representative pressure. Other bases of lesser importance are shown as means of communication, specialized knowledge and skill, and personal qualities of leadership. All of these ratings are meaningful to a reader who is familiar with this organization. As the largest federation of labor unions in the United states it can bring to bear the political influence of a potential voting bloc of 30 to 50 million adult voters (counting approximately 15 million members and dependents). It has lobbyists, legislative and political directors, special organizations like COPE to raise funds, and an aggressive policy that puts direct pressure on members of the Congress during legislative and campaign battles. Its weekly newspaper (*AFL-CIO News*), magazines and pamphlets, public relations and radio programs, and newsworthy spokesmen all combine to give the organization a good means of communication that raters have recognized. Some have expressed their belief that the AFL-CIO has leaders and the specialized knowledge and skill on its staff to give it elements of power. The absence of ratings for such qualities as economic power and social prestige does not mean that they are lacking but only that raters do not consider them principal bases of power.

The *League of Women Voters* provides an interesting power profile for comparison. It, too, represents a large potential bloc of voters, but unfortunately for the organization only a small fraction of women voters are in the association. Still, those women who do belong are respected for their intelligence and their willingness to commit themselves to political action. They often become powerful spokesmen for all women. Therefore the political influence of their organization is high. Their commitment to political action by lobbying and participation in public hearings gives them a power base because of their ability to bring repre-

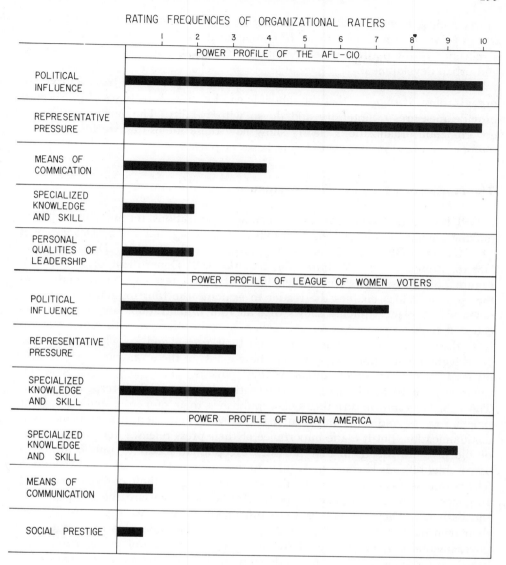

Figure 7.2   Power profiles of three associations.

sentative pressure on the Congress and other legislative bodies and officials. Their staff and their members represent specialized knowledge and skill. One example of staff expertise is their environmental specialist, a Ph.D. who has studied water resources and water legislation and has participated in the direction of pressure campaigns to improve water protection and water quality.

Urban America, which is now combined with the Urban Coalition, has a distinctive power profile. Note that raters see the power of this organization resting almost solely on its specialized knowledge and skill, which is in recognition of the trained architects, engineers, housing specialists, and economists that make up its staff. A few raters also recognize that Urban America's magazine, *Architectural Forum,* is a special means of communication. Its social prestige rating is a reflection of the position of leadership that this association has won in housing and urban development.

These three profiles indicate various ways in which power can be mobilized by organizations. It suggests that the schedule can locate various bases of power and provide measures of intensity and do so with validity. The power profiles of governmental organizations clearly show how these intensities are identified by the organizational raters and different bases of power.

The Profiles of Four Powerful Government Organizations

It will be recalled that four governmental organizations received high power ranking among the top 20: the U.S. Office of Housing and Urban Development (1); the U.S. Office of Economic Opportunity (3); the U.S. Department of Health, Education and Welfare (5); and the U.S. Department of Labor (8). Figure 7.3 clearly shows where their bases of power rest and the magnitude of that power. It also enables the reader to examine the four organizations simultaneously. A glance quickly shows that all four organizations are powerful because of their economic power and governmental authority, with minor support from their means of communication, and their specialized knowledge and skill. No private organization can approach these giants in the economic assets at their disposal or the power of authority they possess. Their large staffs assemble numerous experts in all phases of the activities that occupy their respective offices. The U.S. Government Printing Office publishes their numerous bulletins, pamphlets, reports, and other informational guides to give them a superb means of communication, but it is the importance of their press releases and the eagerness of the press to use them that provides exceptional access to public attention. Their chief officials become spokesmen in the press and over radio and television. The nonrated areas of power are almost as revealing of their power functioning. In general, they do not generate political influence; they are the receptors, not the initiators. They are not pressure instruments; efforts to apply pressure for their own interests are usually counterproductive. The raters do not judge these governmental organizations as deriving any principal base of power from social prestige, personal qualities of leadership, moral and religious persuasion, or military influence.

The reader will note that the power bases have been divided in Figure 7.3 into two classifications: institutional bases of influence and personal bases of influence. This division differentiates those bases that derive largely from the power attributable to the structure of the office and not to the incumbent. The personal bases, on the other hand, refer to qualities that derive from the people who compose the leadership staff and membership of the organization. For the powerful governmental organizations power is largely institutional in character, centered on economic power, governmental authority, and means of communication, whereas only specialized knowledge and skill reflects the staff's composition. Of course, they are products of the institutionalized procedures of civil service and appointment by superiors.

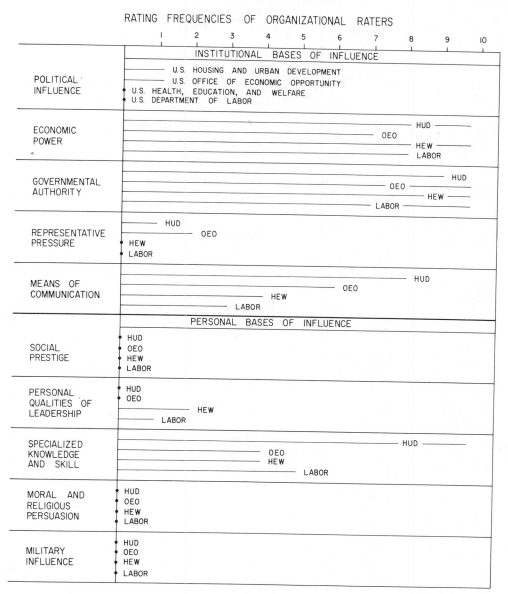

RATING FREQUENCIES OF ORGANIZATIONAL RATERS

Figure 7.3   The power profiles of four powerful governmental organizations.

The Profiles of Five Powerful Government-Related Private Associations

The five government-related private associations reveal power bases that contrast in significant measure with government organizations. Figure 7.4 is a comparative chart of organizational ratings for the U.S. Conference of Mayors, the National League of Cities, the International Association of City Managers, the National Association of Counties, and the Council of State Governments. Note that the

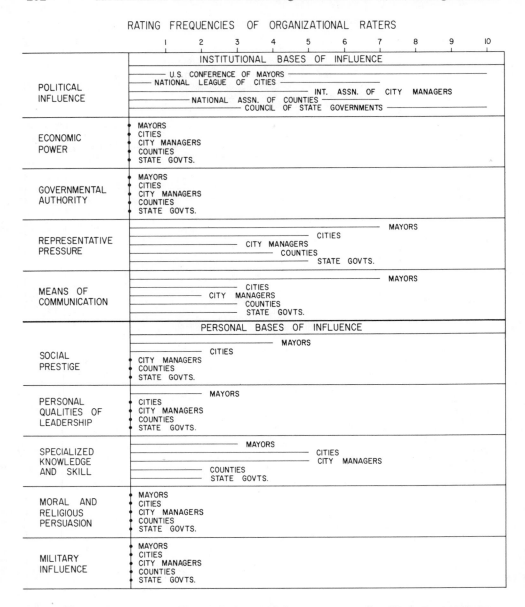

RATING FREQUENCIES OF ORGANIZATIONAL RATERS

	1	2	3	4	5	6	7	8	9	10

INSTITUTIONAL BASES OF INFLUENCE

POLITICAL INFLUENCE
— U.S. CONFERENCE OF MAYORS —
— NATIONAL LEAGUE OF CITIES —
— INT. ASSN. OF CITY MANAGERS
— NATIONAL ASSN. OF COUNTIES —
— COUNCIL OF STATE GOVERNMENTS —

ECONOMIC POWER
• MAYORS
• CITIES
• CITY MANAGERS
• COUNTIES
• STATE GOVTS.

GOVERNMENTAL AUTHORITY
• MAYORS
• CITIES
• CITY MANAGERS
• COUNTIES
• STATE GOVTS.

REPRESENTATIVE PRESSURE
— MAYORS
— CITIES
— CITY MANAGERS
— COUNTIES
— STATE GOVTS.

MEANS OF COMMUNICATION
— MAYORS
— CITIES
— CITY MANAGERS
— COUNTIES
— STATE GOVTS.

PERSONAL BASES OF INFLUENCE

SOCIAL PRESTIGE
— MAYORS
— CITIES
• CITY MANAGERS
• COUNTIES
• STATE GOVTS.

PERSONAL QUALITIES OF LEADERSHIP
— MAYORS
• CITIES
• CITY MANAGERS
• COUNTIES
• STATE GOVTS.

SPECIALIZED KNOWLEDGE AND SKILL
— MAYORS
— CITIES
— CITY MANAGERS
— COUNTIES
— STATE GOVTS.

MORAL AND RELIGIOUS PERSUASION
• MAYORS
• CITIES
• CITY MANAGERS
• COUNTIES
• STATE GOVTS.

MILITARY INFLUENCE
• MAYORS
• CITIES
• CITY MANAGERS
• COUNTIES
• STATE GOVTS.

Figure 7.4   The power profiles of five powerful government-related private associations.

principal bases of power are political influence and representative pressure. The function of these organizations is essentially to put pressure on legislators and government officials. The U.S. Conference of Mayors, the Council of State Governments, and the National League of Cities rank especially high. Minor bases of power are means of communication and specialized knowledge and skill. The importance of the city and the organizations directly related to their problems are highlighted by the influence of the Conference of Mayors, the League of Cities, and the Association of City Managers, among which the mayors hold the most political influence, potential for pressure, and social prestige. The state government and the counties must take secondary importance. The greater specialized knowledge and skill of the League of Cities and the Association of City Managers are recognized by the raters. As in government organizations the strength of the power base of these private associations is located in institutional bases and not in the personal. Most of the powerful organizations have a kind of "supraindividual" character, their power resting on structure, function, and resources. Occasionally an outstanding leader will provide a personality base of power that reinforces the organization he leads. A more permanent base is the staff that commands respect for its knowledge and skill. In some cases the prestige of the members becomes a crucial element. This is shown clearly in the following profiles.

The Profiles of Five Powerful Private Associations
Combining Economic Power and Political Influence

The ideal private association from the standpoint of power would be one with the economic power and governmental authority of a large federal department and the political influence and representative pressure exhibited by government-related private associations. If such an association could also provide social prestige, leadership, and specialized knowledge or skill, it would reach maximum effectiveness. Five private associations tend to approximate that ideal type. They are the National Association of Manufacturers, the National Alliance of Businessmen, the Chamber of Commerce of the United States, the Ford Foundation, and the National Urban Coalition. Figure 7.5 presents the power profiles of these organizations in which their power assets and liabilities can be clearly seen. Their political influence, economic power, and representative pressure (in varying degrees) are high, as is their social prestige, but they lack the power that governmental authority confers. Neither can they match the means of communication of a governmental organization and the specialized knowledge and skill of the large civil service staff.

Figure 7.5 shows that the NAM and the Chamber of Commerce, which represent the largest business groups in the country, have the edge on political influence and economic power. The National Urban Coalition, which lags in last position on these qualities, has high representative pressure, social prestige, and respect for personal qualities of leadership, all which attributes are understandable when it is realized that this organization is deliberately structured to project the power of a broadly based coalition of top leaders in business, labor, government, religion, civic affairs, and civil rights. The Urban Coalition has a remarkable group of prestigious leaders on its policy—making board and a respected president in John Gardner.

Three of the organizations are definitely reinforced by the leadership of one man. The Ford Foundation is led by McGeorge Bundy who is carried in our study as a key influential in Megalopolis. The National Alliance of Businessmen began under the leadership of Henry Ford II, who provided great encouragement for other top business leaders to assume various regional positions. John Gardner is also recognized as a key influential in Megalopolis, and his leadership

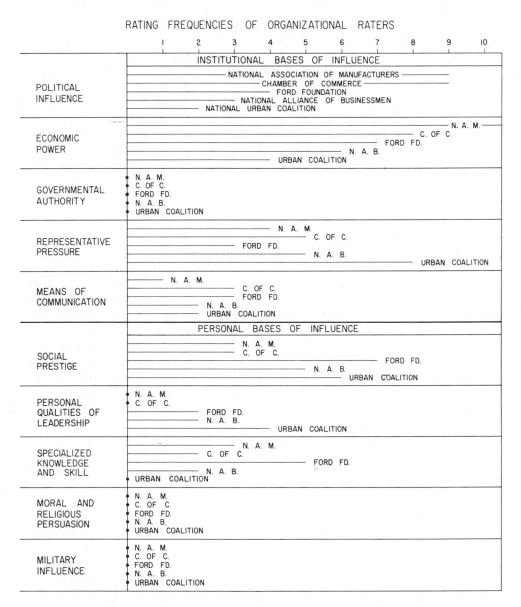

RATING FREQUENCIES OF ORGANIZATIONAL RATERS

Figure 7.5   The power profiles of five private associations combine economic and political influence.

at the National Urban Coalition (and now also of Common Cause) has attracted much attention to these organizations. In contrast, the National Association of Manufacturers and the U.S. Chamber of Commerce elect their president for a yearly term. No staff director commands the leadership visibility and prestige of the other three organizations. Their members are, however, respected for the positions in the business community, and their political influence and economic power are felt not only in their business organizations but in numerous channels such as political parties, welfare contributions, and community leadership.

The Profiles of Three Powerful Civil Rights Associations

Civil rights associations have never been more important in the history of the nation. In ranking the top 20 most powerful urban-oriented associations, the organizational raters put the National Urban League in the fourth position, NAACP in the ninth, and the Congress on Racial Equality (CORE) in the eighteenth. These organizations are recognized as those best able to represent black people, to achieve political and legislative objectives, and to mediate between blacks and whites in time of crisis. It should be understood that Whitney Young was alive and leading the National Urban League when these ratings were made. No one will dispute the fact that this leader had an influence that transcended the organization he represented. He was able to engage the white community as well as the black with his vigorous, intelligent, and militant brand of leadership. NAACP is also led by a remarkable leader in Roy Wilkins who has spent a lifetime with it in various capacities. Roy Innes, in contrast, is the new leader of CORE and not so well known. It is also true that the National Urban League and NAACP are much older organizations.

Both Whitney Young and Roy Wilkins are recognized as key leaders in Megalopolis and have served widely. Whitney Young had reached a peak position in his career at the time of his death and the scope of his acquaintance and participation sociogram shown in Chapter 5 will be recalled.

Figure 7.6 compares the power-base ratings of the three civil rights organizations. Their power is shown as resting on their political influence and representative pressure. Judges give scattered ratings to means of communication, personal qualities of leadership, and specialized knowledge and skill. It is also interesting that for the first time some ratings were registered for the moral and religious persuasion that the National Urban League and NAACP are able to command. No ratings were given to economic power, governmental authority, or military influence.

Because Whitney Young and Roy Wilkins have been such focal figures, it is interesting to speculate how these organizations will derive power with Whitney Young gone and when Roy Wilkens is no longer able to guide NAACP. The power analysis shows that the greater strength of these organizations (as is true of all organizations that persist) is to be found in the institutional bases of influence. If important functions are carried out and the staff is competent, the loyalty of the members remains and new leaders appear. The organization serves as a protective vessel ensuring permanence as leaders come and go. The unsung, unnamed members of the staff hold things together through thick and thin while the members provide the basis of financial and moral support. Power is not a "one time thing"; an analysis of the top 20 shows that it is "various."

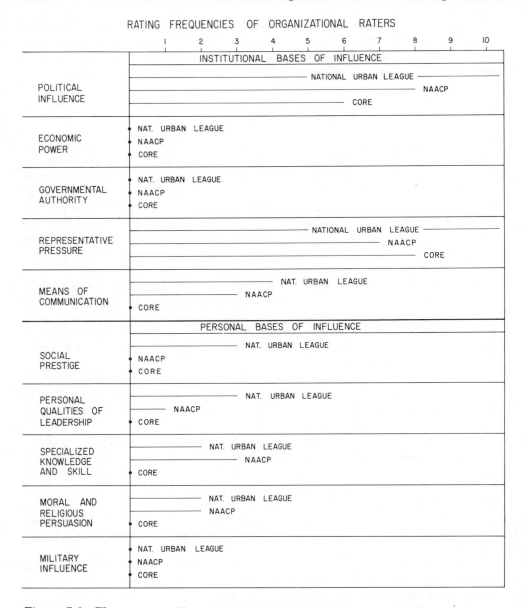

Figure 7.6   The power profiles of three powerful civil rights associations.

Acquaintance and Working Relations of the Top 20
Most Powerful Urban-Oriented Organizations

It will be recalled that the organization officials were asked to describe their acquaintance and working relations with the initial 37 top organizations selected for the study. Figure 7.1 introduced earlier, showed the organizational acquaintance and working relations scale employed.

These relationships were sought because they provide data on the linkage pattern of organizations and on the coalitions formed between organizations when some issue or legislative interest is actively defeated or won. The nature of the linkages reveals a great deal about the manner in which power and influence is mobilized. Such linkages and coalitions and the accompanying power process have constituted the heart of this research after securing identification of the most influential associations and leaders in urban-oriented and environmental quality problems.

It has been pointed out that the most influential urban-oriented organizations divide into such groups as U.S. government agencies, government-related voluntary, civil rights, business, labor, and women's associations, foundations, and general urban affairs like the National Urban Coalition.

To secure the working relationships between these organizations is a difficult job. The magnitude can be appreciated if one thinks of the thousands of employees in the major agencies of the Federal Government, any one of whom may have one or more contacts with other government departments or with the voluntary associations. Even in a small association with a staff of 10 to 20 the problem of getting the total pattern and getting it accurately described is a large order. This problem was discussed earlier and it is repeated here only to call attention to certain limitations that must be considered in any interpretation of the data on working relations. The problem seemed so important that a start was undertaken. In Figure 7.7 the end product is displayed.

This sociogram shows the relationships of the top 20 influential urban-oriented organizations and the 17 organizations of lesser influence. The numbers placed in the circles of the top 20 represent their power ranking. The solid line connecting any two organizations indicates a check against 4 or 5 on the scale and denotes working together or supporting one another on some issue or program. A single-headed arrow is unidirectional; a double-headed arrow is a reciprocal relationship affirmed by the raters. The figure makes clear that the heaviest volume of working activity takes place between the top ranked organizations. Moreover, the large role played by the government agencies is sharply outlined by the magnitude of the various working relationships set up within and between these agencies and the private associations.

The origin of these relationships can be traced to two factors: ideological orientation of the organization and its program interest. In Chapter 11 we demonstrate that all organizations establish reputations as supportive or hostile to the aims and programs of various organizations. Ideological similarities between organizations attract; ideological opposites repel. The AFL-CIO and the Chamber of Commerce, for example, are not likely to have many working relationships (if any), but the National Alliance of Businessmen work closely with the Chamber of Commerce and the National Association of Manufacturers. They think alike, they overlap in membership, and they find it mutually helpful to support joint activity.

Program interest sometimes transcends ideological molds. Two organizations who want to press for legislative acts or programs because of their common interest in a given activity will often fight side by side even when they seem unlikely bed fellows from an ideological comparison of their reputations.

Figure 7.7, which is essentially heuristic, is drawn to present the possibility of showing organizational interaction. We are making efforts to provide more rigorous measures of this interaction. In Chapter 8 the working relation between urban-oriented organizations and environmental quality organizations are studied and interaction coefficients are determined. Finally in Chapter 11, titled The Measurement of Organizational Interaction: Toward a Sociology of Associations, the research challenges of this emerging field of study are explored.

Notes

1. For a study of interorganizational bases of community power compare Robert Perrucci and Mark Pilisuk, "Leaders and Ruling Elites: The Interorganizational Bases of Community Power," *American Sociological Review,* **35** (December 1970), 1040–1057.

2. Important reference books included *Washington: A Comprehensive Directory of the Nation's Capital; Its People and Institutions,* Vol. II, Potomac Books, 1518 K. Street, N.W., Washington, D.C.; *U.S. Government Manual,* Government Printing Office, Washington, D.C., 1968; *Directory of National Trade and Professional Associations. Encyclopedia of Organizations,* Vol. I and II, Gale Research Company, Detroit, 1973. Other references that provided evaluations were Floyd Hunter, *Top Leadership, U.S.A.,* University of North Carolina, 1959, pp. 13–15. Hunter's list proved to be valuable on the initial assembly. See also Robert H. Connery and Richard Leach, *The Federal Government and Metropolitan Areas,* Harvard University Press, Cambridge, 1960.

3. The five judges who worked in Washington for governmental and private organizations have had extensive experience. Their present titles are urban housing administrator, U.S. government agency; executive secretary, civil rights organization; director of urban affairs, national business association; urban program specialist, national research foundation; director of urban policies, association of government officials.

4. The raters included (1) Legislative Director, Council of State Governments; (2) Legislative Director, National League of Cities; (3) Director of Community Relations Service, U.S. Conference of Mayors; (4) Division Director, Office of Economic Opportunity; (5) Assistant Director of National Relations, National Urban Coalition; (6) Urban Affairs Director, Chamber of Commerce of the United States; (7) Assistatnt Urban Affairs Director of Chamber of Commerce of the United States; (8) Director of Urban Affairs, League of Women Voters; (9) Director of Public Affairs, Urban America; (10) Assistant Director of Urban Affairs: National AFL-CIO; (11) Program Director, W. E. Upjohn Institute for Employment Research; (12) Staff Research Associate, The Potomac Institute; (13) Vice President, Director, Industrial Environment, National Association of Manufacturers; (14) Assistant Director, Urban Affairs, Ford Foundation; (15) Director of Public Relations, National Urban League; (16) Assistant Executive Director, National Association for the Advancement of Colored People; (17) Manager-Civic and Governmental Affairs, National Industrial Conference Board; (18) Executive Director, National Association of Counties; (19) Special Secretary, National Association of Broadcasters; (20) Executive Director, American Institute of Planners; (21) Executive Secretary, the Business Council; (22) Director of Task Force on Urban Education, National Educational Association; (23) Executive Director, National Federation of Business and Women's Associations; (24) Executive Director, National Federation of Business and Women's Associations; (24) Executive Director, International Association of City Managers; (25) Executive Secretary, Washington Office, American Bankers Association.

5. It must be remembered that these rankings were made in the fall of 1968 and winter of 1969. Changes have taken place. The National Urban Coalition and Urban America have merged. The Republican administration in Washington has made alterations in programs and priorities of governmental agencies. The ability of various associations to influence government leaders and officials has shifted with some improving and some losing. One of my

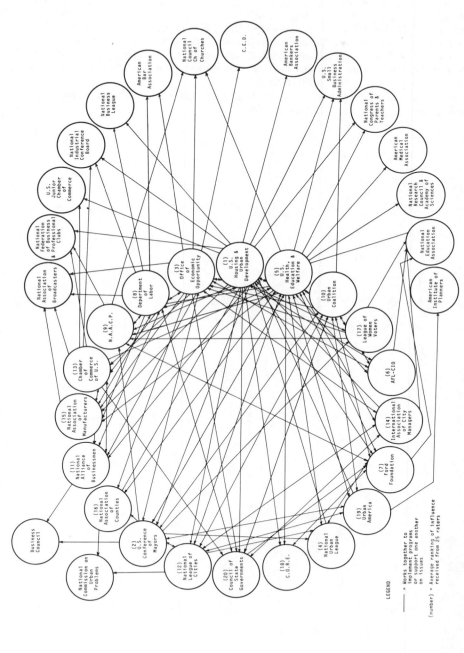

LEGEND

——— = Works together to
        implement programs
        or support one another
        on issues

(number) = Average ranking of influence
           received from 25 raters

Figure 7.7 Working relations within and between the top 20 influential urban-oriented organizations and between the 17 organizations of lesser influence.

former raters was asked to make an evaluation of the top 37 organizations in June 1970. He cited the following as gaining in power since his last rating in October 1968: National League of Cities, U.S. Conference of Mayors, U.S. Chamber of Commerce, National Association of Manufacturers, National Urban League, National Urban Coalition, National Education Association, Ford Foundation, and American Institute of Planners. He cited the following as less powerful: U.S. Department of Housing and Urban Development, U.S. Department of Health, Education and Welfare, U.S. Office of Economic Opportunity, U.S. Small Business Administration, Committee on Economic Development, National Council of Churches, National Alliance of Businessmen, League of Women Voters, and Congress of Racial Equality. He also specified that none of these organizations have dropped out of the list of the top 20 most powerful organizations.

6. Copies may be secured from the author. Write to D. C. Miller, Department of Sociology, Indiana University, Bloomington, Indiana, 47401.

PART FOUR

Environmental
Influence Systems
in Megalopolis
and its Subregions

The research design in Chapter 3 describes a model in which three influence networks are shown. The first is a Megalopolis Generalized Influence Network composed of powerful leaders and organizations in the Atlantic Urban Region who are working on urban problems. Part 3 has just described the structure and modes of decision making for this network.

The other two networks are the Megalopolis Environmental Quality Influence Network and the Delaware River Basin Influence Network. One is concerned with the powerful *environmental* leaders and organizations of Megalopolis and their modes of decision making. The other contains the powerful leaders and organizations that function in the Delaware River Basin and who are responsible for water supply and water quality in four northeastern States. Each of these networks is directed toward ever more specific problems and was selected for study in order to observe decision making in smaller social systems and with more limited and direct goals.

Part 4 is a research report of these two environmental networks. It not only describes the efforts made to identify the relevant structures and decision-making processes but also attempts to define the interrelationships in all three of the influence networks.

CHAPTER EIGHT

Influence Systems and Decision Making in Megalopolis and its Subregion:

The Problem of Environmental Quality

James L. Barfoot, Jr. and Paul D. Planchon, Research Associates, were major contributors to the research and writing of this chapter.

The study of environmental leaders and organizations was directed to that specific part of the regional power structure in which the search was for powerful and active leaders and organizations in the environmental quality area. That area was defined as including problems of air pollution, water pollution, and solid wastes.[1]

Three objectives were set out: (a) to identify the powerful leaders and organizations, (b) to discover their patterns of decision making, and (c) to relate the Megalopolis Generalized Influence Network to the Megalopolis Environmental Quality Influence Network by seeking the degree of overlap and the nature of the working relationships between them.

It was believed that this phase of the research would yield more information about decision-making processes because of the focus on a specific problem. In addition, the determination of the overlap between the two influence networks would provide a test of the impact possibilities of powerful urban-oriented leaders and organizations when related to environmental problems.

The Search for Powerful Environmental Quality Leaders and Organizations

The research required two stages:

1. Assembling preliminary lists and ranking the most powerful environmental leaders and organizations by using a variety of research methods: documents, informants, and reputational techniques.[2]

2. Sending a specially designed questionnaire to a group of approximately 130 organizations, 91 of which responded. This group included those of highly reputed influence and others not rated at all. These organizations represented the various interest groups, multi- and single-purpose associations, and several political and geographic levels and units in the region.[3]

Respondents were asked to name persons and organizations active and influential in specific issues of environmental pollution.

Decision-making activity was probed. A report on the findings with data secured in the two stages is presented.

The First Stage: Identification of Powerful
Environmental Leaders and Organizations

Work on the preliminary list began with an analysis of documents and exploratory interviews to determine the organizations and leaders that were active in this public policy area. When the lists were developed, they were presented to a group of informants who were asked to rate separately the relative influence of the organizations and leaders.

Before securing the ratings from the informants, the interviewers were careful to state and explain the conceptual boundaries of the study. First it was explained that its focus was on public decisions related to pollution. Second the Megalopolis region was defined and the informants were shown a map of the region. Finally, it was stressed that the concern was with activity and not necessarily with location or residence in the region.

The question asked the informants reads as follows:

> Regardless of the positions they take or how you feel about them, which of these organizations (individuals) would you rate as being most powerful in initiating, supporting, or vetoing activities that affect policies concerned with environmental pollution in this region?

This question was followed with another:

> Are there any organizations (individuals) you can think of who were not included in this list that you would rate as having comparable influence?[4] How would you rate them?

The informants placed the organizations and/or individuals whose names had been transcribed on index cards into four piles: very powerful, powerful, not so powerful, and don't know or have insufficient knowledge to rate. Scores of 1, 2, and 3 were assigned to the first three categories, respectively. These data were tabulated by summing up the raw scores by the number of times rated. The result was a set of final ratings that ranged from a high of 1.0 to a low of 3.0.

Table 8.1 contains a list of the 36 organizations rated most influential by the informants. They are arranged in the table according to influence scores; the highest rating is indicated by the lowest score. A score of 1 means that all informants who rated that particular organization considered it "very influential." The lowest rating in this top group is 1.9. The 36 organizations were selected from more than 200 organizations on which ratings were obtained. Note that Table 8.1 is divided into two sections. These two sections contain 8 and 28 organizations, respectively. Although all should be viewed as "very influential," there is a cutting point that separates the two groups (1.3–1.5)[5] which is interpreted to mean that "A" and "B" are different in their degrees of influence, but within each group all organizations are considered equal.

TABLE 8.1   REPUTED TOP 36 MOST INFLUENTIAL ENVIRONMENTAL ORGANIZATIONS (1968)

Organization	Influence score
Group A	
Federal Water Pollution Control Administration (now designated as Federal Water Quality Administration)	1.0
U.S. Senate Committee on Public Works	1.0
U.S. Senate Committee on Interior and Insular Affairs	1.0
U.S. House of Representatives Committee on Public Works	1.0
U.S. House Committee on Science and Astronautics	1.0
U.S. Army Corps of Engineers	1.1
Bureau of the Budget, Natural Resources Division	1.2
U.S. Chamber of Commerce	1.3
Group B	
Citizens Committee on Natural Resources	1.5
The Conservation Foundation	1.5
Federal Power Commission	1.5
National Association of Manufacturers	1.5
Izaak Walton League of America	1.6
League of Women Voters of the United States	1.6
National Rivers and Harbors Congress	1.6
Forest Service of the U.S. Government	1.6
Fish and Wildlife Service of the U.S. Government	1.6
National Park Service	1.6
National Wildlife Federation	1.7
Water Resources Council	1.7
National Air Pollution Control Administration	1.7
National League of Cities	1.7
American Iron and Steel Institute	1.7
Manufacturing Chemists' Association	1.8
Bureau of Mines	1.8
Wildlife Management Institute	1.8
Council of State Governments	1.8
National Audubon Society	1.8
Sport Fishing Institute	1.8
National Association of Counties	1.8
Water Pollution Control Federation	1.9
Sierra Club	1.9
Bureau of Outdoor Recreation	1.9
U.S. Conference of Mayors	1.9
National Coal Association	1.9
National Parks Association	*

* The National Parks Association received a rating of 1.0, but it was based on so few returns that the score was not considered sufficiently representative of the raters to justify its inclusion in Group A. It is an organization that has wielded strong veto power and cannot be ignored. It was tentatively placed in Group B.

Observe that all 36 organizations listed in Table 8.1 represent segments of the legislative and executive branches of the Federal Government or national voluntary associations. No regional, state, or local organization appears on this list. This finding was supported in a supplementary manner by comments made by the informants during the interviewing process. There was a tendency among the informants to view Eastern Megalopolis as (a) a segment of the more general national environmental quality issue area, and/or (b) constituting several subregions which varied, according to the kind of residual (environmental quality problem) being considered (air pollution, water pollution, or solid wastes). Most respondents stated that a set of environmental quality leaders who worked on a regional level could not be isolated because Megalopolis was not a meaningful environmental quality region.

The investigation concentrated on the aspect of environmental quality programs or activities that was directed externally toward influencing other actors in the field in matters affecting public policy decisions. A great number of organizations have highly developed programs directed internally toward their own constituencies. These are usually matters of aiding individual waste disposers—private firms and organizations representing firms in particular. It is possible to do both. The National Association of Manufacturers has both internally and externally directed programs. The National Pollution Control Foundation is a good example of an organization whose program is directed primarily toward the problems that the waste dischargers themselves face—not toward public policy decisions. Like many others, its absence on the list of top organizations presumably reflects this difference rather than a lack of accomplishments.

Table 8.2 presents the findings of the search for influential leaders. Listed are the individuals who received the highest ratings by the informants. All individuals obtained scores of 1.7 or lower on a scale of 1.0 to 3.0. This list is interpreted as indicating a group of men reputed to be influential at the time that the study was conducted. In presenting this list, however, the researchers did not mean to suggest that it includes in any way all the most influential individuals in the issue area studied. In one sense the names on this list are symbolic of the kinds of role that make up the dynamics of the decision-making process. Therefore, rather than focus on the particular names, the researchers felt that what is more useful is the roles that these these men fill. In this regard what makes Edmund S. Muskie influential is not that he is a senator from the State of Maine but rather that he holds the position of Chairman of the Subcommittee on Air and Water Pollution of the Senate Public Works Committee. After the data were gathered the Nixon administration changed many of the personnel in the positions listed in Table 8.2. Many of the names would be dropped out and new ones added if another study were undertaken.[6] The role types have much greater stability, however.

Influential Environmental Quality Leaders as Role Types and Constituency Leaders

In all, 46 names appear on this list of influentials. Figure 8.1 is a percentage breakdown by gross-role classifications. The group with the largest representation

TABLE 8.2 NAMES AND POSITIONS* OF REPUTED INFLUENTIALS IN ENVIRONMENTAL QUALITY (1968)

Horace M. Albright	Citizens Committee on Natural Resources, Board of Directors
Wayne N. Aspinall	House of Representatives, Colorado; House of Representatives Committee on Interior and Insular Affairs, Chairman
John A. Blatnik	House of Representatives, Minnesota; House of Representatives Committee on Public Works
Stewart M. Brandborg	The Wilderness Society, Executive Director
David R. Brower	Sierra Club, Executive Director
Stanley A. Cain	U.S. Department of the Interior, Assistant Secretary
Charles H. Callison	National Audubon Society, Executive Director
Henry P. Caulfield	Water Resources Council, Executive Director
Edward P. Cliff	U.S. Forest Service, Chief
Wilbur Cohen	U.S. Department of Health, Education and Welfare, Secretary
Edward C. Crafts	Bureau of Outdoor Recreation, Director
Henry Diamond	The Citizens' Advisory Committee on Recreation and Natural Beauty, Counsel
William O. Douglas	U.S. Supreme Court, Associate Justice
Max N. Edwards	U.S. Department of the Interior, Assistant Secretary
Joseph L. Fisher	Resources for the Future, President
Orville L. Freeman	U.S. Department of Agriculture, Secretary
Maurice K. Goddard	Delaware River Basin Commission, Alternate for Pennsylvania
Ira N. Gabrielson	Wildlife Management Institute, President
John S. Gottschalk	Bureau of Sport Fisheries and Wildlife, Director
C. R. Guttermuth	Wildlife Management Institute, Vice President
George B. Hartzog, Jr.	National Park Service, Director
Bernard F. Hillenbrand	National Association of Counties, Executive Director
Donald Hornig	Office of Science and Technology, Special Assistant to the President
Hubert H. Humphrey	Vice-President of the United States
Henry M. Jackson	U.S. Senate, Washington; Senate Committee on Interior and Insular Affairs, Chairman
Robert E. Jones	House of Representatives, Alabama; House Committee on Public Works
Dr. Thomas L. Kimball	National Wildlife Federation, Executive Director
Warren G. Magnuson	U.S. Senate, Washington; Senate Committees on Commerce, Aeronautical and Space Sciences, and Appropriations

Joe G. Moore, Jr.	Federal Water Pollution Control Administration, Commissioner
Edmund S. Muskie	U.S. Senate, Maine; Senate Public Works Subcommittee on Air and Water Pollution, Chairman
Gaylord Nelson	U.S. Senate, Wisconsin; Senate Committee on Interior and Insular Affairs
Donald E. Nicoll	Administrative Assistant to Senator Muskie
Clarence F. Pautzke	U.S. Department of the Interior, Assistant Secretary
Joseph W. Penfold	Izaak Walton League of America, Executive Director
Boyd L. Rasmussen	Bureau of Land Management, Director
Abraham A. Ribicoff	U.S. Senate, Connecticut; Senate Finance Committee
Laurance S. Rockefeller	The Citizens' Advisory Committee on Recreation and Natural Beauty, Chairman
Fred B. Rooney	House of Representatives, Pennsylvania; House Appropriations Committee
John P. Saylor	House of Representatives, Pennsylvania; House Committee on Interior and Insular Affairs
Anthony Wayne Smith	National Parks Association, Executive Director
Russell E. Train	Conservation Foundation, President
W. Lloyd Tupling	Sierra Club
Joseph D. Tydings	U.S. Senate, Maryland; Senate Committee on Public Works
Stewart L. Udall	Department of the Interior, Secretary
Lee C. White	Federal Power Commission, Chairman
Charles J. Zwick	Bureau of the Budget, Director

*All positions are those held by the persons named at the time of the study, September to December 1968.

on this list is the administrative branch of the Federal Government (37%). Other government groups and their percentage representations are legislative branch of

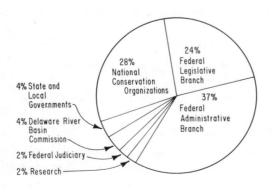

Figure 8.1   Percentage representation among influential leaders by role type.

the Federal Government, 24 percent; Delaware River Basin Commission and state and local governments, 4 percent; the federal judiciary, 2 percent. The remaining representations are those of the voluntary conservation and research organizations, which have 28 and 2 percent, respectively.

Figure 8.1 reveals three main categories of participants in public policy decisions related to environmental quality decision: the administrative and legislative branches of the Federal Government, and the national conservation organizations. Absent from the chart are business leaders. This is not to suggest that business leaders are not active and influential in this issue area. Rather they are not visible leaders. The reasons for this may be several. Businesses are generally concerned with internal plant decisions related to their specific pollution problems and regulations. Of course, public policy regulations are related to in-plant operations, but the federal regulations passed to date have dealt in particular with general standards for river basins and air sheds, not directly with discharges from industrial plants except in interstate enforcement cases. The decisions on method of implementation have not yet been made in most places. Also business leaders have not assumed active leadership because measures to clean up the rivers, air, and land will cost them money. Everyone, including business leaders, will claim to be for some improvement in the quality of the environment, but there are different views on how much is necessary and how to achieve it. It is in this light that one should view the role of business in environmental quality decisions.

In general, leadership in this issue area is carried out by concerned national conservation organizations and Federal Governmental officials in the legislative and administrative branches. Although the conservation leaders have some differences in regard to public policy decisions, they are in general agreement insofar as they favor a continued improvement in the quality of the environment. Both the administrative and legislative branches of the Federal Government have overwhelmingly supported legislation and methods of implementation that will eventually lead to this improvement.

The joint findings on organizations and individuals are not intended to suggest that Megalopolis is controlled from Washington by a group of legislators, bureaucrats, and heads of national voluntary associations. In focusing on a subregion in Megalopolis, it was found that many of these same men and organizations were not the key figures. Instead, many local actors played key roles in the decision-making process. Second, in attempting to study a region that cuts across a number of water, air, and solid wastes sheds, a super-problem-shed group of leaders was not found. Instead, the questions about reputed influence in Eastern Megalopolis elicited responses about a segment of the national leadership in the environmental quality-residuals issue area.

Introduced are a number of variables that have proved to be useful in categorizing and analyzing these data. First, consider the variable, *type of constituency*. Constituency refers to a segment of the general population that is in a position to exert direct influence on the focal organization. Type of constituency is meant to refer to organizations whose constituencies have similar interests. Some constituencies are relatively homogeneous, whereas others often contain segments of the population whose interests conflict. Two examples are the Izaak Walton League of America and the American Iron and Steel Institute. The Sport

Fishing Institute is different in that it represents both sports fishermen and the manufacturers of fishing equipment. Groups such as the House and Senate committees undoubtedly have the most heterogeneous constituencies. The 36 organizations have been listed by type of constituency in Table 8.3: legislative Federal Government, administrative Federal government, state and local governments, business and industry, conservation, civic affairs, and a category labeled water resource.

Among the eight organizations in Group A four are the legislative constituency type, three the administrative type, and one the business and industry type. The constituency types that are not represented in the top eight are the state and local government, conservation, civic, and water-resource organizations. A survey of the total list, however, shows the following distribution: 31 percent of the most powerful organizations are "federal administrative"; 11 percent are "federal legislative"; 22 percent are "national conservation"; 11 percent are "state and local government"; 14 percent are "business and industry"; others, 11 percent.

It will be remembered that among the list of leaders reputed to be influential (see Table 8.2) constituency classifications were basically the same. A category of subregional administration (the Delaware River Basin Commission) and another for research and the federal judiciary were added. There were no individuals who represented business and industry, civic, or water-resource organizations. Thirty-seven percent of the most powerful (reputed) leaders are "federal administrative," 24 percent are "federal legislative," 28 percent are "national conservation," others, 8 percent. The similarity demonstrated between the most powerful organizations by constituency type and the distribution of leaders by role type reinforces the importance of role in contrast to the importance of the individual per se.

Another important classificatory variable is the *purpose* of the organization. This study focused on environmental quality-residuals, but few organizations concerned solely with environmental quality-residuals were found. A threefold classification schema was developed to describe organizations by purpose. In addition to the environmental quality-residual classification, there were "natural resource" and "multipurpose" classifications. Natural resource organizations, as the name implies, are engaged in the conservation and/or development of all or some natural resources. For them environmental quality-residuals are just one of many resource interests, for as multipurpose organizations they do not limit their activities to the natural environment.

Table 8.4 shows the top 36 organizations classified by purpose and power.

Only three single-purpose environmental quality-residual organizations appear in the top 36 and only one of the three is in the top eight.[7] The natural resource and multipurpose organizations are about evenly represented in the top 36, yet it is significant that seven of the top eight are multipurpose. Among the 46 reputed influential one person represents a single-purpose environmental quality-residual organization, 25 are members of natural resource organizations, and 20 work for multipurpose organizations.

These data suggest that the issue area of environmental quality-residuals is not a separate field of activity. Rather it is part of the general decision-making process for all kinds of issue. It is perhaps useful to characterize the issue area of environmental quality-residuals as having three kinds of leader. In order of in-

TABLE 8.3 REPUTED TOP MOST POWERFUL ENVIRONMENTAL ORGANIZATIONS IN MEGALOPOLIS BY TYPE OF CONSTITUENCY

Legislative

House of Representatives Committee on Public Works
House of Representatives Committee on Science and Astronautics
Senate Committee on Public Works (subcommittee on Pollution)
Senate Committee on Interior and Insular Affairs

Administrative

Federal Power Commission
Bureau of Mines
National Park Service
Fish and Wildlife Service of the U.S. Government
Forest Service of the U.S. Government
National Air Pollution Control Administration
Bureau of Outdoor Recreation
Water Resource Council
Army Corps of Engineers
Bureau of the Budget
Federal Water Pollution Control Administration (now the Federal Water Quality Administration)

Organizations of state and local governments

National League of Cities
Council of State Governments
National Association of Counties
U.S. Conference of Mayors

Business and industry organizations

U.S. Chamber of Commerce
National Association of Manufacturers
American Iron and Steel Institute
Manufacturing Chemists Association
National Coal Association

Civic organizations

League of Women Voters of the United States

General conservation organizations

Sierra Club
The Conservation Foundation
National Parks Association
Izaak Walton League of America
Wildlife Management Institute
National Audubon Society
Citizens Committee on Natural Resources
National Wildlife Federation

Water resource organizations

National Rivers and Harbors Congress
Sport Fishing Institute
Water Pollution Control Federation

TABLE 8.4   CLASSIFICATION OF ENVIRONMENTAL ORGANIZATIONS BY
PURPOSE AND POWER

Power	Purpose			
	Exclusively environmental quality residuals	Natural resources	Multipurpose	Total
Group A	1	0	7	8
Group B	2	16	10	28
Total	3	16	17	36

creasing specialization they are (a) general leaders active in many issue areas,
(b) natural resource specialists, and (c) environmental quality-residual specialists. There are few leaders in the last classification.

It is important to note that on the field of environmental quality is a field of
action. The social structure in environmental quality public policy decisions is
seldom unique to the field itself. The evidence is that few organizations devote
their full energies to problems of pollution. The only examples in the list of the
top 36 organizations are the Federal Water Pollution Control Administration, the
National Air Pollution Control Administration, and the nongovernmental Water
Pollution Control Federation. All the rest have extensive interests and activities
beyond environmental quality-residuals. Furthermore, such purely environmental
quality organizations are usually concerned with only one area of environmental
quality—air, water, or land. In addition, much of their energy is devoted to the
implementation of decisions rather than to influencing the decisions themselves.

Four Decision-Making Areas

Most of the social structure in environmental quality decision making is the same
as that involved in public policy decisions in general. Four established areas of
decision making may be identified. The first is concerned with *the preservation or
use of wildlife and wild environments.* Thus the National Park Service, the
Bureau of Outdoor Recreation, and the Fish and Wildlife Service on the public
side and the Sierra Club, the National Parks Association, the Wildlife Federation,
the Conservation Foundation, and the Izaak Walton League on the private side
are drawn in. All are usually most interested in water quality questions. This
"conservationist" type constitutes the largest proportion of organizations active in
environmental qualtiy. Yet conservationists often insist that to them pollution
problems are secondary to land use.

A parallel is the area of decision making concerned with *natural resources as
they relate more directly to economic exploitation,* which attracts such organizations as the Bureau of Mines, the Army Corps of Engineers, Congressional Committees on Public Works, the National Rivers and Harbors Congress, the National

Coal Association, the American Petroleum Institute, and, at the technical study phases, Resources for the Future.

These two areas of decision making interest a third—*environmental quality as it is identified within the general setting of urban problems.* Thus the organizations whose primary interests are in urban problems (or civic interest in general) are drawn into the field. Examples are the private organizations of state and local governments—the National League of Cities, the Council of State Governments, the National Association of Counties, and the U.S. Conference of Mayors. Other examples would include the League of Women Voters. Many federal agencies could also be named.

The fourth area of decision making which overlaps that of environmental quality comes from *business and industry.* Because the assimilative capacity of the environment is a resource to business and industry and therefore a matter of economics, they are implicated if for no other reason than that pollution abatement is likely to become another cost of doing business. Business and industry appear anxious that equitable and economically sound decisions be made about environmental quality. At least, they are concerned that they will not place an inordinate burden upon them. Thus the Chamber of Commerce becomes interested, as does the National Association of Manufacturers, the Manufatcuring Chemists's Association and many individual firms. Industry, as well as business indirectly, finds itself in the structural position of having to respond to the environmental quality challenge as the demand for it increases. Organizations, including firms, or individuals in business and industry may take a defensive position, designed to avoid the costs of pollution abatement as long as possible or they may take varying degrees of positive action. Action, however, tends to be directed toward problems of specific concern to the industry or firm. The findings show that industry seldom directs its attention to public decisions and that when it does the outcomes are often distinctly different from those of others taking part in the decisions.

The Second Stage: Search for Influence Activity Among Environmental Organizations

Influence is a matter of activating potential power. It has at least two important dimensions that potential power lacks. The first is the degree of activation—the extent to which the organization (individual) calls on its resources to exert a change in the behavior of others. The second is the direction of the influence or the goal to which it is directed.

In the environmental quality issue areas, a wide range of degrees of activity and a variety of directions or goals are found. At the same time, there is a diversity of activity—the ways in which power is activated. In the following section the scope, geography, emphasis, and kind of activity in the programs of important organizations in environmental quality are explored. The approach is to describe the top environmental quality organizations and to compare them with other environmental quality organizations that are nationally based.

The data in this section rely heavily on the findings of the questionnaire. Interpretation is also guided by information gathered in interviews, correspondence with the organizations, and their own publications.

Among the reputed most powerful organizations in environmental quality, shown in Table 8.1, 29 of the 36 responded to the questionnaire; seven of the eight in group A and 22 of the group B.[8] In most cases failure to respond can be attributed to the highly controversial nature of the issues or to the difficulty of a bureaucratic agency to respond to questions of a partisan nature.

SCOPE OF ACTIVITY

Two questions were designed to investigate the scope of the organizational programs related to environmental quality-residuals. The first question asked in which of the three environmental quality areas the organization was active within the context of other urban problems. The second question asked whether the organization approached the three areas of air pollution, water pollution, and solid wastes as a unified problem.

Environmental Quality Among Other Urban Problems.   Respondents representing the organizations were asked this question:

> Below is a list of problems that prevail in varying degrees in the Boston-to-Washington urban region. Check those that your organization has worked on during the last three years.
>
> _____ Air pollution
>
> _____ Control of lawlessness and crime
>
> _____ Improvement of public education
>
> _____ Water pollution
>
> _____ Improvement of transportation, traffic movement, and parking
>
> _____ Solid wastes (garbage, litter, dumps, etc.)
>
> _____ Improvement or elimination of poor housing; rebuilding of cities
>
> _____ Improvement and maintenance of roads and streets
>
> _____ Planning and zoning of land; preservation (or improvement) of parks and other natural areas
>
> _____ Unemployment and poverty
>
> _____ Race relations

Table 8.5 shows each of the urban problems listed and the frequency with which those responding to the question reported working on them. It also indicates the frequency with which each of the power levels reported working on each

TABLE 8.5 ENVIRONMENTAL QUALITY AND URBAN PROBLEMS CURRENTLY BEING WORKED ON, BY POWER, AMONG ORGANIZATIONS RATED MOST POWERFUL

Problems	Power		
	Group A	Group B	Total
Water pollution	7	18	25
Air pollution	5	13	18
Solid wastes	5	12	17
Planning and zoning	6	12	18
Transportation	4	7	11
Unemployment	4	7	11
Crime	3	6	9
Education	4	5	9
Housing	4	5	9
Race relations	2	6	8
Roads and streets	2	3	5
Total responding to item	7	21	28

problem. Air and water pollution and solid waste problems are shown together, but the others are arranged in order of decreasing frequency.

The table also indicates that water pollution receives the most attention from the top organizations. Air pollution is in second position. The problem of solid wastes appears to receive the least, with a greater proportion of group A than group B working on it. Following environmental quality problems, planning and zoning of land are most frequently worked on. This reflects the interrelatedness of conservation and pollution and the fact that many of the pollution problems have received attention from conservationist organizations. The technical relationship between the automobile and air pollution probably accounts for the frequency with which improvement of transportation, traffic movement, and parking is studied by the top environmental quality organizations. The high rank of unemployment and poverty probably reflects the general concern with those problems at the time of the investigation.

Table 8.6 like the preceding table, differentiates by power level. It indicates the frequency with which the two categories, group A and group B, report working on (a) environmental quality-residuals problems alone (air pollution, water pollution, and solid wastes), (b) environmental quality problems with the single addition of planning and zoning of land (conservation in terms of land use), and (c) environmental quality plus other urban problems.

The fact that the majority of organizations report working on other problems as well as environmental quality reflects the paucity of interest solely in some aspect of environmental pollution.

GEOGRAPHY OF ACTIVITY

Most of the organizations in the top 36 had main offices in Washington. Some had headquarters offices in New York and one in California, but with few ex-

TABLE 8.6 COMBINATIONS OF ENVIRONMENTAL QUALITY AND
URBAN PROBLEMS CURRENTLY BEING WORKED ON, BY POWER,
AMONG ORGANIZATIONS RATED MOST POWERFUL

Problems	Power Group A	Power Group B	Total
Environmental quality only	1	4	5
Environmental quality plus planning and zoning	0	3	3
Environmental quality plus planning and zoning plus other urban problems	6	12	18
Total	7	19	26

ceptions they also maintained offices in Washington. To discover the geography
of the activity of the organizations studied two questions were asked. One was
designed to obtain the level of the activity—local, state, regional-interstate, or
national. The other was concerned with determining in which specific problem
sheds the organizations may have had an active concern.

Level of Activity.   The first question asked was as follows:

Has the activity of your organization been primarily on the local, state,
interstate, or national level? Check the appropriate blanks.

	Water pollution	Air pollution	Solid wastes problems
Local	————	————	————
State	————	————	————
Regional-interstate	————	————	————
National	————	————	————

The respondent was given the opportunity to indicate more than one level.

Table 8.7 shows the levels of activity by power group among the top rated organizations that responded. Note that this is not a contingency table; each of the
column totals is independent. What is most striking is that most of the organizations indicated the national level as their primary concern. Next was regional-
interstate for water pollution but not for the other two problems. This reflects
the great amount of interstate activity in some of the river basins in Megalopolis.

TABLE 8.7   LEVEL OF ACTIVITY, BY POWER, AMONG ENVIRONMENTAL ORGANIZATIONS RATED MOST POWERFUL

Problem	Power	Local	State	Regional-interstate	National	Total responding to question
Air pollution	Group A	1	2	3	5	7
	Group B	6	5	4	15	22
	Total	7	7	7	20	29
Water pollution	Group A	1	2	3	7	7
	Group B	7	7	10	19	22
	Total	8	9	13	26	29
Solid wastes	Group A	1	2	3	5	7
	Group B	6	5	1	10	22
	Total	7	7	4	15	29

Where air pollution and solid wastes are concerned organizations appear as likely to focus on the state or local level as the regional-interstate. Perhaps one reason why the focus in water pollution has been on regional-interstate as well as national is that both traditionally and by legislation there has been a problem-shed approach to the regulation of water quality. Only recently has similar activity been initiated with gaseous and solid residuals by the Department of Health, Education and Welfare. The difference between group A and group B power levels, although not statistically significant, appears to be that group A shows greater interest at the regional-interstate and national levels.

Problem Sheds Worked in. Among the top-rated organizations the greatest emphasis is on the regional-interstate level with respect to watershed. The question of the extent of such regions remains. Responses to the next question provide indication of regional activity in water, air, and solid waste problems.

> In which of the following environmental quality "problem sheds" has your organization had active concern in the last three years?
>
> Water pollution:
>
> _____ The Connecticut River Basin
>
> _____ The Delaware River Basin
>
> _____ The Susquehanna River Basin

_____ The Hudson River Basin

_____ The Potomac River Basin

_____ Megalopolis in general* (Boston to Washington)

_____ The nation in general*

_____ Others:

Air pollution:

_____ The Boston metropolitan area

_____ The New York City metropolitan area

_____ The Philadelphia metropolitan area (the Delaware Valley)

_____ The Baltimore-Washington, D.C. metropolitan area

_____ Megalopolis in general*

_____ The nation in general*

_____ Others:

Solid waste problems:

_____ The Boston metropolitan area

_____ The New York metropolitan area

_____ The Philadelphia metropolitan area (the Delaware Valley)

_____ The Washington-Baltimore metropolitan area

_____ Megalopolis in general*

_____ The nation in general*

_____ Others:

* Actually the investigators did not consider these areas "problem sheds" by strict definition, but they included to secure comparisons.

Table 8.8 cross-tabulates responses to the question by power level. Here again the column as well as the row totals are independent. For water pollution, although the largest proportion report activity in the "nation in general," no greater proportion reported concern in Megalopolis in general than in any of the river basins. This indicates that, in the case of water, when respondents said regional-interstate they were likely to have been referring to specific river basins.

The pattern is similar for air pollution and solid wastes. Organizations show no greater tendency to focus on the region as a whole than on specific problem sheds. Again, they tend less to focus on any of the regions than on the nation in general.

Concern at the national level probably stems from the nature of the decisions that relate to environmental quality. Enabling legislation that sets national standards originates here. It is the federal administrative agencies that have the responsibility for establishing criteria and enforcement controls. This is true even though actual implementation remains in the hands of state and local authorities. Consequently, it stands to reason that the various environmental quality and other related organizations should concentrate much of their activity at the national level at which so many critical decisions are made. It must be remembered also that many of the "national" organizations owe their existence and allegiance to their nationwide consistencies.

In an examination of the responses to the questions by consistency type it appears to be the administrative governmental agencies and the conservationist organizations that show interest in specific problem sheds. An exception is the League of Women Voters which exhibits active concern with water pollution at almost every level. The remaining categories of legislative, state and local government, business and industry, and water-resource organizations appear to have a national focus with a secondary involvement at the level of Megalopolis in general.

These findings do not rule out the possibility that concern with Megalopolis as an entity has been increasing. Regional urban planning is a new concept. Table 8.9 shows the frequency of activity in Megalopolis by organizations classified by purpose. This table reveals that 40 percent of all the organizations in the responding sample said that they were concerned with water quality in Megalopolis as a whole. Nearly 20 percent said the same for air quality and 31 percent for the solid waste problem. Multipurpose organizations rank especially high in regional response. What is of interest to this study is the nature of the projections. With ever greater concentration of urban population in this integrated area, each of the environmental problems may burst out of older administrative·structures and require regional administration. The problem-shed approach opens the way to such development. Need for control over water, air, and waste demands interstate cooperation around specific subregions, and more interstate compacts may be forecast in future Megalopolis planning. Problem sheds most certainly highlight the importance of subregional planning and control in Megalopolis. Leaders must learn how to deal with problems that lie outside the traditional political boundaries and to interpret these new demands to legislators and the wider publics.

KINDS OF PROGRAM AND ACTIVITY

Program Emphasis.   To determine the character of the programs and the kinds of activity in which the organizations engaged two questions were asked. The

TABLE 8.8 FREQUENCY OF ACTIVE CONCERN IN PROBLEM SHEDS, BY POWER, AMONG ORGANIZATIONS RATED MOST POWERFUL

Water quality problem sheds

Power	River basins					Megalopolis in general	Nation in general	Total responding to item
	Connecticut	Delaware	Susquehanna	Hudson	Potomac			
Group A	4	4	4	4	4	3	7	7
Group B	10	11	11	10	10	9	22	22
Total	14	15	15	14	14	12	29	29

Air quality problem sheds

Power	Metropolitan regions				Megalopolis in general	Nation in general	Total responding to item
	Boston	New York	Philadelphia	Baltimore-Washington			
Group A	2	2	2	2	2	5	7
Group B	5	10	7	8	7	18	22
Total	7	12	9	10	9	23	29

Solid waste problem sheds

Power	Metropolitan regions				Megalopolis in general	Nation in general	Total responding to item
	Boston	New York	Philadelphia	Baltimore-Washington			
Group A	2	2	1	2	1	5	7
Group B	2	4	2	4	4	14	22
Total	4	6	3	6	5	19	29

TABLE 8.9 FREQUENCY OF ACTIVE CONCERN IN PROBLEM SHEDS, MEGALOPOLIS, AND NATION BY PURPOSE AMONG ORGANIZATIONS RATED MOST POWERFUL

Water quality problem sheds

Purpose	River basins					Megalopolis in general	Nation in general	Total responding to item
	Connecticut	Delaware	Susquehanna	Hudson	Potomac			
Environmental only	1	1	1	1	1*	1	2	3
Natural resources	7	7	7	7	8*	5	10	10
Multipurpose	6	7	7	6	5*	6	15	16
Total	14	15	15	14	14	12	27	29

Air quality problem sheds

Purpose	Metropolitan regions				Megalopolis in general	Nation in general	Total responding to item
	Boston	New York	Philadelphia	Baltimore-Washington			
Environmental only	1	1	1	1	1	1	3
Natural resources	1	4	1	3	2	8	10
Multipurpose	5	7	7	6	6	14	16
Total	7	12	9	10	9	23	29

Solid waste problem sheds

Purpose	Metropolitan regions				Megalopolis in general	Nation in general	Total responding to item
	Boston	New York	Philadelphia	Baltimore-Washington			
Environmental only	0	0	0	0	0	0	0
Natural resources	0	1	0	1	2	9*	10
Multipurpose	4	5	3	5	3	10*	16
Total	4	6	3	6	5	19	26

first was concerned with program emphasis; the second dealt with specific kinds of partisan activity. The following was the first question:

Which of the following would be included in a description of your program emphasis?

_____ Advisory   —offering expert opinion on environmental quality or related questions

_____ Research   —inquiry or investigation into environmental-quality questions to uncover facts and working principles

_____ Education   —the dissemination of facts and considerations about environmental quality

_____ Action-oriented—actively working to make a particular point of view felt in public decisions on environmental quality

_____ Other   —(please specify)

Table 8.10 shows the frequency with which each form of program emphasis was claimed by the top 36 organizations. Because the respondents had the latitude of indicating more than one emphasis, the row totals as well as the column totals are independent. *Education* and *Action-oriented* were indicated more frequently than *Advisory* and *Research*. This is not surprising, considering that "education" is a common euphemism for the kind of indirect lobbying that often takes place among nontaxable voluntary institutions with civic concerns.

Although it is not statistically significant, the group B level of power claimed *Advisory* and *Research* as program emphasis less frequently than the other two categories. Note also that most of the group A organizations indicated a program emphasis other than those listed. To get more specific information each kind of partisan activity was probed.

TABLE 8.10 TYPE OF PROGRAM EMPHASIS, BY POWER, AMONG ORGANIZATIONS RATED MOST POWERFUL

Power	Advisory	Research	Education	Action	Other	Total responding to question
			Program emphasis			
Group A	4	3	4	4	5	7
Group B	13	14	16	16	1	21
Total	17	17	20	20	6	28

TABLE 8.11 KINDS OF PARTISAN ACTIVITY ENGAGED IN BY ORGANIZATIONS RATED MOST POWERFUL

	Activity	Total engaged in activity
1.	Testified before Congressional committees, state legislative committees, and committees at the local level.	24
2.	Had a representative who participated in an advisory agency or committee and/or task force report to a government committee.	21
3.	Testified at public hearings.	20
4.	Published brochures and other material about the organization's efforts toward the improvement of enviornmental quality.	14
5.	Conducted research on technical, economic, or political aspects of environmental quality.	16
6.	Prepared detailed statements concerning environmental quality issues, such as the level of quality or how best to achieve a given level of quality.	16
7.	Published a newsletter that informs recipients about current issues, programs, and innovations in the environmental quality field.	14
8.	Encouraged members of the organization to send letters to congressmen, state legislators, and other government personnel.	10
9.	Had membership in an action-oriented association or federation to express interests or environmental quality.	9
10.	Financed research work of other organizations directly or indirectly.	13
11.	Lobbyied in the Congress, state legislatures, or at the local level.	6
12.	Published a professional journal in which technical aspects of environmental quality are discussed.	2
13.	Advertised activities in newspapers or journals to support, oppose, or amend environmental quality recommendations.	4
14.	Other	2
	Total responding to question	27

Partisan Activity. Table 8.11 shows each kind of partisan activity and the frequency with which it was reported to be engaged in by oragnizations rated most powerful. The order in which each activity is presented in the table is the order of the frequency of involvement of the total sample.

The data in this table are based on responses to the following question:

> Listed below are a few of the kinds of program in which organizations that are active in environmental quality public policy decisions

sometimes engage. Check those in which your organization has been active in the last three years.

For each kind of activity respondents were asked to specify whether it was conducted in relation to air pollution, water pollution, or solid wastes.

The frequency of the first three categories shown in Table 8.11 is an indication of the importance placed on governmental activity when environmental quality questions are concerned. Each of these primary activities—testimony before legislative committees; reports by qualified representatives to government committees; testimony at public hearings—is a face-to-face encounter in which decisions are taken or public opinion is mobilized. That "lobbying in Congress, in state legislatures, or at the local level," is reported by only six of the 27 organizations is a reflection more on the formal definition of "lobbying" than on any actual assessment of reality. Many of the attempts at influence that take place should be regarded as lobbying. We cannot, however, expect government agencies or nontaxable voluntary associations to admit readily to such activity, even when it takes place. These organizations usually leave open lobbying to the League of Women Voters, the Citizens Committee on Natural Resources, or the Chamber of Commerce—all of which have more latitude for such action.

Many of the other activities on the list are directed toward specific publics, not the least of which are members of the supporting organization. The "troops" must be kept informed, new members recruited, annual meetings conducted, and new goals set. Sheer organizational maintenance consumes enormous amounts of time, energy, and money.

ISSUES AND IDEOLOGY

A number of critical issues that activate the organizations concerned with environmental quality tend to center about the method of control of waste dischargers and the method of financing abatement of waste discharges. These foci of conflict rouse cries of "polluter" or "clean-water man," as ideological biases are thrust into an environmental battle. The nature of the division may be gaged by examining the positions taken on control of waste dischargers.

Method of Control of Waste Dischargers. The conflict over method of control occurs because of the degree of control of individual waste dischargers. Table 8.12 lists four different types of control, which range from voluntary, setting a specified water-quality standard, direct requirements for the individual waste discharger according to the nature of his plant and discharge, and finally a flat charge by weight, regardless of individual variations. These four methods represent a scale of increasing control and expense. Table 8.12 shows a cross-tabulation of responses by purpose and consistency type among the organizations rated most powerful. Note that voluntary control was rejected completely by almost universal agreement that it is not effective and the same as no control at all. The second alternative, no limitation on discharge except that such discharge cannot result in reduction of water quality, was popular among the multipurpose organizations, many of which were business and industry consistency types. (Note that

TABLE 8.12   PREFERRED METHOD OF CONTROL OF WASTE DISCHARGERS AMONG ORGANIZATIONS RATED MOST POWERFUL BY POWER, PURPOSE AND CONSTITUENCY TYPE

Assuming that the level of water quality in-stream to be achieved (or desired) has been selected, which of the following means of controlling waste discharges do you favor?

1.   Voluntary control by individual plants and municipalities
2.   No limitation on discharges except that such discharges cannot result in reduction in water quality at the point of discharge below the specified standard (as measured in-stream)
3.   Direct requirements imposed on each individual waste discharger in terms of permitted quantity of discharge, permitted characteristics of discharge, or required degree of treatment, that is, secondary treatment (as measured at the pipe)
4.   The establishment of charges on effluents, that is, cents per unit weight (not volume) of waste material discharged, when the level of charge would be high enough to induce sufficient reduction in industrial and municipal waste discharges to achieve or exceed the desired quality level

| | Type of control | | | |
Power	2	3	4*	Total
Group A	3	2	1	6
Group B	4	11	2	17
Total	7	13	3	23
Purpose				
Environmental quality residuals only	0	1	0	1
Natural resource	0	7	1	8
Multipurpose	7	5	2	14
Total	7	13	3	23
Constituency type				
Government-legislative	2	1	0	3
Government-administrative	0	4	1	5
Organizations of state and local governments	0	3	0	3
Business and industry	5	0	0	5
Conservation	0	5	0	5
Civic	0	0	1	1
Water resource	0	0	1	1
Total	7	13	3	23

* This includes one response that indicated both 3 and 4.

business and industry organizations are unanimous in their support of this method of control.) This is not surprising, for business and industry stand to gain the most by provisions that allow the greatest latitude in utilizing the assimilative capacity of water courses. There is always the possibility of employing political leverage to reduce the interquality standard prescribed and thus maintaining a maximum discharge.

By almost two to one the most frequent response was that direct requirements should be imposed on each waste discharger in terms of permitted quantity of discharge. This alternative was most frequently chosen by the group B level of power, the natural resource organizations, and the following consistency types: government-administrative, state and local government, and conservation organizations. This difference now shows that a sharp cleavage exists over the preferred method of control and presents one axis on which power alignments are made when this issue is debated. Another axis is presented when the method of financing pollution abatement is singled out as a specific option.

Burden of Costs of Private Waste Discharges. The question who is to pay the bill for the reduction of pollution is a major issue because the costs can be considerable. There are three options: all costs to be paid by the waste dischargers; all costs to be paid by the public from local, state, and federal funds; some combination of the two. Table 8.13 shows the responses to two options. None of the organizations indicated that the public should bear all the costs of private waste dischargers. The table presents a cross-tabulation of responses by power, purpose, and consistency types. The first glance reveals a sharp cleavage, with almost a clean split between those organizations who want all costs paid by the waste dischargers and those who want a combination of public and private responsibility for the costs.

A closer examination of the table reveals few sharp power alignments. It is apparent that business and industry organizations favor "some combination" in bearing the cost burden. This is not surprising, for this cost option is in correspondence with the choice of business and industry groups to control waste discharge according to individual requirements as already reported. Natural resource organizations, which overwhelmingly (three to one) indicate that all private waste dischargers should bear all the costs, reflect a more general position that the environment is distinctly a public possession rather than an ownerless resource to be exploited freely by private enterprise. Private enterprise on the other hand, believes that a waterway is a public responsibility and is used widely by the public for recreational purposes and for the discharge of municipal wastes. These conditions argue for joint responsibility of private and public users. Here is the crux of the ideological issue which boils over in numerous public debates.

It is clear from the results shown in Table 8.13 that with the exception of these two contending parties there is no other clear pattern. It is the splitting of the organizations on this issue that commands attention. For many the issue is not ideological but rather how to get the job done best.

Environmental Influence Systems and Megalopolis

Two objectives of the chapter have been realized: the identification of powerful environmental leaders and organizations in Megalopolis and the patterns of deci-

TABLE 8.13   PREFERRED METHOD OF FINANCING AMONG ORGANIZATIONS RATED MOST POWERFUL, BY POWER, PURPOSE, AND CONSTITUENCY TYPE

Assuming that the level of water quality has been selected, who, in the case of private waste discharges, should bear the costs of improving water quality or reducing pollution?

_____ All costs should be paid by the waste dischargers

_____ All costs should be paid by the public from local, state and federal funds*

_____ Some combination of the above (please specify)

Power	Paid by waste dischargers	Some combination	Total
Group A	2	4	6
Group B	10	7	17
Total	12	11	23
Purpose			
Environmental quality-residuals only	0	1	1
Natural resource	6	2	8
Multipurpose	6	8	14
Total	12	11	23
Constituency type			
Government-legislative	1	2	3
Government-administrative	3	2	5
Organizations of state and local governments	2	1	3
Business and industry	1	4	5
Conservation	3	2	5
Civic	1	0	1
Water resource	1	0	1
Total	12	11	23

The top of the table shows the heading "Method of financing" spanning the "Paid by waste dischargers" and "Some combination" columns.

* No organizational respondent specified this option.

sion making utilized. The in-fighting over specific issues has not been reported. What has been shown is a structure of great variety. Powerful environmental leaders are operating from the federal administrative branch, the federal legislative branch, national conservation organizations, state and local governments, the federal judiciary, research organizations, and the Delaware River Basin Commission. Although leaders change, these power bases remain.

Most of the organizations do not devote their full energies to environmental quality problems. The major decision-making areas involve organizations concerned with the preservation or use of wildlife or wild environments and with natural resources as they relate more directly to economic exploitation, urban-problem-oriented organizations with environmental concerns, and business and industrial organizations faced with waste discharges that injure the environment.

The variety of special interests is expanded by pollution that ranges from such principal causes as water, air, and solid-waste residuals. Organizations have such different investments that it is not possible to treat environmental quality as a single problem but rather as a multiple one. Although the general public is particularly aroused by air pollution, water pollution, and solid wastes, in that order, powerful environmental organizations are more commonly working on water pollution.

The issues are similarly proliferated, but the cleavages are clearer in the case of water quality. We have seen that the method of control and of financing the improvement of water quality tends to position conservation organizations against business and industrial organizations as such issues as level of water quality and payment for it became matters of public decision.

The structure of power we seek is elusive, however we know that organizations are aware of the appropriate problem sheds that necessitate particular controls. These are regional and interstate in character. Organizations report concern with Megalopolis as a whole, but the immediate demands of water (or air) supply or water (or air) quality in a given basin receive top priority. New forms of governmental administration such as water compacts and air-control districts are being developed to deal with these regional subsystems. Meanwhile, national organizations, both federal and private, housed as they are in Megalopolis, cannot escape the growing interpenetration of environmental quality. The growing urban population of Megalopolis and its increasing industrialization and auto transport continue to demand overall planning and development. The renewed attention to fast interurban mass transportation is only one of the many indications of this regional awareness.

For the researcher the impact of urban-oriented leaders and organizations on environmental leaders and organizations is significant. The discovery of the degree of overlap is the final objective of this chapter.

The Linkage of Environmental Leaders and Organizations with Urban-Oriented Leaders and Organizations in Megalopolis

The search for linkages between urban-oriented and environmental quality leaders and organizations required an examination of the Megalopolis Generalized Influence Network in contact with the Megalopolis Environmental Quality Network.[9] A major theoretical stance was taken in the assumption that urban-oriented leaders and associations were influential in initiating, supporting, or vetoing actions taken by environmental quality leaders and organizations. Furthermore, it was believed that a high degree of support was necessary to increase the resources and personnel directed toward the solution of environmental quality problems and that such maximum support would originate with urban-oriented leaders and associations. There was little known about the ties between the two networks. The task was clear: identify the leaders and organizations reputed to be most powerful in public policy decisions related to environmental pollution and seek out the nature of their linkage with urban-oriented leaders and organizations. Sometimes this linkage can be found in the simple overlap of urban-oriented leaders and associations who become interested in environmental quality problems; at other times the linkage is established by working relationships. Contact points take on significance as sites for influence and decision making. Points of contact are identified as specially arranged conferences, government task forces and committees, government commissions, and boards of private associations in environmental quality. Even government ceremonies may serve to bring the leaders together. The interaction of urban-oriented leaders with specialists in fields closely identified with environmental quality can be traced to the industrial firm and the trade and professional association.

Compositional Overlap of Urban-Oriented Organizations and Environmental Quality Organizations

The identification of urban-oriented organizations was described in Chapter 7 and the 20 most powerful were listed. That list is reproduced in Table 8.14. Since the most powerful environmental organizations are known, the overlap can be determined and those urban organizations that have also received ranking as powerful environmental organizations are identified. The U.S. Chamber of Commerce receives a Group A ranking as an environmental organization; Group B ranking is given to organizations like the U.S. Conference of Mayors, the National League of Cities, the National Association of Manufacturers, the National Association of Counties, the League of Women Voters, and the Council of State Governments. These seven organizations are in a crucial position because they can draw on large resources and skilled profesional staffs to increase the emphasis on environmental problems. This is no little matter, for other urban problems press on them, and struggle for priority determinations is constant.

Although the overlap is relatively small, the degree of common interests in both lists of organizations is high. At least eight other organizations have been active (AFL-CIO, Ford Foundation, Urban America, International Association of City Managers, NAACP, National Urban League, U.S. Department of Housing and Urban Development, and U.S. Office of Economic Opportunity) in the environmental quality area. The major factor that distinguished all 15 in terms of environmental quality involvement is the kind of activities in which they engage. In general, the degree ranges from making resolutions or pronouncements about the need for environmental management, to lobbying for or supporting specific pieces of legislation, to hiring staff specialists. Each degree necessitates a larger commitment of resources, time, and personnel. Only a relatively few have hired environmental specialists and given them full-time assignments. Such organizations include the U.S. Chamber of Commerce, the National Association of Manufacturers, the League of Women Voters, and the Ford Foundation. Others may have joined this list since the research was completed.

Few organizations devote their full energies to an area of environmental quality. As reported earlier, this is equally true of those that we have identified as "environmental quality" organizations. Only five of the 26 most powerful said that

TABLE 8.14   THE TOP 20 MOST POWERFUL URBAN-ORIENTED ORGANIZATIONS (FINAL LIST, 1968) AND OVERLAPPING IDENTITY AS POWERFUL ENVIRONMENTAL ORGANIZATION

Rank as urban-oriented organization	Classification rank as environmental organization	Most powerful urban-oriented organizations
1	Group B	U.S. Department of Housing and Urban Development
2		U.S. Conference of Mayors
3		U.S. Office of Economic Opportunity
4		National Urban League
5		U.S. Department of Health, Education and Welfare
6		AFL-CIO
7		Ford Foundation
8		U.S. Department of Labor
9		National Association for the Advancement of Colored People
10		National Urban Coalition
11		National Alliance for Businessmen
12	Group B	National League of Cities
13	Group A	Chamber of Commerce of the United States
14		International Association of City Managers
15	Group B	National Association of Manufacturers
16	Group B	National Association of Counties
17	Group B	League of Women Voters of the United States
18		Congress of Racial Equality
19		Urban America
20	Group B	Council of State Governments

they were working solely on environmental quality problems (air pollution, water pollution, and solid wastes).

A great overlap occurs between the top organizations in the urban-oriented and environmental quality areas in terms of multiple activity in the field of urban problems. This is also true of top officials in these organizations. The separation of the two types of organization is only a distinction between degrees of emphasis and priority. The high overlap between the two classes can be gaged by their working relations.

Working Relations Between Urban-Oriented and Environmental Quality Organizations

Working relations are links that indicate a coming together of powerful urban-oriented and environmental quality organizations. These links were identified by 14 expert judges who were asked to rate the most important environmental quality organizations and to specify the working relations of their organizations with others.[10]

Working relations were ascertained as judges were given a list of the most powerful organizations and asked to indicate the extent of their participation on a five-point scale:

1. Know about their work on environmental problems.
2. Have approached or have been approached for information about environmental problems.
3. Have exchanged ideas about environmental programs or issues.
4. Have worked together on program development.
5. Have supported one another on environmental issues.
Please name issue.

These judges agreed with the environment officials from the 91 environmental organizations in Megalopolis that the most powerful private urban-oriented organizations with environmental programs are the U. S. Chamber of Commerce, the National League of Cities, the National Association of Manufacturers, the League of Women Voters, the U. S. Conference of Mayors, the Council of State Governments, and the National Association of Counties. Officials representing these organizations (see note) have described their working relations with other top environmental quality organizations (see Figure 8.2). In the center of the figure are the seven urban-oriented organizations, which are among the top environmental quality organizations, and 19 other top environmental quality organizations. The lines connecting the organizations represent the working relationships reported by the seven urban-oriented organizations. Reciprocal choices are not included. Solid lines represent "supportive" contacts and dotted lines represent "informative" contacts. The organizations at the top of the figure represent private organizations and those at the bottom represent executive and legislative committees and agencies in the Federal Government.[11]

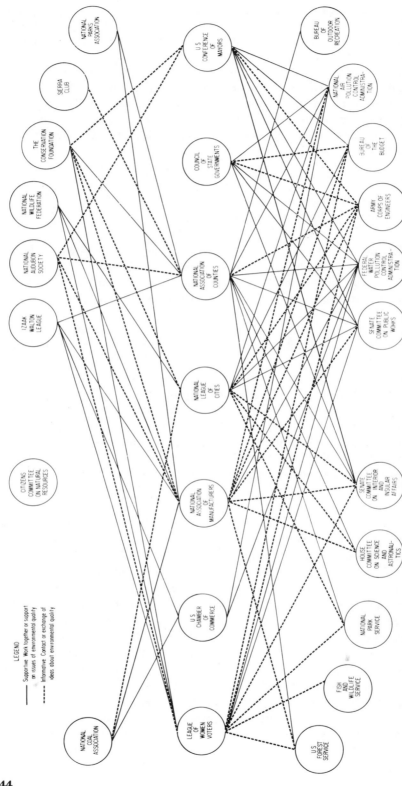

Figure 8.2 Working relationships between urban-oriented organizations and other environmental quality organizations as indicated by urban-oriented organizations only.

244

Table 8.15 describes the working relations between the urban-oriented organizations and the government and private organizations presented in Figure 8.2. The working relations are given in terms of coefficients of interaction and divided into informative, supportive, and total categories.[12] The coefficient of interaction is the actual number of contacts between the classes of organization, divided by the total number of possible contacts between them.

The interaction coefficients reveal that the urban-oriented organizations tend to have a wider range of total contacts with government organizations. The pattern is similar when the coefficients of interaction within the informative and supportive categories are compared. Among the private organizations there are more contacts of a supportive nature with the urban organizations. Officials of urban organizations report that their informative and supportive contacts with government organizations are equal. Yet overall there is the tendency toward a wider range of contacts of a supportive nature with both governmental and private organizations.

The Linking of Urban-Oriented and Environmental Quality Leaders

Two separate investigations have identified 26 of the most powerful urban-oriented leaders and 46 of the most powerful environmental leaders. Chapter 5 described the top of the top among the urban-oriented leaders of Megalopolis. The list held the names of John V. Lindsay, Nelson A. Rockefeller, Bayard Rustin, Whitney Young, Arthur J. Goldberg, David Rockefeller, Richard J. Hughes, A. Philip Randolph, Kenneth B. Clark, John K. Galbraith, Roy Wilkins, the Reverend Leon Sullivan, Walter E. Washington, McGeorge Bundy, Paul N. Ylvisaker, James Rouse, Richardson Dilworth, George Meany, Joseph Clark, Kingman Brewster, John Collins, Terrence, Cardinal Cooke, Cornelius W. Owens, Robert C. Weaver, Andrew Heiskell, and Milton Eisenhower. These leaders were selected from a total of 200 key leaders by top leaders who considered them most influential in the "shaping of urban policy and programming for the Boston-to-Washington urban region."

TABLE 8.15 INTERACTION COEFFICIENTS AMONG SEVEN URBAN-ORIENTED ORGANIZATIONS AND OTHER ORGANIZATIONS WITH ENVIRONMENTAL QUALITY PROGRAMS, AS REPORTED BY THE URBAN-ORIENTED ORGANIZATIONS

	Contacts with seven urban-oriented organizations		
	Informative	Supportive	Total
Governmental N = 11	.26	.27	.53
Private N = 8	.13	.23	.36

This chapter has listed the most powerful environmental quality leaders identified by the same reputational techniques from a large population of leaders. A
comparison of the lists of urban-oriented and environmental leaders indicates that
there is almost no overlap. Only Laurance S. Rockefeller appears on the two lists.

Among the powerful urban leaders many, however, have had considerable experience with environmental quality problems. One might list John V. Lindsay,
Nelson A. Rockefeller, Richard J. Hughes, Joseph Clark, Richardson Dilworth,
and Paul N. Ylvisaker. Most of these men have played important roles in the
Delaware River Basin Compact. All by virtue of their responsibilities have faced
problems of increasing air pollution and solid wastes. As we have seen, the demands of other urban problems (race relations, unemployment and poverty,
housing, public education, crime, etc.) competed for their attention and their
urgency drained away their energies from environmental activity. It is only one
step further to define the problem of environment as a federal responsibility.

The omission of senators, congressmen, and cabinet officials from the urban-
oriented list automatically reduced the possibility of overlap, an omission that becomes especially significant when the discussion of environmental role types is
recalled. In general, environmental leadership is provided by concerned national
conservation organizations and Federal Governmental officials in the legislative
and administrative branches. Although conservation leaders have some differences on public policy decisions, they are in general agreement insofar as they
favor a continued improvement of the quality of the environment. Although the
administrative and legislative branches of the Federal Government may have different positions on some aspects of the desired outcomes and policy implementation, they have overwhelmingly supported legislation that will eventually lead to
improvement in the physical environment. Generally urban-oriented leaders defined the environmental issues as those to be settled by government and environmental specialists. Whereas most would profess their active concern, our data
show that they personally put low priority on environmental problems and only
a few have given active attention to their improvement.

In the population of urban-oriented leaders 6 percent listed their interest in
air pollution, 3 percent in water pollution, 2 percent in wastes, and 4 percent in
planning, zoning, and preservation of open land—a total of 15 percent. When
asked to report those problems on which they were working hardest, the same
results were found. Only one in 20 said that they were working hardest on air
pollution, water pollution, or solid wastes. Although small in number, this group
of leaders may increase as environmental needs grow more demanding. Moreover, the role of top urban leaders as a supportive force must be reckoned with.
If government and conservation leaders are to find support (and votes) for more
energetic efforts in environmental quality, urban-oriented leaders and organizations must provide a back up. If progress is to be made, each will need the other.
Where do the twain meet?

Contacts and Working Relations Between Urban-Oriented
and Environmental Quality Leaders

Key urban leaders and top environmental quality leaders may meet in a number
of places which have significance for their identification, the establishment of

contact and working relations, and the conduct of policy making. The first requirement is to identify the influential persons who are actually in contact. Important official ceremonies in public or private life offer the social analyst this
opportunity because the guests or participants represent a (sociometric) selection. President Johnson's bill-signing ceremony for the four major conservation
bills of 1968 is one example. More than 400 leaders were brought together on
that occasion.

The attendance of key leaders in urban and environmental quality fields at
specially arranged conferences again produces a list of participants represent a
(sociometric) selection. The Swarthmore Regional Conference on Environmental
Problems of the Delaware Valley in 1968 assembled a group believed to be influential in environmental problems. In these two cases, the White House ceremony and the Swarthmore Conference, the burden was heavy on those responsible for bringing people together to make sure that they missed no one of real
influence or whose activity deserved recognition.

Contacts made in the conduct of policy making may be identified by analyzing
the board of directors or trustees of private environmental quality associations;
16 on our list of 36 are private. Each has a board of highly selected personnel,
and each board seeks to retain men of large influence who will commit themselves to the work. This can be illustrated by the board of directors of Resources
for the Future. All 14 men on the Board are well known and have built outstanding careers in their professional lives—some by work in business, economics,
and public service, some by their specific contribution to environmental quality
study and action. Their policy-making decisions set the pattern and direction of
the association.

Executive and legislative government at federal, state, and local levels rely on
lay and government committees for study, advice, and sometimes administrative
action. The Federal Government reaches out for personnel in all parts of the
United States. The selection may have political coloration but there is always the
effort to bring together people "who count"—that is, who can command respect
and influence others. The President of the United States can appoint task forces,
advisory committees, and councils. Before taking office President-elect Nixon
appointed a 50-member Task Force on Resources and Environment which reported to him on January 9, 1969. The composition of that force is of interest because it represented a combination of men and associations. An analysis of this
task force opens perspective (or speculation) on the prestige evaluations of the
President and his advisers. This task force strongly recommended naming a
Special Assistant for Environmental Affairs working out of the White House. The
President's response to this recommendation was to set up an Urban Affairs Council in February 1969 and a new cabinet-level Committee on Environment in June
1969. This Committee was composed solely of high government officials. The
President and Vice President served as titular chairman and vice-chairman, but
the key man was the President's science adviser, Dr. Lee A. Dubridge, who
served as executive secretary. The Secretaries of Agriculture, Commerce, Health,
Education and Welfare, Housing and Urban Development, and Transportation
were the other members. President Nixon described the committee as comparable
in its field to two other White House policy advisory groups—the National Security Council and the Urban Affairs Council. In announcing its establishment the
President said, "the quality of the American environment is threatened as it has

not been threatened before in our history." This act and the composition of the committee now indicates the rising priority of environmental quality and identifies the responsibility of the departments designated. It is important to note a parallel action by the President—the establishment of a 15-member Citizens Advisory Committee on Environmental Quality headed by Laurance S. Rockefeller. The former 12-member Advisory Committee on Recreation and Natural Beauty appointed by President Johnson was moved intact into the new advisory group and three new appointments were made.[13] The composition of this advisory group and the new appointments are indicators of the cross-contact of environmental and urban leaders.[14] As environmental quality climbs to higher priority, it is expected that the distinction between urban-oriented and environmental quality leaders will become less meaningful. At this time the extent of their mutual involvement is a significant indicator of the commitments made to the importance of environmental quality. In January 1970 the President created a three-man Council on Environmental Quality, headed by Russell Train, Assistant Secretary of the Interior, stating that this council would report to him directly. It would advise him and serve in environmental quality as the Council of Economic Advisors serves in economic matters affecting the nation.[15]

Other contact points are the Federal Water Resources Council and the Federal Air Pollution Control Council. Common lobbying activities of urban-oriented and environmental quality leaders are another important form of contact. The new Environmental Protection Agency should play an increasing role as a center of activity.

A systematic analysis of committee work on environmental problems in trade and voluntary organizations and on government boards, commissions, and councils would reveal urban-oriented leaders who are growing in experience. Studies of the interests and motivations of these leaders would provide the knowledge necessary for the development of new leaders. It is probably safe to say that nobody knows today how leaders develop their commitments to environmental quality problems—especially those who are badgered by competing demands for their services.

Summary of Findings

1. Most of the structure in environmental quality decision making is the same as that in public policy decisions in general. Few organizations devote their full energies to an area of environmental quality. The only examples of wholly specialized organizations from the list of the top 36 engaged in environmental quality are the Federal Water Quality Administration, the National Air Pollution Control Administration, and the nongovernmental Water Pollution Control Federation. All the rest have extensive interests and activities other than environmental quality as related to the management of residuals.

2. Four established decision-making areas in environmental quality are (a) that concerned with the preservation or use of wildlife and wild environments; (b) that concerned with natural resources as they relate more directly to economic exploitation; (c) that concerned with environmental quality as it is identified in the general setting of urban problems; and (d) that concerned with the interests of business and industry in environmental quality.

3. A great deal of overlap occurs between the top organizations in the urban-oriented and environmental quality areas in terms of multiple activity in urban problems.

4. The most powerful urban-oriented organizations with high repute in environmental quality programming are the Chamber of Commerce of the United States, National Association of Manufacturers, the League of Women Voters of the United States, the National League of Cities, the Council of State Governments, the National Association of Counties, and the U. S. Conference of Mayors.

5. The most powerful environmental quality organizations are the Federal Water Pollution Control Administration, the U. S. Senate Committee on Public Works, the U.S. Senate Committee on Interior and Insular Affairs, the U.S. House of Representatives Committee on Public Works, the U.S. House of Representatives Committee on Science and Astronautics, the U.S. Corps of Engineers, and the Bureau of the Budget, Natural Resources Division.

6. Government and private organizations join together to shape environmental policy. They exchange information, develop legislative programs, and support one another on issues.

7. Operational interests in environment are divided among regional and interstate problem sheds, the nation, and Megalopolis as a whole.

8. Little overlap occurs between top urban-oriented leaders in Megalopolis and the most powerful environmental leaders.

9. One in 20 urban-oriented leaders work hardest on environmental problems.

10. Points of contact for urban-oriented and environmental quality leaders include government ceremonies, conferences, government task forces and committees, government commissions, boards of private associations in environmental quality, and industrial firms and associations.

Notes

1. It should be noted that environmental quality and environmental pollution are used interchangeably to refer to those environmental quality problems that are caused by the discharge of wastes (residuals) into the water, air, and land environments; hence the subsequent use of the term "environmental residuals."

2. Reputational technique is employed in two ways in the identification. In the first stage it was used to secure persons and organizations believed to be powerful and active in environmental quality in general. In the questionnaire stage the issue of specific reputational technique was emphasized. Respondents were asked to name persons and organizations active and influential in specific issues of environmental pollution. A copy of the Megalopolis Environmental Quality Inventory, Mailing History and Report of Returns may be examined in Appendix A.

3. As for the sample of 91 organizations that answered the questionnaire, randomness has been assumed for the purpose of statistical tests of association, even though the sample is biased. No descriptive inference is made from this sample to the whole population of organizations that influences decision making in Megalopolis.

4. It was not assumed that the informants were aware of any theoretical distinctions between power and influence. The two concepts were used interchangeably in the research operations and are used interchangeably in this report.

5. This cutting point is simply a break in the continuum and is therefore arbitrary. It is useful, however, in separating out the top eight organizations of greater influence from those powerful organizations of somewhat lesser influence.

6. A resurvey was made in June 1970. Although important changes had occurred, a high proportion of the earlier personnel remained unchanged or occupied new positions of influence.

7. This is not surprising in light of the fact that few organizations devote 100 percent of their efforts to residuals problems.

8. Note that high returns can be secured from organizational officials because they have a more direct responsibility and concern for systematic information directly relevant to their work.

9. See Chapter 3.

10. The panel of judges included, James Watt, National Chamber of Commerce; Julius F. Rotheman, National AFL-CIO; Mrs. C. F. S. Sharpe, National League of Women Voters; Don Alexander, National League of Cities; Fred Jordan, National Urban Coalition; James Martin, Council of State Governments; John Field, U.S. Conference of Mayors; J. William Bethea, Urban America; Blair Bower, Resources for the Future; Roger McClanhan, National Industrial Conference Board; Bernard Hilderbrand, National Association of Counties; Daniel W. Cannon, National Association of Manufacturers; Herbert E. Striner, W. E. Upjohn Institute; Mr. Bernard Russel, Housing and Urban Development. These men are all well qualified to make the rankings. They are all in positions which enable them to observe and read about the actions of the organizations. All have a long tenure in Washington, D. C. All are in the forefront of their own organizations. Most are in the thick of issues and their resolutions. At least four are registered lobbyists.

11. This pattern represents the report of an official of each of the seven urban-oriented organizations. It must be regarded as illustrative rather than as a definitive statement. Note that "supportive" means that the rater indicated working together or supporting an organization on issues of environmental quality; "informative" means contact or exchange of ideas about environmental qualtiy with another organization.

12. As shown in Figure 8.2, supportive relationships indicate working together or giving support on issues of environmental quality; informative relationships indicate contact or exchange of ideas about environmental quality.

13. Committee members include Edmund N. Bacon, Joseph H. Davis, Rene J. Dubos, James H. Evans, Jean Fassler, Grace T. Hamilton, Wesley Hodge, Tom McCall, Willard F. Rockwell, Jr., John Ben Sheppard, Leland L. Sillin Jr., Thaddeus F. Walcowicz, Harry M. Weese, Gordon K. Zimmerman, and Henry L. Diamond, counsel.

14. The Citizens Advisory Committee on Environmental Quality has released a handbook for social action leaders titled *Community Action for Environmental Quality*, U. S. Government Printing Office, Washington, D. C., 60 cents.

15. Robert Cahn of the *Christian Science Monitor* and Boston is a second member from Megalopolis to be appointed to the new council. The other member is Dr. Gordon J. F. McDonald of California.

CHAPTER NINE

Influence Systems and Decision Making in a Specific Subregion: The Delaware River Basin and the Issue of Water Quality Levels

James L. Barfoot and Paul D. Planchon, research associates, assumed the major responsibility for this study. Most of this chapter rests on the research and writing of James Barfoot. Data on linkage patterns were collected by Paul Planchon. Echelon analysis was contributed by the principal investigator.

The Delaware river runs through four of the heaviest populated states of Megalopolis. It is the source of water for a score of major cities and provides recreational facilities for millions of people. The issue over water quality standards for the Delaware estuary is an example of social conflict in which the stakes, both social and economic, are high.

In 1966–1967 a decision had to be made. Various parties at interest were given an opportunity at public hearings to indicate which of the five levels of water quality they preferred and to propose modifications. A decision was made by the Delaware River Basin Commission on the information gathered at these hearings.

This chapter is a report on a supplementary study, the purpose of which was to probe intensively into the decision-making factors affecting a subregion of Megalopolis. It was hoped that a Delaware River Basin Influence Network would be uncovered and that its relation to the wider megalopolitan environmental and generalized networks might be determined.

The Setting: The Delaware River Basin

The Delaware River Basin, which consists of all the drainage area of the Delaware River and its tributaries, serves sections of four states (see Figure 9.1). In Delaware it reaches from Cape Henlopen through Wilmington to the Pennsylvania line. The boundary between New Jersey and Pennsylvania is the river itself. The basin in New Jersey stretches from Cape May to the New York state line. In Pennsylvania it spreads over an area extending across the entire eastern portion of the state, and in New York it includes much of the Catskill Mountains in the southeastern section of the state. It also contains the major cities of Wilmington, Delaware, Camden and Trenton, New Jersey, and Easton, Chester, Reading, Philadelphia, and Allentown, Pennsylvania. In all it constitutes an area

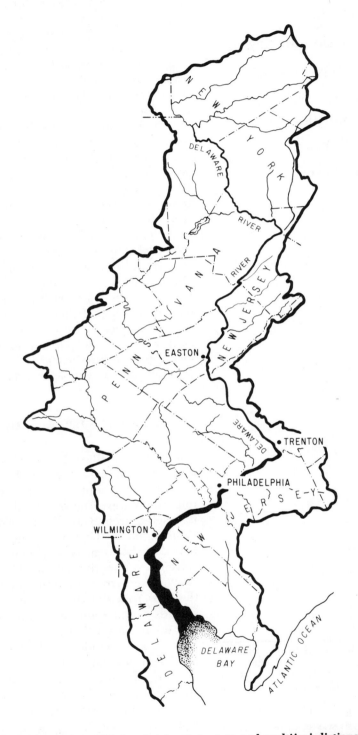

Figure 9.1   Delaware River Basin, showing interstate and multijurisdictional aspects.

252

of 13,000 square miles in at least part of 38 counties and a major portion of 25 more, but it is only a fraction of the total served, in one way or another by the river. That region includes all of the states of Delaware and New Jersey, New York City, and a small part of Connecticut. Although its inhabitants are not affected by the river to the same degree, they make up about one-eighth of the population of the entire country.[1]

The Delaware River rises as two streams in the Catskill Mountains of New York and descends to Liston Point, Delaware, where it becomes the Delaware Bay. It has nine major tributaries.[2]

Important points in the course of the river are (a) the two branches in New York's Catskill Mountains, from which New York City gets much of its water supply, (b) the Kittaninny Mountains and the Delaware Water Gap, above which the Tocks Island Dam is being built to create a large lake in the Valley near Stroudsburg, Pennsylvania, and (c) the estuary which flows for 85 miles from the fall line near Trenton, New Jersey, to Linton Point. Most of the estuary is navigable and the greatest population of the basin is concentrated on its banks.[3]

It is not a large river. Its 370-mile length ranks it seventeenth among the streams that enter tidewater in the United States. At Trenton, where it joins the estuary, its rate of flow is 5 million gallons a minute. Record high flow for the river occurred in 1955 as the result of Hurricane Diane. A record low flow occurred in 1965.[4] These events constitute part of the challenge the river has presented to its users in recent years. The response to this challenges was a series of important decisions that became the subject of this study.

Industry in this river basin includes chemicals, cement, iron, petroleum, clothing, airplanes, paper, fertilizer, and heavy and light machinery. It is one of the largest building centers in the world and supports a comparably large shipping industry.[5]

The Delaware River as a Social Problem

When it came into being the Delaware River Basin Commission was charged with the development and implementation of a comprehensive plan for water resources in the basin as a whole.[6] Among other difficult problems the Commission inherited from its predecessor, the Interstate Commission on the Delaware River Basin (INCODEL), was the pollution of the lower estuarine reaches of the river. This heavily populated and industrialized area was subject to low levels of dissolved oxygen due to a concentration of oxygen-demanding wastes discharged into the river. The result was that during warm weather the river was subject to unsightly septic or anaerobic conditions which gave off unpleasant odors and were hazardous to aquatic life.[7]

The use of water for domestic purposes depends on the kinds of pollutants contained in it. It is always more expensive to treat water at higher levels of pollution to make it safe for drinking, but once it requires any treatment at all the added expense of conditioning increasingly poorer qualities is not excessive. Water that is clean enough for recreational use must often be treated in proportions comparable to more polluted water.

The quality of water used for industrial purposes is a highly technical question that varies from situation to situation. Much of the water employed by industry is needed for cooling, which can tolerate low quality levels. Again the cost principle is the same: if any treatment at all is required, the incremental costs to treat poorer quality water are relatively low.

Related to recreational use is the use of water by aquatic life that will be allowed to survive. It is true, for example, that many popular fish will live at lower pollution levels.[8]

Aesthetic enjoyment of water, which must be considered a use, is mostly visual and to some extent olfactory. Aesthetic levels of bodies of water are yet to be quantified. Recreational uses are easier to quantify. Here the presence of certain concentrations of pathogenic bacteria have served as an indication of relative safety. Thus a hierarchy of uses may be identified—from swimming and maximum body contact to boating with minimum body contact to no contact at all.[9]

If the amount of dissolved oxygen in the water is depressed by an overload of organic wastes, bacteria that do not use free oxygen will take over in a process, that is said to go on anaerobically, in which case an unpleasant odor will be given off.[10] The significance is that a threshold exists at which polluted water becomes radically more objectionable. This illustrates a quality of water that generate many of the issues that arise; that is, water (and the environment in general) can assimilate a certain amount of wastes without objectionable odors only if the conditions are right. In this view there are optimum levels and methods of waste discharge. The nature of the body of water, the amount of wastes discharged, the method and timing of the discharges, and even the weather all affect its capacity to assimilate the wastes without the development of objectionable conditions.

The variety of uses and the multiplicity of factors affecting water quality indicate the complexity in which the issue of water-quality level is embedded. These variables not only bring about a clash of interests (e.g., business versus conservationists) but also the confrontation of technical specialists who debate the methods of water control.

Before the Delaware River Basin Commission was established there were more than 895 traditional government units in the four states that might have claimed jurisdiction: states, counties, cities, towns, townships, boroughs, and villages. In addition, 19 different federal agencies were active in the Delaware Basin. Such multiplicity made unified control of the river an impossibility. The development of an effective administrative unit will overall powers is a regional issue with historic roots.[11]

The Delaware River Basin Commission and Water Pollution

After a long political struggle the Delaware River Basin Commission was created on November 2, 1961, when the President of the United States and the Governors of New York, Pennsylvania, New Jersey, and Delaware signed their names to the Delaware River Basin Compact. Prior approval had been granted by the Congress of the United States and the state legislatures of the four states. Thus the first federal and state Compact gave the Commission primary authority to implement comprehensive multipurpose planning, coordination, and effectuation of the development of water resources in the Delaware River Basin.[12] Its first major problem was founded on the growing need to protect, develop, and allocate the water supply of the growing cities along its waterway.[13] Water quality was soon to become a major problem.

In July 1966 the Federal Water Pollution Control Administration released a preliminary report on the Delaware Estuary[14] which indicated that waste discharges in combination with other factors had placed such a heavy burden on the assimilative capacity of the estuary that near Philadelphia a condition prevailed during the spring and summer in which no dissolved oxygen was present in the water. This not only interfered with the recreational and aesthetic enjoyment of the river but threatened the procreation and survival of game and commercial fish. In addition, indications of the presence of microorganisms harmful to humans posed a health hazard.[15]

During the development of a comprehensive study by its advisory committees a confrontation between the two segments of the public concerned with water quality took place. These segments were the supporting public, pressing for improved water quality for the river, and the target public, or the waste dischargers themselves.[16] This confrontation was characterized by much dialogue and reorientation on both sides—in particular, among the waste dischargers who participated the most. These events set the tone of the ensuing issue.

The Commission analyzed and evaluated the findings and the five alternative levels of pollution abatement (the objective sets) offered by the comprehensive study.

Five Water Quality Levels and the Related Objective Sets

An action program or "objective set" was formulated around each water quality standard. Each objective set was really a package with a specified price tag. It took into consideration the different needs of different sections of the estuary and the changes of season.[17] The costs associated with each set made the options a focus of controversy.

Objective set I was the highest level considered. It would allow great increases in water-contact recreation and ensure safe passage of migratory fish. It would cost an estimated $460 million dollars, but because the techniques it required are not well understood this figure was considered uncertain; 160 to $350 million dollars estimated benefits in recreation would result from this set.

Objective set II would allow an increased but restricted area of water-contact recreation and aquatic life would face some danger, particularly the more sensitive species. It did, however, provide for the passage of certain migratory fish during season. The costs would be between 215 and 315 million dollars; between 140 and 320 million dollars in recreation benefits were thought to result from this set.

Objective set III would allow for most of the benefits that objective set II would provide but no special provision was made for the passage of fish. The set would cost 85 to 155 million dollars and would benefit recreation to a value of 130 and 310 millions.

Objective set IV would show only a small increase over the level of quality provided by objective set V, which was the level in 1964. Primarily, the chances of septic conditions occurring in the estuary would be greatly reduced. This set would cost 65 to 130 million dollars but would produce 120 to 280 million dollars in recreation benefits.

Objective set V referred to the prevailing level. The Delaware Estuary Study pointed out that this level was not satisfactory and that a dangerous condition of water pollution menaced the river.[18]

The Design and Method of the Supplementary Study

Our research sought to identify the various decision makers and factors associated with decision making as controversy over the adoption of a water quality standard was underway. The Delaware River Basin Commission gave the various parties at interest an opportunity to indicate which of the alternative objective sets they preferred and to state their arguments. Ultimately, a decision was to be made. The ensuing issue provided the investigators with a circumscribed setting in which to study the parties whose preferred outcomes were explicit and on which debate was on public record. The issue itself is an example of social conflict in its most frequent form; circumscribed and nonviolent controversy. The stakes, both political and economic, were high. The higher the quality standards adopted, the greater the costs to the interests who used the river to dispose of wastes. On the other hand, continuation of the old conditions promised political costs.

The design involved three methods of collecting information: (a) subject interviews (b) informant interviews, and (c) documents. The sample of subjects consisted of people who testified at the hearings on water quality standards for the estuary. They were usually the representatives of collectivities with interests in using the river either for waste-disposal or in some other way that required a high level of water quality.[19]

These subject-respondents were interviewed to gather the necessary information that could not be found in documents, a procedure that also served to validate and supplement the data obtained from documents and informants. The subjects of the analysis were agencies of state and local governments, citizens and professional associations, business and industrial organizations, businesses, and various coalitions of individuals and groups with interests in the outcome of the issue. Both sides of the issue were represented. Testimony included statements to back the positions taken and additional information to clarify the issue.

Thirty-five subject-respondents who represented some 60 organizations (depending on how affiliated organizations are divided were interviewed. To supplement this 20 informants were interviewed. The subject-respondents were asked standard questions designed to allow quantification and statistical analysis later on. Interviews with informants varied according to their areas of knowledge.[20]

The Authorities and the Partisans

The actors in the issue of water quality can be divided into authorities and partisans according to their roles in the decision-making process. The authorities were the individuals and organizations who in an official capacity performed a central role in making the decisions. The partisans were those who took sides on the issue.

THE AUTHORITIES

The two important authorities are the Federal Water Pollution Control Administration and the Delaware River Basin Commission.

The Federal Water Pollution Control Administration in 1966 concluded the Delaware Estuary Comprehensive Study, which was built on earlier studies by the U. S. Public Health Service and the U. S. Army Corps of Engineers. In the final study three advisory committees, the Policy Advisory Committee, the Technical Advisory Committee, and the Water Use Advisory Committee, brought together representatives of more than 100 state, interstate, and federal agencies which had the legal power to abate pollution. Because of this wide representation, the study carried unusual weight. Its role in formulating the standards for the estuary was unique.

First, rather than making a single recommendation, it provided several alternative options for decision makers to use in deciding on standards. Second, it made at least a partial analysis of the "needs" of the people along the estuary in terms of improved water quality as an integrated part of its output. Finally, its advisory committee, whether or not entirely by design, provided a forum for the confrontation between the economic demands that strained against expensive pollution abatement and the demand for improved quality that strained toward extensive antipollution measures.

The Delaware River Basin Commission. The Delaware River Basin Commission was the central authority on standards for the estuary. It had the power to make the decision and to make it binding. It adopted the Delaware Estuary Comprehensive Study Preliminary Report as the technical basis for its decision and was the central point toward which those attempting to influence the decision directed their efforts.

The Delaware River Basin Commission consists of five voting members: the elected governors of the four states and a federal representative serving at the pleasure of the President of the United States. Each commissioner or his alternate is entitled to one vote: no action of the commission shall be taken at any meeting unless a majority of the membership shall vote in favor thereof.[21] This type of federal-state partnership was unique at the time of the creation of the commission. Subsequently the Congress of the United States acted on legislation that would extend this federal-state arrangement to other river basins.[22]

THE PARTISANS AND THEIR POSITIONS ON DESIRED STANDARDS OF WATER QUALITY

Partisans, either directly or indirectly attempt to exert influence on the authorities toward achieving an outcome of the issue consonant with their own goals. Partisans can be classified by the general character of their organizations or individuals roles. Major types have been identified as business or industrial firms, business or industrial associations (e.g., the National Association of Manufacturers), public administration (government agencies or elected officials), public legislation (elective officials), general civic and conservation organizations, advisory committees, and others that are unclassified. Note that three parties dominated: business and industry, civic and conservation groups, and government. Table 9.1 shows the distribution of live testimony given at the hearings on the subject by partisans, as classified above.[23] Note that those who favored objective set II (47), the higher set of standards, outnumbered those who favored objective set III (41)), but that the vote was close. Only four parties recommended set I, the highest objective.[24] The votes expressed a majority will, but they do not explain why the standard eventually adopted by the Commission more closely resembled objective set II than any other.

The division of the major parties on objective sets is clearly shown. Conservation, government, and other public groups overwhelmingly favored I and II, the higher objective standards; business and industrial firms and their allied associations prefer red, almost unanimously, the lower standard, objective set III. The fact that no one recommended objective sets IV and V conceals the fact that many persons, especially in business and industry, considered objective set IV adequate. That no one took a public position to that effect is a reflection of the solidarity with which business and industry presented their arguments.

TABLE 9.1   STANDARDS FAVORED BY MAJOR TYPES AMONG PARTISANS TESTIFYING AT HEARINGS

| | Standards favored | | | |
| | Objective sets | | | |
Type	I	II	III	Total
Business or industrial firms		2	14	16
Business or industrial associations			14	14
Public administration (government agencies, elected officials	1	10	6	17
Public legislative (elected officials)		7		7
General civic organizations		6	1	7
Conservation organizations	3	17		20
Advisory committees		1	4	5
Other		4	1	5
Total	4	47	41	92

The split between these major parties is best understood as a cleavage of interests: the "clear water" interests which wanted higher standards for many different values versus the "waste dischargers" composed largely of business and industry but also including some municipal governments which sought to keep down their costs of operation. This cleavage of interests is demonstrated in Table 9.2, which shows the frequency of testimony (both live and written) for the dif-

TABLE 9.2   STANDARDS FAVORED BY RELATION TO DISCHARGING OF WASTES AMONG PARTISANS TESTIFYING AT HEARINGS

	Standards favored			
	Objective sets			
	I	II	III	Totals
Waste dischargers			19	19
Representatives of waste dischargers		7	18	25
Clear water partisans (do not discharge waste or represent waste dischargers)	4	40	3	47
Totals	4	47	40	91

ferent objective sets recorded for categories: waste dischargers, representative of waste dischargers, and clear water partisans who do not discharge wastes or represent waste dischargers. The dividing line between those organizations that represented waste dischargers and those that did not is necessarily vague. It could be argued that everyone is a waste discharger, and it sometimes seems strange that representatives of municipal sewage systems and large industrial plants are standing together for lower standards.

The categorization of Table 9.2 is based on a list of major waste dischargers obtained from the Delaware River Basin Commission.[25] If an organization (usually a firm or municipality) was on the list or was known to be a waste discharger, it was categorized as a waste discharger. If a substantial portion of the membership or constituency (50% or more) of any other organization were waste dischargers, the partisan was classified as representing a waste discharger. Those not discharging wastes nor representing waste dischargers were classified by their common label—"clear water" partisans.

The relation between partisans and standards is straightforward. No waste dischargers supported anything higher than objective set III. Most of the associational representatives of waste dischargers went along and supported the same standard. Altogether 37 of the 40 who favored the lower standard were among the waste dischargers or their representatives. On the other side, the clean water partisans favored the higher objective sets, I and II, by an overwhelming margin. Only three supported objective set III.

These findings argue that values associated with the desired level of water quality hold the key to the reasons for preferred choice of water quality levels.

Value Assumptions of the Partisans.   The waste dischargers hold that the river is a part of the public domain and is open to multiple use, including waste discharges, as long as public health and recreational activities are not injured. Business and industry point to the large tax outlays made to the public treasury to assist in the necessary treatment of water to maintain these standards. This premise and its supporting legitimation make it fairly easy for all business and industrial groups (and some municipal waste dischargers) to arrive at consensus.

The clear water partisans, which include conservationist organizations, sportsmen's groups, public concern organizations, state regulatory agencies, legislative bodies, and numerous political figures, are more heterogeneous and are divided by a variety of value assumptions: (a) the goal of re-establishing water-related recreation where it had been prevented by low-quality conditions, (b) the value of pleasant surroundings in which to live and the goal of aesthetically pleasing water areas, (c) the value of maintaining the ecology in a "healthy" state as insurance of a safe and ecologically useful environment for man and the accompanying goal of "healthy" water, (d) the moral responsibility of man to other life forms, and (e) preventing violations of the public domain.

There are obvious interrelationships among these values. Collectively, the goals seek one end, that is, high water quality. There are, however, wide differences in the importance attached by clear water partisans to the various value assumptions. This makes consensus difficult, for they presume to speak for "higher" values that do not yield to economic criteria. It was of great significance for the course and probably the outcome of the issue that among these categories of values only that of recreation could be quantified by the comprehensive study with the techniques available at that time. This was central to the issue because there was little agreement on the monetary value to be placed on the other values. Yet the moral responsibility of man to other forms of life was a very real motivation among many dedicated conservationists, as personal interviews disclosed. This is the kind of value that is seldom articulated openly and it received the least weight in the dialogue over standards for the estuary.

Preventing violations of the public domain is a value that holds that no one has the right to discharge wastes into the water at all. Obviously, this value is in direct opposition to the waste dischargers investment in the assimilative capacity of the Delaware River. There is a growing belief that the use of the river for wastes by industry and municipalities is a transgression on the public domain.

Partisans argued among themselves over the legitimacy of many of these value assumptions. Business and industrial partisans did not regard the "demand" for water quality higher than objective set III as justified and argued that there was no justification for the value of a clean river for aesthetic reasons. They insisted on their right to discharge wastes as long as they did not violate health standards.

Among the "clear water" partisans many refused to accept any use of the river to discharge wastes but others claimed that this was an extreme position and not tenable. They made their appeals on recreational, ecological, or aesthetic grounds.

Decision-Making Strategy and Consensus of the Partisans Strategy

Two questions became important decision making. Did the partisans differ in the strategies they chose with respect to their relations with other organizations?

What behavior of the partisans was associated with consensus on water quality levels?

A cooperative strategy was operationally defined as one in which a partisan leader or organization had considerable communication with organizations or individuals holding differing views. By contrast, a defensive strategy became one in which a partisan made contact with others only when they held similar views. This is admittedly a narrow definition for the two terms but such concepts do help us to understand the decision-making process.

On the basis of interviews and documents, it can be concluded that most organizations used a defensive stategy by these definitions. It was more characteristic of business and industry than of those advocating the higher set of standards. In contrast, civic organizations, including the League of Women Voters, adopted cooperative strategies. Similarly, government agencies employed cooperative strategies more often than private voluntary associations, especially the more specialized conservation organizations.

Consensus

It became apparent that waste dischargers and those representing waste dischargers achieved the highest consensus and consistently supported objective set III. There was less solidarity among those supporting the higher objective sets.

Actually objective set III represented a predetermined compromise on the part of business and industry. In interviews the opinion was often expressed that objective set IV or even V was adequate water quality protection for the needs of industry. In the final analysis this position was tempered by three factors. In the various federations and confederations of business and industry—the Chambers of Commerce, the American Manufacturers Association, and the organizations representing specific industries—the issue was well discussed before public positions were taken. These were often occasions of much controversy, the issue itself, but in general the contention was confined intramurally.

The first factor tempering the positions supporting objective sets IV and V was the consideration on the part of many that certain economic advantages might accrue from a clean river. The tourist industry and certainly water-related recreational industries stood to benefit from a cleaner river. This factor, however, was overshadowed by a second consideration.

Public opinion at the time of the issue was becoming increasingly hostile toward waste dischargers. Any firm or industry was in the position of standing to lose public credit if it appeared not to have the public interest in mind on pollution matters. According to the interviewees, this factor greatly affected the position taken by industry and business.

The final factor was actually a matter of strategy. Many persons representing firms were persuaded to support objective set III by the implication that a solidary front in favor of a predetermined compromise would be persuasive toward avoiding the most costly standards.

The fact that some conservation organizations did recommend objective set I is an indication of the relative lack of solidarity on the part of organizations and individuals supporting the higher standards. Unlike the case of business and industry, there was no common forum at which a predetermined position could be thrashed out. Even the meetings of the Recreation, Conservation, Fish and Wildlife Subcommittee of the Delaware Estuary Water Use Advisory Committee experienced difficulty in obtaining participation.

The difficulties of the "clear water" partisans to achieve consensus, especially for a higher water level, can be traced back to the technical study phase when a recommended decision on standards was taken for the Delaware Estuary Comprehensive Study. Of particular relevance to the issue as a whole was the activity surrounding the advisory committees.

The stated purpose of the Water Use Advisory Committee was to make a better determination of the needs of the valley, but from the beginning its functions were far more than that. This committee enabled the interests concerned with water use in the valley to confront one another in an effort to reach consensus on the use of the river. Although the committee did recommend an objective set to be adopted as standards, objective set III, this investigator detected that consensus was never reached primarily because of the failure of "clean water" demands to be well articulated in this bargaining or confrontation stage. The result was that the "clean water" interests—those interested in uses that require high standards—failed to experience the education and adjustment that the waste discharging interests had. The parties interested in high standards did not enter into a consensus-making effort which might have effected a compromise.

During the meetings of the advisory committees the waste dischargers were intimately involved in working out many of the technical problems. They began to understand and have confidence in the study, especially the mathematical model. For the clean water interests this was not paralleled to the same extent. It is true that the advisory committees contained representatives of almost all interests insofar as it was possible to arrange it through the mechanism of voluntary organizations.

An interpretation of these observations is that there were two barriers to effective inclusion of clean water interests. One is mechanical. Most clean water interests were represented by voluntary associations. As already mentioned, business and industry, with a direct economic interest in the outcome of the issue, were motivated to include the activity of the advisory committees as part of the jobs of the men representing them. This could not be the case for the conservationist, sportsmen, or public interest associations—all voluntary.

A second possible barrier is the social class bias of voluntary organizations. Sociological studies of affiliation with voluntary associations indicate that participation is not so widespread as once thought. Typically, the wage-earning classes experience less participation in voluntary associations than the white-collar and upper middle classes. If a constituency of hunters and fishermen interested in "clean water" existed in the wage-earning class, it would not be likely to find a voice in a voluntary association.

That political figures—elected officials, usually—articulate the public demand for higher standards is consistent with this interpretation. When other channels are weak or unrepresentative, the demand for a clean environment finds its way through the political system. Politicians have been quick to recognize the positive image afforded by an antipollution stance and have probably contributed to the increased demand. To the public pollution is indefensible.

Objections to pollution-abatement programs, however valid, are difficult to support without endangering the image of the interest one represents.

THE FINAL DECISION

The central authorities in the decision were the Delaware Estuary Comprehensive Study and, more important, the Delaware River Basin Commission, which had the final word. As reported earlier, objective set II was selected, a victory for the "clear water" partisans. Whatever may have been the deciding influences, the factor most closely associated with which an objective set was supported by a given party at interest was whether the party was (or substantially) representing waste dischargers. This cleavage with the clear water interests has been amply demonstrated. What is not known is the extent to which the decision on standards incurred political judgment. The decision was made by the Commissioners, most of whom are elected officials. It is probable that anticipation of the desires of the voting public did affect the actions of these men.

There are several notions regarding the pattern of influence internal to the Commission which led to the selection of higher alternatives. This research was unable to find clear evidence to support or deny these theories, but three of them deserve attention for their relevance and credibility.

The first theory concerned the position of the Delaware River Basin Commission staff. Although the Commission staff, like that of the Delaware Estuary Comprehensive Study, never took public positions on the issue (unlike the Comprehensive Study), it had an apparent leaning toward the higher standards. In general, it was the observation that Comprehensive staff supported objective set III, whereas the Commission staff supported objective set II, both having persuasive arguments to bolster their positions.

Within this theory the Commission staff, because of its contacts with the Commissioners and their alternates, was able to convince them of the advantages of choosing a higher set of standards. The arguments centered around four things: (a) the fact that the projected costs of objective sets II and III would be nearly the same after the passage of several years, (b) the idea that higher standards would provide clearer enforcement leverage for the Commission to use with waste dischargers, (c) the opportunity of reaching the higher value by regionalization, and (d) the cultural assumption of the value of cleanliness itself.

A second theory about the pattern of influence within the Commission concerned the behavior of the state water quality regulation agencies and the governors of New York and Pennsylvania, in which antipollution public action has been comparatively vigorous. The theory stated that Governor Nelson A. Rockefeller, the Commissioner representing New York, could easily support high standards. His state had recently passed a bond issue for the support of municipal pollution-abatement plant construction, which indicated a mandate for antipollution action. At the same time he did not have to answer through the political system to the parties at interest in the Delaware Valley who would have to shoulder the immediate costs of pollution abatement.

Similarly, the state government departments concerned with the regulation of water quality in Pennsylvania favored a set of standards consistent with their own internal standards, which were high, and interpreted the federal guidelines to indicate that objective set II was the most compliant. The theory stated that they, along with the Commission staff, persuaded the Commissioner from Pennsylvania, Governor Raymond P. Shafer, and his alternate to support standards based on objective set II. These two, plus the vote of Commissioner Stewart L. Udall, who represented the United States, would have been sufficient to adopt the higher standards.

A *third theory* received less support from respondents supporting the higher standards but was current among many of those supporting the less costly standards. It *centered around the representative to the Commission from the Federal Government,* Stewart L. Udall, U. S. Secretary of the Interior. This theory stated that Udall persuaded the governors to support the higher set by convincing them that the Federal Government would not approve standards based on objective set III.

To repeat, there was insufficient evidence to affirm or deny any of these theories. There may be a degree of credibility in each of them. However, they do serve to illustrate the importance of the political judgment phase of the decision and its relative isolation from previous activities in the issue.

Reconstruction of the Delaware River Basin Influence Network

The study of a specific issue has revealed many decision-making factors and processes, but only the outline of an influence network has emerged. We know that the partisans were divided into waste dischargers (and their representatives) and clear water partisans and that the clear water partisans exerted the winning influence. This means that business and industry and their representatives were defeated by a loose coalition of conservation groups, sportsmens' organizations, civic groups, organizations of state and municipal governments, and various political figures of influence. Indeed, the final decision was made by the four governors of New York, Pennsylvania, New Jersey, and Delaware; the Secretary of the Interior represented the Federal Government.

To understand the linkage pattern of leaders and organizations the concept of echelon appears to be most appropriate.

The Concept of Echelon

"Echelon" derives from military usage and refers to a steplike formation of units of troops in which each unit moves progressively to the left or right of the one preceding it. This concept has been applied more loosely to various formations (ships, aircraft, combat forces, and organizational personnel in general).

The echelon concept fits well the power arrangements observed as key and top leaders of Megalopolis interconnect with environmental leaders and with Delaware River Basin water resource leaders. It is equally applicable to the corresponding organizations in these categories. This concept is needed to contrast with hierarchical power rankings which refers to persons arranged in order of rank, grade, or class within a given system. The echelon pattern allows for a description of order without imposing a chain of command, which may exist but is not implied. Most frequently a mix of hierarchical and lateral power and influence characterize the echelon. These power arrangements are shown in Figure 9.2, which illustrates three formations of leaders involved at the policy-making level in the Delaware River Basin water resource program. The first formation

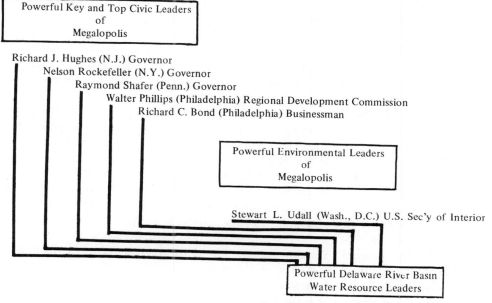

Figure 9.2 Echelon of powerful leaders designated as interlinked in decision-making involving Delaware River Basin water resource problems.

lists some of the most powerful urban-oriented leaders in Megalopolis, the second, its the most powerful environmental leader, and the third, the water resource leaders active in the Delaware River Basin, all of whom were identified in a study of Delaware River Basin problems by Paul Planchon. He assembled a list of leaders who occupied various formal positions of leadership in the Delaware River Basin. Positions were selected to ensure two conditions: that the major institutional segments would be represented and that all positions were in some way related to water resource development. Questionnaires were sent (see Appendix A for format) to 162 leaders and usuable returns were received from 81 (50% return).

One question stated:

> Suppose there were a major water resource problem confronting the
> Delaware River Basin as a whole—one that required a group of men
> whom nearly every one would accept and who could rally the support
> of most segments of the river basin. Whom would you select to make
> up such a group, regardless of whether you know them?

A total of 144 persons were nominated and a power rating was established for
each leader based on the frequency of his nomination. Table 9.3 lists the names
of the first 21 leaders in order of rank and gives their organizational identifications. It is this list that provided the basic data for the echelon figure. Leaders
like Richard J. Hughes, Nelson Rockefeller, Raymond Shafer, Walter Philips, and
Richard C. Bond were identified earlier as key and top urban-oriented leaders
of Megalopolis as described in Chapter 4. Likewise, Stewart L. Udall, was
placed among the environmental leaders of Megalopolis as cited in Chapter 8.
The remaining leaders are those directly related to the Delaware River Basin and
have organizational identification with water resource problems. The power ratings of these leaders have been checked for validity by asking respondents to list
specific issues and indicate which persons were most influential in the decision-
making process. Most of the leaders with high power ratings appeared as influential issue leaders, as the Issue Influence Rating in Table 9.3 shows.[26] Many of
these leaders were found by James Barfoot to be among those leading the parties
at interest in the hearings on water quality standards before the Delaware River
Basin Commission.

Leaders like James F. Wright, Maurice Goddard, Samuel Baxter, Paul Felton,
and H. Matt Adams, who were directly connected with the water resources of
the Delaware Basin can refer to other megalopolitan leaders for advice and various kinds of assistance, but leaders of voluntary organizations are not tied to any
direct chain of command. Even alternates to the Delaware River Basin Commission have considerable latitude in their decision-making power. The mix of lateral
and hierarchical power is demonstrated in an echelon system in which private
leaders and organizations can exert influence high enough to contest governmental authority.

Echelon of Powerful Organizations Interlinked in Water
Resource Problems in the Delaware River Basin

Organizations that participated in decision making relating to water resource
problems can also be discovered in an echelon arrangement. Figure 9.3 is a pattern of powerful megalopolitan urban-oriented and environmental organizations
and environmental organizations active in the Delaware River Basin. The megalopolitan organizations were described earlier in Chapters 4 and 8. The organizations active in the Delaware River Basin were found through two sources: in
a study made by Syracuse University researchers of organizational activity
around seven major issues on the Delaware and in James Barfoot's study of water
quality standards.

TABLE 9.3 POWERFUL LEADERS DEALING WITH WATER RESOURCE PROBLEMS IN THE DELAWARE RIVER BASIN

Leadership ranking	Power rating	Issue influence	Organizational affiliation
James F. Wright	20	Yes	Delaware River Basin Commission, Director
Maurice Goddard	20	Yes	Pennsylvania Alternate to the Delaware River Basin Commission
Samuel Baxter	19	Yes	City of Philadelphia Water Commissioner
Paul Felton	16	Yes	Water Resource Association of the Delaware River Basin, Executive Director
Richard J. Hughes	14	Yes	Governor, State of New Jersey Delaware River Basin Commission
Nelson Rockefeller	12	Yes	Governor, State of New York Delaware River Basin Commission
Raymond Shafer	12	Yes	Governor, State of Pennsylvania Delaware River Basin Commission
H. Mat Adams	11	Yes	New Jersey Alternate to the Delaware River Basin Commission
Russell W. Peterson	10	No	Governor, State of Delaware Delaware River Basin Commission
Frank Dressler	10	No	Tocks Island Regional Advisory Council, Executive Director
Harold L. Jacobs	8	No	Delaware Alternate to the Delaware River Basin Commission
Stewart L. Udall	7	Yes	Former U. S. Secretary of Interior Delaware River Basin Commission
Vernon Northrop	7	No	Former U. S. Alternate to the Delaware River Basin Commission
R. Stewart Kilborne	7	No	New York Alternate to the Delaware River Basin Commission
Walter Phillips	5	No	Commission on Regional Development, Consultant
Richard C. Bond	4	No	Philadelphia businessman
Thomas Dolan	4	Yes	Wissahickan Valley Watershed Association
James Kerney	4	No	Trenton Times, Publisher
William Scranton	4	No	Former Governor of Pennsylvania
William Halladay	4	Yes	Oil Company Representative
Lloyd L. Falk	4	Yes	Delmarva Ornthological Society
Power ratings of	3		12 individuals
Power ratings of	2		18 individuals
Power ratings of	1		93 individuals

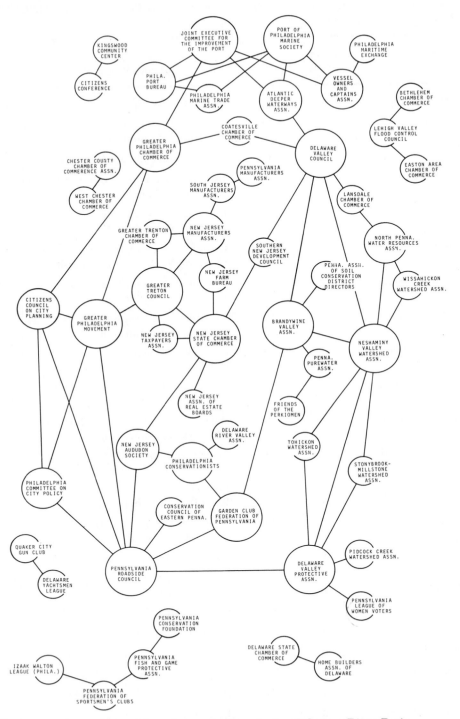

Figure 9.3   Interrelationships of organizations in the Delaware River Basin.
SOURCE: Roscoe C. Martin, Guthrie S. Birkhead, Jesse Burkhead, and Frank J. Munger, *River Basin Administration and the Delaware,* Syracuse University Press, 1960, p. 57. Size of organizational circle reflects its importance as a link in the network.

The first study identified parties at interest involved in such specific proposals as (a) the 40-foot Delaware channel, a navigation improvement; (b) Round Valley, a water supply reservoir for New Jersey; (c) Tock's Island Reservoir for flood control, stream flow regulation, and future water supply; (d) The Schuylkill Pollution Control Program; (e) Bear Creek Reservoir; (f) INCODEL basinwide plan for water supply; and (g) Public Law 566 which specifies small watershed development.

Several hundred citizens' organizations in the Delaware River Basin were identified. Each was asked to indicate the areas of action in which it was interested. A questionnaire was then constructed and sent to a sample of 72 of the larger organizations interested in water resource problems which was asked to indicate action actually taken on the seven specific proposals listed. Figure 9.3 is a suggestive demonstration of the interlocking interests of the organizations responding. This interlocking is charted from the results of one of the questions which inquired with what other organizations the respondent association cooperated. The size of the organizational circle shown reflects its importance as a link in the network—defined as the number of times it was mentioned—rather than as implied political or other strength.[27] Barfoot's study on parties at interest based on the Commission's hearings on water quality standards validates many of the same organizations as the most powerful. These echelon arrangements are shown in Figure 9.4. Note that the urban-oriented organizations include the U. S. Chamber of Commerce, the National Association of Manufacturers, the League of Women Voters, the National Association of Counties, the Council of State Governments, and the U. S. Conference of Mayors. The environmental quality organizations include the Izaak Walton League, the National Audubon Society, the Water Resources Council, the Conservation Foundation, and numerous federal agencies. On the Delaware itself the list contains many affiliates. One finds the Water Resources Association of the Delaware River, the Pennsylvania Department of Forest and Waters, the New Jersey State Chamber of Commerce, the Greater Philadelphia Chamber of Commerce, the Pennsylvania League of Women Voters, the Council on Regional Development, the New Jersey Audubon Society, the Wissahicken Valley Watershed Association, the Pennsylvania Conservation Foundation, the Tocks Island Regional Advisory Council, and the New Jersey Manufacturers Association.

We observe again the echelon character of the linkage. The Delaware Basin associations can look to national associations for advice, financial assistance, and leadership. No direct chain of command is involved, for all the member associations have wide latitude, if not full autonomy of action. The role of lateral power and influence is highlighted by the echelon arrangement.

Major Factors Affecting the Echelon Arrangements of Leaders and Organizations

A number of major factors may be identified as associated with echelon power arrangements: (a) the nature of the issue, (b) the stage of the issue, (c) the strategy required, and (d) the official position of the leader or organization. A description of the operation of each of these factors follows.

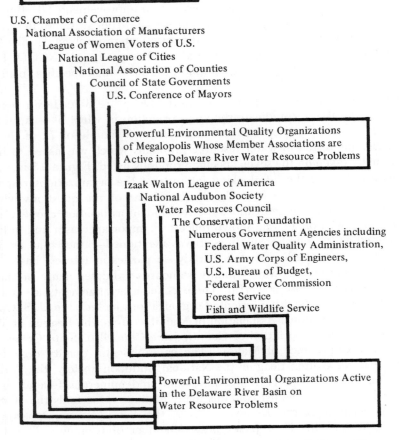

Powerful Urban-Oriented
(And Environmental) Organizations
Of Megalopolis

U.S. Chamber of Commerce
National Association of Manufacturers
League of Women Voters of U.S.
National League of Cities
National Association of Counties
Council of State Governments
U.S. Conference of Mayors

Powerful Environmental Quality Organizations
of Megalopolis Whose Member Associations are
Active in Delaware River Water Resource Problems

Izaak Walton League of America
National Audubon Society
Water Resources Council
The Conservation Foundation
Numerous Government Agencies including
Federal Water Quality Administration,
U.S. Army Corps of Engineers,
U.S. Bureau of Budget,
Federal Power Commission
Forest Service
Fish and Wildlife Service

Powerful Environmental Organizations Active
in the Delaware River Basin on
Water Resource Problems

Water Resources Association of Delaware River
Penn. Dept. of Forest and Waters
N.J. State Chamber of Commerce
Greater Philadelphia Chamber of Commerce
Penn. League of Women Voters
Council on Regional Development
N.J. Audubon Society
Wissahickon Valley Watershed Association (Penn.)
Penn. Conservation Foundation
Tock Island Regional Advisory Council (Penn.)
N.J. Manufacturers Association

**Figure 9.4   Echelon of powerful organizations interlinked in water resource problems
in the Delaware River Basin.**

The *nature of the issue* activates different leaders and organizations according
to their different interests and claims. A controversy over decentralization of
schools in New York will most certainly bring about a different power arrangement than housing redevelopment in the same city. In the Delaware River Basin
a flood control project will activate different organizations and leaders than a
water quality standards decision. As a matter of fact, in setting water quality

270

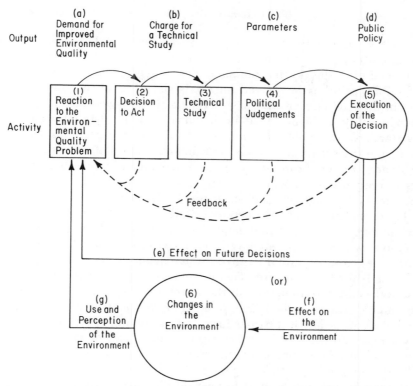

Output

(a)
Demand for
Improved
Environmental
Quality

(b)
Charge for
a Technical
Study

(c)
Parameters

(d)
Public
Policy

Activity

(1)
Reaction
to the
Environ-
mental
Quality
Problem

(2)
Decision
to Act

(3)
Technical
Study

(4)
Political
Judgements

(5)
Execution
of the
Decision

Feedback

(e) Effect on Future Decisions

(g)
Use and
Perception
of the
Environment

(6)
Changes in
the
Environment

(or)

(f)
Effect on
the
Environment

Figure 9.5   Elemental phases in the generalized decision-making process in environmental quality (devised by James Barfoot, Jr., and Paul D. Planchon).

standards on the Delaware three different decisions had to be reached. One had to do with the creation of a new agency and the establishment of its domain of jurisdiction, its delegated powers, its constituency, and the relation of the constituency to the Commission. A second involved the selection of standards such as the specification of tolerance levels. Finally, methods of implementing the standards, which included financing, the requirements made of waste dischargers, and the means of measuring and monitoring wastes once they were found in the environment, had to be resolved. It was observed that the better known and reputedly more powerful leaders were active in the creation of the Delaware River Basin Commission. Many of these leaders were not active in the other two decisions. The decisions on water quality standards precipitated activity by a group of leaders who represented diverse interests in the valley, but they were not of the stature and repute of those who created the Commission. The decisions related to the implementation of the standards mainly involved technical specialists and the waste dischargers themselves. It can be concluded that if a reseascher wishes to observe the roles of the most powerful leaders, he must identify the most critical issues whose saliency draws the top decision makers to their debate and resolution.

The *stage of the issue* is an important factor in determining the leaders that are active at a given time in the process of decision making. Figure 9.5 is a schema that relates five different elemental phases in the process of issue resolution: reaction to the environmental quality problem, decision to act, technical study, political judgments, and execution of the decision. Different leaders and organizations may play varying parts at each of these activity levels. The process has a number of feedbacks that can affect the various activities as the determination of public policy is hammered out. It is shown as an on-going process as changes in the environment may at any time activate new reactions to the environmental quality problem. It has been shown that the determination of water quality standards brought about differential roles for the partisans, the commission staff, and the basin commissioners at different stages of the issue.

The *strategy required* can influence the activation and role pattern of different leaders and organizations. Militant, cooperative, defensive, and passive strategies may be employed to fight or gain consensus. In the Delaware water quality issue it will be remembered that a cooperative strategy was utilized by many partisan leaders and organizations when organizations or individuals held different views. A defensive strategy was employed when partisans shared common views. Together, they grouped around a given water quality standard and held fast to their demands for that standard. The attempt to secure a winning power alignment introduced a certain fluidity to the search for consensus.

Last, the importance of the *official position of the leader or organization* cannot be minimized, especially if it carries formal grants of authority. The power of the commissioners and their alternates is clear in all phases of policy making. The leaders who head the voluntary organizations are considered the natural spokesmen. They can speak for their organizations. It is their task to mobilize and concentrate influence and bring it to bear on the policy makers.

The Distinctive Character of the Linkage Relationships in Decision Making on Water Quality in the Delaware River Basin

The tracing of the water quality issue has verified the central propositions set forth in the theoretical base described in Chapter 3. It was stated that policy decisions affecting innovation, control, and order are not something generally achieved by an administrator or group at any one unit or level but a process that spans and links persons and groups at local, state, regional, and national levels. Administration is not a process that flows down from one level to the next but is related to the interaction of levels and component groups.

The use of the echelon concept has been suggested in this chapter to give meaning to the power arrangement that introduces so much lateral power into the interaction of levels and groups. This gives the linkage relationship its distinctive character as issue resolution occurs within a subregion such as the Delaware River Basin. The premise that top urban-oriented leaders and associations are influential in initiating, supporting, or vetoing actions taken by environmental quality leaders and organizations is borne out. These broad-gage leaders not only have high formal power but also carry great informal influence that reaches beyond environmental leaders to the broader publics in which they operate. In their ties with environmental leaders we see how subregional power structures function as issues develop in Megalopolis. The power arrangements are often loose, as judged by a comparison with a hierarchy of vertical power chains within an organization. They rest on fluid formal links and often temporary, informal ties, but the decision-making process has its own kind of social cement. Parties at interest come together and leaders and organizations interact and sort out areas of consensus and difference. Different levels—national, regional, state, and local— relate as their interests draw them together or as the "lower" levels call on the "higher" levels for advice, assistance, and leadership. In this way regional substructures assemble power arrangements. It has been our contention that key and top urban-oriented leaders are repeatedly called on for just such activity and in their interactions come to know one another. Mega-leaders, who operate across Megalopolis, provide the binding units of the incipient power structure that is so well established.

Notes

1. Roscoe C. Martin, Guthrie S. Birkhead, Jesse Birkhead, and Frank J. Munger, *River Basin Administration and the Delaware*, Syracuse University Press, 1960, pp. 19–25.
2. U.S. Department of the Interior Geological Survey, *River Basins of the United States. Series: The Delaware* (no date).
3. *Ibid.*
4. *Ibid.*
5. *Ibid.*
6. Allen V. Kneese and Blair T. Bower, *Managing Water Quality: Economics, Technology, Institutions,* The Johns Hopkins Press, Baltimore, 1968, pp. 277–278.
7. *Ibid.,* p. 225.
8. *Ibid.,* p. 22.
9. *Ibid.,* p. 37.
10. *Ibid.,* p. 16–17.
11. Roscoe Martin et al., *op. cit.*
12. *Ibid.*
13. The Commission is empowered to deal with water supply, pollution control, flood protection, watershed management, recreation, hydroelectric power, and the regulation of withdrawals and diversions.
14. Delaware Estuary Comprehensive Study, Federal Water Pollution Control Administration, U.S. Department of the Interior, Philadelphia, July, 1966.
15. Delaware River Basin Commission, *Annual Report,* 1967, p. 6.
16. Both the present use of these concepts and part of the original idea for the advisory committees came from Ward Goodenough of the University of Pennsylvania. See Ward Goodenough, "Agency Structure as a Major Source of Human Problems," *Journal of Public Health,* **55** (July 1965).
17. Description from the Delaware Estuary Comprehensive Study, Federal Water Pollution Control Administration, U. S. Department of the Interior, Preliminary Report and Findings, Philadelphia, July 1966, pp. viii-ix.
18. The five "objective sets" represented alternative levels of quality for alternate costs derived from a mathematical model for the analysis of water quality management in the region. This model may be examined in *The Delaware Estuary Comprehensive Study: Preliminary Report and Findings ibid.,* p. 226.
19. An ideal design for the study of selection of standards would do two things that this study could not do: (a) it would study a large number of subjects, longitudinally, over time; (b) it would take a sample of similar issues and follow the same procedure. Because adequate resources were not available a much more modest design was adopted. It was a survey design, primarily retrospective and cross-sectional in time.

20. The Delaware River Basin Interview Schedule, devised by James L. Barfoot, is reproduced in Appendix C.

21. *Delaware River Basin Compact*, Section 2.5.

22. Water Resources Planning Act, Public Law 89-80, 89th Congress, S. 21, July 22, 1965.

23. Table 9.1 excludes testimony that did not specifically recommend a particular objective set.

24. There was no public testimony for the lowest standards, objective sets IV and V.

25. Delaware River Basin Commission, Waste Discharge-Delaware Estuary (a map and list), May 1967.

26. Respondents were given a list of six major issues in the Delaware River Basin. They were asked to name two on which they were most active. For each of the two they were asked, "Please name four people who you think have been most influential on this issue." A "yes" in the issue influence column means that this person was identified as having been influential in two or more issues listed by the respondent.

27. Roscoe Martin, Guthrie S. Birkhead, Jesse Burkhead, and Frank J. Munger, *River Basin Administration and the Delaware*, Syracuse University Press, 1960, pp. 30–60. Figure 3 is shown on p. 57.

PART FIVE

Research Problems of Regional Sociology

The sociology of urban regions is only in its infancy. This primitive state of knowledge contrasts with urban sociology or the study of cities. Sociologists have long been interested in the life of the inner city and have extended their interests to the suburb, the satellite city, the planned city, and the metropolitan area. Because research techniques are not easily applied to macrounits, sociologists and urban geographers alike have seldom ventured beyond the boundaries of a metropolitan area. It is true that the region has challenged some sociologists who looked for significant geographical units in which distinctive culture patterns might be identified. In the United States the intermingling of peoples and ideas is great and this search has not been especially fruitful. Howard Odum's *Southern Region* was greeted with acclaim as he identified a "southern culture" in the United States and demonstrated with painstaking care some of the distinctive patterns distributed over many southern states.[1] There the delineation stopped, however, and today many of the patterns identified by Odum have long since been greatly modified by migration and the increasing industrialization and urbanization of the South.

The current search for the integration and linkage of cities into urban systems was described in Chapter 1, System Characteristics of Megalopolis. This research has attempted to make two original contributions to this incipient stage of urban systems. Each was conducted in Megalopolis with the purpose of establishing new techniques for detecting social linkages between leaders and organizations within the urbanized region. Chapters 10 and 11 are reports of these probings, and it is hoped that they will stimulate future research. Chapter 10 describes the measurement of contact and clique structures of leaders who employ both conventional documentary and new computer techniques. Chapter 11 continues with a search for the measurement of organizational interaction. It is believed that research work will eventually open a new field of sociology that may be called the sociology of associations. Both measurement problems, that of clique interaction among leaders and working relations among associations, are challenges on the research frontier. Researchers of the future seem destined to make major progress in these two areas of regional sociology.

CHAPTER TEN

The Measurement
of Contact and
Clique Structures

The social scientist has two principal sources of data on the interaction of leaders. The records of organizations which indicate the composition of the board of directors, the officers, and the membership provide one source. Powerful leaders who become active in organizations tend to become even more active and establish multiple memberships. If organizational records are available, these multiple bases of organizational identity can be discovered. They provide an index of a leader's power and influence. When the leader is an officer or on a policy-making board, it is also possible to observe the members with whom he interacts. His circle of interaction can be progressively described, as associates in one organization in which he is functioning are compared with others in which he is active. If measures of a leader's power are available, such as current work position, reputed power, or a record of participation in national or local issues, this enables the researcher to "tag" powerful leaders and examine their activities in voluntary organizations or government agencies. The observer scans the records for committee appointments or previous official appointments. A pattern of interaction can often be determined which illumines past behavior and is predictive of future activity. Organizational records do constitute secondary data, however, and they leave unanswered many questions, such as the informal pattern of interaction, for which it is necessary to turn to a primary source.

Problems of Data Collection

The primary source is a sociometric pattern of leaders who know one another and choose to work together on civic matters. These data must as a rule be secured by a statement from the leaders themselves. Sometimes direct observation of contacts can be employed, but this method has many limitations, even in the best of situations. Access to the places of leader inter-

Lloyd V. Temme, Research Associate, is chiefly responsible for the data analysis and writing of this chapter; data collection and editing by principal investigator.

action is generally highly restricted. Public meetings represent the best opportunity and patterns are most easily discovered in small communities, but even when the researcher has obtained permission to observe, let us say in the working office of the leader, there is a real possibility that the most important centers of decision making for that leader will be in private places, unknown to and concealed from the observer. Obviously the same defensiveness can plague the researcher who seeks a listing or ranking of powerful leaders with whom his respondent interacts in decision making. The researcher must do everything possible to reduce the defensiveness of each respondent. Figure 10.1 shows a channel opened by the researcher to provide the acceptance of a questionnaire or interview. This channel is clear only after fears are dispelled and a pride system satisfied. A powerful leader may have a more sensitive pride system than one who has not achieved high leadership. A powerful leader knows that he occupies an important position and he expects that he will be asked to deal only with important matters. The researcher must convince the respondent of the legitimate character of the research activity and establish confidence in himself and the importance of his work. Because he is attempting to secure data from very busy men whose time is of great monetary value, these requirements are understandable. The researcher may have to consider carefully the particular doubts that must be dispelled to obtain agreement to cooperate. The leader may entertain many *personal fears*: that he will be quoted out of context, either verbally or in publication, in a way that will damage him or his organization; that his sociometric choices will make many other friends unhappy if they discover that he underrated their power or influence. There are *socially rooted fears* that others stand ready to attack any one in the "establishment." Leaders increasingly dislike appearing in any "power structure" and certainly do not want to assist in establishing one for public consumption. Some hold beliefs that no social research is worthwhile and that no one in the organization should be bothered. Some are afraid that the organization will be regarded as supporting the conclusions of the study or will

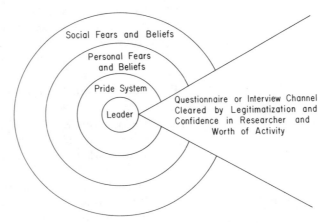

Figure 10.1   The opening of a questionnaire or interview channel through the fears and pride system of a leader.

become subject to injurious action. Indeed, there is enough anxiety in the contemporary political climate to arouse nameless alarm. The social researcher must understand and try to alleviate them by validating himself and his research. He will find his own faith in social research sorely tested by the personal screens and obstructions that make his work difficult. A feeling of frustration may dog him, especially if he believes that his respondents do not appreciate the value of his endeavor and share with him the belief that the research is for "the good of knowledge and of mankind." It must be said that the successful researcher dare not entertain the luxury of such feelings. His job is to get the research data not by trickery or deception but by understanding the social and psychological problems of validation and then employing the appropriate techniques.

Documentary Analysis for the Detection of Leadership Interaction

In this chapter we discuss measuring personal interaction by the documentary and sociometric analysis employed in this research study. Because the documentary approach was used first, it is discussed first. Records do not resist once they have been secured. It is not always easy to secure them, however. Private organizations are just that and executive officers are under no special obligation to release even a list of members. Since officers and board members can be harassed, they often demand that their addresses or telephone numbers not be disclosed. Sometimes they do not want their names paraded publicly. Fortunately most organizations do not impose these limitations and will provide the names of officers, board members (and sometimes members) on request. In addition, there are reference volumes that are helpful. Those most useful to this study are the following:

> *The Encyclopedia of Associations*, Vol. I, II, and III. Gale Research Co.
> *The Directory of National Trade and Professional Associations*.
> *Washington: A Comprehensive Directory of the National Capitol: Its People and Institutions*, Potomac Books.
> *U. S. Government Manual*
> *The Congressional Staff Directory*

Many of the *Who's Who* volumes are helpful for they list the organizational affiliations of the people listed.

Establishing Multiple Bases of Membership

The search for multiple bases of membership began with a look at the most powerful organizations. Floyd Hunter had said that the best starting point for anyone interested in a quick estimate of national leadership was the membership lists of the Business Council, the Committee for Economic Development (CED), and the National Industrial Conference Board (NICB).[2] This recommendation was accepted in the belief that many top business leaders would be identified and that those living or active in Megalopolis could be sorted out. It seemed useful to add the National Alliance of Businessmen (NAB) because this organization was engaged in direct social action in its program for the training of the hard-core unemployed. Headed by Henry Ford II, it was rated as one of the most powerful urban-oriented associations and attracted top business leaders as volunteer workers.

Among the four associations the Business Council is commonly regarded as the most prestigious body of businessmen in the United States. Its membership list (1968) included 191 men, 78 of whom, or 41 percent, were located in (or were influential in) the East. Thirty of them also held membership on the Committee for Economic Development and some were active on the National Industrial Conference Board and in the National Association of Manufacturers (NAM). The 1963 and 1968 lists of the Business Council were used to provide a time span in which to gage the range of multiple membership. The selected Business Council members are listed on the left side of Table 10.1 and their ratings as active, graduate, or honorary members are given. Their 1968 positions in CED are then given as chairman or vice-chairman of the Research and Policy Committee, chairman or vice-chairman of the Board of Trustees, and trustee or member of the Research and Policy Committee. Memberships in NICB or NAB are listed for anyone who was also active in the Business Council and CED. The analysis required that the selected member satisfy common membership in two organizations and then pass through two more sieves to determine whether additional memberships were recorded. In this manner multiple memberships were identified and their extent demonstrated for four voluntary associations of businessmen (and some professionals).

Table 10.1 does not exhaust the multiple membership of the 30 businessmen shown. If a list of members actively working in the National Alliance of Businessmen were examined, it would show that they overlapped in many other organizations; for example, two key leaders in NAB, Louis Cabot of Boston and Stuart Saunders, were members of NICB. These overlappings are significant for one reason. They represent opportunities for interaction—indeed, multiple opportunities. It is in this manner that leaders come to know one another, and as they are accepted they are drawn into more activity unless they decline.

For the social researcher analysis of membership in powerful organizations provides two things: first, the identification of many national or regional leaders who are usually especially powerful in their own communities, and, second, an index of interaction represented by the number of multiple memberships. This index of interaction is more suggestive than definitive, but it is an important step in the discovery of group configurations.

An analysis was also made of two urban-oriented organizations that draw leaders from different walks of life: the Urban Coalition and Urban America, which have now merged. In addition, various governmental commissions and committees were reviewed: the *National Commission on Urban Problems,* Paul Douglas, Chairman; the *National Advisory Commission on Civil Disorders,* Otto Kerner, Chairman; the *National Advisory Council on Economic Opportunity;* and the *President's Commission on Equal Opportunities in Housing.* Certain names appeared and were repeated in 1968. For labor, George Meany, Walter Reuther, A. Philip Randolph, and I. W. Abel; for civil rights, Roy Wilkins and Whitney Young; for government, Edward W. Brooke, John V. Lindsay, Nelson Rockefeller, and James H. J. Tate; for civic leadership, John W. Gardner, Kenneth Galbraith, Daniel Moynihan, James Rouse, and Kingman Brewster.

Often the pressure on the top man was so great that his appointment brought his "second" man into action; for example, everyone knew that Bayard Rustin had the backing of veteran labor leader A. Philip Randolph.

The identification of powerful leaders committed to urban problems is a slow process; the piecing together of working relations is akin to an intelligence operation. A researcher reads books like Theodore White's *The Making of a President*, Stewart Alsop's *The Center; People and Power in Political Washington*, Theodore C. Sorenson's *Decision Making in the White House*, *The Republican Establishment* by Stephen Hess and David S. Broder, Stephen Birmingham's *Social Establishment in America*, E. Digby Baltzell's *The Protestant Establishment*, G. William Domhoff's *Who Rules America* and *The Higher Circles*, Floyd Hunter's *Top Leadership U. S. A.*, Ferdinand Lundberg's *The Rich and Super Rich*, Daniel S. Greenberg's *The Politics of Pure Science*, Peter H. Clark's *The Business Man as Civic Leader*, Charles R. Adrian's *Governing Urban America*, *The Makers of Public Policy* by Joseph R. Mouser and Mark W. Cannon, and everything else he can find that is relevant to economic, political, or social leadership. He seeks out informants and he conducts interviews. He watches for the recurrence of names and the influence imputed to certain leaders. Step by step, names and organizations begin to sort themselves out.

Analysis of documents is laborious and at best a preliminary step, yet it is helpful in assembling a list of powerful leaders and organizations. It proved to be valuable in their final identification in Megalopolis as described in Chapters 4 to 7.

Interviews and questionnaires lead to primary data, which convey what the key and top leaders can (or will) tell the researcher about their acquaintance and contacts with other leaders. Fortunately we were able to collect an excellent body of this primary sociometric data to detect contact and clique structures.

The Sociometric Determination of Contact and Clique Structures[3]

In the initial questionnaire 100 key leaders described their relations with each of the other 200 key leaders on the list.[4] It will be recalled that each had been asked to check how well he knew the others with such choices as "don't know," "have heard of," "know little," "know well," or "know socially." These responses are called the *acquaintance data*. Each leader was also asked whether he had had business, civic, or social contacts with each of the others in the preceding years, hereafter called the *general contact data*. He was also asked whether he had worked on a committee dealing with urban problems with each of the others, hereafter called the *committee contact data*.

The Definition of a Sociometric Link

The first step in determining contact and clique structures was the definition of a *sociometric link* between two people. Three essentially independent sets of data

TABLE 10.1 SELECTED EASTERN MEMBERS OF THE BUSINESS COUNCILS OF 1963 AND 1968 WHO EXHIBIT OVERLAPPING MEMBERSHIP ON THE COMMITTEE FOR ECONOMIC DEVELOPMENT, NATIONAL INDUSTRIAL CONFERENCE BOARD, AND NATIONAL ALLIANCE OF BUSINESSMEN

Position of selected member of business council		Overlapping membership position in CED 1968	Membership in NICB	Membership in NAB
Robert B. Anderson	(63) Active (68) Active	Trustee		
S. Clark Beise	(63) Active (68) Graduate	Trustee, member research and policy		
Roger Blough	(63) Active (68) Graduate	Trustee	Trustee	
John T. Connor	(63) Active (68) Active	Trustee		
John H. Daniels	(63) Active (68) Active	Trustee		
Donald R. David	(63) Active (68) Honorary	Trustee		
William A. Hewett	(63) Active (68) Honorary	Trustee, member research and policy		
J. Ward Keener	(63) Active (68) Graduate	Trustee	Trustee	
Ralph Lazarus	(63) Active (68) Graduate	Trustee, member research and policy		
David Packard	(63) Active (68) Graduate	Trustee		
Marion B. Folson	(63) Graduate (68) Honorary	Trustee, vice-chairman research and policy		
G. Keith Funston	(68) Active	Trustee		

283

were available. Within the acquaintance data, which constituted an ordinal scale, the range of possible responses lay between "don't know" and "know socially," but because no well-tested technique existed to handle ordinally scaled sociometric data is was decided to sacrifice the extra information gained by the scale and to accept an operational definition that a computer program could handle. Considering what is usually meant by a sociometric link between persons, that is, the flow of communication in at least one direction, a response of "know well" or "know socially" was defined as constituting a *sociometric link of acquaintance.* If the respondent had checked that he had had business, civic, or social contacts with another leader, they were considered a *link of general contact;* similarly, for joint participation on a committee dealing with urban problems the contact was defined as a *link of committee contact.* For these three sets of data, then, the acquaintance, general contact, and committee contact, we had for each respondent a list of his sociometric choices and, if desired, could ascertain three different linkage structures.

One of the major goals of the leadership research was to investigate the possible existence of informal social networks connecting the major cities of Megalopolis. In Chapter 4 sociograms were drawn to display acquaintance contacts and the environmental problem activities of the key leaders. The drawing of sociograms, although preserving all the information, is limited to small numbers of persons. After a certain size the lines become unintelligible. The good uses to which a computer can be put are well attested by the data assembled here. The computer scanned 100^2, or 10,000, responses to a single link criterion and in 30 seconds furnished a data display that listed all reciprocated choices in the population. Clerical time for the same operation would have exceeded two full work days.[5] The computer has a greater range than merely the capacity to record rapidly. With appropriate programming it can sift the data and detect clique patterns that would otherwise be denied the researcher. This research has utilized the work of Duncan MacRae, James S. Coleman, and others, who contributed computer techniques that have made new discoveries possible.

Only recently has sociometry been given a firm grounding in the theory of informal association. For many years the prolific construction of scales and diagrams was justified by practical applications in various formal associations.[6] Although a wide variety of techniques has been advanced for conducting sociometric analyses, few, until recently, have achieved the methodological rigor of other techniques used in the analysis of social science data.[7] A new approach to sociometry that can be applied to clique analysis has appeared in the literature. Before presenting the methods available it is necessary to define such concepts as clique, sociometric status, projected status, received status, and attenuation.

BASIC CONCEPTUAL CONCEPTS

The term *clique* is commonly used to refer to a small group of persons with high in-group cohesion or solidarity. Decision-making cliques in community power studies are often reported as characterized by leaders who are the spokesmen for their followers. The clique's all-important decisions are made as a social unit. The sociometric data available to us does not permit an analysis of clique dynamics, but it can determine clique structure. Homans has provided an interactional concept of a clique that is useful for this purpose.

... a group is defined by the interactions· of its members. If we say that individuals, A, B, C, D, E . . . form a group, this will mean that at least the following circumstances hold. Within a given period of time A interacts more often with B, C, D, E . . . than he does with M, N, L, O, P . . . whom we choose to consider outsiders or members of other groups. B also interacts more often with A, C, D, E . . . than he does with outsiders, and so on for the other members of the group. . . . This is what we do crudely in everyday life when we say that certain persons "see a lot of one another," "go around together," "work together," or "associate with one another," and that they make up a clique, a gang, a crowd, a group.[8]

This interactional concept leads to an operational definition:

A clique is a group of at least three individuals, the majority of whom choose and are chosen by one another.

This definition releases the researcher from the stricture of imposing all mutually reciprocated choices on a group in order that it may be considered a clique.

Sociometric Status. The research can be forwarded if it is possible to differentiate the cliques and rank them on a popularity continuum. Sociometric status, as employed here, is defined as the position of any individual in an informal structure based on his popularity in being chosen by others. An index of sociometric status can be constructed for a clique by taking into account everyone's sociometric choices.

Projected and Received Status. A given individual may make choices of others and/or receive choices from others. A projected status score may be secured by counting the number of choices each respondent makes; a received status score may be the number of choices received in a given population or group. Such scoring of projected or received statuses does not take into account any differences between who is chosen and who chooses. If a respondent chooses "important" people, a true projected status score should reflect his choices, and, similarly, if one is chosen by "important" people, a true projected status score would also include such distinctions. For this reason traditional measures of status were rejected for the analysis. A model used for the construction of a status index for projected and received statuses was developed.[9] The projected and received status indices made possible by this model consider the relative status of those being chosen and of those choosing. The indices are also improved by their correction for attenuation. The meaning of this term must be explained.

Attentuation. Before current techniques were available sociometric analysis was carried out by making the assumption that each link was a direct connection between two or more persons and that each had the same strength as all others. When we examine sociometric data closely, the difference between direct and indirect sociometric links is evident. Figure 10.2 shows the sociometric choice trees that resulted from direct and mediated choices as six individuals made their selections and their candidates then made theirs. A sociometric link between two

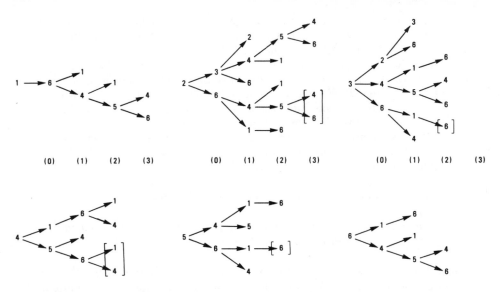

Figure 10.2   Sociometric choice trees for six individuals.

people becomes *attenuated* when the link between them is not direct but inter-
mediated by other individuals. An attenuation constant is introduced in the
computational procedure such that appropriate weights are assigned, depending
on the relative strength of all connections, direct and indirect. The projected
status score is computed by multiplying the appropriate attenuation constant by
the number of direct or indirect choices an individual makes. The same procedure is used in computing the received status score except that the appropriate
attenuation constant is multiplied by the number of direct or indirect choices an
individual receives.[10]

The Calculation and Interpretation of Clique Determination and Status Indices.
The goals set out in this probe of contact and clique structures included a determination of existing cliques in the Megalopolis key leader population and the
determination of status indices which would reflect the "importance" of the
leaders and the full impact of all direct and indirect choices. These difficult objectives require elaborate and rigorous computer programs. The factor analytic
method of clique determination and the status indices allow the researcher to
map and rank the informal structures of any population. Although these techniques had been applied only to small, self-contained sociological units, their
application to a region such as Megalopolis seemed feasible. If there is a basis
for future regional development in Megalopolis, the informal associational patterns should possess the same properties as any other sociological unit. Informal
patterns have demonstrated great importance in decision making in smaller units
and possession of the informal leadership structure in a region could prove to be
of high value. The research challenge is to find and describe it.

The Determination of Cliques

Many methodological contributions have emerged from the area of sociometry, in which mathematical applications and models have been used increasingly. The history of sociometry is a varied and interesting one, and Glanzer and Glaser review the more important avenues of approach used throughout the 1950's.[11] The main approach to the identification of cliques have been the sociogram, matrix manipulation, and factor analysis. Davis and Leinhardt have recently applied graph theory techniques and have demonstrated ability to extract cliques and ranking systems from sociometric data.[12] Nosanchuk applied the sociogram, the matrix manipulation, and the factor analytic methods to fictitious data and found that only factor analysis yields unambiguous results with groups of varying structure. Factor analysis best permits objectivity in partitioning the group into cliques and revealing the affiliations and cleavages in the groups.[13]

James Coleman has recently developed a technique of analyzing sociometric data based on multidimensional scaling procedures.[14] In his method a sociogram is drawn in three or four dimensions in which the location of its points would not be arbitrarily determined for artistic convenience but by a mathematical solution to a given set of data. This method provides the advantage of reducing the time (conventional methods may require as long as 50 hours) required to secure an accurate sociogram. The major disadvantage is that the number of dimensions into which the structure may be mapped is limited.

The most favored technique for clique identification is the factor analytic model. The application of factor analysis to sociometric data was first done by MacRae and the technique consists of two main routines: principal component analysis and the rotation of the components to varimax simple structure.[15] This technique was adopted for use with the Megalopolis data.

THE CALCULATION OF STATUS INDICES

Clique membership and identification are necessary to establish the structure of the informal group network. Equally important is the determination of the relative status of each member and of the clique as a whole. This knowledge enables the researcher to find the most effective subgroup structures within the larger informal social system.

In the calculation of status scores the direct and indirect choices are tabulated by a network construction process. Individual i makes direct choices to j, k, l, . . . , all of whom make direct choices to n, p, q, . . . Thus individual i is connected to n, p, q, . . . , by j, k, l, . . . When the attenuation constant is multiplied by the varying numbers of individuals who appear in different cycles, and a sum is derived for each, projected status scores result. When these choice networks are constructed for all individuals, the number of times an individual appears in a cycle over the choice networks of all others is multiplied by the appropriate attenuation constant and summed over all cycles. Received status scores result. The effect of this procedure is that if several high-status individuals choose our individual i whose score is being computed, i will receive "credit" not only for those directly received choices but also for all the people who have chosen him through intermediaries. Thus a relatively isolated individual who nevertheless is chosen by a few high-status individuals will be indirectly connected by one intermediary to many others. A model of this network has been built into a set of mathematical equations but will not be introduced.[16]

Projected and received status scores may be interpreted in a more general fashion. A high score on either scale could be interpreted as an indicator that the individual is tightly bound into the social fabric of the population being studied. Thus the measure lends itself to usage as an index of centrality or connectedness. The flow of communications could be studied by using these indices because individuals with high scores are immediately seen as possessing information-dispensing capabilities. Also, because the projected and received indices are computed independently, the individual's place in the social network can be viewed in two ways: where he is placed by others, using the received score, and where he places himself, using the projected score.

By finding the mean status scores of the individuals in a clique the status indices can be applied to the cliques themselves. Most of the same interpretations made for individuals can, when appropriate, be transferred to cliques. The advantage of employing status measures to both individuals and cliques is demonstrated in the following analysis.

The Leadership Cliques of Megalopolis Determined by a Contact Criterion

To determine the cliques that may exist among the key leader population in Megalopolis the general contact data were subjected to direct factor analysis.[17]

After varimax rotation loadings were found for each of 10 choosing and 10 chosen factors. To detect clique structure the sum of the squares of the loadings of the factors must be computed.[18] Using the criterion of a high loading on both chooser and chosen factors, nine cliques were found.[19] The membership of the cliques is shown in Table 10.2.

COMPOSITION OF THE CLIQUES

The nine cliques represented what may be considered highly interacting groups, enmeshed in a broader social network. The sociograms in Chapter 4 described that broader network across Megalopolis. The cliques, now identified, provide a sharper view of the subgroups and the boundaries that separated them. We know definitively that smaller groups of leaders from different cities shared common patterns of interaction. These groups can be examined for their residential and occupational affiliations.

Classification of Residential and Occupational Affiliations of the Clique Members

Clique composition classified by residence and occupation is presented in Table 10.3. Although the larger cliques (1, 2, and 3) were dominated by leaders from

TABLE 10.2 MEMBERSHIP OF NINE CLIQUES BASED ON THE GENERAL CONTACT DATA

					Cliques				
1		2		3	4	5	6	7	8	9

1		2		3		4	5	6	7	8	9
33	56	43	78	3	12	27	16	43	18	15	31
43	59	68	79	4	14	28	21	44	20	16	43
47	60	69	80	5	16	29	22	56	27	42	47
49	61	70	81	6	17	30	23	88	35	43	72
50	63	71	82	8	18	31	24	93	39	44	
51	65	72	83	9	20	91	26	94	58	56	
53	66	73	84	10	43	92	47	95		87	
54	67	74	85	11			51	97			
55		75	86				95	100			
		77									

Note. Individuals with underscored ID numbers are members of more than one clique.

one city, there was considerable diversity in area of leadership and at least two cities were represented in every clique. Some leaders bridged cliques with multiple memberships. Thirty-one leaders, underscored in Table 10.2 and identified as multiple clique members, possessed high capacity to extend influence over the region.

Relative Status of Leaders and Cliques

The next problem encountered in the research relates to the leaders and cliques in the Megalopolis population. Quantitative measurements promised to provide increasingly sharper understanding of the potentials in the informal social system. To this end the two indices, the projected and received status scores, were computed for all 100 respondents. Based on the membership of the nine cliques listed in Table 10.3, the projected and received scores were grouped so that mean scores could be calculated for each clique. The results appear in Table 10.4. A high score on projected status means that clique members generally chose high-status individuals or they placed themselves in a fairly high place in the social network. A high score on received status means that others generally placed the clique member high on the status hierarchy.[20] The true status of a clique is best repre-

TABLE 10.3 CLASSIFICATION OF RESIDENTIAL AND OCCUPATIONAL AFFILIATIONS OF CLIQUE MEMBERSHIP*

Cliques

1	2	3	4	5	6	7	8	9
Philadelphia	*Baltimore*	*Boston*	*New York*	*Boston*	*Washington*	*New York*	*Boston*	*New York*
Business Labor Politics Religion Civic	Business Labor Politics Religion Civic	Business Labor Politics Civic Religion	Labor Politics	Civic	Business Politics Religion Civic	Labor Religion	Civic	Politics Civic
New York	*New York*	*New York*	*Washington*	*New York*	*New York*	*Boston*	*New York*	*Philadelphia*
Politics Civic	Civic	Civic	Labor Politics	Business	Civic	Religion	Civic	Business
				Philadelphia Business	*Philadelphia* Politics	*Philadelphia* Religion	*Philadelphia* Politics	*Baltimore* Business
				Washington Politics			*Baltimore* Civic	

* The full list of members is shown in Table 10.1. This table presents the appropriate classification of the clique member. One or more members may be represented by each classification.

TABLE 10.4   MEAN PROJECTED AND RECEIVED STATUS SCORES FOR NINE CLIQUES

	Cliques								
	1	2	3	4	5	6	7	8	9
Projected score	112.37	119.49	102.96	99.12	80.68	120.84	80.78	131.87	127.63
Standard deviation	38.33	19.16	26.52	19.98	22.41	26.99	20.14	22.52	30.46
Received score	116.83	134.84	95.91	97.30	93.10	104.87	72.00	173.50	151.85
Standard deviation	41.67	39.56	46.50	27.13	41.60	72.35	27.66	38.97	62.73

sented by the received scores because they reflect what others ascribe to the members of the clique The rankings of the cliques by their received and projected scores are compared in Table 10.5.

The high correlation between these rankings is clear, but some variation is undoubtedly due to sampling error as the wide standard deviations suggest.[21] Cliques 8 and 9, two of the smaller cliques of four members, ranked highest in true status, as shown by their received scores, and their rankings on mean projected scores were consonant. At the bottom were cliques 5 and 7. The widest variation was shown by clique 6, which ranked fifth on the basis of its received scores and third on its projected scores. Higher projected scores revealed the general upward direction that individual member choices tended to take. Their true status is shown at variance because they received choices from individuals on lower levels.

The Clique Pyramid Showing Relative Status of the Nine Cliques

If the cliques were arranged on a status hierarchy with their positions determined by both projected and received scores, the pyramid in Figure 10.3 would result.

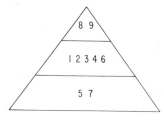

Figure 10.3 Pyramid showing the relative status of the nine cliques in Megalopolis.

TABLE 10.5   RANKINGS OF THE CLIQUES BY THEIR MEAN RECEIVED SCORES AND PROJECTED SCORES

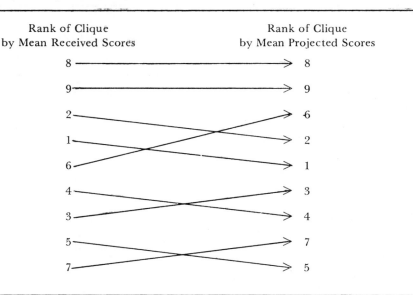

| | |
| Rank of Clique by Mean Received Scores | Rank of Clique by Mean Projected Scores |

Cliques 8 and 9 had the highest status. Cliques 1, 2, 3, 4, and 6 occupied medium status positions; 5 and 7 were at the bottom of the hierarchy.[22]

Analysis of specific cliques leads to a number of observations. Cliques 8 and 9 at the top of the status hierarchy were small. They were represented by three to four cities and the status of their members was high. Cliques 1, 2, 3, and 6 were large, with in-city cliques predominating: a majority of their members came from Philadelphia, Baltimore, Boston, and Washington, respectively. Furthermore, the medium-sized cliques, 4, 5, and 7, had broader bases in Megalopolis. New York has the unique distinction of having had clique members in every one of the nine cliques. Obviously, New York leaders served to bridge them. The overall character of the clique structure is marked by the interaction of a few leaders who worked on committees together and made other contacts that tied their cities to the larger social network of Megalopolis.[23]

Conclusion

The research demonstrates that sociometric techniques can be applied to study the interaction patterns of leaders in a large sociological unit. Whether Megalopolis is expanding its common base by leader integration is a question that cannot be answered here, but at least the existence of a definitive base has been documented. Two properties of an informal structure, clique differentiation and status positions, support the hypothesis that Megalopolis is connected not only by formal organizations but by informal associations as well. The existence of such a base provides evidence for a common framework so necessary to the handling of common regional problems like environmental quality control.

Notes

1. Howard W. Odum, *Southern Regions of the United States,* University of North Carolina Press, Chapel Hill, 1936.

2. Floyd Hunter, *Top Leadership: U. S. A.,* University of North Carolina Press, Chapel Hill, 1959, p. 33.

3. The computer analysis of the sociometric data was under the direction of Lloyd V. Temme, Research Associate, now Project Director, Bureau of Social Science Research, Inc., Washington, D.C.

4. Although the 100 key leaders had provided complete reports on all 200 key leaders, the lack of reciprocal data from the nonrespondents left an incomplete set of data. Various tests of bias had shown that the 100 respondents could be regarded as a representative sample. With such an assumption, the analysis of the interconnected choices of 100 leaders became the population. This decision, of course, reduced the total possible sociomatrix by one-fourth, but it did make the analysis more manageable because even with the computer the determination of clique structures was difficult.

5. Computer programs are being written by Charles Kadushin that will produce machine-drawn sociograms, a badly needed contribution. See Charles Kadushin, "Analysis of Sociometric Data with the Aid of Computers." Research Proposal to the National Science Foundation, Teachers College, Columbia University, New York, 1970.

6. For examples of how sociometry has been used in an applied way see Mary Northway, *A Primer of Sociometry,* 2nd ed., University of Toronto Press, 1967, and J. Alex Murray, "A Sociometric Approach to Organizations Analysis," *California Management Review,* **13** (1970), 59–67. Although the methodology employed by these authors is primitive, their works do demonstrate the uses to which sociometry has been put.

7. For an excellent review of methodology in sociometry up to 1959 see Murray Glanzer and Robert Glaser, "Techniques for the Study of Group Structure and Behavior: I. Analysis of Structure," *Psychological Bulletin,* **56** (1959), 317–332. Cf. Paul Hare, Edgar F. Borgata, and Robert F. Bales, *Small Groups,* 2nd ed., Knopf, New York, 1966.

8. George Homans, *The Human Group,* Harcourt, Brace, and World, New York, 1960, pp. 84–85.

9. The description of the status index is available from Lloyd Temme to interested readers by request. See footnote 23 for his address.

10. As an approximation of the strength of direct and indirect sociometric links, the relative influence between individuals i and j, when mediated by k individuals, is c^k. In the present research we set c equal to 0.5, such that the strength of a sociometric link between two individuals, mediated by one other, is one-half that of a direct link, one-fourth that of a direct link when the link is mediated by two others, and so on.

11. Glanzer and Glaser, *op. cit.*

12. James A. Davis and Samuel Leinhardt, "The Structure of Positive Interpersonal Relations in Small Groups" unpublished manuscript, 1967. This article will appear in Joseph Berger, Morris Zelditch, Jr. and Bo Anderson, *Sociological Theories in Progress,* 2 vols. Houghton Mifflin, Boston, 1966–72. Cf. James A. Davis, "Clustering and Hierarchy in Interpersonal Relations: Testing Two Graph Theoretical Models on 742 Socio-Matrices," *American Sociological Review,* **38** (1970), 843–851.

13. Terrance Nosanchuk, "A Comparison of Several Sociometric Partitioning Techniques," *Sociometry,* **26** (1963), 112–124.

14. James S. Coleman, "Clustering in N-Dimensions by Use of a System of Forces," *Journal of Mathematical Sociology* 1, 1970, 1–47.

15. Duncan MacRae, "Direct Factor Analysis of Sociometric Data," *Sociometry,* **23** (1960), 360–371. MacRae has shown that the principal components of a sociomatrix can be extracted by using Hotelling's iterative method and that each subgroup or clique will correspond to a separate dimension in factorial space. Given the sociomatrix, X, where $x_{ij} =$

1 if there is a choice directed to individual j from i and $x_{ij} = 0$ if there is no such choice, and using an iterative procedure called direct factor analysis discussed more fully by MacRae, a column vector and a row vector, or conjugate pairs of eigenvectors, emerge as a factor solution representing the chooser matrix, one of the column vectors, can be interpreted as all thse individuals choose the same individuals, and conversely for the chosen matrix, or individuals with high loadings in a row vector are chosen by the same people. The factor matrices may then be rotated independently by the varimax criterion. This rotation would yield a maximum number of independent dimensions, or cliques, in factorial space but would preserve overlapping membership where it occurs. In terms of clique determination, using Homan's definition of clique, a clique would consist of those people who both choose and are chosen by the same people or the individuals who have high loadings on the same chooser and chosen factors. The communalities that are computed in this procedure represent the sum of squares of an individual's choices accounted for by the factor matrix, and when compared with the number of choices he actually made can be interpreted as a measure of goodness of fit. Also the factor sum of squares gives the amount of variation in the total sample explained by one factor and the sum of those squares for all factors, hence can be used as another goodness-of-fit measure. There is one problem, however, with this method of clique determination: a criterion for stopping factoring has not yet been developed. The criterion used in the present research was to extract more factors than necessary and include only those that yielded a clique—the chooser and chosen factors had to yield at least three individuals with high loadings (greater than 0.8) on both factors. Whether this criterion can be translated into an eigenvalue criterion is questionable. A criterion for stopping rotation has been included in the computer program and considerable computer time can be saved by using it, but there is no certain way at present of stopping factoring, yet yielding all the significant factors. The criterion for stopping rotation is that there must be at least three high loadings per factor for that factor to be included, but the correspondence question is still not solved.

16. This model is available to interested researchers. Write Lloyd Temme at the address shown in footnote 23.

17. The application of "direct factor analysis" is treated fully in Duncan MacRae, Jr., *Issues and Parties in Legislative Voting*, Harper and Row, 1970.

18. Communalities can be interpreted as an indication of the extent to which an individual's actual choices are represented by the factors.

19. The sum of the sums of squares for the chooser factors is 681.8. The total sum of squares for the sample of 100 is 1024.0; that is 1024 choices were given, including self-choices. Therefore the factors "explain" 66 percent of the total variation in the sample. Another measure of goodness of fit of the model, the extent to which the factor structure corresponds to a varimax simple structure, is given by the varimax rotation criterion function, which has a range of zero to one. For these data the function is 0.52 for the chooser factors and 0.53 for the chosen factors. This function measures the extent to which the rotated factors fit the theoretical model of simple structure, when the loadings on each factor tend toward zero or one.

20. The mean scores are not totally independent of one another because several individuals appear in more than one clique; hence their scores were used in computing means for several cliques. Regardless of overlapping membership, however, the relative status of each clique was desired, and because the cliques themselves are analytically independent in factorial space clique means for the status indices reflect the relative status of one clique opposed to another.

21. See Table 10.4 for the range of these deviations.

22. The interpretation of the ranking should take into account that only one point in time is being considered; dynamic processes that occur in leader interaction are obscured. It must be remembered that there is considerable overlapping, for many leaders belonged to more than one clique. Relying on clique status to determine the structure of informal association obscures individual movements taking place between members.

23. A computer program to analyze sociometric data for clique differentiation and status positions has been developed around Duncan MacRae's formulations. Lloyd Temme will make
this program available to interested researchers. Write him at the Bureau of Social Research, Inc., 1990 M Street N.W., Washington, D.C. 20036.

CHAPTER ELEVEN

The Measurement of Organizational Interaction: Toward a Sociology of Associations

A sociology of associations is struggling for birth. The theory and the functional elements are assembled and only a synthesizer to breathe life into the separate parts is lacking. David Sills, who has codified sociological aspects of voluntary associations, stresses various structural and internal aspects like types, extent, nature of membership, organization processes, and functions for individuals and society.[1] *The Government of Associations*, a book of readings edited by Sills (and William A. Glaser), adds such themes as the influence of associations on society, the nature of leadership, problems of government, organizational goals, communication and decisions, organizational means, internal divisions, and organizational change.[2] It is interesting that both writers hesitate to proclaim that a full-fledged sociology of associations has arrived. Similarly, in March's comprehensive *Handbook of Organizations* no mention of this field is made—the word association does not even appear in the subject index.[3]

Perhaps what has been most lacking is a grasp of interorganizational relations and enough research to show how interactional processes function. As early as 1961 Levine and White wrote,

> Sociologists have devoted considerable attention to the study of formal organizations, particularly in industry, government, and the trade union field. Their chief focus, however, has been on patterns within rather than between organizations. Studies of interrelationships have largely been confined to units within the same organizational structure or between a pair of complementary organizations such as management and labor.[4]

Almost independently a group of theorists and researchers have been developing a body of knowledge to give substance to this new area of interorganizational interaction and relationship.[5]

Andrew Collver has developed an outline and a bibliography to bring together current research and theory on relations among organizations. His outline is presented here:

1. General theoretical discussions of the nature of communities and societies and the place of autonomous organizations therein.
2. The origin and development of organizations; their characteristics, inventories, and classifications.
3. General discussions of the relation between organizations and their environments.
4. Elementary concepts of relations between two organizations.
5. Theoretical discussions of more complex interorganizational systems—organization—sets, intergroup networks, functional subsystems, or industries.

Problems of Associational Sociology Deriving from the Eastern Leadership and Organizational Study

The design of this research study led the research operations deeper and deeper into problems of complex interorganizational relationships. What is most significant is that the focus became fixed on the interrelation of national voluntary associations both among themselves and in interaction with federal agencies. No social scientist had ever undertaken a systematic study of this kind. What we discovered was a dynamic web of relationships. Since most of the powerful national associations interested in urban problems are located in Washington, the arena of interaction is in a small and concentrated area of the capital city. Even those with national heaquarters elsewhere tend to have Washington offices; therefore access to organizational officials is made relatively easy. Interviews with them on the rating of the power of various organizations (both voluntary and public) and the working relations of organizations opened up the discussion of associational interaction. The initial problem of rating organizations—how to rate an organization powerful in one specific area (such as HUD) but with little or no power in others—became acute, especially when the judge was asked to rate the National League of Cities or the U.S. Conference of Mayors which have broad interests and wide-ranging programs. There were questions raised by the ideological positions taken by some organizations. How do you rate an organization with a powerful veto that is always fighting against change and doing little to improve a problem area? How do you evaluate a militant civil rights organization that has great potential power but is intransigent in its relations with most of the other powerful organizations?

Other problems were presented in the interpretation of working relations described by organization officials as those with which their organizations had cooperated. It became apparent that both in this rating and in working relations in other organizations officers were influenced by two factors: ideological orientation and program interests of the referent organizations.

These discoveries opened the door to a number of inquiries. Each points to an enlarging area of study—association interaction. A proposed outline of the field is presented at the end of this chapter.

Discussions of research problems in associational interactions are presented in the following order:

1. The influence of program interest and ideology in the thinking of organizational officials as they evaluate referent organizations.
2. The influence of ideological position on the cooperative and conflict relations established with referent organizations.
3. The measurement of acquaintance and contact as they affect the working relations of organizations.
4. The invoicing of organizational orientations and activities undertaken for political action.
5. The formation of confederations and mergers for augmenting organizational power and the advancement of common interests.

The Influence of Program Interest and Ideology in the Thinking of Organizational Officials as They Evaluate Referent Organizations

STEREOTYPING

Stereotype judgments are normal in the thinking of all persons about government and voluntary organizations. The range of both is so large, their programs so comprehensive, and changes so ever present that the mind can take in but a fraction of the relevant information that is necessary to understand fully a federal agency or a national association. Stereotype judgments are fragmentary, drawn from what an observer has read, heard, or seen in bits and pieces over time. Although they are incomplete, they have the advantages of revealing the elementary but crude bases of judgment. It is the stereotype that quickly reveals the extent of attraction, repulsion, or indifference of the rater to other organizations. Table 11.1 shows the influence rankings and stereotype judgments of a high federal official with a long career as a civic worker in Washington. His judgments are shown in the verbatim terms in which he made them.

A study of these judgments demonstrates that many factors enter: the interests of the organization, its ideological position, power, action orientation and degree of activity, and quality of leadership. Among these factors the interest of the organization and its ideological position loom largest. They show up especially when cooperative and conflict relations between organizations are examined.

The Influence of Ideological Position on the Cooperative and Conflict Relations Established with Referent Organizations

THE IDEOLOGICAL SPECTRUM OF ORGANIZATIONS

Each government agency and private association represents certain economic and political interests which are revealed in the formulation and execution of policy. It is perhaps misleading to say that each organization has a given ideological position because organizations display great flexibility and think of themselves as acting independently on each issue. Yet each organization has its normative or

TABLE 11.1 STEREOTYPE JUDGEMENTS OF URBAN ORIENTED ORGANIZATIONS BY AN OBSERVER

Influence ranking		
2	Urban America	"Has focus on housing but it has begun to work with street gangs."
1	National Association for the Advancement of Colored People	"Won many legal battles. Has fought consistently, solidly for Negro gains. Now is target of Black Militants."
3	National Association of Manufacturers	"Lags behind. Take veto positions on progressive legislation."
3	Business Council	"Not very important, has backward outlook."
3	Committee for Economic Development	"Lost their punch. Need new mission."
3	National Industrial Conference Board	"Not action-oriented — research outfit."
2	National Congress of Parents and Teachers	"Long fight to integrate these groups but the battle was won. They do work for quality education."
1	National Urban League	"An organization that has fought and won solid progress for the Negro."
2	National Educational Association	"Is in fight with American Federation of Teachers. Has done a lot for teachers but now torn over whether it should advocate teachers strikes."
1	U.S. Department of Health, Education and Welfare	"A wide-ranging organization with difficult tasks. It has had and has great creative leadership."
2	Small Business Administration	"Just getting in to help Negro businessmen. It has had an instruction program for small businesses that has been basic."

	Organization	Rank	Comment
	National Council of Churches	1	"They have carried the fight for integration once they were won over."
	U.S. Conference of Mayors	2	"Potentially powerful but they can't get much done without money."
	National Alliance of Businessmen	1	"Fighting to get hard-core unemployment reduced. Making some progress."
	National League of Cities	2	"More educational than action-oriented."
	International Association of City Managers	3	"Professional association. That's it."
	National Research Council of National Academy of Science	3	"Not action-oriented."
	Ford Foundation	1	"Have done a great job. Not afraid to move into controversy."
	American Bankers Association	3	"Haven't done much but they have programs relative to business firms and lower interest for Negro businessmen."
	AFL-CIO	2	"Have helped labor greatly, but have lagged in racial matters, especially in building trades. They can press more now."
	American Medical Association	3	"Always laggards, not socially oriented."
	U.S. Department of Housing and Urban Development	2	"An important program but red tape ties up action. Last housing bill was emasculated."
	U.S. Office of Economic Opportunity	3	"Some ideal efforts in poverty fight but they are undermined by Black Militants."
	Chamber of Commerce of the United States	2	"They're coming around but they don't really back significant programs."

301

TABLE 11.1   STEREOTYPE JUDGEMENTS OF URBAN ORIENTED ORGANIZATIONS BY AN OBSERVER   (*Continued*)

Influence ranking		
3	Council of State Governments	"Get tied up in red tape and political clearances."
3	American Bar Association	"Lag on most urban matters. Have program for legal assistance that is good."
2	U.S. Junior Chamber of Commerce	"Has some new leadership that will make its mark."
3	National Association of Broadcasters	"They have an opportunity to be a leader but can they take the role? That is the question."
2	Urban Coalition	"I don't think they see the real obstacles. Businessmen don't really understand slum problems and they need money."
1	League of Women Voters	"They work and take stands but they need money."
3	American Institute of Planners	"They have the professional expertise – not action-oriented."
3	National Federation of Business and Professional Women's Clubs	"Nice ladies but they just don't get things done."
3	National Business League	"A Negro small business club. They are without a program."
3	National Commission on Urban Problems	"Not action oriented."
1	U.S. Department of Labor	"Doing an important job – job training for hard-core unemployed and job upgrading."

model position in a political continuum reading right to left or from reactionary to revolutionary. An effort to establish a scale is shown in Table 11.2 in which categories are named in sequence, from reactionaries, traditionalists, neotraditionalists, reformers, crisis reformers, and revolutionaries. These categories are defined as positions in the support of capitalism and the role of government in funding and implementing social action. A tentative placement of various organizations has been made to establish the general position or range of positions usually taken on issues and programs.

Granted that this table is only a rough approximation, such data are used by observers in evaluating organizations and making personal estimates of their functions. This fact can be seen clearly as soon as an observer is asked to make ratings of an organization's influence. The crisis reformer commonly gives a lower rating to those organizations that do not assume the "progressive" position to which he adheres. Such an observer will speak of these "less progressive" organizations as "lagging," "not action-oriented," or "exercising veto power." The government agencies that association members approach and the officials they choose to work with may be strongly conditioned by their ideological coloration. Government officials act in like manner toward given associations.

OVERALL SOCIOMETRIC SUPPORTIVENESS PATTERNS

An exploratory effort was made to identify these ideological affinities and repulsions as government agencies view the most influential urban-oriented associations. An official at the Office of Economic Opportunity was given a deck of 37 cards with the names of the most influential associations and asked to select those that would be most supportive, generally supportive or less supportive if the OEO needed help in securing a budget or perhaps in fighting for its survival. (In the fall of 1968 after the Republican victory OEO was regarded as the most vulnerable agency of government. The general belief was that it would be eliminated or most of its functions transferred to the more permanent departments—HEW, HUD, and Labor.) The OEO official made the selection shown in Figure 11.1. The organizations rated most supportive, generally supportive, and less supportive appear in successive circles. These ratings were not repeated by any other observers in the organization and the researcher does not know if the rating is a reliable one, nor can anyone affirm that the organizations shown actually took the position in which they are placed. However, this one important divisional head viewed the associational world in the way the figure describes it and acted accordingly. The reason for his views seems to stem largely from the ideological positions of the associations. Obviously this is a researchable question.

Another exploratory interview was held with a divisional head, an official of long tenure at the Department of Housing and Urban Development. A similar rating was prepared, but this time a second rating was conducted. Again the official was asked to examine the deck of 37 cards with the listed associations and to rate them as most supportive, generally supportive, or less supportive. He was then asked to relate his ratings to the budget requests of the agency and to its major policies and decisions. When he had completed the rating, an identical deck of cards was given him to consider and rate the associations he regarded as giving most opposition, sometimes opposing, or offering little opposition to the efforts of the agency to carry out its programs (see Figure 11.2).

Reactionaries	Traditionalists	Neotraditionalists	Reformers	Crisis reformers	Revolutionaries
Capitalism should be free to respond to supply and demand in consumer and labor markets; the problem of inflation is major for all segments of the population and should receive top priority; unemployment is a safety valve in a dynamic economy	The capitalistic system as it is now functioning under loose government controls is the best answer to urban problems; expanded private employment will reduce unemployment and poverty, thus enabling more people to better their lives in housing, their education, and their lives in general; meanwhile law and order should be established with tight controls.	Private business and government should establish a partnership in which tax incentives and subsidies will be made available to train and educate hardcore unemployed and others with low education and skill capacity; an expanded private housing effort is required and will be possible only with tax incentive or subsidies to builders who build for the low-income market	Public programs are necessary in order to meet urban needs; the Federal Government must raise and distribute large sums of money to cities and states to increase public housing, better schools, and improved rapid transit	Democratic capitalism should be reshaped into new priorities and goals; massive federal aid is necessary and should be poured into the inner city if the society is to be saved from riots, crime, and the threat of revolutionary chaos; new programs and new directions are needed; black community programs must get the highest priority; poverty and unemployment must be abolished	The capitalistic system and its establishment tools must be destroyed and replaced with a socialist system; black power must be established and increased by a continuous application of terroristic or pressure activities and policies of separatism by which the black community will achieve greater control
Many trade Associations	Republican Party	National Association of Manufacturers	American Institute of Planners	National Urban League	Black Panthers
Business council				NAACP	SNCC
				U. S. Conference of Mayors	Black United Front

National Industrial Conference Board

Chamber of Commerce

Urban America

National League of Cities

U.S. Council of State Governments

Urban Coalition

American Bankers Association

Committee of Economic Development

Southern Christian Leadership Conference

American Medical Association

National Alliance of Businessmen

Democratic Party

CORE

AFL–CIO

International Association of City Managers

National Business League

National Federation of Business and Professional Women's Clubs

Ford Foundation

League of Women Voters

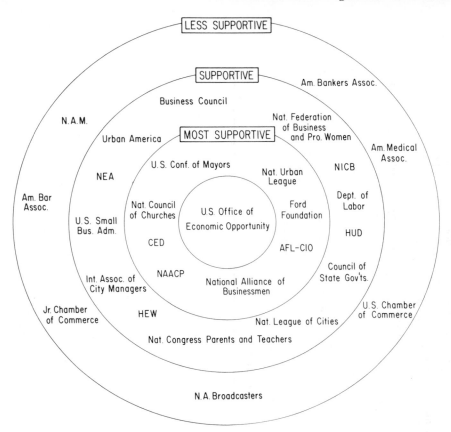

Figure 11.1   Ratings by a divisional head of the U.S. Office of Economic opportunity.
of the perceived supportive character of the 37 top urban-oriented associations. Associa-
tions rated as "don't know" are not shown.

This analysis shows the character of the perceived structure of relation as government officials view that part of the "outside" world with which they commonly work. The degree to which the parties approach one another and the type of relationship established are suggested by these sociograms.

It will be noted that the AFL-CIO was perceived as most supportive by the OEO official. Over at HUD, however, the official called the AFL-CIO generally supportive, but indicated that it is one of the organizations that gives HUD most opposition. A division head at AFL-CIO was asked to rank the same 37 top urban-oriented associations, first according to support and then to opposition bearing on the AFL-CIO. Figure 11.3 shows his pattern of perceptions. He, too, indicated that the AFL-CIO is generally supportive of HUD and OEO but that his own organization sometimes opposes HUD.

Each official was asked whether he thought that other officials in his organization would agree in generally with his perceptions. All three answered that they believed there would be high agreement. One said, "we are pretty well brainwashed as to who goes along with us and who is in opposition." Another said,

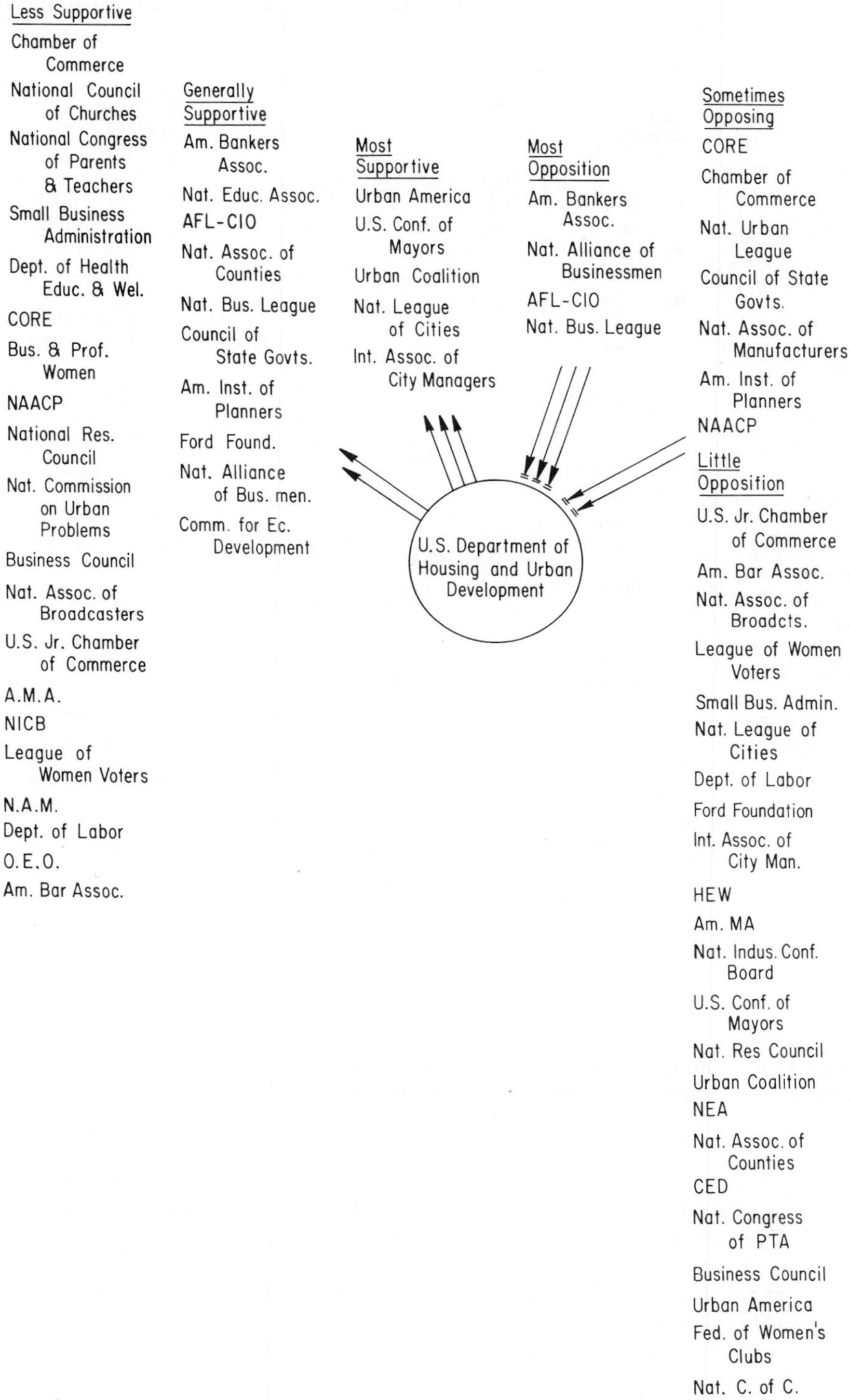

Less Supportive
Chamber of
  Commerce
National Council
  of Churches
National Congress
  of Parents
  & Teachers
Small Business
  Administration
Dept. of Health
  Educ. & Wel.
CORE
Bus. & Prof.
  Women
NAACP
National Res.
  Council
Nat. Commission
  on Urban
  Problems
Business Council
Nat. Assoc. of
  Broadcasters
U.S. Jr. Chamber
  of Commerce
A.M.A.
NICB
League of
  Women Voters
N.A.M.
Dept. of Labor
O.E.O.
Am. Bar Assoc.

Generally
Supportive
Am. Bankers
  Assoc.
Nat. Educ. Assoc.
AFL-CIO
Nat. Assoc. of
  Counties
Nat. Bus. League
Council of
  State Govts.
Am. Inst. of
  Planners
Ford Found.
Nat. Alliance
  of Bus. men.
Comm. for Ec.
  Development

Most
Supportive
Urban America
U.S. Conf. of
  Mayors
Urban Coalition
Nat. League
  of Cities
Int. Assoc. of
  City Managers

Most
Opposition
Am. Bankers
  Assoc.
Nat. Alliance of
  Businessmen
AFL-CIO
Nat. Bus. League

U.S. Department of
Housing and Urban
Development

Sometimes
Opposing
CORE
Chamber of
  Commerce
Nat. Urban
  League
Council of State
  Govts.
Nat. Assoc. of
  Manufacturers
Am. Inst. of
  Planners
NAACP

Little
Opposition
U.S. Jr. Chamber
  of Commerce
Am. Bar Assoc.
Nat. Assoc. of
  Broadcts.
League of Women
  Voters
Small Bus. Admin.
Nat. League of
  Cities
Dept. of Labor
Ford Foundation
Int. Assoc. of
  City Man.
HEW
Am. MA
Nat. Indus. Conf.
  Board
U.S. Conf. of
  Mayors
Nat. Res Council
Urban Coalition
NEA
Nat. Assoc. of
  Counties
CED
Nat. Congress
  of PTA
Business Council
Urban America
Fed. of Women's
  Clubs
Nat. C. of C.

Figure 11.2   Ratings by a divisional head of the U.S. Department of Housing and
Urban Development of the perceived supportive and opposing character of the 37 top
urban-oriented associations.

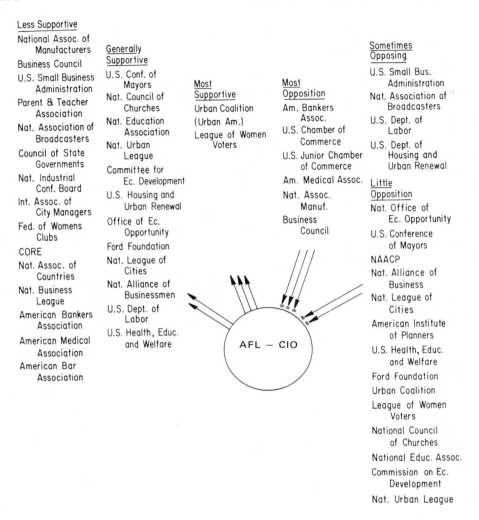

Figure 11.3   Ratings by a divisional head of the national AFL-CIO of the perceived supportive and opposing character of the 37 top urban-oriented associations.

Of course, some organizations are controversial. The Ford Foundation is a good example. Some of my fellow managers think the Ford Foundation was largely responsible for stirring up all that controversy in New York over community control of the schools, and they are angered over the Jewish-Negro antagonism that was brought about. Others, however, think the Ford Foundation is doing a great job and want us to work more closely with the Foundation.

What is important about the sociogram of support and opposition is its potential as a tool for predicting working relations and the degree of political support that organizations can depend on. It is also a tool of analysis for interpreting decision-making resolutions. To be knowledgeable about power in Washington is to have a kaleidoscopic understanding of all the combined sociograms. The ablest movers learn much by intuition and the experience that accompanies a long life along the Potomac. Social science could shorten the time necessary for the newcomer to find out who's who and what's what. Stereotypes and sociograms are a first step; knowledge of the parties at interest in the associational network is a second.

MAJOR PARTIES AT INTEREST OF THE ASSOCIATIONAL NETWORK

We have said that ideological position and interest are determiners of contact and working relations. Interest can override ideological obstacles. Government agencies have large sums of money and authority to get things done. Associations have political muscle that can be supportive or opposing. Most possess implementing staffs and a vast grass roots apparatus so necessary to community-based programs. Associations represent firms, commercial establishments, mass communications media, governments, churches, schools, and universities—indeed, every facet of business, government, and social activity. Figure 11.4 attempts to show some of the major parties at interest in the associational network. The Federal Government appears with the Departments of Health, Education and Welfare, Justice, Housing and Urban Development, and Labor and the Small Business Administration. HEW and Justice are shown as having important federal-state relations; HUD and OEO exemplify federal-city relations. Competing and supportive national agencies conflict and cooperation among other departments is common. Figure 11.4 then shows how the Congress, the executive agencies, and the Supreme Court relate themselves to urban programs. Private associations, private enterprise, governments, and universities and colleges are described as major interest parties with programs, funds, and personnel to offer.

TANDEM AND MULTIPLE RELATIONS BETWEEN ASSOCIATIONS AND
GOVERNMENT AGENCIES

In the midst of the array of interests the private association is a permanent agent and watchdog that seeks to advance or thwart various government programs. The parties at interest often find that they need one another, and from common need bonds are developed. Tandem or pair relations can be clearly discerned. Perhaps the tightest are those of the National Alliance of Businessmen and the Department of Labor. The association is private but it works so closely with the Department of Labor that both call their connection a "partnership." The Alliance encourages private companies to participate in JOBS (Job Opportunities in the Business Sector) and to sign a contract with the Department of Labor if they need financial assistance to underwrite the extraordinary costs of training disadvantaged persons for the jobs they provide. As the result of these ties each party, private and public, has a strong stake in the outcome.

Other organizations, by their special character, are drawn to particular agencies. The National Educational Association cooperates with the U. S. Office of Education and Urban America[6] with HUD, whose tandem relations are strengthened by the fact that Urban America can provide HUD with a bridge to the businessmen and professionals who are interested in public housing opportunities and contracts. Urban America can bring these business and professional people together with HUD officials who plan to promote new housing and renewal projects under private contract. Urban America through its contracts can also give political support to HUD by helping to marshal the building contractors and planning officials and other associations like the Urban Coalition, National League of Cities, and U. S. Conference of Mayors. HUD, in turn, can provide Urban American with funds for conferences, seminars, and research study. Other ties are knit by the reciprocal exchange of personnel. Former HUD personnel are found in Urban America; former Urban America personnel may go to HUD.

As association programs expand new relationships may be forged. Urban America is developing ties with the Office of Economic Opportunity in its work with street gangs. It has also developed ties with the Department of Transportation in its study of urban transportation.

Informal ties among the associations tend to expand their acquaintance in government agencies. The U. S. Conference of Mayors and the National League of Cities have many overlapping memberships. It is reasonable to believe that almost all mayors associated with the Conference of Mayors belong to the National League of Cities, for their programs and leadership are highly similar.

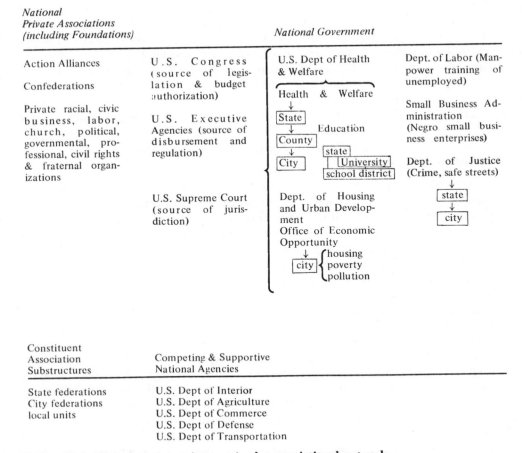

Figure 11.4 Major parties at interest in the associational network.

Likewise their mutual contacts and working relations with government agencies are similar but also jointly expanded by their independent activities.

The Council of State Governments and the U. S. Governors Conference have a closer relationship because they share a common staff. A similar expansion of working relations can be observed because of their own organizational bonds.

The Chamber of Commerce and the National Association of Manufacturers not only work closely with government agencies but they are also tied into far-ranging contacts with trade associations like the American Petroleum Institute and the National Coal Association. The Chamber of Commerce and the NAM have a multiplicity of agency contacts. Their large staffs are in touch with all federal departments and many of its divisions. Because each association staff man is a specialist, his work carries him into particular sectors of government. He can contribute knowledgeability and contactability. A total staff combines collective knowledge and collective contacts that can be measured. Certainly the staffs of the Chamber of Commerce, the NAM, and the AFL-CIO would rank high in any such measurement as a result of the scope of their interests.

National Private Enterprise	State, County and Municipal Governments	Universities and Colleges
Banks	Health	Teaching
Investment houses	Welfare	Research
Research Organizations	Education	Administration
Manufacturers	Crime	Professional Organizations
Builders	Air & Water Pollution	American Association of University Professors
Merchants		American Association for the Advancement of Science
Utilities		American Association of Universities
Transport		National Academy of Sciences
Communication		

Constituent Branch Firms	Constituent Government Substructures	Constituent Private and Public Institutions
Distributed in the various 50 states	50 state 3,072 counties 5,445 cities 134,833 schools	2,008 Higher Institutions

Figure 11.4 (Continued)

The Measurement of Acquaintance and Contact as They
Affect Relationships of Organizations

THE LEADERSHIP ACQUAINTANCE-A-SCOPE

Organizations are known as collective entities with interests, ideological positions, programs and resources. They are also known by the leaders they keep—both professional and lay. In the search for the most powerful urban-oriented and environmental quality leaders of Megalopolis many organizational officials were interviewed. Because they were asked to judge lists of leaders (and add names) representative of five major metropolitan areas, it was necessary to gain some estimate of their acquaintance with these leaders. Let us call this special knowledge by the term leadership acquaintability. The measuring instrument used to make personal estimates of the judges acquaintability is called an acquaint-a-scope, described briefly in Chapter 4. It will be recalled that the five major metropolitan areas—Washington, Baltimore, Philadelphia, New York, and Boston—are placed in the left-hand column. A row of five leader classifications—business, labor, government, religious, and civic, appears at the top to complete a matrix of 25 cells. Each judge was given a table and asked to check boxes in which he felt he could recognize some of the most important leaders in each occupational grouping who were active in urban affairs. Lists were made for those boxes in which acquaintance was marked.

The acquaint-a-scope was scored as follows: by giving one point for each check a maximum score of 25 was possible. Thirty-five judges received scores ranging from 3 to 25; the average score was 13. This means that most judges had considerable leadership acquaintability outside their own communities. These personal acquaint-a-scope measures showed a number of patterns—the localite pattern in which the respondent indicated he knew leaders in the local community; the occupational pattern in which he checked leaders in his own occupational classification in the major metropolitan areas; and the Megalopolite who knew leaders in all classifications in the major metropolitan areas. We speculated in Chapter 4 that leadership acquaintability is acquired in chronological stages according to the patterns described above; that is to say, the Megalopolite must first acquire knowledge of local leaders; this acquaintability takes place as he becomes active in urban affairs in his own community and assumes larger responsibilities over time. As this process gets underway he is also moving up the career ladder which opens up opportunities to travel and make contacts with more and more occupational leaders in other communities. He becomes a Megalopolite only if his occupation or his civic activities provide wider acquaintance across Megalopolis. This kind of leadership acquaintability takes time and effort. It is a quality of older leaders, now in their fifties and sixties. It is exceptional for a younger man, but it can happen. Government or foundation officers who travel extensively and have wide-ranging contacts can achieve it. At least, that is what our data show. The highest score of 25 was made by a Ford Foundation executive who had been a federal official with the Department of Housing and Urban Renewal in Washington for many years.

STAFF LEADERSHIP ACQUAINTABILITY AND CONTACT

Higher acquaintability, often highly valued, is regarded as an organizational resource, and a man's salary can reflect this quality. What is not so often appreciated is that an organization is a collection of officials whose joint acquaint-ability can be a collective resource. This was revealed for the first time to an executive secretary who was serving as a judge. After checking perhaps 12 of the 25 boxes he said, "That represents the leaders I know, but I believe that my staff would be able together to check all 25 boxes." He called in a staff man who did indeed add five more boxes to the acquaint-a-scope. The executive then ex-claimed, "This gives me an idea for staff training. I want my people to know a wider range of leaders." He might have added that it also gave him an idea for recruiting: to find new personnel who could fill gaps in the staff leadership ac-quaintability. For the researcher the possibility of determining a total staff leader-ship acquaintance score also presents itself. Figure 11.5 is an instrument that could be filled out by staff members who would reveal acquaintance and contact with a selected group of leaders of special importance to the work of the organi-zation. This instrument can be scored 1 to 5, starting with a score of 1 for "have heard of," 2 "for know little," 3 for "know well or socially," 4 "for approached on public problems in last three years," and 5 for "worked on committee with him in last three years. A summation of scores by all staff members would provide a picture of leadership acquaintance.

ORGANIZATIONAL ACQUAINTABILITY AND CONTACT

Just as a staff leadership acquaintability and contact score can be determined, so can an organizational acquaintability and contact score be identified and measured by using the Organizational Acquaintance and Working Relationship Scale (see Appendix B). In this instrument organizations are listed and the re-spondent marks the following: "know about their work in urban field," "have approached or have been approached for information about urban problems," "have exchanged ideas about urban programs," "have worked together on pro-gram development," "have supported one another on issues." Name the issue. In this study one major official always represented the entire organization in his marking. What the researcher needs for the highest reliability and validity is a composite of the working relations of major staff officials.

Please look at the following list of leaders that live and work on the North East seaboard. Indicate your acquaintance with each and whether you have worked on any committees with him in the past three years.

Name of leader	Do not know	Have heard of	Know little (by reading or con-tact)	Know well or socially (visit with him at home or meet in town)	Approached on public problems during last three years	Worked on committee with him during last three years

Figure 11.5   Leadership Acquaintanceship and Working Relationship Index for organi-zational staff.

ORGANIZATIONAL WORK BACKGROUND ANALYSIS OF STAFF PERSONNEL

An intensive examination of a given organization which is seeking to establish staff working relations would first involve an analysis of the organization's work background. Table 11.3, Organizational Work Background Analysis of Staff Personnel, is an instrument devised for this purpose. The personnel director can provide these data for major staff personnel. Two tests have been made: one for Resources for the Future, the other for the Fels Institute of Local and State Government. A personnel list was used, and symbols shown on the right-hand side of the figure indicated work background characteristics applicable to each staff man. A potential contactability score can be derived for any staff member in this manner.

CURRENT STAFF MEMBER AND ORGANIZATIONAL CONTACTS

An actual contactogram can be constructed for each staff man by asking him to indicate his current contacts (in the last year) in various sectors: private associations, business firms, universities, government, and special committees. Figure 11.6, a staff member's contactogram, shows the contacts and working relations of an official of Resources for the Future. Note that his contacts are mainly in government, university, and private association sectors. Figure 11.7 an organization contactogram, outlines the combined working relations of an organization. This is heuristic figure based on rough estimates of major staff personnel at Resources for the Future. Both figures suggest the kind of interactional data needed for more intensive research work. Figure 11.8 Check List of Common Activities of Organizational Personnel, provides a more detailed analysis of working relations. These activities could be derived with time estimates to increase precision.

TABLE 11.3   ORGANIZATIONAL WORK BACKGROUND ANALYSIS OF STAFF PERSONNEL

1.	Has worked for federal, state, or local government in an authorized position	(G)
2.	Works for federal, state, or local government now and is on loan or leave of absence	(G_n)
3.	Has worked for a university in an authorized position	(U)
4.	Works for a university now and is on assignment or leave of absence	(U_n)
5.	Has worked for a private research or action agency	(R)
6.	Works for private research or action agency now and is on loan or leave	(R_n)
7.	Has worked for private enterprise in an authorized position	(P)
8.	Works for private enterprise now and is on loan or leave	(P_n)
9.	Has worked for military in an authorized position	(M)
10.	Works for military now and is on loan or leave	(M_n)

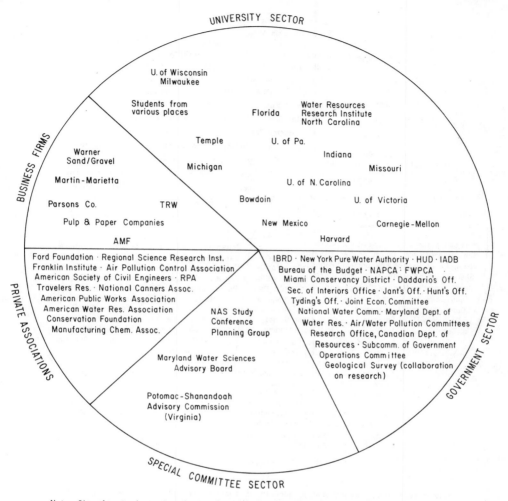

UNIVERSITY SECTOR

U. of Wisconsin
Milwaukee

Students from
various places

Florida

Water Resources
Research Institute
North Carolina

Temple

U. of Pa.

Indiana

BUSINESS FIRMS

Warner
Sand/Gravel

Michigan

Missouri

Martin-Marietta

U. of N. Carolina

Parsons Co.

TRW

Bowdoin

U. of Victoria

Pulp & Paper Companies

New Mexico

Carnegie-Mellon

AMF

Harvard

PRIVATE ASSOCIATIONS

Ford Foundation · Regional Science Research Inst.
Franklin Institute · Air Pollution Control Association
American Society of Civil Engineers · RPA
Travelers Res. · National Canners Assoc.
American Public Works Association
American Water Res. Association
Conservation Foundation
Manufacturing Chem. Assoc.

NAS Study
Conference
Planning Group

Maryland Water Sciences
Advisory Board

Potomac-Shanandoah
Advisory Commission
(Virginia)

IBRD · New York Pure Water Authority · HUD · IADB
Bureau of the Budget · NAPCA · FWPCA
Miami Conservancy District · Daddario's Off.
Sec. of Interiors Office · Jant's Off. · Hunt's Off.
Tyding's Off. · Joint Econ. Committee
National Water Comm. · Maryland Dept. of
Water Res. · Air/Water Pollution Committees
Research Office, Canadian Dept. of
Resources · Subcomm. of Government
Operations Committee
Geological Survey (collaboration
on research)

GOVERNMENT SECTOR

SPECIAL COMMITTEE SECTOR

Note: Size of sector is rough estimate of magnitude of contact. University, 40 per cent
because of research grants; government, 20 per cent; private associations, 20 per cent;
business firms, 8 per cent; special committees, 12 per cent.

Figure 11.6 Staff member contactogram.

Invoicing Organizational Orientations and Activities
Undertaken for Political Action

Acquaintanceship and contact is an influence resource. The association staff
member may be constantly seeking to cultivate an increased area of contact
through working ties, lunches, cocktail parties, and dinners. This is considered
part of his work.

The association as a collective body may undertake a number of activities to
influence decisions in favor of their objectives. Blair T. Bower of Resources for
the Future has assembled a list of activities undertaken by groups attempting to

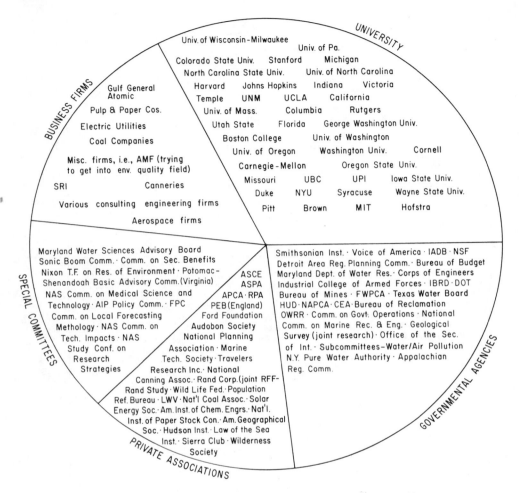

Note: Size of wedge proportional to quantity of contact for category. Universities,
      30 per cent (because of grants); government, 25 per cent; special committees,
      15 per cent; private business firms, 15 per cent; private associations, 15 per cent.

Figure 11.7   Organization contactogram.

influence environmental quality decisions. They may be generalized to include
associations of all kinds.

LIST OF ACTIVITIES UNDERTAKEN BY ATTEMPTING TO
INFLUENCE POLICY DECISIONS

Continual lobbying on Capitol Hill, in state legislatures, and at the local level.
   Testifying at public hearings; for example, on air quality standards.
   Testifying before Congressional committees, legislative committees at state
level, and committees at local government level.

Kindly check if members engage in these activities:

————————— 1. Requests for information by telephone, letter, or by office appointment

————————— 2. Research collaboration or writing

————————— 3. Seminar contact and participation

————————— 4. Professional meetings

————————— 5. Trade association meetings

————————— 6. Civic meetings

————————— 7. Committee work across government, university, and private associations

————————— 8. Noon lunches with officials in the various sectors (government, universities, and private associations)

————————— 9. Friendship contacts made during social occasions such as dinners, bridge clubs, or outdoor activities.

—————— 10. Consulting to private and governmental organizations

—————— 11. Requests for information, reactions to proposals.

—————— 12. Discussions with visitors of all types

—————— 13. Review of manuscripts

—————— 14. Monitoring of research underway

Figure 11.8 Checklist of common contact activities of organizational personnel.

"Generating" outpouring of letters from members to the Congress and state legislatures.

Publishing brochures about (company) efforts in environmental quality improvement (air and water pollution control, etc.)

Financing research work on environmental quality problems, by individual company and industrial association activities; for example, the American Petroleum Institute, the National Coal Association, and the National Council for Air and Stream Improvement.

Assigning one or more staff people to attend various meetings wherever they are held; for example, water meetings in the Delaware Basin, interagency meetings, and INCODEL and DRBC conferences.

Taking memberships in "citizen" groups; for example, Water Resources Association of the DRB.

TABLE 11.4 LOBBY RECORD FOR THE FIRST AND SECOND QUARTERS OF 1968 FOR THE 37 TOP URBAN-ORIENTED ASSOCIATIONS*

Name of association	Period registered; registered lobbyists	Expenditures
Urban America		
National Association for the Advancement of Colored People →	2 registered lobbyists	No expenditures given
National Association of Manufacturers →	3 registered lobbyists	No expenditures given
Business Council		
Committee for Economic Development		
National Industrial Conference Board		
National Congress of Parents and Teachers →	Registered in second quarter	$234.83
National Urban League		
National Educational Association		
U.S. Department of Health, Education and Welfare		
U.S. Small Business Administration		
National Council of Churches		
U.S. Conference of Mayors		
National Alliance of Businessmen		
National League of Cities		
International Association of City Managers		
Ford Foundation		
AFL-CIO	11 registered lobbyists; registered first and second quarter	$59,744.78
Other labor organizations	Extensive	
National Research Council and National Academy of Science		

American Bankers Association	6 registered lobbyists	$36,071.26
American Medical Association	9 registered lobbyists; registered both quarters, 1968	$16,733.03
U.S. Department of Housing and Urban Development		
U.S. Office of Economic Opportunity		
Chamber of Commerce of the United States	5 registered lobbyists; registered second quarter, 1968	Total reported expenditure, $15,685.84
Council of State Governments		
American Bar Association	1 registered lobbyist	$30
National Association of Broadcasters	1 registered lobbyist	
Urban Coalition		
League of Women Voters		
American Institute of Planners		
National Federation of Business and Professional Women's Clubs →	Listed in first quarter	Receipts $27,205.50 Total reported expenditure $1,970.08
National Business League		
National Commission on Urban Problems		
U.S. Department of Labor		
U.S.Jr. Chamber of Commerce		
National Association of Counties		
CORE		
Environmental American Petroleum Institute	5 registered lobbyists; registered second quarter	$14,379.85
National Coalition Association	2 registered lobbyists	$4,499.95

* From Congressional Record, Vol. 114, No. 141, August 29, 1968, pp. H8197-H8227.

Participating in advisory committees and/or task forces to government agencies; for example industry and water users committees in connection with the Delaware estuary study and the Delaware Basin Commission. Placing members on "prestigious" committees or task forces, for example, the President's Water Pollution Advisory Board, the National Water Commission, and the President's Task Force on National Beauty.

Preparing detailed statements on quality issues such as level of standards, time focus, continuous or noncontinuous, on the assimilative capacity of the environment, on the effects of quality changes on receptors, and on the costs of quality control.

Preparing newspaper and journal advertisements to reduce pollution or improve quality or to oppose particular decisions; for example to study the Grand Canyon.

Publishing a professional journal in which technical aspects of environmental qualities are discussed.

Assigning a top-level corporate executive to be responsible (corporationwide) for air and water pollution activities or environmental quality problems (a significant trend in this direction in the last 5 to 10 years, as at Allied Chemical and Dow Chemical).

Proposing counterplans to those of government agencies responsible for environmental quality, from complete opposition to small modification.

Hiring outside consultants to prepare and/or give testimony on environmental quality issues, such as level of standards and effects of changing quality.

These activities are an indication of the many ways to win friends and influence others. The list is far from exhaustive. The informal ties, the friendships and contacts are not listed. The indebtedness developed by free dinners, gifts, "consultant fees," speaking engagements, and fees are not shown.

LOBBYING

Everything that is legal can be utilized by a nonprofit organization. If, however, an association wishes to approach legislators to press their objectives on pending legislation, it must recognize that it must re-establish itself as a profit-making organization or establish an auxiliary association to collect its lobby funds. Moreover, under the Federal Lobby Act it must register its lobbyists for the period in which they will be active and report their expenditures. The lobby record for the first two quarters of 1968 is given in Table 11.4 for the top 37 urban-oriented associations.

PROPOSED BASIC FILE OF ORGANIZATIONAL ORIENTATIONS

The lobby record shows that some organizations make vigorous efforts to influence legislation. What they do depends on their functions and the demands of their clients. Figure 11.9 is an Organizational Program and Policy Orientation Check List. It sets out eight dimensions that affect an organization's policies programs, and working relations. These dimensions include its program emphasis, program values and objectives, action policies, political coloration, power ranking, top leadership reservoir, size of total membership, the direction of power as applied to secure objectives, and its lobbying record. This check list would constitute the basic file for the study of associations.

1. Program emphasis

    ———— Advisory   ———— Research and   ———— Action-oriented
                   information

2. Program values and objectives

    ———— Stable, well   ———— Partial acceptance;   ———— Precarious; program
           accepted   occasional attacks   is constantly on
                             on budget   defensive for survival

3. Action policy

    ———— Unilateral   ———— Limited   ———— Broad based
                       coalitional   coalition

4. Political coloration

    ———— Takes no stands   ———— Takes stands but   ———— Endorses and
           and is nonpartisan   claims nonpartisan   identifies with a
                           position   political party

5. Power ranking

    ———— High (top 20)   ———— Intermediate   ———— Low (unranked)
                       (top 20 to 40)

6. Top leadership reservoir (as shown by board membership, officers, and members)

    ———— Large (20 or more   ———— Medium (10 to 20 top or   ———— Small (under 10 top
           top or key leaders)   key leaders)   or key leaders)

7. Size of total membership, all affiliates

    ———— Above 500,000   ———— 50,000-to-500,000   ———— Under 50,000

8. Direction of power as applied to secure objectives

    ———— Predominant emphasis is upward toward the top policy makers in private and public
           organizations

    ———— Predominate emphasis is downward toward its own state and local affilities

    ———— Emphasis is twofold: vigorously upward toward policy makers and downward toward
           local and state bodies

9. Record of lobby registration and positions taken on pending legislation

Figure 11.9   Organizational program and policy orientation checklist.

The Formation of Confederations and Mergers for Augmenting Organizational Order and Advancement of Common Interests

THE NEW RESEARCH CHALLENGE: THE INTERACTION OF CONFEDERATIONS

The increase in urban legislation and the growth of funded urban programs in public and private organizations presents a volume of activity that staggers the imagination and swamps the capacity of an individual memory. On June 1, 1970, the Office of Economic Opportunity published the second edition of the Catalog of Federal Assistance Programs. This 701-page book contains descriptions of the 459 domestic assistance programs of the Federal Government. A similar compilation of programs sponsored and funded by private associations and foundations does not exist. Unquestionably it would be much greater in length. It is probably reasonable to say that no one person could give off the top of his head a thorough and accurate account of the programs of the top 37 urban-oriented associations in the area of urban affairs. If he could do so, he would have to make a constant effort to keep currently informed because of the numerous changes taking place. This situation is one definition of complexity. Professionals, social workers, association personnel, scholars, and interested lay members all suffer from an ignorance of the total scene. Each person masters only a part of it.

The Federal Government responds to such problems by establishing national and regional councils; for example, the National Urban Affairs Council, the President's Citizens Advisory Committee on Environmental Quality, and regional councils of federal agencies that deal with state and local programs for urban problems.

The associations have also been responding by establishing confederations, which usually begin as an impulse to get similar organizations together for the purpose of exchanging information. The idea of a clearing house easily catches hold in the complex multitudinous and ever-changing pattern of contemporary activities. Later, the problem of making their influence felt as a body becomes urgent and the need for a lobbying arm is claimed. In the evolution of a confederation many functions may be undertaken such as

> exchanging program and policy information,
> fixing goals,
> revising priorities,
> securing appropriate legislation,
> planning campaigns for increased governmental appropriations,
> securing changes in governmental regulations,
> planning educational campaigns and recommendations for local action, and
> assessing dangers to its interests from political and governmental sources and public opinion and discussing plans for counteraction.

SOME MAJOR CONFEDERATIONS AFFECTING URBAN AFFAIRS

Among the major confederations that affect urban affairs are the public interest groups located in Washington, Chicago, and New York: the AFL-CIO Confederation of craft and industrial unions, the UAW and Teamsters Alliance for Labor Action, the National Council of Churches, the U. S. Catholic Conference, and the Urban Action Exchange. Many others could be listed. Those mentioned tend to represent the major segments of the urban community regarded by the Urban Coalition as significant in urban influence. Reading from left to right are the sectors and the representative confederations:

Government	Business	Labor	Religion	Civil rights
Public interest groups	Urban Action Exchange	AFL-CIO UAW-Teamsters Alliance for Labor Action	National Council of Churches U.S. Catholic Conference American Jewish Conference National Conference of Christians and Jews	Urban League NAACP CORE Southern Christian Leadership Conference

Strictly speaking, no confederation exists for civil rights groups, but the Urban League and the NAACP are broadly based coalitions of interest. The appearance of confederations of this magnitude now confronts the researcher with a new problem in associational interaction. He must accept a larger unit for study and the accompanying social processes as confederations interact. A brief outline of these confederations follows.

The Public Interest Groups. Forty-one associations make up the public interest groups located in Washington, Chicago, and New York. Membership is made up of local and/or state public officials. Their roster, as of November 1968, is given in Table 11.5. Representatives of these groups who humorously call themselves PIGS meet monthly to exchange information and make various plans for implementation. They have their own lobbying organization called the Urban Action Council and a registered lobbyist. The potential influence of this confederation must be considered substantial. It can be noted that it contains seven of the associations on the list of 37 top urban-oriented organizations: the American Institute of Planners, the Council of State Governments, the International City Managers Association, the National Association of Counties, the National Governor's Conference, the National League of Cities, and the U. S. Conference of Mayors.

Urban Action Exchange. This confederation proposed by the U.S. Chamber of Commerce, was in the formative stage in late 1968. It was suggested that an urban action exchange could be a voluntary effort by national business, trade, and professional organizations and associations. Two principal functions could be served:

First, as a means of exchanging information and know-how among national organizations and, second, as a means of helping national organizations work together through their state and local affiliates and members to promote broad cooperative efforts to meet community problems. A classified list of members invited to the Urban Action Exchange Luncheon is shown below.

Note that there are 54 organizations, of which 40 are business associations; the remainder are in government and the professions. From our list of the top 37 urban-oriented organizations we find the American Bankers Association, the National Association of Broadcasters, the American Bar Association, the American Medical Association, the U. S. Chamber of Commerce, the U. S. Conference of Mayors, the National League of Cities, the National Association of Counties, the International City Managers Association, and the National Governors Conference.

The vigor of this confederation is not known. However, luncheons held in October 1968 attracted representatives from many other associations not originally listed, including the NAACP, CORE, the National Urban League, the National Federation of Business and Professional Women's Clubs, the League of Women Voters, the National Associations of Manufacturers, the National Industrial Conference Board, the National Business League, the AFL-CIO, National Junior Chamber of Commerce, and the National Clean Up, Paint Up, Fix Up Bureau.

What is significant is that a confederation gap exists and that the Chamber is taking the lead in bringing business, professional, government, and civil rights

Airport Operators Council International
Mr. J. Donald Reilly, Acting Executive Vice-President
1700 K Street, N.W.
Washington, D.C. 20006   296-3270

American Association of Port Authorities
Mr. Paul Amudsen, Executive Director
501 Southern Building
Washington, D.C.   RE 7-0043

American Association of School Administrators
Dr. Forest E. Conner, Executive Secretary
1201 — 16th St. N.W.
Washington, D.C. 20036   223-9400

American Association of State Highway Officials
Mr. A. E. Johnson, Executive Secretary
917 National Press Building
Washington, D.C.   NA 8-2438

American Institute of Planners
Mr. Robert L. Williams, Executive Director
917 — 15th St. N.W.
Washington, D.C.   783-0666

American Public Power Association
Mr. Alex Radin, General Manager
2600 Virginia Avenue
Washington, D.C. 20037   333-9200

American Public Welfare Association
Mr. Guy R. Justis, Director
1313 East 60th Street
Chicago, Illinois 60637   FA 4-3400

Harold Hagen, Washington Representative
815 — 17th Street, N.W.
Washington, D.C. 20006   St 3-2541

American Public Works Association
Mr. Robert D. Bugher, Executive Director
1313 East 60th Street
Chicago, Illinois 60637   FA 4-3400

Mr. Leo Weaver, Director
Washington Office
1755 Massachusetts Ave.
Washington, D.C. 20037   265-1718

American Society of Planning Officials
Mr. Israel Stollman, Executive Director
1313 East 60th Street
Chicago, Illinois 60637   FA 4-3400

American Society of Public Administration
Mr. Don Bowen, Executive Director
1225 Connecticut Avenue, N.W.
Suite 300
Washington, D.C. 20037   659-9160

American Transit Association
Mr. Robert Sloan, General Secretary
815 Connecticut Ave., N.W.
Washington, D.C. 20006   223-5770

American Water Works Association Inc.
Mr. Eric Johnson, Executive Secretary
2 Park Avenue
New York, New York 10017   MU 4-6696

Building Officials Conference of America
Mr. Richard L. Sanderson, Executive Director
1313 East 60th St.
Chicago, Illinois 60637   FA 4-3400

Council of State Governments
Mr. Brevard Crihfield, Executive Director
1313 East 60th St.
Chicago, Illinois 60637   FA 4-3400

Institute of Traffic engineers
Mr. Burton W. Marsh, Executive Secretary
2029 K St., N.W., Sixth Floor
Washington, D.C. 20006   223-3650

International Association of Assessing Officers
Mr. Paul V. Corusy, Executive Director
1313 East 60th Street
Chicago, Illinois 60637   FA 4-3400

International Association of Auditorium Managers, Inc.
Mr. Charles R. Byrnes, Executive Director
20200 Ashland Avenue
Chicago Heights, Illinois   754-6292

International Association of Chiefs of Police, Inc.
Mr. Quinn Tamm, Executive Director
1319 – 18th St. N.W.
Washington, D.C. 20036   265-7227

International Association of Fire Chiefs
Mr. Donald M. O'Brien, Executive Director
232 Madison Avenue
New York, New York 10016   MU 3-7287

International Bridge, Tunnel and Turnpike Association, Inc.
Mr. W. A. Rusch, Executive Director
1225 Connecticut Avenue, N.W.
Washington, D.C. 20036   659-4620

International City Managers' Association
Mr. Mark E. Keane, Executive Director
1140 Connecticut Avenue, N.W.
Washington, D.C. 20036   293-2200

International Institute of Municipal Clerks
Mr. Frank R. Dotseth, Executive Director
Museum of Science and Industry
Lake Front and 57th Street
Chicago, Illinois 493-1215

Joint Council on Urban Development
Mr. Darrel Stearns, Executive Director
1707 H Street, N.W.
Washington, D.C. 20006   298-5925

Municipal Finance Officers Association
Joseph F. Clark, Executive Director
1313 East 60th Street
Chicago, Illinois 60637   FA 4-3400

TABLE 11.5 PUBLIC INTEREST GROUPS LOCATED IN WASHINGTON, CHICAGO, AND NEW YORK WITH MEMBERSHIP MADE UP OF LOCAL AND/OR STATE PUBLIC OFFICIALS — NOVEMBER 1968* (*Continued*)

National Association for Community Development
D. Richard Wenner, Executive Director
1832 Jefferson Place
Washington, D.C. 20037   296-2875

National Association of Counties
Bernard Hillenbrand, Executive Director
1001 Connecticut Avenue, N.W.
Washington, D.C. 20006   628-4701

National Association of Housing and Redevelopment Office
John D. Lange, Executive Director
2600 Virginia Avenue
Washington, D.C. 20037   333-2020

National Association of Tax Administrators
Charles F. Conlon, Executive Director
1313 East 60th Street
Chicago, Illinois 60637   FA 4-3400

National Governors' Conference
Brevard Crihfield, Secretary and Treasurer
1313 East 60th Street
Chicago, Illinois 60637   FA 4-3400

Charles Byrley, Director
Washington Office
1735 DeSales Street, N.W.
Washington, D.C. 20036   393-2662

National Institute of Municipal Law Officers
Charles Rhyne, General Counsel
839 — 17th Street, N.W.
Washington, D.C. 20006   347-7996

National League of Cities
Patrick Healy, Executive Director
1612 K Street, N.W.
Washington, D.C. 20007

National Municipal League
Alfred Willoughby, Executive Director
47 East 68th Street
New York, New York 10021   535-5700

National Recreation and Park Association
Dr. Sol Prezioso, Executive Vice-President
1700 Pennsylvania Avenue, N.W.
Washington, D.C. 20006   223-3330

National School Boards Association
Harold V. Webb, Executive Director
1233 Central Street
Evanston, Illinois   869-7730

Mr. August W. Steinhilber
Director for Federal and Congressional Relations
1616 H Street, N.W., Suite 505
Washington, D.C. 20006   737-2292

National Institute of Government Purchasing, Inc.
Albert H. Hall, Executive Vice-President
1001 Connecticut Avenue, N.W.
Washington, D.C. 20006   DI 7-9357

Public Administration Service
H. G. Pope, Executive Director
1313 East 60th Street
Chicago, Illinois 60637   FA 4-3400
Ralph Spear, Washington Representative
1755 Massachusetts Avenue, N.W.
Washington, D.C. 20036   265-5355

Public Personnel Association
Kenneth O. Warner, Director
W

National Service to Regional Councils
Richard Hartman, Executive Director
1700 K Street, N.W., 13th Floor
Washington, D.C. 20006   296-8069

1313 East 60th Street
Chicago, Illinois 60637   FA 4-3400

U.S. Conference of Mayors
John Gunther, Executive Director
1707 H Street, N.W.
Washington, D.C. 20006   298-7535

Water Pollution Control Federation
Dr. Ralph Fuhrman, Executive Director
3900 Wisconsin Avenue, N.W.
Washington, D.C. 20016   362-4100

* Published by the National League of Cities

associations together. This is not only a loose confederation but a coalition, analogous to the efforts of the Urban Coalition.

A Classified List of National Associations Invited to the UAE Luncheon

RETAIL

> American Retail Federation
> Menswear Retail Association of America
> National Association of Chain Drugstores
> National Association of Food Chains
> National Automobile Dealers Association
> National Retail Merchants Association
> Variety Stores Association

UTILITY

> American Gas Association
> Edison Electric Institute

FINANCE

> American Bankers Association
> American Industrial Bankers
> Mortgage Bankers Insurance
> National Consumers Finance Association
> United States Savings and Loan League

INSURANCE

> American Insurance Association
> American Mutual Insurance Alliance
> Institute of Life Insurance
> Life Insurance Association of America
> National Association of Independent Insurance Agents
> National Association of Life Underwriters

CONSTRUCTION

> Associated General Contractors of America
> National Association of Homebuilders of the United States

TRANSPORTATION

> American Transit Association
> Transportation Association of America

COMMUNICATION

> American Advertising Federation
> National Association of Broadcasters

SERVICES

American Hotel and Motel Association
American Petroleum Institute
National Restaurant Association

PROFESSIONAL ASSOCIATIONS

American Bar Association
American Institute of Architects
American Medical Association

MANUFACTURING

American Apparel Manufacturers
American Iron and Steel Institute
Grocery Manufacturers Association of America
Institute of Scrap Iron and Steel
National Tire Dealers and Retreaders Association
National Tool, Dye, and Precision Machining Association

REAL ESTATE

National Association of Building Owners and Managers
National Association of Real Estate Boards
Urban Land Institute

MISCELLANEOUS

American Society for Training and Development
National Employment Association
National Recreation and Park Association
Chamber of Commerce of the United States

LOCAL AND STATE GOVERNMENTS

Citizens Conference on State Legislatures
Advisory Commission on Intergovernmental Relations
United States Conference of Mayors
National League of Cities
National Association of Counties
International City Managers' Association
National Municipal League
National Governor's Conference
National School Boards Association

If the Urban Action Exchange does not prove successful, the business community will continue to look for general guidance from the Chamber of Commerce or from the National Association of Manufacturers. It is interesting to speculate about the possibility of a merger of these two organizations. The Chamber is often thought of as representing "Main Street" and the NAM as the "factory district," but in ideology and objectives they are seldom far apart.

The Labor Confederations.   Labor organizations have an early history of federations led by the founding of the National Labor Union in 1866 and superseded by the Knights of Labor in 1866—both largely conglomerates of craft unions. In 1886 the American Federation of Labor (AFL) was organized when the Knights amalgamated with the new Federation of Organized Trades and Labor Unions. The Congress of Industrial Unions (CIO) was founded in 1934 by John L. Lewis of the United Mine Workers who brought together such large industrial unions as the United Auto Workers, the United Rubber Workers, and the Amalgamated Association of Iron, Steel and Tin Workers. In 1957 the AFL-CIO merged all the largest unions in the country. The expulsion of the Teamsters and the resignation of the United Auto Workers from the AFL-CIO has now set the stage for two major labor confederations. The AFL-CIO with its 13,600,000 members is still the largest and most prestigious body. Twenty-seven major unions are represented on its executive council:

United Steel Workers of America

Communications Workers of America

National Maritime Union of America

International Printing Pressmen and Assistants' Union of North America

International Ladies' Garment Workers' Union

International Union of United Brewery, Flour, Cereal, Soft Drink and Distillery Workers of America

Retail, Wholesale and Department Store Union

Industrial Union of Marine and Shipbuilding Workers of America

Seafarers' International Union of North America

Brotherhood of Railway, Airline, and Steamship Clerks, Freight Handlers, Express and Station Employees

United Packinghouse, Food and Allied Workers

United Brotherhood of Carpenters and Joiners of America

International Union of Electrical, Radio and Machine Workers

International Brotherhood of Electrical Workers

American Federation of Musicians

International Association of Bridge and Structural Iron Workers

Glass Bottle Blowers Association of the U.S. and Canada

United Papermakers and Paperworkers

Textile Workers Union of America

Amalgamated Clothing Workers of America

Brotherhood of Sleeping Car Porters

United Association of Journeymen and Apprentices of the Plumbing and Pipe Fitting Industry of the U.S. and Canada

International Association of Machinists and Aerospace Workers

Retail Clerks International Association

Building Service Employees' International Union

International Alliance of Theatrical Stage Employees and Moving Picture Machine Operators of the U.S. and Canada

International Union of Operating Engineers

Altogether the AFL-CIO federates 130 national unions and numerous state organizations and city central bodies as well as the directly affiliated local unions. As described earlier, the AFL-CIO has a long history of fighting for legislation to alleviate unemployment, poverty, and sickness and to promote education, adequate housing, and welfare efforts in general.

The Alliance for Labor Action was founded in May 1969 by the United Auto Workers and the Teamsters, the world's two largest unions with a combined membership of 3.5 million. ALA urges a massive federal commitment to help rebuild and rehabilitate urban areas, relieve traffic congestion, eliminate air and water pollution, improve Social Security benefits, develop a national welfare system, and establish uniform standards for unemployment insurance and workmen's compensation.

It has pledged full support of a comprehensive program of an assured minimum income for all workers, including a $2 minimum wage, a guaranteed income allowance, federal pension reinsurance, and the guarantee of a job at decent pay for every person able and willing to work, with the government acting as the employer of last resort.

Other goals include strict enforcement of civil rights laws, equal opportunity in all areas of life, increased aid to schools, legislation to protect consumers, and a total war against poverty.

The conference emphasized the necessity for a thorough readjustment of national priorities if these goals are to be achieved.[7]

The late Walter Reuther of the United Auto Workers must be considered the promoter of this alliance. It was he who led the United Auto Workers out of the AFL-CIO, charging the federation with sluggishness in the pursuit of labor ideals and social action for all working people. The new alliance has now pledged to "rededicate the labor movement to its original purpose: ideals which will revitalize our talents and resources for the total communitty good."[8]

Among other things the alliance hopes to make its unions models of racial equality. These efforts can spur the craft unions of the AFL-CIO, especially in the building trades, to faster action in removing racial discrimination.

As a political force each federation is a giant and will have great influence in the choice of leaders and legislative action undertaken in the campaign to solve urban problems. Each will lobby extensively and continue to make large donations to political campaigns.

Religious Confederations. The split of religion into the three major faiths, Protestant, Catholic and Jewish, has the effect of dividing religious federations along the same lines. Thus Protestants have the National Council of Churches, Catholics, the American Catholic Conference, and Jews, the American Jewish Conference. Many other confederations exist. One that has attempted to provide a unification of the three mayor faiths is the National Conference of Christian and Jews. It is an effective organization, but it does not speak as an integrated confederation of all religions. Yet the importance of federation has been increased by the antisemitism exhibited in the New York City schools and in other isolated sections of the United States. An increase in black antisemitism could have serious repercussions in the efforts to solve inner-city problems.

Civil Rights. Three major organizations exist in this area and many factional organizations represent varying degrees of militancy and types of objective. A confederation of existing organizations is almost unthinkable. Consolidation of interests has been achieved largely by the NAACP, the Urban League, and CORE, all of which have been described in earlier chapters. It would be useful to identify organizations that reflect the orientation of middle-class blacks and those of the more militant factions. At the present time it appears that the NAACP, the Urban League, parts of CORE, and the Southern Christian Leadership Conference could find a common ground and a base for confederation. The March on Washington on August 28, 1963, represented a confederated effort, but it did not spawn a confederation.

The National Urban Coalition. The National Urban Coalition is an alliance of leaders, not associations. Its examination is useful because the influential leaders that compose the national coalition and the various urban coalitions are members and officers of a large number of organizations. When they come together, they represent the ideas of these organizations and transmit to them ideas developed in the coalitions. Problems of communication and support in an organization of highly diversified membership are all developed in the urban coalitions. Many are being met for the first time and the behavior exhibited by participants must be considered a frontier in leadership research.

Confederation in Environmental Organizations. The confederation impulse is also found in the environmental quality area. The only mention to be made here is of the Water Pollution Control Federation. Fifty-six worldwide member associations compose it. Such countries as Israel, India, Mexico, South Africa, the United Kingdom, Sweden, Australia, Canada, and the Netherlands are represented.

The Natural Resources Council of America is an "organization of organizations." The major function of the Council is to bring together the staffs of various conservationist organizations. In 1969 it had a membership of 38, of which the League of Women Voters is one.

The National Watershed Congress was conceived and fostered by more than 20 of the nation's leading industrial, agricultural, and conservationist organizations. Members among the urban-oriented associations from our list of the top 37 are the U. S. Chamber of Commerce, the National Association of Countries, the National Association of Manufacturers, and Urban America.

The Clean Waters Association is also a vigorous new confederation of conservationist organizations.

The Future of Associations: Implications for the Urban Problems and Research Study

Executives of 30 leading trade and professional associations met in Washington in December 1964 for the specific purpose of analyzing, discussing, and predicting the future of associations. They agreed that America's trade, professional, and technical associations will undergo great structural and functional change in the near future. The most compelling force for change is that imposed by the Federal Government. The individual unit cannot finance itself satisfactorily before government agencies or legislation bodies. Collective representation by the associations is increasingly necessary to finance the required apparatus. Indeed, for the associations to be effective mergers will be mandatory.

Tomorrow's association will be a large umbrella organization that will represent all those within its industry or profession. Overlapping organizations serving the same interests will disappear, absorbed by the umbrella associations.[9] Professionally trained executives will have far greater responsibility than they are given today and thus will speed the merger process. Committees will tend to become bodies of technicians and specialists assisted by highly qualified staff people.[10] In the next decade we will have the corporate association, which will be vastly more effective in its total than its various uncoordinated components are today. It will be efficiently managed and well financed. The association of 1975 will directly reflect the sophistication of the industry or profession it serves.[11]

These predictions are made with the full appreciation that the mergers "will develop great controversy. Associations and association executives must find ways of concentrating on the human equations in the decade of change immediately ahead."[12] Loyalties, desire for participation, and special interests could effectively brake these mergers as fully integrated units. Confederation is a more likely form. Joint meetings and joint committees could be utilized. Councils representing groups of organizations may become more common, especially for joint lobbying. The development of public interest groups, which utilize monthly meetings for clearing house purposes and the Urban Action Council for lobbying, is a case in point. The AFL-CIO represents a long and successful evolution (in spite of its difficulties). Its guiding principle is the autonomy of its constituent unions and their locals in the company of cooperative and coordinating organizations formed by these units at central, state, and national levels. If trends are truly pressing for consolidation of associations, the confederation is a model that will allow joint cooperation with a minimum of political friction.

The movement toward consolidation is taking place, however. A recent study indicates that members' overall attitudes toward associations have become quite favorable. Substantial majorities of business and professional men characterize their membership in an association as "very valuable."[13]

Nearly three-fourths of all members say they would be willing to serve at the rate of one hour a week for a three-year term if asked to do so by their elected officers. When asked if they thought that associations should increase or decrease their lobbying and legislative activities, 41 percent responded do more, 3 percent, do less, 38 percent, no change, 18 percent, other or no opinion; 51 percent of the members of professional associations said do more. These findings must be interpreted to show that a substantial number of members want their associations to increase their lobbying and legislative activity. This finding takes on special significance as a subsequent question is examined. Should the associations be concerned only with legislation that affects their memberships or should they also be concerned with legislation that affects people in general? Fifty-four percent of all members said the association should be concerned with legislation that affects people in general and 38 percent said legislation that affects only members. Sixty-eight percent of the members of professional associations urged concern with legislation that affects people in general and only 28 percent said legislation that affects only its membership.

This broad mandate indicates a supportive attitude for efforts to increase the general welfare of all people. Those fighting for effective legislation and funds in the remediation of urban problems can count on a wide base of support. The 47 associations represented in the study are business and professional groups with specific economic interests, and their members might be expected to withhold their support of possibly conflicting action. They have not done so.

Toward a Sociology of Associations

A sizable volume of research work and theoretical formulation is available on voluntary organizations and their role in the community and society. What has been lacking is any knowledge of associational interaction. This chapter has suggested various ways in which this void might be filled. The field of associational interaction refers to the study of the structure and functioning of voluntary associations as they interact among themselves, with government agencies, and with businesses, foundations, universities, and other private agencies. It includes the processes of competition, cooperation, and conflict as decision making takes place in and between associations, their affiliates, governmental agencies, and other private bodies. The national level provides an optimum opportunity to observe these processes. Key elements in the analysis include power ranking of organizations, links or working relations between organizations, and coalition formation. The trend toward confederation is both an example of linking and coalition as confederations utilize interchange of information and lobbying for political action.

An enormous amount of research work is indicated at the national level where almost no study has been undertaken. The description of the most influential urban-oriented organizations demonstrates a complex of government agencies and associations that have close working relationships in the efforts made to alleviate urban problems. At the center are the big four of government:

> Department of Housing and Urban Development
> Office of Economic Opportunity
> Department of Health, Education and Welfare
> Department of Labor

These divisions of government represent reservoirs of money, technical and trained staffs, and authority to act.

Influential government voluntary associations with the closest ties to these giants include the U. S. Conference of Mayors, the National League of Cities, the International Association of City Managers, the National Association of Counties, and the Council of State Governments. Members of these organizations have direct participation in the planning and implementation of municipal, county, state, and national programs.

The civil rights organizations such as the NAACP, the National Urban League, and CORE have a new importance because of the heavy involvement of blacks in the programs of the inner city—employment, housing, education, welfare, and crime.

Business and labor also have large stakes in government and respond through their associations. The leaders in the business community are the Chamber of Commerce, the NAM, and the National Alliance of Businessmen, Labor means the AFL-CIO, although the Alliance for Labor Action will be watched.

Broad interests are represented by such organizations as the League of Women Voters, the Ford Foundation, the Urban Coalition, and Urban America. These associations have the special function of drawing diverse groups together and finding common ground.

All are being faced with common decisions on four crucial issues.[14] The first deals with federal assistance to alleviate urban problems. The issue is whether broad bloc grants should be made to states or whether the grants should be categorical made to cities, private enterprise, universities, and the like. The U. S. Governors' Conference and the Council of State Governments want bloc grants; the U. S. Conference of Mayors and the National League of Cities are asking for categorical grants. The contest is severe because Republican administrators are pledged to a "new federalism." Most voluntary organizations probably lean toward categorical grants. None can escape the issue.

The second issue has to do with questions of association direction. New pressures that demand coalition participation in policy making are rising, which brings up the question of board membership and committee composition. Problems of integration are being introduced as minority groups clamor for representations. The association may be asked to change its manner of governance and to undertake the accommodation of minority elements. No association can ignore the moral or political of "black power."

This issue elaborates to a third. The question is whether centralization or decentralization should be practiced in dealing with affiliates and in planning community programs At the community level the issue is unilateral or community-controlled. As an example, the Ford Foundation found itself at the center of vehement controversy over community control of New York public schools.

A fourth issue also concerns the relation of associations to metropolitan areas. The needs of the inner cities for housing, schools, and services clash with suburban demands for protection of residential property and the quality of the school systems. Contests occur over taxes, services, pollution, and bussing of school children. Associations concerned with urban problems cannot ignore these matters. Metropolitan and regional governments are at the apex of these controversies.

Government agencies and private associations find themselves facing these issues together. As the biggest issues of our day they call for decisions on priority of needs, policy decisions on administration and finance, and even moral and philosophic reconciliation. In the process businesses, universities, foundations, and churches become involved, and within this interactional context a dynamic sociology of associations will find meaning and substance.

Notes

1. David L. Sills, "Sociological Aspects of Voluntary Associations," *International Encyclopedia of the Social Sciences,* **16,** 362–379.

2. William A. Glaser and David L. Sills, *The Government of Associations*, Selections from the Behavioral Sciences, The Bedminister Press, Totowa, New Jersey, 1966.

3. James G. March, Ed., *Handbook of Organizations*, Rand McNally, Chicago, 1965.

4. Sol Levine and Paul E. White, "Exchange as a Conceptual Framework for the Study of Interorganizational Relationships," *Administrative Science Quarterly* 5 (March 1961), 583–584. See also Amitai Etzioni, "New Directions in the Study of Organizations and Society," *Social Research*, 27 (1960) 223–228; Nicholas Batchuk and John N. Edwards, "Voluntary Associations and the Integration Hypothesis," *Sociological Inquiry* (Spring 1965), 149–162.

5. Andrew O. Collver, Bibliography (105 citations) on the Interrelations of Organizations (mimeo, Distributed to working scholars August 1, 1967, University of Michigan, Ann Arbor. On February 1, 1967 Professor Collver distributed a mimeographed report on 21 research scholars actively engaged in interorganizational analysis. For current information, consult Professor Collver, Department of Sociology, SUNY, Stony Brook, New York. Paul E. White also reports work on an exhaustive bibliography of interorganizational research reported in American periodical literature between 1960 and 1970. The Johns Hopkins University, School of Hygiene and Public Health, Department of Behavioral Sciences, Baltimore, Maryland. Some selected articles that attempt to establish field definitions include Roland L. Warren, "The Interorganizational Field as a Focus for Investigation," *Administrative Science Quarterly*, 12 (December, 1967), 396–419. James D. Thompson, *Organizations in Action*. McGraw-Hill, New York, 1967; William M. Evans, "An Organizational-Set Model of Interorganizational Relations," in M. F. Tuite, M. Radnor, and R. K. Chisholm, Eds., *Interorganizational Decision Making*, Aldine, Chicago, 1972.

6. Urban America has now merged with the National Urban Coalition.

7. *U.A.W. Solidarity*, 12, No. 7 (July, 1969), p. 9.

8. Teamster General Vice-President Frank E. Fitzsimous, *ibid.*, p. 7.

9. *Associations in the Next Decade*, Chamber of Commerce of the United States, 1965, p. 2.

10. *Ibid.*, p. 3–4.

11. *Ibid.*, p. 5. It is interesting to observe that these predictions have been borne out.

12. *Ibid.*, p. 3.

13. *Members Appraise Associations by Opinion*. A study of association members in 47 leading trade and professional organizations. Chamber of Commerce of the United States, Washington, D.C., 1966, p. 1.

14. These issues were discussed in detail in Chapter 6 and viewed through the eyes of regional leaders.

PART SIX

The Future of
The Megalopolitan
Community

The destiny of urban man in the United States has been written. He is already changing from Metropolitan Man to Megalopolitan Man. Currently more than 70 percent of all inhabitants dwell within 231 standard metropolitan areas. Only three of the 50 states contain no metropolitan areas —Alaska, Vermont, and Wyoming,[1]—and even they are experiencing increasing urbanization. The significant trend is the rise of megalopolises. With each passing year, as population increases, metropolitan areas are reaching out to one another to form new urban regions or urban systems.

An urban region has been defined by one political scientist as two or more contiguous standard metropolitan statistical areas.[2] Such an operational definition makes it possible to determine that 18 urban regions containing 40 percent of the nation's population now exist.

It will be recalled that three major megalopolises delineated in projections to the year 2000 by Kahn and Wiener will have axes between such polar cities as Boston and Washington ("Bos-Wash"), Chicago and Pittsburgh ("Chipitts"), and San Francisco and San Diego ("Sansan"). Other megalopolises are projected as arms reaching from Chicago to Milwaukee, Chicago to St. Louis, and Chicago to Louisville and Cincinnati. The Mohawk Bridge (Buffalo-Hamilton-Toronto) will link two great megalopolises—Bos-Wash and Chipitts.[3] Thus a new stage of regional growth will culminate in an urban succession as the metropolitanization of the United States reaches megalopolitan proportions.

By A.D. 2000 it is expected that 90 percent of the population will be living in a megalopolitan community or along a connecting arm. It can also be expected that these will be the areas in which the problems of government will pose their greatest challenge.

One regional geographer has said:

> There are three dimensions to the geographic region—natural, cultural, and political—

each of which presents different problems—the greatest single need of the regionalist is a series of systematic studies of culture forms and complexes per se.[4]

In this monograph a search for a regional power structure, environmental quality decision-making patterns, and organizational interaction has been undertaken. The findings have been presented for a current period. Now it is proposed that some projections for the future be attempted. The key question is, "What is the future of Eastern Megalopolis as a sociological and governmental unit?"

Some answers are put forward in this final chapter, which has been titled *From Localism to Regionalism: The Widening of Community Consciousness* and in which the growth of Eastern Megalopolis is examined more carefully by observing the population changes in the major metropolitan areas. The dispersal of urban problems to connecting areas is also discussed. The growing elaboration of governmental forms is associated with the levels of civic activity in the region and the growth of regional consciousness is treated. What the region means now to the inhabitants and what it may mean later are significant to an understanding of future society.

Notes

1. U.S. Department of Commerce, Bureau of the Census, *Statistical Abstract of the United States*, 1970, p. 17.
2. Charlton F. Chute, "Today's Urban Regions," *National Municipal Review*, **45** (June-July 1956).
3. Described in Chapter 1, drawn from Herman Kahn and Anthony J. Wiener, *The Year 2000*, Macmillan, New York, 1968. See also Figure 1.5, Formation of Megalopolitan Systems, U.S.A. and Southern Canada, 1965–2000, on p. 20, this volume.
4. George W. Hoffman, "Development of Regional Geography in the United States," in *Economic Regionalization*, Dr. Miroslav Macka, Ed., *Academic*, Prague, 1967, p. 48.

CHAPTER TWELVE

From Localism
to Regionalism:
The Widening of
Community
Consciousness

The indicators of growing social and economic interaction were discussed in Chapter 1. Although the flow and spatial patterns of such things as telephone calls, telegrams, visitors, and travel generally show conclusively the movement of social objects, these indicators only reflect the presence of social interaction between the major cities of Megalopolis. More knowledge is needed of the bonds that provide social cohesion. This research has focused on the direct social interaction of leaders and organizations. Another area of interest, the spread of common social problems as they take on an interstate and regional character, has not been fully studied. The environmental quality problems of water and air pollution and the disposal of solid wastes were examined in earlier chapters, and their interstate and regional character are shown heuristically in Figure 12.1, which also illustrates other problems that are compelling regional consideration. Perhaps the most visible is transportation. Interstate highway systems are a necessity and regional planning has been a must. Every freeway is not only a problem for the metropolitan area but also for Megalopolis. The increase in numbers of autos and trucks is ever demanding of more roadbed, and high-speed railroads are increasing their schedules. The New York to Washington Metroliners have proved their usefulness and extensions to Boston are underway. Air traffic at airports has become a major concern. Airport locations, especially between New York and Philadelphia and Baltimore and Washington have drawn these cities into land-use agreements.

The need for recreational space is real for all of Megalopolis. The long weekend, numerous holidays, and vacation periods have put enormous pressure on the existing facilities. There are not enough beaches, parks, and open places to accommodate megalopolitan leisure. It is well known that federal facilities are poorly balanced across the United States. The large areas of public lands lie in the Western states where the

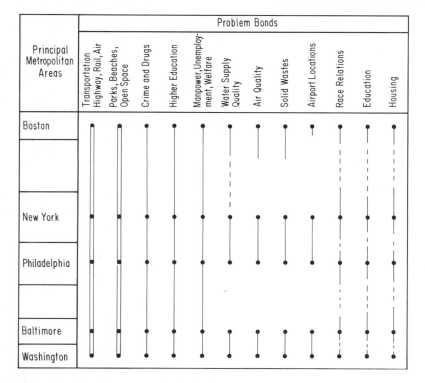

Figure 12.1 Heuristic diagram projecting assumed gradients for selected social problems in Megalopolis.

population is lowest. The East, which has the largest population, has the fewest facilities. It must somehow solve its own problems.

Crime and drug abuse require the close cooperation of the police forces throughout the region. The frequent movement of criminals of all kinds demands the closest interstate scrutiny.

The availability and financing of higher education has a special significance. In no region has private education been so prevalent. Major universities in the five cities include Harvard and M.I.T. in Boston, Columbia and New York University in New York, the University of Pennsylvania and Temple in Philadelphia, Johns Hopkins in Baltimore, and American, Georgetown and Catholic U. in Washington. These are but a few of the many fine private institutions on which parents and students of Megalopolis rely heavily, and movement up and down Megalopolis is considerable. All need philanthropy and federal funds, and all must compete with the area's strengthened public universities.

Manpower, unemployment, and welfare are problems shared by each of the major cities. Manpower, when needed, is sought along the "Bos-Wash" axis. Demands in one city draw labor from all the others when surpluses exist. Likewise, unemployment and poverty is a push to labor mobility unless the resident state has superior welfare benefits. New York has first-hand knowledge of the way higher welfare benefits draw people into the city and limit their mobility.

Water supply and quality are problem shed concerns that are related to major river basins; New York and Philadelphia are bound together by the Delaware,

Baltimore and Washington by the Potomac. Air quality and solid waste disposal draw the same cities together because of their proximity. Boston, more than 200 miles away from New York, has its own problems, but it is not unaffected by the needs of other cities to the south. New York in particular is constantly searching for greater supplies of water in the northern hinterland.

Race relations, public education, and housing are commonly regarded as local responsibilities, but as we have shown in Chapter 6 they can generate regional issues. Each city finds that is is grappling with common issues and examines carefully the experience of others. Political leaders and organizations exchange information and advice, and experts may shuttle back and forth between the cities as problems intensify. There is always the possibility that a crisis in one city will spread quickly to others.

These are some of the major problems that are increasing in scope to provide the kind of interstate and regional concern that gives meaning to regionalism. The elaboration of government forms to deal with them is inevitable. Civic activity has already been heightened and the next section describes this behavior.

Broader Levels of Civic Activity and the Growth of Government Across Megalopolis

Problems of urban civilization do not respect the traditional boundaries established for rural life. The result is that the efforts of government to plan and control are often blocked not only by the inadequate power of the city but also by jurisdictional battles between city, suburb, and state. Nonetheless, the spread of civic participation and the innovation of new agencies are productive of bursts of civic activity.

Eight Civic Activity Levels

In the most comprehensive classification eight activity levels are related to the following:

1. Central city.
2. Metropolitan area.
3. Multicounty area.
4. State.
5. Multistate and subregional.
6. Megalopolis.
7. Section.
8. Nation.

Table 12.1 describes these levels and lists the major issues and prevailing groups associated with them. It will be noted that these levels become ever broader until the nation itself completes the area of largest domain. An understanding of all this activity is required because it is on these levels that leaders and organizations act and interact, and it is in their multitudinous overlapping that regionalism gains social significance. A brief description of each level follows.[1]

TABLE 12.1 CIVIC ACTIVITY LEVELS WITH ASSOCIATED ISSUES AND GOVERNMENTAL AND NONGOVERNMENTAL AGENCIES AND ORGANIZATIONS

Civic activity level	Central City	Metropolitan area	Multicounty area	State	Multi-state and subregional areas	Megalopolis	Section	National
Some major issues	Taxes; subsidizations of the suburbs; threats to central business district; integration of schools; revenue sharing by state and Federal Governments; community participation and control; metropolitan government	Financing and establishing jurisdiction over sewage, water, police, fire, schools, housing, airport, cemetaries; land use and zoning; annexation; community participation and control	Land use, planning and jurisdiciton; representation on policy-making boards of agencies; taxing power of agencies over county units	Revenue sharing, taxes; state support of education, welfare, roads; relation of state agencies to cities and multicounty agencies	Subregional land use and resource planning, pollution control; relation between Federal Government and state agencies	Highway, recreational, and airport planning and financing; crime and drug control; manpower and welfare accommodation	Issues that compel sensitivity to Eastern interests, such as tariffs, banking, securities and export trade	Federal aid to education, welfare, housing and urban renewal; crime prevention and control

Agencies of government	Municipal forms of mayor-council and city manager council; metropolitan area planning councils	Special districts; city-county consolidations; highway and air transport, Metropolitan multicounty	Area water and sewage commissions; highway and air transport agencies; multicounty planning commissions and councils	Governor legislature; State government; State commissions	Regional commissions; federal interstate agencies; compact agencies of two or more states; regional offices of federal agencies	Regional governor's conference; informal cooperation among mayors	National legislators in Congress acting as an Eastern bloc	Eastern legislators acting as individual representatives on national level
Non government organizations	Citizens movements and other voluntary organizations	Metropolitan citizens' groups	Multi county groups of citizens or voluntary organizations	State trade associations; manufacturers' groups; state conservancy association; various professional and semi professional interest groups	Provate-non government organizations	Private planning associations, professional, scientific and cultural associations headquartered in major cities	Powerful Eastern leaders and organizations in Eastern sectional societies	National organizations of industrial, commercial, scientific, and cultural groups

1. CENTRAL CITY

The central cities of Megalopolis have suffered a common fate, for population and industry have moved out at a rapid date. The 1960 census revealed that the largest cities of the United States (except Los Angeles) were declining for the first time. York Wilbern has titled this trend, *The Withering Away of the City*.[2] New problems have descended on these cities with a rush. The influx of blacks, the loss of tax base, and threats to the central business districts have all compounded difficulties that are revealed as problems of race relations, education, housing, crime, unemployment and poverty, transportation, planning and zoning, environmental pollution, and drug abuse.

Major issues have developed over taxes, subsidization of city services for the suburbs, revenue sharing by the state and the Federal Government, integration of schools, community participation and control, and metropolitan government.

To solve these problems the central city has tried to annex adjoining areas in order to widen its tax base. It has fought for metropolitan government or, at least, metropolitan area planning. It has sought categorical grants in aid from the Federal Government for housing, schools, welfare programs, and every other form of assistance available to buttress its badly strained finances.

Annexation and metropolitan government proposals have usually resulted in long and often fruitless battles with the suburbs. Federal help has been most effective, and this assistance that has introduced a new agency—the Metropolitan Area Planning Council—which has power to wield because to qualify for funds many federal grants require area planning proposals. Cooperation is needed among leaders and agencies in the central city and suburbs. The Area Planning Council may have no formal authority, but without its approval federal funds cannot be secured. The creation of this council, which works closely with the traditional mayor-council municipal government, is the first significant step toward a widening of regional consciousness. By this new mechanism the central city and suburbs are learning to reconcile their differences and reach agreement. In finding common grounds, they discover new identities of purpose.

2. METROPOLITAN AREA

From 1950 to 1970 most major cities watched growth take place in the suburbs. While many were experiencing decline suburban growth was soaring, in many places by 100 percent or more. Suburbs may be of many types. Although difficult to classify, most of them will include characteristics of more than one of the following:

1. Dormitory suburbs, built on undeveloped land for the purpose of absorbing the city's overflow.

2. Industrial suburbs centered on large manufacturing establishments.

3. Enclaves or suburbs that retain their independent legal status but are completely surrounded by the core city.

4. Recreational suburbs, characterized as places to which people go to relax, play, and escape.

5. Once autonomous communities, which were independent municipalities, probably serving as marketing towns, and which have been overrun by a metropolitan community.

6. Heterogeneous suburbs that serve many purposes and combine many features of the other five.[3]

This wide variety of suburban types suggests an equally wide variation in personal interests and motivation which has brought suburbanites to their chosen location. Wealthy, middle-class, and working class live in the suburbs and in most cases are segregated by class and race. Most have escaped from the central city only for residential purposes. They commute to work in the central city and use it for much of their shopping and recreation. The suburbs promise ownership of homes with more open space, independence from big municipal government, access to the decision-making centers of local government, and greater control of municipal services and level of financing. Many have been drawn to the suburbs by the belief that they can get a better way of life for lower taxes. Actually, many services are more expensive because of the lesser density of the population. The major portion of the tax appropriations goes toward the support of schools, and as population increases one school board issue follows another with regularity. Each issue results in raised taxes. The increase in population density originates needs for other urban services. Water and sewage systems must be installed, streets paved, and storm sewers laid. Fire and police protection must be expanded, and street lights become desirable. Each new service must be paid for with additional levies.

These problems fall on the mortgage- and debt-ridden suburbanite. Furthermore, the open space and the intimacy of the small suburb may have disappeared with shocking rapidity. It begins to look and feel like a heavily urbanized area—indeed, like the central city. In desperation people seek solutions in special districts, incorporation, new state legislation, annexation, city-county consolidation, or metropolitan area planning and government.

The search for an adequate governmental form to meet the diverse value patterns of suburbanites has been one of experiment and conflict. Nowhere in the United States does the sociological and economic metropolitan area coincide with a single government unit. Numerous arrangements have been tried, but no current trend toward the adoption of a particular form exists. The special district which is an organized unit of government with substantial autonomy deserves attention. However, it has its own tax program and usually its own bonding authority and incorporates many government services, such as water, sewage, fire protection, schools, and cemeteries. The need for an area-wide approach to these problems exists in both rural and urban districts. Whereas other solutions have been politically impractical, the special district makes possible the provision of government services when and where they are most needed and limits the financial burden on residents most directly affected. By leaving the political status quo undisturbed the social need is met with little resistance. Most ad hoc districts serve a single purpose, although multipurpose districts are in use and are authorized by some states. In Boston the Massachusetts Metropolitan District Commission was created by the state in 1919 by consolidating three districts which furnished sewage, water, and park services. In 1952 refuse disposal was added. In 1929 a separate Boston Metropolitan District provided rapid transit, and in 1947 a Metropolitan Transit Authority was established to operate a previously privately operated elevated railway system.

Annexation is another way of meeting metropolitan area problems. Although annexations have increased in number and importance, they seldom produce a single metropolitan government. The reason is that state laws generally provide that outlying areas may be annexed only after a referendum has been held and the annexation has been approved by the voters of the area and the central city as well. It requires only the threat of higher taxes or loss of political independence and control to arouse vigorous opposition.

City-county consolidations have been attempted, but only a few have succeeded. They usually meet with failure at the polls for the same reasons that annexation is resisted.

Metropolitan government runs into the same thorny political problems. This economically feasible solution is not politically acceptable. Norton Long has noted that

> the search for metropolitan government is the search for a potential metropolitan governing class, the institutions through which it can function and a set of ideal goals which it can embody and which will render its leadership legitimate in the eyes of the people.[4]

This explains the slow progress toward metropolitan government. There is no consensus on goals, no acceptable governing group, and institutions have not evolved. The increase in political control by blacks in the central city and the disparate character of the suburbs have exacerbated the problem of consensus. An issue like busing alone is sufficient to arouse fears antagonistic to cooperation.

It is in the suburbs that the high walls of provincialism have been erected. The defenses are formidable, but if they should crumble regionalism might be greatly expedited. There are challenges to this suburban isolation that do point to change. The metropolitan area is becoming similar in its urban characteristics as population densities increase and megalopolis becomes the predominant urban form.

The rise of special districts, the increase of annexation and city-county consolidations (in spite of opposition), and the growing demands for area planning all point the way to future changes in political values held by inhabitants of metropolitan areas. The sociological city is struggling for its life. In that struggle federal and state authorities have been responsive. The availability or withholding of federal and state funds, depending on area planning and cooperation, is a powerful weapon.[5] The central city may have to continue to be the instigator of programming, but the reluctant suburbs will find themselves in an increasingly receptive mood as their own urban problems begin to approximate the city's. Metropolitan citizen groups are slowly providing the leadership bridges to amalgamate city and suburbs. Meanwhile, the national and international economy throws its own net over the region and the nation.

3. MULTICOUNTY AREA

Problems of the metropolitan area spill over into adjacent counties. Water supply, sewage, highway, and air transport are some of the services that demand intra-county cooperation. Planning commissions, solid waste management agencies, and area water and sewage commissions represent the government agencies that must cope with these problems. The Twin Cities Metropolitan Council, created by the Minnesota legislature in 1967 by an enabling act designed to provide unified direction for a domain of seven counties embracing Minneapolis and St. Paul and about 130 smaller municipalities in the surrounding countryside, is being watched as a national model of multicounty government. It was given responsibility and specified authority for sewage, water supply, airport location, highway routes, and the preservation of open space. It has its own source of revenue and is not dependent on voluntary contributions from the 150 constituent municipalities. It is charged with making overall plans "for the orderly physical, social and economic growth of the Twin Cities Area." It reviews all plans and projects of local government and special agencies such as the Airport Commission. If it is found that any of them conflict with the regional plan, the Council can suspend them. It is also empowered to review local requests for federal aid.[6]

Other cities have attempted similar plans: Nashville, Miami, Jacksonville, Seattle, and, most successfully, Toronto. Mayor Richard Lugar of Indianapolis recently proposed an eight county metropolitan area planning council which he called necessary to avoid losing 11 million dollars in federal funds for water pollution and park land development.[7]

In Megalopolis the best known multicounty district is the Port of New York Authority. It is, however, a joint agent of the states of New York and New Jersey rather than a unit of local government. To keep the classification scheme adopted here, it must wait its turn as an example of multistate planning.

What is significant about the multicounty area regional council is that it can become a better sociological adaptation while evading the vigorous political opposition that accompanies metropolitan government proposals.[8] It has the capability of drawing able central city leaders into municipal government at a time when their suburban residential loyalties are isolating them from city problems. Moreover, if regional consciousness must grow in a linear fashion from smaller to ever larger units, multicounty planning is a vital step along the road. This linear notion of regional consciousness is discussed in the next section. At the moment it should be recorded that nongovernment groups, such as water-shed associations, multicolony groups of the League of Women Voters and suburban citizens associations, are building public interest at this level.

4. STATE

The state carries out two functions that are highly important to the citizen. First of all, it allocates funds to counties and cities for public schools, state colleges and universities, roads, welfare, crime control, health, and a growing list of serv-ices. The controversial federal revenue sharing plan seems to be gaining favor. At least President Ford and most governors are firmly committed. At the beginning of his second term President Nixon announced his intention to scrap 70 federal aid programs in such areas as education, law enforcement, job training, and urban community development and to replace them with cash grants totaling nearly seven billion dollars (1974). This expenditure of funds is part of a deliberate plan to decentralize federal responsibilities and to increase the power of the individual states. It is argued that the state is in the best position to coordinate the needs of its subunits.

The same argument is often used to bolster the state's second major function as administrative overseer of city and county government. Traditionally, the city and county have been the responsibility of the state, and state law defines matters in which these units act simply as agents. The state-imposed limitation on the power of cities to tax has especially restricted the actions of their governments. Cities have been and still are overwhelmingly dependent on general property taxes. This levy was designed to fit the needs of a frontier society and is not only being challenged in the courts as unconstitutional but is constantly failing to meet the needs of cities, counties, and metropolitan areas. Municipalities have found that the limit of their services comes when the property tax reaches a psychological saturation point. The impatient and annoyed citizen turns desperately to the state or national government for services for which the city "has no money."

These two functions of the state make this unit of government more rather than less powerful. At the same time it has often failed to provide adequate representation. Failing to reapportion itself on population, many states continue to be dominated by farmers and small-town merchants and lawyers who are largely in control of the legislature. State agencies have often failed under political patronage systems to develop the professional and technical skills the cities have at their disposal. Against this background of political domination and control, the relation of the state to its subunits is crucial to program development. The implementation of environmental quality standards for water, air, and land is a hot issue. There are difficult coordination problems between state and multicounty or other intrastate regional agencies; for example, a state water resources or environmental agency with an intrastate environmental agency. National illustrations include the Washington State Department of Ecology vis-à-vis the Pudget Sound Air Quality Control Commission; the California Department of Water Resources vis-à-vis the San Francisco Bay Conservation and Development Commission. Organizations at the state level include state trade associations, manufacturers groups, the state conservancy organizations, such as the Connecticut Conservancy, and various professional and semiprofessional organization such as the Pennsylvania Water Pollution Control Association.

These interrelationships can only begin to suggest the growing net that binds state, cities, and multicounty and metropolitan areas together. They imply increased contact between leaders and organizations over wider ranges of interaction and suggest growth of a wider political consciousness.

5. MULTISTATE AND SUBREGIONAL

Problems at this level are truly interstate or apply to subregions that cross state lines but define explicit areas. Interstate problems involve transportation, manpower, or land-use planning for parks and airport location. Subregions that cross state lines but are not necessarily coterminous include "problem sheds" for water, air, and solid wastes. The Delaware River Basin, the Potomac River Basin, and many Air Quality Control Districts are examples.

At this level it is particularly important to differentiate between two types of "compact" agency. One has been established by an interstate-federal compact. Only two of this kind are currently in existence—the Delaware River Basin Commission and the Susquehanna River Basin Commission. The second is a compact agency which serves two or more states. Compact agencies of two states within Megalopolis are the Port Authority of New York (New York-New Jersey), the Delaware Valley Regional Planning Commission (Pennsylvania-New Jersey), the Pennsylvania-New Jersey Port Authority (the last two are in the process of being subsumed by a new Tri-Pact agency, a three-state regional agency for transportation in the Philadelphia-Camden-Wilmington area). Compact agencies of three or more states are the Tri-State Transportation Agency and the New England Interstate Pollution Control Commission.

Other types of agencies that are not compact play important roles in sub-regional and interstate development. The regional headquarters of HEW, HUD, OEO, Labor, and Small Business Administration are examples of the decentralization of federal agencies to provide more effective adaptation to regional needs. The New England Regional Commission, an interstate effort, plans, develops, and conserves the resources of the states in that region. The Federal Government has offered some financial support.

A fascinating private interstate subregional plan is illustrated by an air pollution control program sponsored by the Regional Conference of Elected Officials. This study covered a vast 11-county, tristate region encompassing the three metropolitan areas of Philadelphia-Camden, Trenton, and Wilmington, located in Pennsylvania, New Jersey, and Delaware, respectively; RCEO's report points out that

> part of the unique commitment to action is reflected in the financing arrangement for the study which involved a grant from the United States Public Health Service and the individual contributions of local units of government throughout the region. Further this study provides new evidence that autonomous local units of government can join together in a cooperative venture to solve a common problem.[9]

The leap frogging and coordinating of governmental agencies is the practical action that makes a regional program possible. This lesson was learned in the Delaware River Basin. Before the Delaware River Basin interstate-federal compact could be achieved there it had to be recognized that 19 federal agencies, 14 interstate agencies, 43 state departments, boards and commissions, and more than 250 public and private water companies[10] had a major interest in the water resources of the Delaware Basin.

The river is a product of nature; water and air pollution is all of man's creation. Air pollution is a new phenomenon, for it has a changing, fluid character that overflows all traditional government jurisdictions. Nothing could so shake and change government boundaries as the authority granted to the Secretary of the Interior under the Air Quality Act of 1967.

The Secretary is directed

> to define atmospheric areas of the nation considering those parameters which affect atmospheric interchange and diffusion of pollutants. In the establishment of such atmospheric areas, parameters such as climate, meteorology, and topography are to be considered.

> The Secretary is further required to define those air quality regions he deems necessary for the establishment of air quality standards to protect public health and welfare. Such air quality control areas shall be defined on the basis of jurisdictional boundaries, urban-industrial concentrations, and other factors including atmospheric regions necessary to provide adequate implementation of air quality standards and after consultation with appropriate state and local authorities.[11]

A sociologist is tempted to anticipate a grant of similar authority to proclaim these environmental areas as true sociological regions deemed necessary to provide adequate protection to public health and welfare. Obviously this is not a practical consideration in this seventh decade of the twentieth century. Like World Government, it asks too much of political man too soon. This brings us to the main object of interest—Megalopolis.

6. MEGALOPOLIS

It was in 1961 that Jean Gottman published his study of Megalopolis and concluded that "as the vast region of Megalopolis grows, regional integration into one interwoven system is bound to progress."[12] More than a decade has elapsed. Megalopolis has grown rapidly in population and pushed its boundaries outward to the north, south, and west. Maps that show the daily flow of telephone calls, highway traffic, airline passenger traffic, and other measures of regional interaction have become black with lines of contact. Open space has steadily yielded to interconnecting urban settlements. Economic integration and social interaction have increased in every dimension, but the compelling question of 1961 is still pertinent. Is Megalopolis emerging as a community?

The answer still remains shrouded in many unknowns. Gottman had concluded that the first evolution toward a megalopolitan community must be achieved in the minds of the people and that many signs indicated that it had already occurred. This research study advances the same proposition. A leadership and organization pattern of megalopolitan concern and interaction is operative. Social problems and issues of megalopolitan dimension have been identified and described. What does not exist is a governmental frame that isolates and defines the political character of Megalopolis as a sociological entity. The Regional Governors Conference and informal cooperation among the mayors of the major cities have provided communication but not definition, power, and authority. Private planning associations like the Regional Plan Association based in New York devote their attention to the North Atlantic seaboard. The most powerful urban-oriented and environmental organizations have their national headquarters in the major cities of Megalopolis, notably New York and Washington. Professional, scientific, and cultural organizations tend to locate their national headquarters in the central cities of Megalopolis. This has the effect of concentrating a great amount of highly educated and trained leadership in Megalopolis and exposing it to the problems of the region. We have said that the incipient power base is in place. Only the future can demonstrate whether the social changes will force regionalism into a political reality.

7. SECTION

Eastern sectionalism is real. The consciousness that one is an Easterner is generally prized by the inhabitants of the New England and the Northeast central states, but the Eastern section is broader than Megalopolis as defined by Gottman, although it is true that the two may one day be almost coterminous. At the political level sectionalism is displayed when legislators in the Congress vote in accordance with economic interests that are characteristically Eastern. Issues that involve tariffs, banking, securities, and export trade will often find legislators of both political parties voting in a bloc. Congressional representatives from the states of Eastern Megalopolis show the following distribution (from North to South):

> Massachusetts, 12; Rhode Island, 2; Connecticut, 6; New York, 41; Pennsylvania, 27; New Jersey, 15; Delaware 1; and Maryland, 8.

This is a total of 112, or 26 percent of the 435 in the House, a substantial clout when delivered in a body. Because metropolitan areas, by virtue of their population, contribute the largest share, Megalopolis can rely on sectionalism to provide strong support of its economic interests. The 16 senators from the eight states also carry supporting weight in the Senate. Powerful Eastern leaders and organizations also come to the support of sectional interests.

Because the states are so embedded in the traditional government pattern, it is entirely possible that Megalopolis will find its real political expression in the Eastern bloc of states in which the major interconnected metropolitan areas are located. It can be noted in Figure 1.5 how the projected growth of Bos-Wash and the interconnecting Chippitts will spread over wider areas of the Eastern states by A.D. 2000. Meanwhile the nation is the macro unit that provides the structure for sectionalism to operate successfully without rupturing the social system.

8. THE NATION

Nationalism is the identity pole around which citizens marshall their strongest loyalties. Nationhood is a psychological reality for most Americans. When Eastern legislators function on the national level, they are expected to act in the national interest but to interpret the needs of their constituencies. These two expectations are not always compatible, for Eastern legislators in the Congress tend to respond to the problems common to the highly urbanized communities they represent. Thus federal support is generally delivered by legislators of both political parties for education, welfare, housing and urban renewal, crime prevention and control, highway and airport development, metropolitan and multicounty area planning, job training, and many other urban-related programs. National organizations of industrial, governmental, commercial, scientific, and cultural groups add political pressure for many urban proposals.

The power of the Federal Government attracts Eastern leaders and organizations who believe that they can achieve maximum results for their programs by working with other sectional leaders in the United States.

In any evaluation of the political power of the East in the national scene the wealth, industry, and leadership concentrated in that section must be given due weight. The fact that the nation's capital is located in Eastern Megalopolis and that most of the powerful national organizations are headquartered there means that officials and officers are exposed to the daily life of Megalopolis in their work, their homes, and their leisure. All national legislators cannot ignore Megalopolis even if their home states are far distant.

The Eight Civic Activity Levels in Review

These eight activity levels demonstrate the width and multiplicity of civic relations in Eastern Megalopolis. The central city, the state, and the nation are the traditional units of sociological and political identification. The section is especially meaningful for Easterners, but it has no formal governmental apparatus. It is a lively concept for the various industrial and professional societies that use the section as a basis of organization.

All the other activity levels are either without formal governmental structures or are struggling to establish or implement new forms of social control to include metropolitan, multicounty, multistate, and subregional areas, and Megalopolis. Planning studies seem to be the first step by which the concrete realities of economic and social life are expressed in statistical and interpretative terms. Time series and future projections begin to awaken more and more people to the dimensions of area needs. Meanwhile insistent problems are spilling over traditional boundaries and demanding wider social and political treatment. How does the citizen some to grasp the widening scope of his interests and the need to respond by supporting new forms of government? How does regional consciousness develop?

THE GROWTH OF REGIONAL CONSCIOUSNESS

A community has both geographic and social dimensions. As a spatial concept it is an area that bounds economic and social functions. As a sociological concept it stresses social interaction in which participants hold sentiments of belonging and establish bonds that knit psychological ties to a given place. The community should feel like "home" to its inhabitants.

The national and international market pulled modern man into a consciousness of the wide area on which his livelihood had come to depend. He became a mobile man by pulling up his community roots to establish himself in jobs that were often available only in more distant labor markets. His desire to establish a home often placed him many miles from his place of work. To satisfy his leisure needs he often found that he must drive farther and farther from his home to discover open recreational space.

Sociologists have studied the character of these shallow community roots and have wondered how contemporary man holds on to any sense of community.

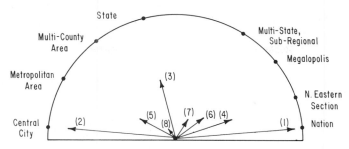

Figure 12.2   A citizen awareness-and-identity arc showing a heuristic modal pattern for a central-city inhabitant in Megalopolis. (Length of vector is an estimation of the strength of awareness and identity).

However attenuated community sentiment may be, persistent realities remain. The individual must live in geographic and social space. He must work, find housing, pay taxes, eat, educate his children, and satisfy his religious and leisure needs. Each of these requirements depends a great deal on what happens in distant centers. We have described eight areas that serve him. What we would like to know is how he responds to them and develops a social consciousness that broadens into identities and loyalties.

Figure 12.2 presents a Citizen Awareness and Identity Arc that describes heuristically a modal pattern for an inhabitant of an *eastern* central city. It shows each of the eight areas that are potential community bases for the central-city inhabitant selected. Each is arrayed on the arc according to its geographic size, beginning with the central city and extending to the nation. The vectors are drawn so that the length of each shows an estimated strength of the awareness and identity felt by the inhabitant. This means that the vector matrix is a psychological model and not an empirical statement of actual social, political, or economic relationships. We are trying to show what consciousness of these eight areas means to our average central-city citizen.

The estimates are based on the following assessments which rank each area in relative awareness and identity strength:

Area	Psychological component
1. Nation	Individual experiences reality of nationhood by payment of income taxes, in labor market potentialities, military service, a historic sense of identity, a label in world relations, and travel.
2. Central city	Inner city resident develops identity with this base for his work, home, and leisure; payment of city taxes, cultural and educational opportunities, pride in sport teams.
3. State	Identification by payment of taxes and highway services received; park and other state recreational facilities, historic sense of identity, pride in state universities and sport teams.

4. Northeastern section	Easterner connotes a cosmopolitan culture pattern. It expresses a rich urban way of life with cultural and educational opportunities. The East often bounds an acceptable area of residence.
5. Metropolitan area	For an inner city resident the metropolitan area establishes an alternate labor market and residential base. Area complements the central city with stores and recreational facilities.
6. Megalopolis	Represents urban life around interesting cities in an Eastern culture; a potential labor market and residence for future mobility, a source of travel and leisure.
7. Multistate, subregional area	Connotes an area distinguished by a distinctive way of life—New England, Delaware region, Potomac Area.
8. Multicounty area	Has meaning because of certain shopping and recreational services available within easy driving distance.

Empirical study may show that alterations in the ranking are required. It is also that great variation would be exhibited around a modal pattern. Almost certainly different patterns can be found for those inhabitants of the suburban part of a metropolitan area. A resident of a multicounty area may view the civic activity levels still differently and have correspondingly different feelings of identity. All that can be said with definiteness is that community consciousness varies enormously. Yet our Megalopolitan Man must live in a world of interlocking communities and must find his social roots in the multiplicity of social networks. How this happens is an intriguing question and three theories are suggested in the final section.

THREE THEORIES THAT EXPLAIN THE GROWTH OF REGIONAL CONSCIOUSNESS

The three theories may be called traditional, linear, and fiat. *The traditional theory* holds that individuals become identified with the most visible governmental entities that direct their affairs. In the United States these entities are the incorporated city, the state, and the nation, all of which become viable because they are the centers of government in which legislation is enacted, officials are elected, and taxes are raised. The press, radio, and television give high coverage to their activities.

The linear theory is based on the premise that socialization of the individual begins as the child experiences life in the home, the neighborhood, the constituent community in a town or city, and finally by travel, residence, or vicarious experience in the metropolitan area, the metropolis, or the nation. Constantinos Doxiadis has developed a system of linear development that he calls Ekistics. Figure 12.3 shows his ekistic grid with a community scale of 15 units. Man is shown as he faces adaptation to such smaller units as the room, dwelling, and dwelling group, to such middle-sized units as the small neighborhood, neighborhood, small town, and town, and finally to the macro communities such as the large city, metropolis, conurbation, megalopolis, urban region, urbanized continent, and ecumenopolis (one-world interconnected urbanized city). The ekistic elements, nature, man, society, shell, networks, and synthesis represent those factors that enter into the socialization of the individual in each community unit with which he is confronted. Projections to A.D. 2000 indicate that a large part of the world's population will come in contact progressively with the macro communities (urban region, urbanized continent, ecumenopolis).[13]

History buttresses the linear theory of social consciousness as men learned how to move from family, tribe, city, state, and nation in their ability to fashion ever larger government units and be identified with them. The sociologist Charles H. Cooley gave considerable attention to this evolutionary process.

> The central fact of history, from a psychological point of view, may be said to be the gradual enlargement of social consciousness and rational cooperation. . . . Throughout modern European history, at least, there has been an evident extension of the local areas within which communication and cooperation prevail, and, on the whole, an advance in the quality of cooperation as judged by an ideal moral unity. . . . The present epoch, then, brings with it a larger and potentially, at least, a higher and freer consciousness. Because of this more conscious relation to the larger wholes—nation, institutions, tendencies—he takes a more vital and personal part in them.[14]

The fiat theory is based on the ability of any traditional authority, city, state, or nation to create new government organizations to transform areas into communities. Examples are the Twin Cities Metropolitan Community (the seven-county multicounty unit described earlier mandated by the Minnesota legislature) and the Metropolitan Government of Indianapolis and Marion County created by the Indiana Legislature. It will be recalled that the Delaware Region became a reality as four states and the Federal Government agreed to a compact that made the Delaware River Basin Commission an authority over water supply and quality (as well as other functions previously cited). The Model Cities Program of the Federal Government has given financial support for the planning of entirely new cities. The decentralizing of such major human and community relations programs as HEW, HUD, OEO, Labor, and Small Business Administration into regional administrations strengthens subregional consciousness. One can speculate that this might be simply a step in the eventual selection of Megalopolis as the most effective planning and administrative unit.

It is not easy to evaluate these programs according to their relative utility. Each captures a part of the reality that is the growth process of regional consciousness. It is likely that man's conception of multibased communities will develop in the different ways suggested. One definitive statement is possible. The fastest way for the weaker community bases (multicounty, multistate, and metropolitan areas and Megalopolis, to be strengthened is by government fiat. New governmental authorities with their own independent sources of finances can heighten the possibilities of the area, crystallize leadership activity, and build new networks of identity.

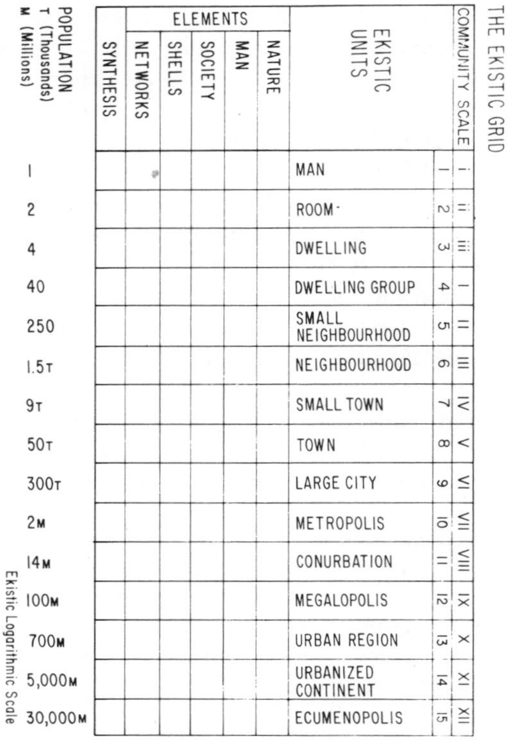

POPULATION T (Thousands) M (Millions)	SYNTHESIS	NETWORKS	SHELLS	SOCIETY	MAN	NATURE	EKISTIC UNITS	COMMUNITY SCALE	THE EKISTIC GRID
1							MAN	— / i	
2							ROOM	2 / ii	
4							DWELLING	3 / iii	
40							DWELLING GROUP	4 / I	
250							SMALL NEIGHBOURHOOD	5 / II	
1.5T							NEIGHBOURHOOD	6 / III	
9T							SMALL TOWN	7 / IV	
50T							TOWN	8 / V	
300T							LARGE CITY	9 / VI	
2M							METROPOLIS	10 / VII	
14M							CONURBATION	11 / VIII	
100M							MEGALOPOLIS	12 / IX	
700M							URBAN REGION	13 / X	
5,000M							URBANIZED CONTINENT	14 / XI	
30,000M							ECUMENOPOLIS	15 / XII	

(Ekistic Logarithmic Scale)

Figure 12.3   The Ekistics Grid.
SOURCE: Ekistics Index, March 1972. By permission of The Athens Center of Ekistics, Athens, Greece.

Ekistic Elements

NATURE

1. Environmental analysis
2. Resource utilization
3. Land use and landscape
4. Recreation and tourism

MAN

1. Physiological needs
2. Safety and security
3. Affection, belonging and esteem
4. Self-realization, knowledge and aesthetics

SOCIETY

1. Public administration and the law
2. Social relations, population trends and cultural patterns
3. Urban change
4. Economic development

SHELL

1. Housing
2. Community facilities: schools, hospitals, etc.
3. Shopping and shopping centers
4. City centers: business and cultural centers

NETWORKS

1. Public utility systems: water, power, sewerage
2. Transportation systems: road, rail, air
3. Communication systems, radio, television, etc.
4. Computers and information systems

SYNTHESIS

1. Physical planning
2. Ekistic theory

Megalopolis as a meaningful sociological community has not arrived, although a power base exists. The rush of urban growth and governmental action hold the key to the future. By A.D. 2000 the decision will be in.

Notes

1. I am indebted to Blair Bower formerly of Resources for the Future, Inc. and now a private consultant for many of the ideas presented in the description of the different levels.

2. York Wilbern, *The Withering Away of the City,* University of Alabama Press, University, Alabama, 1964. This trend continued between 1960 and 1969; the annual rate of growth for all central cities was 0.1 percent, whereas the annual rate outside central cities was 2.7 percent. See *Statistical Abstract of the United States,* 1970, p. 16.

3. Charles R. Adrian and Charles Press, *Governing Urban America,* McGraw-Hill, New York, 1968, pp. 44–47.

4. Norton E. Long, *The Polity,* Rand, McNally & Co., 1962.

5. Title 6 of the 1965 law covering federal financing of community facilities (water and sewer plants) states, "The requirement that a facility given a grant be a part of a unified or official coordinated area-wide system would assure no financing of uncoordinated or fractionated facilities."

6. *Ibid.,* p. 24. Cf. Newsletter of Twin Cities Metropolitan Planning Commission, VI, No. 11, August 1967.

7. "Lugar Asks 8-County Metro Plan Council," *Bloomington Herald-Telephone,* June 10, 1972. This proposal is in response to various federal laws which now require regional review before grants can be approved for water, sewer, transportation, planning, health, and air polluton projects. A 1961 federal housing act includes regional planning and development commissions as possible recipients of funds to help acquire open space land near a metropolitan area for recreation, conservation, or historic-scenic purposes.

8. The regional review requirement for planning project funds is by law required for counties of more than 50,000. Unless counties belong to regional commissions and make regional reviews, they will receive no federal money for water or sewer projects, highways, mass transportation, hospitals, clinics, housing improvement, or construction.

9. Regional Conference of Elected Officials, *Government Organization for a Regional Air Resource Management and Control System,* Fels Institute of Local and State Government, University of Pennsylvania, 1968.

10. Roscoe C. Martin et al., *River Basin Administration and the Delaware,* Syracuse University Press, 1960, p. 51.

11. Air Quality Act of 1967. Section 107. Air Quality Control Regions, Criteria, and Control Techniques, Senate Report No. 403, U.S. Government Printing Office, 1967.

12. J. Gottman, *Megalopolis,* Twentieth Century Fund, New York, 1961, p. 738.

13. C. A. Doxiadis. *Ekistics,* **25,** No. 151 (June 1968), 374–394. Doxiadis predicts that unless the developing civilization of man can be stopped there will be a total of 14 megalopolises by the year 2000, subsequently ensuring a complete and inevitable ecumenopolis, the "universal city of man." See his *Emergence and Growth of an Urban Region,* Vol. 3, Detroit Edison Company, Detroit, 1970, p. 169.

14. Charles H. Cooley. *Social Organization,* Free Press, Glencoe, Ill., 1956, pp. 113, 116.

Bibliography of Large City Power Structures: Theory and Substantive Findings

Adrian, Charles H.: *Governing Urban America,* McGraw-Hill, 3rd ed., New York, 1968 (see especially Chapter 5: Intergroup Activity and Political Power).

Baltzell, E. Digby: *The Protestant Establishment,* Random House, New York, 1964.

Bauer, Raymond A., Lewis A. Dexter, and I dePool: *American Business and Public Policy,* Atherton, New York, 1936.

Birmingham, Stephen: *The Right People, A Portrait of American Social Establishment,* Little, Brown, Boston, 1968.

Cheit, Earl F., Ed.: *The Business Establishment,* Wiley, New York, 1964.

Domhoff, G. William: *Who Rules America?* Prentice-Hall, Englewood Cliffs, N.J., 1967.

Domhoff, G. William: *The Higher Circles: Governing Class in America,* Random House, New York, 1970.

Elias, C. E. Jr., James Gillies, and Svend Riemer: *Metropolis: Values vs. Conflict,* Wadsworth, Belmont, Calif., 1964.

Elizar, Daniel J.: "Megalopolis and the New Sectionalism," *The Public Interest,* Spring 1968, pp. 65–86.

Hess, Stephen, and David S. Broder: *The Republican Establishment,* Harper and Row, New York, 1967.

Hunter, Floyd: *Top Leadership, U.S.A.,* University of North Carolina Press, Chapel Hill, 1959.

Lundberg, Ferdinand: *The Rich and the Super Rich,* Lyle Stuart, New York, 1968.

Maier, Henry W.: *Challenge to the Cities: An Approach to a Theory of Urban Leadership,* Randon House, New York, 1966.

Mathews, Donald: *The Social Background of Political Decision-Makers,* Randon House, N.Y., 1954.

Mills, C. Wright: *The Power Elite,* Oxford Univ. Press, New York, 1956.

Mouser, Joseph R., and Mark W. Cannon: *The Makers of Public Policy, American Power Groups and their Ideologies,* McGraw-Hill, New York, 1965.

Revere, Richard: *The American Establishment,* Harcourt, Brace, and World, New York, 1962.

Rose, Arnold M.: *The Power Structure, Political Processes in American Society,* Oxford Univ. Press, New York, 1967.

Talbot, Allan R.: *The Mayor's Game, Richard Lee of New Haven and the Politics of Change,* Praeger, New York, 1970.

Wolman, Harold: *Politics of Federal Housing,* Dodd, Mead, New York, 1971.

Ziegler, Harmon: *Interest Groups in American Society,* Prentice Hall, Englewood Cliffs, N.J., 1964.

Bibliography for Power Structure and Processes in the Major Cities of Megalopolis

BOSTON

Allen, Robert S.: *Our Fair City,* Vanguard, New York, 1947 (see Louis M. Lyons, "Boston: Study in Inertia," pp. 16–36).

Amory, Cleveland: *The Proper Bostonians,* Dutton, New York, 1947.

Banfield, Edward C.: *Big City Politics,* Random House, New York, 1966 (see "Boston, The New Hurrah," pp. 37–50).

Banfield, Edward C., and Martha Derthick: *A Report on the Politics of Boston,* 2 vols., Joint Center for Urban Studies, Cambridge, Mass., 1960 (mimeographed).

Banfield, Edward C., and James Q. Wilson: *City Politics,* Harvard University Press, Cambridge, Mass., 1963 (see citations to Boston).

Blackwood, George: "Boston Politics and Boston Politicians," in Murray B. Levin, *The Alienated Voter: Politics in Boston,* Holt, Rinehart and Winston, New York, 1960, Chapter 1.

Curley, James M.: *I'd Do It Again,* Prentice Hall, Englewood Cliffs, N.J., 1957.

Long, Norton: "The Local Community as an Ecology of Games," *American Journal of Sociology,* **64,** (November 1958), 251–248.

Myerson, Martin, and Edward C. Banfield: *Boston, The Job Ahead,* Harvard University Press, Cambridge, Mass., 1966.

Seasholes, Bradbury: "Patterns of Influence in Metropolitan Boston: A Proposal for Field Research," in *Current Trends in Comparative Community Studies,* Bert E. Swanson, Ed., Community Studies, Kansas City, Mo., 1962.

NEW YORK

Allen, Robert S.: *Our Fair City,* Vanguard Press, New York, 1947 (see Paul Crowell and A. H. Raskin, "New York, Greatest City in the World," pp. 37–58).

Banfield, E. C., and James Wilson: *City Politics,* Harvard University Press, Cambridge, Mass., 1963 (see numerous citations to New York).

Berube, Maurice R., and Marilyn Gittell, Eds.: *Confrontation at Ocean Hill-Brownsville: The New York School Strike of 1968,* Praeger, New York, 1969.

N. Birmingham, Stephen: *"Our Crowd," the Great Jewish Families of New York,* Harper and Row, New York, 1967.

Buckley, William F.: *The Unmaking of a Mayor,* Viking, New York, 1966.

Campbell, John Franklin: "The Death Battle of the Eastern Establishments," *New York,* 4 (September 20, 1971), 47–51.

Connery, Robert H., and Demetrios Caraley, Eds.: *Governing the City, Challenges and Options for New York,* Praeger, New York, 1969 (see their selected bibliography, pp. 224–227).

Costikyan, E. N.: *Behind Closed Doors,* Harcourt, Brace, and World, New York, 1966.

Hagevik, George H.: *Decision-Making in Air Pollution Control: A Review of Theory and Practice with Emphasis on Selected Los Angeles and New York City Management Experiences,* Praeger, New York, 1970.

Lowi, Theodore J.: *At the Pleasure of the Mayor: Patronage and Power in New York City, 1898–1958,* Macmillan, New York, 1964.

Makielski, S. J.: *Politics of Zoning, New York, 1916-1960,* Columbia University Press, New York, 1965.

Mann, Arthur: *LaGuardia: A Fighter Against His Time,* Lippincott, Philadelphia, 1959.

Morsell, John A.: *The Political Behavior of Negroes in New York City,* Ph.D. dissertation, Columbia University, New York, 1951.

Pilat, Oliver, *Lindsay's Campaign: A Behind the Scenes Diary,* Beacon, Boston, 1968.

Sayre, Wallace S., and Herbert Kaufman: *Governing New York City,* Russell Sage Foundation, New York, 1960.

PHILADELPHIA

Allen, Robert S.: *Our Fair City,* Vanguard, New York, 1947 (see Thomas P. O. Neil, "Where Patience is a Vice," pp. 59–76).

Baltzell, E. Digby: *Philadelphia Gentlemen,* Free Press, Glencoe, Ill., 1957.

Banfield, Edward C.: *Big City Politics,* Random House, New York, 1965 (see Chapter 7, "Philadelphia: Nice While It Lasted").

Crumlish, Joseph D.: *A City Finds Itself: The Philadelphia Home Rule Charter Movement,* Wayne State University Press, Detroit, Mich., 1959.

Gilbert, Charles E.: *Governing the Suburbs,* Indiana University Press, Bloomington, Ind., 1967.

McCullough, John C.: *Philadelphia's Movers and Shakers,* Philadelphia Evening and Sunday Bulletin Co., June 1965.

McKenna, William J.: "The Pattern of Philadelphia Politics, 1956–1963," *Economics and Business Bulletin,* Temple University, **16** (December 1963), 19–24.

Reichley, James: *The Art of Government: Reform and Organizational Politics in Philadelphia.* The Fund for the Republic, New York, 1959.

BALTIMORE

Baratz, Merton S., and Peter Bachrach: *The Politics of Poverty in Baltimore: Preliminary Findings,* Institute for Environmental Studies, University of Pennsylvania, Philadelphia, 1970 (see also by the same authors, *The Community Action Program in Baltimore City,* published as above).

Lukas, J. A.: "Boss Pollack: He Can't Be There, But He Is," *Reporter,* **27** (July 19, 1962), 35–36.

Martin, Harold H.: "The Case of the Bouncing Mayor," *The Saturday Evening Post,* September 24, 1955, pp. 19 ff (story of Mayor Thomas D'Alesandro).

WASHINGTON, D.C.

NOTE   Information about Washington D.C., as a local community is limited except for reports in the local newspapers. Most of the following bibliography is about the power structures and processes generated by the nation's capital city. There is some overlap, however, between the local and the national structure.

Alsop, Stewart: *The Center, People and Power in Political Washington,* Harper and Row, New York, 1968.

Cater, Douglass: *Power in Washington,* Random House, New York, 1965.

Clark, Joseph S.: *Congress: The Sapless Branch,* Harper and Row, New York, 1965.

Clark, Joseph S.: *The Senate Establishment,* Hill and Wang, New York, 1965.

Dexter, Lewis A.: *How Organizations are Represented in Washington,* Bobbs-Merrill, Indianapolis, 1969.

Dexter, Lewis A.: *Sociology and Politics of Congress,* Rand McNally, Chicago, 1969.

Grayson, Cary T., Jr.: *Washington '68,* Potomac Books, Washington, D.C., 1968.

Green, Constance M.: *The Secret City: Race Relations in the Nation's Capital,* Princeton University Press, Princeton, N.J., 1967.

Mathews, Donald: *U.S. Senators and their Word,* University of North Carolina Press, Chapel Hill, 1960.

Pearson, Drew, and Jack Anderson, *The Case Against Congress,* Simon and Schuster, New York, 1968.

Raymond, Jack: *Power at the Pentagon,* Harper and Row, New York, 1964.

Sorenson, Theodore C.: *Decision Making in the White House,* Columbia University Press, New York, 1963.

White, Theodore: *The Making of the President, 1968,* Atheneum, New York, 1969.

White, Theodore: *The Making of the President, 1972,* Atheneum, New York, 1973.

APPENDICES

A. Major Questionnaires, Accompanying Letters, Mailing History, and Report of Returns

1. *Leadership Interaction and Urban Problem Inventory*
2. *Urban Problem Resurvey*
3. *Decision-Making Inventory of MEGA-Leaders*
4. *Megalopolis Environmental Quality Inventory*
5. *Delaware River Basin Questionnaire*

B. A List of All Instruments Used in Collecting Data on Leader and Organizational Roles in Megalopolis

1. Survey Recording Instruments (4)
2. Diagnostic and Scaled Instruments for Leadership Analysis (10)
3. Organizational Interactional Analysis (3)

C. *Delaware River Basin Interview Schedule and Checklist*

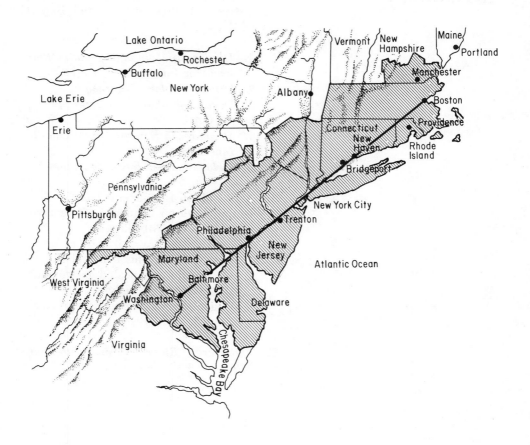

Major Questionnaires,
Accompanying Letters,
Mailing History,
and Report of Returns

1. Leadership Interaction and Urban Problem Inventory

EASTERN LEADERSHIP STUDY directed by Delbert C. Miller, Professor of Sociology and Business Administration, Indiana University, and funded by Resources for the Future, Inc., Washington, D.C.

Field office and mailing address:

Eastern Leadership and Environmental
  Quality Study
Department of Sociology
Indiana University
Bloomington, Indiana 47401

URBAN PROBLEM INTEREST AND AC-TIVITY PATTERN OF CIVIC LEADERS IN THE BOSTON TO WASHINGTON URBAN REGION

1. Check problems in which you have the highest personal interest.
2. Mark the one problem on which you are currently working most intensively.

Note. The researcher is seeking to estimate the degree of interest and current activity pattern of civic leaders engaged in urban problems. All information is confidential and each person will be recorded by code number.

I have most interest in	I am currently working hardest on	Urban Problems
		1. Air pollution
		2. Control of lawlessness and crime
		3. Improvement of public education
		4. Water pollution
		5. Improvement of transport, traffic movement, and parking
		6. Waste (garbage, litter, and dumps)
		7. Improvement or elimination of poor housing: rebuilding of cities
		8. Improvement and maintenance of roads and streets
		9. Planning and zoning of land; preservation (or improvement) of park and other natural areas; beautification
		10. Unemployment and poverty
		11. Race relations
		12. Other (please specify)

In your civic activity on urban problems do you work mainly with leaders associated with (rank in order of the amount of activity):

___ Private voluntary organizations
___ City government agencies
___ State government agencies
___ National government agencies
___ Business organizations
___ Your own firm or organization
___ Universities
___ Independent professionals

LEADERSHIP ACQUAINTANCE AND WORKING RELATIONSHIP INDEX

Please look at the leaders listed. All live and work in the Bos-Wash urban region. Please indicate by ($\sqrt{}$) your acquaintance and civic activity with each. All information is confidential and each person will be recorded by code number.
Note. The researcher is trying to discover the degree of acquaintance and contact in and among such leadership groups as business, labor, politics, religion, and civic affairs in the metropolitan area and the Atlantic urban region.

Name of leader	Acquaintance					Contacts	
	0	1	2	3	4		Worked with him on
						I have had business, civic, or social contacts during last three years	a committee dealing with urban problems during last three years
					Know socially (visit at home or personal contact)		
		Know little (reading or contact)	Know well (reading or contact)				
	Have Don't heard know of						

Boston Leaders (business)

1. Robert Slater

2. Paul C. Cabot

3. Eli Goldstone

4. John M. Fox

5. Roger P. Sonnabend

Boston Leaders (labor)

6. Valentine Murphy

7. Paul Flynn

8. James P. Loughlin

9. Larry Sullivan

10. Salvatore Camilio

Boston Leaders (politics and government) senators, congressmen, and cabinet members have been omitted.

11. John Collins

12. Kevin White

13. Tom Atkins

14. Frank Licht

15. John Winthrop Sears

Name of leader	Acquaintance					Contacts	
	0	1	2	3	4		Worked with him on a committee dealing with urban problems during last three years
	Don't heard know of	Know little (reading or contact)	Know well (reading or contact)	Know socially (visit at home or personal contact)	Have ing or con-	I have had business, civic, or social contacts during last three years	

Boston Leaders (civic affairs civil rights)

16. Melvin King
17. Kenneth Guscott
18. Edward Mason
19. Paul Parks
20. Howard W. Johnson
21. Arthur Schlesinger
22. Nathan Pusey
23. John K. Galbraith
24. James Killian
25. Kingman Brewster

Boston Leaders (religion)

26. Bishop Anson Stokes
27. Reverend James Breeden
28. Reverend James Mathews
29. Reverend Robert Drinan
30. Richard, Cardinal Cushing

New York Leaders (business)

31. Roswell B. Perkins
32. Gustave L. Levy
33. Cornelius W. Owens
34. Thomas S. Gates, Jr.

Name of leader	Acquaintance					Contacts	
	0	1	2	3	4		Worked with him on a committee dealing with urban problems during last three years
	Don't know of	Know little (have heard reading or contact)	Know well (reading or contact)	Know socially (visit at home or personal contact)		I have had business, civic, or social contacts during last three years	
35. Emilio G. Collado							
36. H. I. Romnes							
37. Roger M. Blough							
38. Albert L. Nickerson							
39. Charles F. Luce							
40. Floyd D. Hall							
41. Gilbert W. Fitzhugh							
42. Christian A. Herter, Jr.							
43. James F. Oates, Jr.							
44. Fred J. Borch							
45. Thomas J. Watson, Jr.							
46. C. Douglas Dillon							
47. Andrew Heiskell							
48. George Champion							
49. Frank Stanton							
50. David Rockefeller							

New York Leaders (labor)

Name of leader	Acquaintance					Contacts	
51. Albert Shanker							
52. Peter Brennan							
53. Gus Tyler							
54. Victor Gotbaum							
55. Howard Coughlin							
56. Max Greenberg							
57. Matthew Guinan							
58. Jacob S. Potofsky							

	Acquaintance					Contacts	
	0	1	2	3	4		Worked with him on a committee dealing
						I have had business,	with urban problems during last three years
					Know socially	civic, or contacts during social last three	
			Know little (reading or con-	Know well (reading or con-	(visit at home or personal con-		
Name of leader	Don't heard know of	Have ing or con- tact)	tact)	tact)	tact)	years	years
59. Harry VanArsdale, Jr.							
60. A. Philip Randolph							

New York Leaders (politics and government)

61. Nelson A. Rockefeller							
62. John V. Lindsay							
63. Stanley Steingut							
64. Eugene Nickerson							
65. Herman Badillo							
66. Richard J. Hughes							
67. Percy Sutton							
68. Francis X. Smith							
69. Paul N. Ylvisaker							
70. Paul O'Dwyer							

New York Leaders (religion)

71. Terrence, Cardinal Cooke							
72. Reverend Edler Hawkins							
73. Reverend Milton A. Galamison							
74. Rabbi Marc Tannenbaum							
75. Algernon Black							
76. Monsignor Fox							
77. Reverend L. P. McLaughlin							
78. Reverend Calvin Marshall							
79. Reverend George Younger							

	Acquaintance					Contacts	
	0	1	2	3	4		Worked with him on a committee dealing with urban problems during last three years
Name of leader	Don't heard know of	Have ing or con- tact)	Know little (read- ing or con- tact)	Know well (read- ing or con- tact)	Know socially (visit at home or per- sonal con- tact)	I have had busi- ness, civic, or social contacts during last three years	
80. Reverend Lucius Walker							
New York Leaders (civic affairs and civil rights)							
81. Laurance S. Rockefeller							
82. Arthur J. Goldberg							
83. Bayard Rustin							
84. Whitney Young							
85. Kenneth B. Clark							
86. Roy Wilkins							
87. McGeorge Bundy							
88. Theodore Kheel							
89. Robert C. Weaver							
90. Francis Keppel							
91. Hector Vazquez							
92. I. Ted Velez							
93. Alan Pifer							
94. Charles Abrams							
95. John Doar							
96. T. George Silcott							
97. Franklin A. Thomas							
98. Arthur Ochs Sulzberger							
99. Wallace S. Sayre							
100. Roy Innis							

Name of leader	Acquaintance					Contacts	
	0	1	2	3	4	I have had business, civic, or social contacts during last three years	Worked with him on a committee dealing with urban problems during last three years
	Don't heard know of	Know little (reading or contact)	Know well (reading or contact)	Know socially (visit at home or personal contact)		

Philadelphia Leaders (business)

101.	Crawford H. Greenwalt
102.	John R. Bunting
103.	William L. Day
104.	R. Stewart Rauch, Jr.
105.	John P. Bracken
106.	Gustave G. Amsterdam
107.	Richard C. Bond
108.	Stuart T. Saunders
109.	Robert M. Wachob
110.	Thomas B. McCabe

Philadelphia Leaders (labor)

111.	William Ross
112.	James Jones
113.	Edward F. Toohey
114.	Anthony Cortigene
115.	James J. Loughlin

Philadelphia Leaders (politics and government)

116.	Richardson Dilworth
117.	James H. J. Tate
118.	Arlen Specter
119.	Paul D'Ortona
120.	Joseph Clark

	Acquaintance					Contacts	
	0	1	2	3	4		Worked with him on a committee dealing with urban problems during last three years
					Know socially (visit at home or personal contact)	I have had business, civic, or social contacts during last three years	
			Know well (reading or contact)				
		Know little (reading or contact)					
	Don't heard know of	Have contact)					

Philadelphia Leaders (religion)

121.	Paul M. Washington							
122.	Bishop John Bright							
123.	Reverend Leon Sullivan							
124.	Reverend Robert L. DeWitt							
125.	John Cardinal Krol							

Philadelphia Leaders (civic affairs and civil rights)

126.	William L. Rafsky							
127.	Herman Wrice							
128.	Gaylord P. Harnwell							
129.	Maurice B. Fagan							
130.	Millard E. Gladfelter							
131.	Clarence Farmer							
132.	Samuel Evans							
133.	Mrs. Albert M. Greenfield							
134.	Raymond Pace Alexander							
135.	Walter Phillips							

Baltimore Leaders (business)

136.	Robert Levi							
137.	Nicholas V. Petrou							
138.	William Boucher III							
139.	Walter Sondheim, Jr.							
140.	James Rouse							

	Acquaintance					Contacts	
	0	1	2	3	4		Worked with him on
						I have had busi-ness,	a com-mittee dealing with
				Know	socially	civic, or	urban
			Know	well	(visit at	social	prob-
			little	(read-	home	contacts	lems
			(read-	ing or	or per-	during	during
		Have	ing or	con-	sonal	last	last
	Don't	heard	con-	tact)	con-	three	three
	know	of	tact)	Know	tact)	years	years

Baltimore Leaders (labor)

141. Dominic Fornaro

142. Jacob J. Edleman

143. Edward Gutman

144. Jacob Blum

145. Charles A. Della

Baltimore Leaders (politics
and government)

146. Samuel Daniels

147. Robert Embry

148. Edgar Ewing

149. Thomas J. D'Alesandro, Jr.

150. Theodore R. McKeldin

Baltimore Leaders (religion)

151. Frederick J. Hanna

152. Vernon N. Dobson

153. Marion C. Bascom

154. Rabbi Morris Lieberman

155. Laurence, Cardinal Shehan

Baltimore Leaders civic affairs
and civil rights

156. Milton Eisenhower

157. Parren Mitchell

	Acquaintance					Contacts
	0	1	2	3	4	
	Don't heard know of	Have ing or con- tact)	Know little (read- ing or con- tact)	Know well (read- ing or con- tact)	Know socially (visit at home or per- sonal con- tact)	I have had busi- ness, civic, or social contacts during last three years	Worked with him on a com- mittee dealing with urban prob- lems during last three years

158. Homer Favor

159. Mrs. Joseph Levi

160. Furman Templeton

161. George Gelston

162. Mrs. Juanita Mitchell

163. Eugene M. Feinblatt

164. Walter Lively

165. Lincoln Gordon

Washington Leaders (business)

166. George Olmsted

167. Thornton W. Owen

168. L. A. Jennings

169. William Calomiris

170. Stephen Ailes

Washington Leaders (labor)

171. P. I. Siemiller

172. Jacob Clayman

173. Joseph D. Keenan

174. Paul Jennings

175. George Meany

176. James A. Suffridge

177. David Sullivan

178. Andrew J. Biemiller

179. Jerry Wurf

180. Joseph A. Beirne

Washington Leaders (politics
  and government)

181.	Channing Phillips
182.	Flaxie Pinkett
183.	Walter E. Washington
184.	John W. Macy, Jr.
185.	Frederick A. Babson

Washington Leaders (religion)

186.	Bishop Paul Moore, Jr.
187.	Reverend Philip R. Newell, Jr.
188.	Rabbi Richard G. Hirsch
189.	Bishop Smallwood Williams
190.	Reverend Walter E. Fauntroy

Washington Leaders (civic affairs
  and civil rights)

191.	Carl Shipley
192.	Kermit Gordon
193.	H. Carl Moultrie
194.	Mrs. David Scull
195.	G. Franklin Edwards
196.	Carl T. Rowan
197.	Clarence Mitchell, Jr.
198.	Sterling Tucker
199.	Marion Barry
200.	John W. Gardner

NOW PLEASE LOOK OVER THE LIST AND NOMINATE 25 LEADERS THAT COULD BEST REPRESENT THE BOSTON TO WASHINGTON URBAN REGION IN THE SHAPING OF URBAN POLICY AND PROGRAMMING FOR THE REGION.

Simply put the NUMBERS of your nominees here. See list. The order is not important. (All information is confidential and each person will be recorded by code number only. This information is for research purposes only.)

Other names not on the list to which you would give higher priority. (Please do not name senators, congressman, or cabinet members. They have been omitted.)

In my choices I have given most weight to the criterion that states the following:

___ A leader should be able to work with other business, labor, government, religious, and civic leaders.

___ A leader should commit himself to the work required.

___ A leader should be able and willing to influence others.

For me the most valuble contacts dealing with urban problems in civic work and policy making have generally been with leaders from (rank 1 through 5)

___ BUSINESS   ___ LABOR   ___ POLITICS-GOVERNMENT   ___ RELIGION
___ CIVIC AFFAIRS

My most frequent to least frequent contacts with *groups of leaders* can be ranked 1 through 5 as (1 equals most frequent)

___ BUSINESS   ___ LABOR   ___ POLITICS-GOVERNMENT   ___ RELIGION
___ CIVIC AFFAIRS

My best to poorest knowledge of leaders and organizations *in the major cities* of the Atlantic urban region can be ranked from 1 through 5 as

___ BOSTON   ___ NEW YORK   ___ PHILADELPHIA   ___ BALTIMORE
___ WASHINGTON

In civic activity do you personally find it most rewarding to work at the

___ LOCAL LEVEL ___ STATE LEVEL ___ NATIONAL LEVEL ___ ALL THREE

I find that I can be most effective in civic policy making

___ in face to face contact with another person
___ on the telephone
___ in letters
___ in committee activity
___ by talking to large groups
___ by talking with small groups of leaders meeting informally

As you watch different issues of high importance develop in urban life would you say that leaders generally change according to the issue or that the same group generally makes the decisions, regardless of the issue?

___ Leaders generally change with the issue at stake.
___ Same group of leaders generally makes the decisions, regardless of the issue.
   COMMENTS:

Thank you for your assistance. A report will be mailed to you as soon as a summary is possible. Reference to persons will be made only by a confidential code number.

Delbert C. Miller

Letter from Delbert C. Miller accompanying the Leadership Study:

Eastern Leadership and Environmental Quality Study

DEPARTMENT OF SOCIOLOGY — INDIANA UNIVERSITY
BLOOMINGTON, INDIANA 47401

Sponsored by
RESOURCES FOR THE FUTURE
1755 Massachusetts Avenue, N.W.
Washington, D. C. 20036

My teamworkers and I have just completed eight months of intensive interviewing of leaders and organizations in the cities of Boston, New York, Philadelphia, Baltimore and Washington. We have sought to identify influential leaders and organizations that are active in urban problems. The list shown in the questionnaire contains 200 leaders; another 200 could have been added.

The purpose has been to find out if there is any *regional identity—a viable community of interest stretching from Boston to Washington.* A partial answer would be forthcoming if the acquaintance and contacts of leaders in this highly urbanized area were known.

Some leaders say that many segments of American life have been out of touch with one another—and, in many cities, are still out of touch. Is this true? I would like to contribute to social science research more adequate information about leadership communication and the human boundaries of Megalopolis.

I am completely dependent on your help. Your answers to the questions enclosed will make it possible to ASSESS LEADERSHIP IN THE EAST AS IT HAS NEVER BEEN DONE BEFORE. You are a leader identified by the panels of knowledgeable persons as of high importance in the life of your city and the Eastern region. Your knowledge (and contacts with other leaders) is basic for this study.

The search is for a better way of solving problems. Behind the effort is a critical question. Can Americans develop the capacity to organize and work in coalitions and interstate or regional compacts if urban problems demand them? My research sponsor, *Resources for the Future*, would like an answer as it pertains to problems of water quality and air pollution. Other urban problems pose the same question.

The questionnaire can be completed in less than 15 minutes. All data will be held in strict confidence. *Each person will be recorded by a code number and any publication will list only an anonymous number.* The analysis is carried out on a university campus and no access will be permitted to the data—not even to our sponsor.

Please take time to fill out the questionnaire. This could be the most effective contribution you could make to urban problems in a brief allocation of time. We need your experience and each missing name will weaken the research. A stamped addressed envelope is enclosed for your use. A report of the results will be made to you in midsummer 1969.

MAILING HISTORY AND REPORT OF RETURNS FOR THE LEADERSHIP
INTERACTION AND URBAN PROBLEM INVENTORY

Three mailings were made. The first complete mailing was sent to all 200 key and 200 top leaders on April 11, 1969. A follow-up mailing went to those leaders who had not answered 18 days later (April 29). Another follow-up mailing was made 15 days later (May 14). In each follow-up a short appeal for a return was attached to another copy of tthe questionnaire. Each mailing tended to produce a net cumulative effect. On May 21, five weeks after the initial mailing, the record of returns stood as follows:

	Number of returned questionnaires	Proportion of total population
Key leaders	74	37 percent
Top leaders	52	26 percent

Questionnaires continued to arrive throughout June and until July 2. Analysis was begun shortly thereafter. The record of returned questionnaires had increased with the following final record:

	Number of returned questionnaires	Proportion of total population
Key leaders	100	50 percent
Top leaders	78	39 percent

Two more questionnaires were returned, one in late August, the other in October. These leaders had been out of the country when the questionnaires were sent out and were completed on their return.

The final returns are gratifying. This was no ordinary population. The leaders were among the most important in Megalopolis and probably the busiest. The questionnaire reached persons who could not have been easily interviewed. All had offices at some central point, but many were more likely to be away from them than in them. Busy people can "sandwich" questionnaires into their schedules (probably when they answer their mail) when they cannot (or will not) yield valuable interview time.

Some researchers have suggested that a telephone call could have been used effectively either as a follow-up or for actually seeking an interview. This would have required extensive long-distance telephoning. The length and character of the questionnaire argued against it. We know that in many cases it would not have succeeded; for example, letters were received from aides of leaders like John Lindsay and Nelson Rockefeller in which they stated that their chiefs could not devote time to research inquires, not matter how deserving, because of the press of other compelling administrative responsibilities.

The final response pattern is shown in Table A-1, which provides a breakdown of responses of key and top leaders from the business, labor, political-governmental, religious, and civic sectors in each of the five major cities of Megalopolis. A number of findings have significance for future researchers.

TABLE A.1 RESPONSE PATTERN OF KEY AND TOP LEADERS BY OCCUPATIONAL GROUPING AND MAJOR URBAN AREA, MAY 1969 TO LEADERSHIP INTERACTION and URBAN PROBLEM INVENTORY (10-page questionnaire, $N = 176$)

Urban region	Type of leader	Business			Labor			Politics-government			Religion			Civic affairs			Totals by city		
		N	max	%	N	max	%	N	max	%	N	max	%	N	max	%	N	max	%
Boston	Key	5	5	100	3	5	60	2	5	40	4	5	80	6	10	60	20	30	67
	Top	1	5	20	1	5	20	2	5	40	2	5	40	2	10	20	8	30	27
New York	Key	6	20	30	4	10	40	3	10	30	8	10	80	5	20	25	26	70	37
	Top	4	20	20	3	10	30	0	10	0	3	10	30	4	20	20	14	70	20
Philadelphia	Key	5	10	50	3	5	60	2	5	40	3	5	60	8	10	80	21	35	60
	Top	5	10	50	3	5	60	1	5	20	4	5	80	6	10	60	19	35	54
Baltimore	Key	5	5	100	5	5	100	2	5	40	3	5	60	5	10	50	20	30	67
	Top	2	5	40	5	5	100	4	5	80	3	5	60	8	10	80	22	30	73
Washington	Key	2	5	40	3	10	30	4	5	80	2	5	40	2	10	20	13	35	37
	Top	0	5	0	6	10	60	0	5	0	2	5	40	7	10	70	15	35	43
Totals by occupation	Key	23	45	51	18	35	51	13	30	43	20	30	67	26	60	43	100	200	50
	Top	12	45	27	18	35	51	7	30	23	14	30	47	27	60	45	78	200	39

1. Key leaders responded in greater percentage (50 percent) than top leaders (39 percent). The best explanation is that the questionnaire carried the names of all key leaders, which is perhaps a unique situation because every key leader could see his own name and the name of every other key leader who was receiving the questionnaire. It is believed that this facilitated response. Top leaders were asked to respond to their interactions with *key* leaders. They did not know the names of the other top leaders.

2. In frequency of return the following leaders ranked from high to low religion, labor, civic affairs, business, politics-government.

3. In frequency of return the following cities ranked from high to low: Baltimore, Philadelphia, Boston, Washington, New York.

These three findings can provide predictive probabilities to future researchers of Megalopolis and may be generalized to the occupational groupings of leadership populations in the urban areas of the United States.

2. Urban Problem Resurvey

Eastern Leadership and Environmental Quality Study

Field Office: DEPARTMENT OF SOCIOLOGY — INDIANA UNIVERSITY
                            BLOOMINGTON, INDIANA 47401
                                                    Sponsored by
                                                    RESOURCES FOR THE FUTURE
                                                    1755 Massachusetts Avenue, N.W.
                                                    Washington, D. C. 20036

URBAN PROBLEM INTEREST AND ACTIVITY PATTERN OF CIVIC LEADERS
IN THE BOSTON TO WASHINGTON URBAN REGION

1. Check problems in which you have the highest personal interest.
2. Mark the *one* problem on which you are currently working most intensively.

Note. The researcher is seeking to estimate the degree of interest and current activity pattern of civic leaders engaged in urban problems. All information is confidential and each person will be recorded by code number.

Have you changed your interest and activity in urban problems during the last year?

Yes   No

If yes, what interests and activity have changed?

INTEREST CHANGES   ACTIVITY CHANGES
(indicate by number of problem
shown on p. 366)

How would you account for these changes?

Letter from Delbert C. Miller accompanying Urban Problem Resurvey:

Eastern Leadership and Environmental Quality Study

BLOOMINGTON, INDIANA 47401

Field Office: DEPARTMENT OF SOCIOLOGY — INDIANA UNIVERSITY

Sponsored by
RESOURCES FOR THE FUTURE
1755 Massachusetts Avenue, N.W.
Washington, D. C. 20036

Dear Citizen of Megalopolis:

In April 1969 I sent a questionnaire to 400 top leaders of Megalopolis I had identified by polling expert judges in Boston, New York, Philadelphia, Baltimore, and Washington. You were one of those leaders.

I have completed various phase of my research and have sent you a brief report of my findings. A more definitive report is in the printing office and a copy will be sent to you in the next few weeks.

You will recall that I have been searching for answers to these questions:

Who are the business, labor, political, religious, and civic leaders of this region?

What are the urban problem interests of these leaders?

Do leaders know one another—in their own cities? In the various major cities of the region?

Are leaders working together on urban problems—from Boston to New York to Philadelphia to Baltimore to Washington?

Now, I am seeking the answer to another question:

HAVE THERE BEEN ANY CHANGES IN URBAN PROBLEM INTEREST AND ACTIVITY AMONG TOP LEADERS OF MEGALOPOLIS DURING THE LAST YEAR?

Please help me find an answer to this question by completing the one-page follow-up questionnaire that is enclosed. It can be filled out in 2 to 3 minutes. All data will be held in strict confidence. Each person will be recorded by a code number and any publication will list only an anonymous number. The analysis is carried out on a university campus and no access will be permitted to the data—not even to our sponsor.

A report of these results will be made to you in a few weeks. It will tell you what leaders are doing now and what changes have occurred in urban interest and activity. Please respond even if you were not among the less silent majority who answered on the first round.

MAILING HISTORY AND REPORT OF RETURNS FOR THE URBAN PROBLEM RESURVEY

Two mailings were made of the urban problem resurvey. The first was sent to all 200 key and 200 top leaders on June 23, 1970. Three weeks later, on July 14, a follow-up mailing was made. The record of returns for the two mailings show the following:

	First mailing	Proportion of returns
Key Leaders	68	34 percent
Top Leaders	58	29 percent

	Second mailing	Proportion of returns
Key Leaders	12	6 percent
Top Leaders	29	15 percent

Total return from key leaders = 80, a 40 percent return.
Total return from top leaders = 87, a 44 percent return.

Note that returns are lower for key leaders (40 percent) and higher for top leaders (44 percent). This time the names of key leaders were not carried on the questionnaire. The response rate is down 10 percent and the questionnaire is much shorter—a simple one-page sheet. On the other hand, the top leaders responded with a close proportion to the earlier survey (44 percent compared with 39 percent).

Although a higher rate of return might have been predicted for the much shorter questionnaire, the reason for the actual return is probably due to the content of the urban problem resurvey. Its purpose was to determine changes in problem interest and activity in the 14-month interval. As subsequent findings showed, leaders generally made no important changes and were probably not challenged to answer such inquiries.

The final response pattern is shown in Table A.2, which provides a breakdown of responses from key and top leaders (as shown in Table A.1) to those from the business, labor, political-governmental, religious, and civic sectors in each of the five major cities of Megalopolis. A number of findings have significance in validating the response patterns established 14 months earlier.

1. Ranking hierarchies established by response from the occupational groupings of leaders showed high similarity:

RANKING HIERARCHY OF QUESTIONNAIRE RETURNS BY OCCUPATIONAL GROUPING, KEY AND TOP LEADERS, 1969 AND 1970

1969	1970
Religion (highest)	Religion
Labor	Business
Business	Civic affairs
Civic affairs	Politics-government
Politics-government (lowest)	Labor

TABLE A.2 RESPONSE PATTERN OF KEY AND TOP LEADERS BY OCCUPATIONAL GROUPS AND MAJOR URBAN AREAS, JULY 1970 TO URBAN PROBLEM INTEREST AND ACTIVITY PATTERN SURVEY (1-page questionnaire; $N = 167$)

Urban region	Type of leader	Business			Labor			Politics government			Religion			Civic affairs			Totals by city		
		N	N max	%	N	N max	%	N	N max	%	N	N max	%	N	N max	%	N	N max	%
Boston	Key	3	5	60	2	5	40	3	5	60	4	5	80	3	10	30	15	30	50
	Top	1	5	20	1	5	20	1	5	20	4	5	80	5	10	50	12	30	40
New York	Key	5	20	20	0	10	0	1	10	10	7	10	70	5	20	20	18	70	26
	Top	7	20	35	3	10	30	3	10	30	3	10	30	10	20	50	26	70	37
Philadelphia	Key	5	10	50	1	5	20	3	5	60	4	5	80	7	10	70	20	35	57
	Top	7	10	70	3	5	60	1	5	20	4	5	80	3	10	30	18	35	51
Baltimore	Key	5	5	100	4	5	80	2	5	40	2	5	40	6	10	60	19	30	63
	Top	4	5	80	3	5	60	3	5	60	2	5	40	6	10	60	18	30	60
Washington	Key	3	5	60	1	10	10	2	5	40	1	5	20	1	10	10	8	35	23
	Top	1	5	20	5	10	50	2	5	40	3	5	60	2	10	20	13	35	37
Totals by occupation	Key	21	45	47	8	35	23	11	30	37	18	30	60	22	60	37	80	200	40
	Top	20	45	44	15	35	43	10	30	30	16	30	53	26	60	43	87	200	44

Note that religious leaders have the highest response in both years. Business-civic and political-governmental leaders rank in high similarity. Labor provides the major shift. Labor dropped from second to fifth position. Because the re-survey focused solely on urban problem activity, it may be that local labor leaders are not strongly committed to urban problems in general or, at least, are diverted by their high concern with economic bargaining.

2. Ranking hierarchies by cities established a similar pattern:

RANKING HIERARCHY ON RESPONSE
RETURNS BY CITIES, KEY AND TOP
LEADERS, 1969 AND 1970

1969	1970
Baltimore (highest)	Baltimore
Philadelphia	Philadelphia
Boston	Boston
Washington	New York
New York (lowest)	Washington

Baltimore, Philadelphia, and Boston remained in their respective positions— 1, 2, and 3. Washington and New York changed theirs in the two lowest rankings:

3. Decision-Making Inventory of MEGA-Leaders

Eastern Leadership and Environmental Quality Study

Field Office   DEPARTMENT OF SOCIOLOGY — INDIANA UNIVERSITY
                                 BLOOMINGTON, INDIANA 47401
                                              Sponsored by
                                              RESOURCES FOR THE FUTURE
                                              1755 Massachusetts Avenue, N.W.
                                              Washington, D. C. 20036

1. You have indicated to us that you are active in trying to get something done about certain urban problems. What have you worked on most during the last three years? Please check that problem.

___ UNEMPLOYMENT AND POVERTY   ___ RACE RELATIONS
___ EDUCATION ___ HOUSING ___ CRIME ___ PLANNING AND ZONING
___ ENVIRONMENTAL POLLUTION
___ OTHER (SPECIFY)

2. With what persons on the list of Eastern leaders (see pp. 367-376) have you communicated about this problem or worked on committees or projects during the last three years? Please underline names on the list and add others that apply. (This information will be held in strict confidence.)

3.   From the list of persons with whom you have worked please name four people who you think have been most influential and describe their principal contributions.

4.   Please tell me what you have tried to accomplish.

5.   Would you say that your interest and activity has been primarily

___ LOCAL   ___ STATE   ___ INTERSTATE-REGIONAL
___ NATIONAL   ___ ALL LEVELS

6.   What did you do to get things done?

_____ Direct contact with key governmental leaders
_____ Direct contact with key business leaders
_____ Direct contact with key labor leaders
_____ Direct contact with key religious leaders
_____ Direct contact with key civic and civil rights leaders
_____ Testifying before special committees or public hearings
_____ Raise money
_____ Organizing mass citizen support (radio, TV, telephone, newspapers, etc.)
_____ Lobbying at state or federal levels
_____ Working through organizations
_____ Others (please specify)

Comment:

7.   If you have worked with organizations, please check the list (see p. 193) and note their contributions briefly.

Organization (list number)   Contribution

8.   What was the nature of the opposition you encountered?

9.   What did you do to counteract this opposition?

10. What have you accomplished?

11. How would you rate your accomplishments in getting results?

___ VERY EFFECTIVE   ___ EFFECTIVE   ___ SOMEWHAT EFFECTIVE
___ NOT EFFECTIVE AT ALL

12. What was the pattern of action—the important events or actions that influenced the outcome of your efforts?

13. What sources of power and influence do you consider most important for leaders who have tried to be effective in working on the problem you have indicated?

14. What specific experiences have you had that illustrate the importance of these power sources?

15. If you were responsible for assembling the strongest task force to work on the urban problem you have discussed and were asked to pull together leaders and organizations located in Eastern Megalopolis, what would your choices be? Please look at the lists of persons and organizations and enter the numbers of your choices (again, see pp. 367-376, 193).

Leaders	Organizations
Number _____	Number _____
Number _____	Number _____
Number _____	Number _____
Number _____	Number _____
Number _____	Number _____
Number _____	Number _____
Number _____	
Number _____	Others not listed:
Number _____	

Others not listed:

16. The issues listed below are in connection with the policy and administration of urban problem agencies and organizations. For the issues in which you have been involved please indicate how active you were.

	Very Active	Active	Not involved
(1) Metropolitan area government or planning with the issue:			
(a) strong support of central city versus			
(b) strong support of suburbs.			
(2) Revenue sharing by the Federal Government with the issue:			
(a) bloc grants to states versus (b) specific program grants to cities.			
(3) Community participation and control of public organizations and institutions with the issue:			
(a) centralized versus (b) decentralized control of schools, poverty programs, etc.			
(4) Executive control of organizations by direct line control or representative coalition of community members with the issue (a) agency-directed versus (b) coalition-directed policy formulation and administration [exemplified in National Alliance of Businessmen (business directed) and Urban Coalition (directed by representatives of business, labor, government, religion, and civil rights)].			

(5) Other (please specify)

17. Please select an issue on which you have been active and describe your position.

Issue No. (   )

18. How did you attempt to influence the outcome of the issue?

19. Can you give the names of three or four leaders and organizations on the lists of leaders and organizations who you know have participated and were generally in favor of the (a) side of the issue?

Leaders   Organizations

Others (not listed)   Others (not listed)

20. Can you give the names of three or four leaders or organizations on the lists of leaders and organizations who you know have actively participated and were generally supportive of the (b) side of the issue?

Leaders   Organizations

Others (not listed)   Others (not listed)

YOU HAVE FINISHED. THANK YOU VERY MUCH. Please return all the pages of your questionnaire.

MAILING HISTORY AND REPORT OF RETURNS FOR THE
DECISION-MAKING INVENTORY OF MEGA LEADERS

This questionnaire was sent to 80 key and top leaders who had the highest scores on interaction between other key and top leaders in different cities of Megalopolis.

Two mailings were made. The first was completed on June 1, 1971. A follow-up was sent out one month later. Fifty-two completed questionnaires were received (68 percent). This return was better than those recorded for the *Leadership Interaction and Urban Problem Inventory* and the *Urban Problem Resurvey*. Various reasons can be given. The population was specially selected, as the accompanying letter pointed out: "The analysis of the data shows that you are one of the most active of the 200 key leaders in our sample. You emerged as the kind of leader that other leaders turn to."

This important appeal suggested that the researcher had made a serious *continuing* research effort. The letter also stated that, "since the fall of 1968 my co-

Letter from Delbert C. Miller accompanying Decision Making Inventory:

Eastern Leadership and Environmental Quality Study

Field Office: DEPARTMENT OF SOCIOLOGY — INDIANA UNIVERSITY
BLOOMINGTON, INDIANA 47401

JUNE 1, 1971

Sponsored by
RESOURCES FOR THE FUTURE
1755 Massachusetts Avenue, N.W.
Washington, D. C. 20036

Since the fall of 1968 my coworkers and I have been working on a study of urban problems as they relate to the Eastern Seaboard. We have identified influential leaders and organizations active in Boston, New York, Philadelphia, Baltimore, and Washington.

You have assisted us graciously by answering our questionnaires in 1969 and 1970 and we have sent you two reports of our research.

Our analysis of the data shows that you are one of the most active of the 200 key leaders in our sample. You emerged as the kind of leader other key leaders turn to.

You are now central to our study. I need to learn more about how leaders get things done on specific problems. Please help me with the attached schedule. I wish I could sit down and discuss these matters with you. Because I cannot I have set down what my questions would have been if you had granted me an interview.

The search is for a better way of solving problems. Already your assistance has helped me to transmit new knowledge. I have published numerous articles for professionals, a small book for environmental quality specialists, two handbooks for active social leaders, and have made numerous addresses. Now I want to know more about the way Eastern leaders get things done, especially when they are drawn in from the major cities.

The questionnaire can be completed in less than 15 minutes. All data past, will be held in strict confidence. Each person will be recorded by a code number and any publication will list only an anonymous number. The analysis is carried out on a university campus and no access will be permitted to the data—not even to our sponsor.

Professor Jean Gottman of France, who has made the only study of Eastern Megalopolis, has just written me that no one has studied the total area since he completed his study in 1961. More knowledge of the Eastern Seaboard as a region awaits on the willingness of leaders like you to assist in this research.

I need your experience in order to tie all of my previous findings together and should like to hear from all of you. I will keep you informed of results.

workers and I have been working on a study of urban problems as they relate to the Eastern Seaboard." "You assisted us in 1969 and 1970." "You are now central to our study. I need to learn more about how leaders get things done on specific problems." "Already your assistance has helped me to transmit new knowledge."

Other features in the appeal included the following:

> The short time required ("less than 15 minutes")
> Confidentiality
> Lack of research on Eastern Megalopolis
> Importance of tying research together
> Contribution that the leader can make
> Report of results promised
> University and RFF sponsorship

What seems most crucial is that the population was identified as select and that each leader was being asked to contribute to a research effort in which he had a continuing part. It should be pointed out the researcher was making a third consecutive contact with a special group of leaders singled out for their knowledge. Most of them answered the first two questionnaires sent to 200 key and 200 top urban-oriented leaders of Megalopolis.

4. Megalopolis Environmental Quality Inventory

QUESTIONNAIRE ON ENVIRONMENTAL QUALITY

Please express your opinion about the following questions:

1. Below is a list of problems that prevail in varying degrees in the Boston to Washington urban region.

(a) Please indicate in rank order (1 to 11) the urgency or priority that your organization assigns to the solution of these problems
(b) Check those problems that your organization has worked on during the last three years.

(The list reproduced here was the same as that shown in the Leadership Interaction and Urban Survey on p. 366.)

Note. If your organization has not been engaged in the solution of problems concerning air pollution, water pollution, or solid wastes, please check here and return the questionnaire ___. You need not answer the other questions.

2. Has your organization a unified program that combines problems of air pollution, water pollution, solid wastes, and/or others?

___ YES ___ NO   If yes, what is included in the program?

3. If you have specialized staff personnel working on environmental quality questions, indicate how many.

___ AIR POLLUTION   ___ WATER POLLUTION
___ SOLID WASTE PROBLEMS   ___ A COMBINED PROGRAM

4. About what percentage of your staff time is devoted to environmental quality questions?

___ AIR POLLUTION   ___ WATER POLLUTION
___ SOLID WASTE PROBLEMS   ___ A COMBINED PROGRAM

5. About what percentage of your organization's total budget is devoted to environmental quality questions?

___ AIR POLLUTION   ___ WATER POLLUTION
___ SOLID WASTE PROBLEMS   ___ A COMBINED PROGRAM

6. Has the activity of your organization been primarily on the local, state, interstate, or national level? Check the appropriate blanks.

	Water pollution	Air pollution	Solid waste problems
Local			
State			
Regional-Interstate			
National			

7. Which of the following would be included in a description of your program emphasis?

___ Advisory	offering expert opinion on environmental quality or related questions
___ Research	inquiry or investigation into environmental quality questions to uncover facts and working principles
___ Education	the dissemination of facts and considerations about environmental quality
___ Action oriented	actively working to make a particular point of view felt in public decisions on environmental quality
___ Other (please specify)	

8. Listed below are a few of the activities in which organizations that are active in environmental quality public policy decisions sometimes engage. Check those in which your organization has participated in the last three years.

Testifying at public hearings

___ AIR POLLUTION   ___ WATER POLLUTION   ___ SOLID WASTES

Testifying before congressional committees, state legislative committees, and committees at the local level

___ AIR POLLUTION   ___ WATER POLLUTION   ___ SOLID WASTES

Encouraging members of the organization to send letters to congressmen, state legislators, and other governmental personnel

___ AIR POLLUTION   ___ WATER POLLUTION   ___ SOLID WASTES

Publishing a newsletter that informs recipients about current issues, programs, and innovations in the environmental quality field

___ AIR POLLUTION   ___ WATER POLLUTION   ___ SOLID WASTES

Doing research on technical, economic, or political aspects of environmental quality

___ AIR POLLUTION   ___ WATER POLLUTION   ___ SOLID WASTES

Publish brochures and other material about your organization's efforts toward the improvement of environmental quality

___ AIR POLLUTION   ___ WATER POLLUTION   ___ SOLID WASTES

Providing financial assistance for research work of other organizations directly or indirectly

___ AIR POLLUTION   ___ WATER POLLUTION   ___ SOLID WASTES

Membership in an association or federation that is "action oriented" to express your interests on environmental qualtiy

___ AIR POLLUTION   ___ WATER POLLUTION   ___ SOLID WASTES

Participating in an advisory agency or committee and/or task force to a governmental committee

___ AIR POLLUTION   ___ WATER POLLUTION   ___ SOLID WASTES

Preparing detailed statements concerning environmental quality issues such as the level of quality or how best to achieve a given level of quality, etc.

___ AIR POLLUTION   ___ WATER POLLUTION   ___ SOLID WASTES

Publishing a professional journal in which technical aspects of environmental quality are discussed

___ AIR POLLUTION   ___ WATER POLLUTION   ___ SOLID WASTES

Newspaper or other journal advertising concerning activities to support, oppose, or amend environmental quality recommendations

___ AIR POLLUTION   ___ WATER POLLUTION   ___ SOLID WASTES

Lobbying in Congress, in state legislatures, or at the local level

___ AIR POLLUTION   ___ WATER POLLUTION   ___ SOLID WASTES

9. For the organizations listed in the chart please complete the following operations:

(a) In column 1 indicate by a check mark those organizations with which your organizations has a close "identity of interest."

(b) In columns 2 through 6 check those boxes that best describe the nature of any contacts that your organization has had with these organizations during the last three years.

Name of organization	(1) Identity of interest	(2) Know about their work	(3) Have approached or have been approached for information	(4) Have exchanged ideas about environmental quality issues	(5) Have worked together on program development	(6) Have supported one another on issues (please name issue)
Citizen's Committee on Natural Resources						
National Park Service of the U.S. Government						
Forest Service of the U.S. Government						
U.S. Chamber of Commerce Pollution Committee						
National Audubon Society						
National Association of Manufacturers						
National Coal Association						
Bureau of Sport Fisheries and Wildlife						
Atomic Energy Commission						
Interstate Sanitation Commission						
National Wildlife Federation						
Regional Plan Association						
Bureau of Outdoor Recreation (New York)						
Bureau of the Budget						

	(1) Identity of interest	(2) Know about their work	(3) Have approached or have been approached for information	(4) Have exchanged ideas about environmental quality issues	(5) Have worked together on program development	(6) Have supported one another on issues (please name issue)
Army Corps of Engineers						
Federal Water Pollution Control Administration						
National Parks Association						
Izaak Walton League of America						
Sierra Club						
American Petroleum Institute						
The Conservation Foundation						
League of Women Voters of the United States						
National League of Cities						
U.S. Senate Committee on Interior and Insular Affairs						
U.S. House of Representatives Committee on Science and Astronautics						
Senate Committee on Public Works						
National Air Pollution Control Administration						

10. In which of the following environmental quality "problem sheds" has your organization had an active concern in the last three years?

Water pollution in

___ the Connecticut River Basin
___ the Delaware River Basin

___ the Susquehanna River Basin
___ the Hudson River Basin
___ the Potomac River Basin
___ the Northeastern urban region in general (Boston to Washington)
___ the nation in general
___ Others:

Air pollution in

___ the Boston metropolitan area
___ the New York metropolitan area
___ the Philadelphia metropolitan area (the Delaware Valley)
___ the Baltimore-Washington metropolitan area
___ the Northeastern urban region in general (Boston to Washington)
___ the nation in general
___ Others:

Solid waste problems in

___ the Boston metropolitan area
___ the New York metropolitan area
___ the Philadelphia metropolitan area (the Delaware Valley)
___ the Baltimore-Washington metropolitan area
___ the Northeastern urban region in general (Boston to Washington)
___ the nation in general
___ Others:

Questions 11 through 15 are related to the organization and administration of a water management agency for a river basin as a whole. Assume that the region in which water quality is a problem involves a multicounty, interstate region, such as the Delaware, Hudson, Potomac, or Connecticut river basins.

11. If an agency were set up to deal with the question of water quality management, which of the following best describes the "range of responsibilities" that you feel is most advisable? check one alternative.

___ Data collection, research, and establishment and enforcement of water quality standards
___ Those powers stated above and the powers for planning of facilities and measures to improve water quality, such as reservoirs to provide dilution water and waste treatment plants
___ All powers stated above and the powers to finance and construct facilities such as waste treatment plants
___ All powers stated above and the powers for the operation of facilities and montoring networks, authority to levy charges on effluents and/or water withdrawals (sell water)
___ All powers stated above, but within an agency with responsibility for all facets or aspects of water resources management, including—in addition to water quality management—flood damage reduction, water supply, navigation, water-based recreation, hydropower, etc.
___ No agency necessary

12. What kind of agency would you prefer to have perform the range of functions you have designated in the preceding question?

___ Parallel agencies (i.e., with some responsibilities and authorities) in each of the affected states
___ Regional interstate agency
___ Interstate-federal agency
___ Federal agency
___ Other (please specify)

13. For the kind of agency you have designated, should the members of the governing board be

___ elected by the people within the area of jurisdiction of the agency
___ appointed by the governors of the states involved
___ appointed by the President of the United States
___ appointed by the President and by the governors of the respective states
___ the regularly elected governors of the states involved
___ Cabinet officials of the states involved, when such officials have special competence in water (or air) management, such as the head of the health department
___ Congressmen from the congressional districts within the agency's area of jurisdiction
___ Some combination of the above, such as part of the board appointed by the governors and part elected by the people within the area
___ Other (please specify)

14. Assuming that the level of water quality instream to be achieved (or desired) has been selected, which of the following means of controlling waste discharges do you favor?

___ Voluntary control by individual plants and municipalities
___ No limitation on discharges except that such discharges cannot result in reduction in water quality at the point of discharge below the specified standard (as measured instream)
___ Direct requirements imposed on each individual waste discharger in terms of permitted quantity of discharge, permitted characteristics of discharge, or required degree of treatment, that is, secondary treatment (as measured at the pipe)
___ The establishment of charges on effluents, that is, cents per unit weight (not volume) of waste material discharged, at which the level of charge would be high enough to induce sufficient reduction in industrial and municipal waste discharges to achieve or exceed the desired quality level

15. Assuming that the level of water quality has been selected for private waste discharges, who should bear the costs of improving water quality or reducing pollution?

___ All costs should be paid by the waste dischargers
___ All costs should be paid by the public from local, state, and federal funds
___ Some combination of the above (please specify)

Letter from James L. Barfoot, Jr., and Paul D. Planchon accompanying Megalopolis Environmental Inventory:

Eastern Leadership and Environmental Quality Study

Field Office: DEPARTMENT OF SOCIOLOGY — INDIANA UNIVERSITY
BLOOMINGTON, INDIANA 47401

Sponsored by (mailing address)
RESOURCES FOR THE FUTURE
1755 Massachusetts Avenue, N.W.
Washington, D. C. 20036

Our study is under the sponsorship of Indiana University and Resources for the Future, Inc. One of its purposes is to learn about leaders and organizations that play important roles in the determination of public policy on environmental quality in the Boston to Washington urban region.

Using the term environmental quality to refer to the complexities that result from the disposal of wastes from human consumption and production, we have chosen to concentrate on air and water pollution and the problems produced by solid wastes. The interests involved in the making of public policy in these areas are diverse and numerous. Because of the difficulty of making personal visits it has become necessary to gather as much information as possible by mail. By answering the enclosed questions about your own organization you will help to ensure that our data include all points of view.

Kindly check the questions and send them to us. (Some of them may not be completely appropriate for your own organization—please answer those that are.) Add information and make comments as you will. We are particularly interested in your working definition of pollution and your ideas on the "intangible" benefits of abatement.

All the information will be confidential. We will neither quote nor identify anyone. It is the collective pattern that is important. The number we have placed on the questionnaire is for the purpose of identification in data analysis.

It would be most helpful if you could enclose a brochure describing your organization; its purposes, its programs, and the size of its annual expenditures.

MAILING HISTORY AND REPORT OF RETURNS FOR MEGALOPOLIS
ENVIRONMENT QUALITY INVENTORY

This questionnaire was mailed to 130 organizations identified as the most powerful in environmental problems. The first step in their identification was the compilation of a list based on documentary sources. Informants were then asked to rate the organizations they believed were most powerful and active in Megalopolis in environmental quality problems in general. They were also encouraged to add their own choices not already on the list. The frequency of the votes received from some 30 "judges" determined the final list of 130.

A complete mailing and follow-up yielded 91 returns (70 percent). This high response can be accounted for because of these reasons:

1. The questionnaire was sent to national organizations in which officials are appointed to give special attention to requests for information.

2. Most of the organizations were located in Washington, where the research work of Resources for the Future is well known. Most organizational leaders are personally acquainted with members of the RFF staff. This is equally true of many organizational leaders outside Washington.

3. It is likely that these organizations have not been so heavily burdened with questionnaire demands as the larger and more broadly based urban-oriented organizations.

4. The appeal of the accompanying letter stresses the importance of getting the organization's point of view. This is regarded as vital because of the diverse and numerous interests of the parties concerned with environmental problems.

Among these reasons the most significant is probably the first: specific responsibilities assigned to paid officials of national organizations to provide information when requested. The contrast of such a respondent population with a top leadership population makes clear how larger percentage returns are possible for one that bears a specific informational responsibility in contrast to one that does not.

5. Delaware River Basin Leadership Questionnaire

Listed below is a set of problem areas in water resource development which prevail in varying degrees in the Delaware River Basin.

(a) Please indicate in rank order (1-7) the urgency or priority that you assign to the solution of these problems. (Place ranks in column 1 below.)

(b) At the present, how do you think priorities are being assigned to these problems in the decision-making process of the Delaware River Basin as a whole? (Rank present priorities in column 2 below.)

Water Resource Problems	1	2
Water supply		
Flood control		
Fish and wildlife		
Watershed development		
Water-based recreation		
Pollution control		
Hydroelectric power		
Others (please specify)		

1.   Would you say that your interest and activity in water resource problems have been primarily local, state, interstate-regional, or national in scope?

___ LOCAL   ___ STATE   ___ INTERSTATE-REGIONAL   ___ NATIONAL

2.   Which of the following best describes the Delaware River Basin (New York to Delaware)?

    ___ A region in which all water resource uses are physically interrelated.

    ___ A set of smaller subregions in which only a few water resource uses are physically related to the region as a whole.

    ___ A set of smaller subregions in which water resource uses are physically localized in nature.

    ___ Other (please specify)

3.   In which of the water resource problem areas listed in question 1 have you devoted most of your time and effort?

4.   In your opinion how effectively have these problem areas been managed by the Delawar River Basin Commission in the last five years?

	Very Effectively	Somewhat Effectively	Ineffectively
Water supply			
Flood control			
Fish and wildlife			
Watershed development			
Water-based recreation			
Pollution control			
Hydroelectric power			

5.   Here is a list of resources to which individuals have access in varying degrees. Some of the resources are characteristics of individuals and others of relationships between individuals and groups. Please indicate which resources you possess to a high degree.

    ___ Money and credit

    ___ Control of jobs

    ___ Control of mass media

    ___ High social status

    ___ Knowledge and technical skill

    ___ Popularity and personal qualities

    ___ Legality

    ___ Coalitional support

    ___ The right to vote

    ___ Social access to regional leaders

    ___ Commitments of followers

    ___ Manpower and control of oranization(s)

    ___ Control of interpretation of values

    ___ Others (please specify)

6.   In your judgment which of the following statements best describes the leadership pattern for water resource issues in the Delaware River Basin?

    ___ A relatively small number of leaders have greater influence than other participants and the same leaders are influential in virtually all water resource issues.

    ___ There are separate groups of influential leaders for most water resource issues and in each issue there are leaders who have greater influence than other participants.

___ There are separate groups of influential leaders for most all water resource issues and in each issue the leaders are only slightly more influential than the other participants.

___ Highly active people tend to participate in many types of water resource issue rather than in particular issues and there is little difference in the relative influence of leaders and other participants.

7.   Suppose there was a major water resource problem confronting the river basin as a whole—one that required a group of men nearly everyone would accept and who could rally the support of most segments of the river basin. Who would you select to make up such a group, whether you know them or not (list names, not titles).

8.   How would you rate yourself in comparison to the men you have listed:

___ An equal in terms of the question stated.

___ Would not select myself but these men would seriously consider what I might suggest.

___ Have a good deal of regional influence but not with these particular leaders.

___ My influence is limited to a small group of people.

___ I do not consider myself an influential person.

9.   Below is a list of issues in the Delaware River Basin. Some are past issues; others are still being debated. For the issues in which you attempted to influence the Delaware River Basin Commission in some way please indicate how active you were.

Issues	Very active	Active	Not involved	Relative importance
Water quality objective sets				
Sunfish Pond controversy				
Regional sewage plants				
1965-1966 drought decisions				
Waste load allocations				
Hydroelectric power at				
Tocks Island				
Metering of water in entire basin				
and service area				
Shad fish in the Delaware				

10. How would you rank (1-8) the relative importance of these issues for the river basin as a whole? Place ranks in column labeled "relative importance."

11. In which one of the preceding issues were you most active?
How did you attempt to influence the outcome of the issue?
Refer to the list of "activities" and place a check against your activities in this issue.

List of Activities

Direct contact with key state or federal leaders
Direct contact with key business leaders

Direct contact with key conservation leaders

Direct contact with state or federal water resource agencies

Indirect contact, through intermediaries, with state or federal leaders, business leaders, or conservation leaders

Testifying before special committees or at public hearings

Organizing mass citizen support by telephone or telegraph, in letter writing campaigns, or in radio or T.V. announcements

Newspaper or other journal advertising

Presenting research findings to support particular policy alternatives

Lobbying at state or federal levels

Others (please specify)

Others (please specify)

Describe your position on this issue briefly.

Refer to the list of "means of influence."

Means of Influence

Constraints: Constraints are the threat of withholding support, or by giving support to another party, when you have previously supported that person or group; appealing to a higher authority e.g., the courts or higher legislative body).

Inducements: Inducements involve an exchange of specific goods or services in a quid pro quo relationship. Promises are made for future support (i.e., political support on another issue or campaign contributions) or old political debts are collected.

Persuasion: Persuasion involves changing the minds of the decision makers without offering inducements or constraints. It also involves getting the decision makers to accept the same outcomes preferred by the influencer.

How would you characterize the manner in which you attempted to influence the Delaware River Basin Commission?

___ CONSTRAINTS　　　___ INDUCEMENTS　　　___ PERSUASION

Please name four people who you think have been most influential on this issue.

12. In which issue were you next most active?

How did you attempt to influence the outcome of this issue?

Others (please specify)

Describe your position on this issue briefly.

How would you characterize the manner in which you attempted to influence the Delaware River Basin Commission?

___ CONSTRAINTS　　　___ INDUCEMENTS　　　___ PERSUASION

Please name four people who you think have been influential on this issue.

13. Please supply the following information from 1963 to the present:

Membership in water resource voluntary associations (name and offices)
Water resource committees or commissions (name and offices)
Business or professional organizations (like Chamber of Commerce or National Association of Civil Engineers)
Elective or appointive governmental offices (office title and dates of office)

14. What is your occupation?

15. By whom are you employed?

16. What is the highest educational level you have attained? Please circle:

___ EIGHTH GRADE OR LESS   ___ HIGH SCHOOL
___ TWO YEARS OF COLLEGE   ___ FOUR YEARS OF COLLEGE
___ MASTERS DEGREE   ___ PROFESSIONAL DEGREE
___ PhD   ___ OTHER

17. If you have an educational speciality, indicate what it is.

18. What was your personal income before taxes in 1968?

___ No answer
___ Below $5000
___ $5000 to $9999
___ $10,000 to $14,999
___ $15,000 to $19,999
___ $20,000 to $29,999
___ $30,000 to $49,999
___ Above $50,000

19. What is your place of residence?

20. What is your political identification?

___ DEMOCRAT   ___ INDEPENDENT   ___ REPUBLICAN   ___ OTHER

MAILING HISTORY AND REPORT OF RETURNS FOR THE
DELAWARE RIVER BASIN QUESTIONNAIRE

This population was composed of leaders identified as occupying various formal positions of leadership in environmental organizations in the Delaware River Basin area. Questionnaires were sent to 162 leaders and usable returns were received from 81 (a 50 percent return). This return is lower than that received from officials of national organizations and may be explained for the following reasons:

Many of the local organizations have no pronounced commitment to provide public information and their officials have neither the time for nor the outlook suitable to this activity. They are hired to serve their own members and therefore put their interests first.

The questionnaire seeks information on specific issues in the Delaware River Basin and asks for nominations of the most influential environmental leaders in that area. Respondents may not have this information or be unwilling to share it.

APPENDIX B

A List of All
Instruments Used in
Collecting Data on
Leader and
Organizational Roles
in Megalopolis:

A Special Display of
the Leadership
Acquaint-a-Scope,
the Organizational
Acquaintance and
Working Relationship
Index, and Other
Selected Instruments

I. Survey Recording Instruments

1. ORGANIZATION BASIC INFORMATION LIST

   This form contained the name of the organization, the national address, general type, urban problem focus levels (national, regional, and local) on which it operated, important policy makers in the areas of its concern, and potential contacts for follow-up interviewing. Data were secured from an organization executive.

2. ORGANIZATIONAL PROGRAM AND POLICY ORIENTATION CHECK LIST

   This form contained categories for program emphasis (advisory, research, action-oriented), action policy (unilateral, limited coalitional or broad-based coalition), political coloration (nonpartisan, took a stand but claimed nonpartisan position, endorsed and identified with a political party), role (pace setters or followers), top leadership reservoir, top leadership turnover rate, and program values and objectives. Data were secured from an organization executive. The check list is presented as Figure 11.9 on p. 321.

3. INTERVIEW INFORMATION COVER SHEET

   This form was designed to assemble information from the interview of an influential or informant describing influentials. It contained his name, address, organization, and who referred the researcher to him. The type of interview was checked (general leadership, environmental quality, river basin, or other). All significant background information of the interviewee was recorded.

4. LEADERSHIP ACQUAINT-A-SCOPE

   This instrument was constructed to ascertain the knowledgeableness of the informants who submitted nominations and rated influential leaders in Boston, New York, Philadelphia, Baltimore, and Washington. Leader nominations were sought for Business,

Labor, Governmental, Religious, and Civic areas of activity. Placed opposite the five major cities, a matrix of 25 cells was created.

The Acquaint-a-Scope was placed in front of a knowledgeable informant who was asked to check the boxes in which he felt he could recognize some of the most important leaders who were active in urban affairs. The informant was told that lists of leaders had been prepared for each of the 25 boxes represented, and if he checked any of them the researcher would feel free to give him appropriate matching lists of leaders for rating.

This information provided a practical base for rating leaders (and getting new names), and was also a measure of the informant. It indicated his scope of acquaintance, both locally and in the region. Each block could be given a score with a range of 0 to 25. Informants with large scores were constantly sought and their judgments were considered more seriously. They represented the fuller scope of megalopolitan leaders in their comparative judgments.

II. Diagnostic and Scaled Instruments for Leadership Analysis

1. URBAN PROBLEM INTEREST AND SALIENCY INDEX

This instrument was designed to establish priorities among urban problems as designated by leaders and to indicate their own interest and working patterns. They were asked (a) to indicate the order of importance and urgency assigned to 11 urban problems (air pollution, control of lawlessness and crime, improvement of public education, water pollution, improvement of transport, traffic movement, and parking, waste disposal, improvement of housing, improvement of roads and streets, planning, conservation, and zoning, unemployment and poverty, and race relations); (b) to check problems in which they had the highest personal interest; and (c) to mark those on which they were working hardest at that time.

2. REGIONALISM INDEX OF ADMINISTERED AUTHORITY

This index was constructed to provide leaders judgments of the level on which various urban problems should be administered. The 11 problems cited were listed and the respondent was asked, "Regardless of where the money or guidelines come from, what is the level on which these problems can best be administered?" They were then asked to check the appropriate authority. The levels among which they were asked to choose were

FEDERAL AUTHORITY
REGIONAL AUTHORITY
INTERSTATE AUTHORITY
STATE AUTHORITY
METROPOLITAN AREA AUTHORITY
CITY AUTHORITY

3. LEADERSHIP ACQUAINTANCESHIP AND WORKING RELATIONSHIP SCALE

This scale measured five degrees of acquaintanceship held by one leader toward another. It was used this study to secure the acquaintance of 200 key and 200 top leaders with a specified population of 200 key leaders in Megalopolis. A local community leadership occupational, or a total megalopolitan score was secured. Similarly, scores were given for contacts and working relationships—that is, for general business, civic, or social contacts and/or for urban committee working relationships. This scale is reproduced in Appendix A: Leadership Interaction and Urban Problem Survey.

4. URBAN ORGANIZATIONAL WORKING RELATIONSHIP AND IDENTITY OF INTEREST SCALE

This scale measured the working relations of one organization with others; together their relationships revealed a matrix of working patterns. The scale had five points. An organization official looked at the various urban problem-oriented organizations of which his organization is one. He was asked to check those boxes that best described the nature of any contacts his organization had had with the other organizaions during the last three years. A rater could check none or all of the five scale items; the last item was regarded as a measure of the intensity of the work relationship. This scale is shown in Figure 7.1.

5. ENVIRONMENTAL WORKING RELATIONSHIP AND IDENTITY OF INTEREST SCALE

This scale was used specifically for environmental quality organizations that had been rated as most powerful in Megalopolis. The only difference was that the organizational rater was asked to mark the organizations with which his organization had a close identify of interest. After this selection, he was asked to describe the nature of contacts for those organizations on the Scale. This use provides a more direct sociometric selection.

6. KEY LEADER SELECTION AND POWER PROFILE ANALYSIS

This instrument was used to construct power bases for key leaders. The leader respondent was asked to select 10 to 15 persons from a list of powerful leaders and to indicate their principal bases of power and influence. These data made it possible to draw profiles of power for key leaders and to identify differential bases for business, labor, political, religious, and civic leaders. A segment of this analysis form is shown.

Key Leader Selection and Power Profile Analysis

Look again at the list of leaders. Regardless of how you feel about them or their opinions, please select 10 or 15 who are the most powerful in initiating, supporting, or vetoing activities in the development of urban programs or policies in the Boston to Washington urban area or in the nation in general. Add names of your own choosing if they do not appear on the list. List the names of leaders selected and indicate the principal bases of their power and influence.

Types of Power or Influence

1. *Economic power* (based on wealth or contacts with wealthy persons and organizations)
2. *Political influence* (based on position or contacts in political organizations)

3. *Governmental authority* (based on formal authority of a position in government)
4. *Representative pressure or collective action* (based on the representation of a group or organization as a lobby or pressure instrument or the ability to mobilize large numbers of people to protest, strike, or picket)
5. *Moral and religious persuasion*
6. *Military influence* (direct or by access)
7. *Means of communication* (control or access of mass communication)
8. *Social prestige* (family lineage or upper class standing)
9. *Specialized knowledge or skill* (trained expertise)
10. *Personal qualities of leadership* (well liked or esteemed, organizational ability, or charisma)

Types of power

Names of chosen leaders   1 2 3 4 5 6 7 8 9 10

7. ORGANIZATIONAL SELECTION AND POWER PROFILE ANALYSIS

The same instrument can be applied to organizations. A list of powerful organizations is presented and organizational raters are asked to select 10 to 15 powerful organizations and to indicate their principal bases of power and influence. See application of this analysis in Figures 7.2, 7.3, 7.4, 7.5, and 7.6.

8. SPECIALIZED LEADERS SELECTION FORM

This form was employed to identify leaders in various institutional sectors and to build a comprehensive list for subsequent rating. Informants were asked, "What leaders on the northeastern seaboard of the United States in the various sectors listed are the most powerful in initiating, supporting, or vetoing acts in their own groups in the development of urban programs or policies." The sectors listed were (1) business; (2) politics and government; (3) mass Communication; (4) education; (5) religion; (6) labor; (7) military; (8) health and welfare; (9) recreation; (10) independent professions; (11) race relations; (12) conservationists; (13) water pollution; (14) air pollution.

9. URBAN COALITION POLICY COMMITTEE SURVEY

This form was developed to identify potential policy-making coalitions. A segment of the form is shown.

Urban Coalition Policy Committee Survey

If a regional agency were set up to deal with problems of cities (employment, housing, education, transport, and race relations) in the Boston–Washington area, what groups and leaders would be most important for developing policy and ensuring broad support for a wide-scale attack on these problems?

Group	Key eastern leaders in group

10. ENVIRONMENTAL QUALITY LEADERS POLICY COMMITTEE SURVEY

This form is the same as that of the urban coalition policy committee survey but has been adapted to environmental quality groups and leaders.

Environmental Quality Policy Committee Survey

If a regional agency were set up to deal with problems of environmental quality (water, air, and conservation) in the Boston–Washington area, what groups and leaders would be most important for developing policies and ensuring broad support for a wide-scale attack on these problems?

Group	Key eastern leaders in group

III. Organizational Interactional Analysis

A set of forms was developed to assess the interaction of private organizational personnel among business, government, university, and private associations. All these forms are displayed in Chapter 10.

1. Associational personnel analysis of work background in other organizations
2. List of common contact activities of organizational personnel
3. Individual and group contactograms showing personnel and organizational interactional patterns for given organizations

APPENDIX C

Delaware River Basin
Interview Schedule

I'm interested in three things: first, why the parties at interest chose to recommend the levels that they did—both their stated reasons and the origin of those reasons; second, how they went about making their points of view felt; third, in general how they participated in the decision-making process.

Your responses to the questions will not be for publication. They will be held confidential. We are interested only in the collective patterns.

1. Desired outcomes:

   a. Your testimony at the hearing indicated that your organization recommended objective set ___ for the estuary area. Is this correct?

   b. Does this represent any change in the position taken by your organization during the course of the issue? If so, how?

2. Range of acceptable outcomes:

   a. Your testimony indicates that although you preferred objective set ___ you would have agreed to objective set ___. Is this correct?

   b. If the above date is not available, what other objective sets would your organization have found acceptable?

3. What interests do you feel you and your organization represented in the debate over the level of water quality?

4. What were the intangible costs and benefits associated with the different objective sets and how valuable were they?

5. Perception of range of alternatives: present-day technology may make possible many measures that are effective in reducing pollution significantly, but whether such measures are taken is often determined by other sets of considerations, including the cost balanced against the perceived benefits and the various political and social demands. The following questions are designed to learn something of the way in which your organization viewed the alternatives open to public action.

a. Which objective set best described the condition of the river in 1964?

    1   2   3   4   5

b. If the money were available and the decisions were made to do so, which objective set could have been obtained by 1975, given the present level of technological development?

    1   2   3   4   5

c. If the decisions were made to do so, which objective set could have been achieved by 1975, considering the cost of doing so, both public and private, balanced against the benefits and the technological constraints?

    1   2   3   4   5

d. Finally, taking into consideration the two factors of cost and technology, what level of quality was likely to be achieved by 1975, given the various social and political pressures involved?

    1   2   3   4   5

6. Perception of the opposition:

    a. During the course of the issue did you think that there existed among the alternatives an optimal choice that would provide the greatest benefits (tangible or intangible) for the least cost for all concerned? Which level represented this choice?

    b. During the course of the issue did your organization feel that the primary task was that of protecting the interests it represented or one of determining an optimal level?

    c. What organizations or interests do you feel were in opposition to your point of view in the issue?

    d. Which of them do you think was the most powerful? The most effective?

    e. At that time did you think that the opposition was prepared to compromise with your point of view?

    f. If they did compromise, did you anticipate it to be a matter of influence—a cease-fire line between opposing demands—or did you feel that they were genuinely seeking an optimal level that would produce the greatest benefits for the least cost?

7. Cooperative activity: the respondent is given a deck of cards on which the names of organizations appear.

    a. With which of these organizations did your organization have contact or work with on the subject of the water quality issue of the Delaware?

(Respondent divides cards.)

b. Now divide them into two stacks: (1) those that your organizaion approached and (2) those that approached your organization or that you met or worked with through a third party.

(Respondent divides cards. Now there are three stacks.)

8. Optional:

   a. Do you think the level chosen by the Commission was too high or too low? If so, how much?

   b. Regardless of what you think about the level chosen, do you think that the Commission is implementing its pollution–abatement program in the best way? If not, how would you suggest they change it?

9. Which, if any, on this list of methods did your organization use to make its position felt in the decision-making process?

   Testifying at public hearings.
   Testifying before Congressional committees, state legislative committees, and committees at the local level.
   Encouraging members of the organization to send letters to congressmen, state legislators, and other governmental personnel.
   Publishing a newsletter that informs subscribers about current issues, programs, and innovations in the environmental quality field.
   Conducting research on technical, economic, or political aspects of environmental quality.
   Publishing brochures and other material about your organization's efforts toward the improvement of environmental quality.
   Financing research work of other organizations directly or indirectly through associational ties.
   Taking membership in an association or federation that is "action"-oriented to express your interests on environmental quality questions.
   Appointing a representative who participated in an advisory committee and/or task force to a governmental committee.
   Preparing detailed statements concerning environmental issues such as the level of quality or how to best achieve a given level of quality.
   Publishing a profssional journal in which technical aspects of environmental quality is discussed.
   Preparing newspaper or other journal advertisements concerning activities to support, oppose, or amend environmental quality recommendations.
   Lobbying in Congress, in state legislatures, or at the local level.
   Others:

10. Below is a list of problems that prevail in varying degrees in the Boston to Washington urban region.

    a. Please indicate in rank order (1 to 11) the urgency or priority that your organization assigns to the solution of these problems.

    b. Check those problems that your organization has worked on during the last three years.

The list reproduced in this questionnaire is the same as that in the Leadership Interaction and Problem Survey and the Urban Problem Resurvey.

Party at Interest Data Schedule: Checklist

1. Name of organization _____

   Address of organization _____

2. Name of individual representing the organization at the hearing _____

   Title _____

   Occupation _____

3. Name of respondent _____

   Title _____

   Occupation _____

4. Level of organization

   __ CITY   __ COUNTY   __ STATE   __ BASIN WIDE   __ REGION
   __ NATION   __ OTHER

5. Purpose of the organization

   __ PROFIT   __ PUBLIC ADMINISTRATION   __ PUBLIC LEGISLATION
   __ GENERAL CIVIC GOALS   __ CONSERVATION   __ RESEARCH
   __ EDUCATION   __ REPRESENT BUSINESS   __ BEAUTIFICATION AND
   AESTHETICS   __ HEALTH   __ COLLECTIVE BARGAINING
   __ PROFESSIONAL ASSOCIATION   __ OTHER
   __ BROAD SCOPE   __ NARROW SCOPE

6. Nature of internal constituency

   __ MEMBERSHIP   __ FEDERATION OF ORGANIZATIONS   __ VOTERS
   __ STOCKHOLDERS OR OWNERS
   __ HETEROGENEOUS   __ HOMOGENEOUS
   __ INCLUDES WASTE DISCHARGERS   PERCENT __

7. Inferred interest

   __ SPORTS FISHING   __ COMMERCIAL FISHING   __ WATER SPORTS
   __ WILDLIFE PRESERVATION   __ AESTHETICS   __ WATER FOR
   DOMESTIC USE   __ WATER FOR INDUSTRIAL USE   __ RIVER TO
   DISPOSE OF WASTE   __ RIVER WATER TO COOL   __ IRRIGATION
   __ WASTE DISPOSAL   __ HIGHER QUALITY
   __ MULTIPLE INTEREST   __ SINGLE INTEREST

8. Power index ___ (from informant sources)

9. Activity index ___ (from informant sources)

10. DECS advisory committee membership

___ POLICY COMMITTEE   ___ TECHNICAL WATER USE   ___ INDUSTRY
___ LOCAL GOVERNMENTS AND PLANNING AGENCIES
___ RECREATION   ___ CONSERVATION, FISH AND WILDLIFE
___ GENERAL PUBLIC

11. ___ WASTE DISCHARGER; ___ REPRESENTS WASTE DISCHARGERS

INDEX